MUIRHEAD LIBRARY OF PHILOSOPHY

AN admirable statement of the aims of the Library of Philosophy was provided by the first editor, the late Professor J. H. Muirhead, in his description of the original programme printed in Erdmann's *History of Philosophy* under the date 1890. This was slightly modified in subsequent volumes to take the form of the following statement:

'The Muirhead Library of Philosophy was designed as a contribution to the History of Modern Philosophy under the heads: first of different Schools of Thought—Sensationalist, Realist, Idealist, Intuitivist; secondly of different Subjects—Psychology, Ethics, Aesthetics, Political Philosophy, Theology. While much had been done in England in tracing the course of evolution in nature, history, economics, morals and religion, little had been done in tracing the development of thought on these subjects. Yet "the evolution of opinion is part of the whole evolution".

'By the co-operation of different writers in carrying out this plan it was hoped that a thoroughness and completeness of treatment, otherwise unattainable, might be secured. It was believed also that from writers mainly British and American fuller consideration of English Philosophy than it had hitherto received might be looked for. In the earlier series of books containing, among others, Bosanquet's *History of Aesthetic*, Pfleiderer's *Rational Theology since Kant*, Albee's *History of English Utilitarianism*, Bonar's *Philosophy and Political Economy*, Brett's *History of Psychology*, Ritchie's *Natural Rights*, these objects were to a large extent effected.

'In the meantime original work of a high order was being produced both in England and America by such writers as Bradley, Stout, Bertrand Russell, Baldwin, Urban, Montague, and others, and a new interest in foreign works, German, French, and Italian, which had either become classical or were attracting public attention, had developed. The scope of the Library thus became extended into something more international, and it is entering on the fifth decade of its existence in the hope that it may contribute to that mutual understanding between countries which is so pressing a need of the present time.'

The need which Professor Muirhead stressed is no less pressing today, and few will deny that philosophy has much to do with enabling us to meet it, although no one, least of all Muirhead himself, would regard that as the sole, or even the main, object of philosophy. As Professor Muirhead continues to lend the distinction of his name to the Library of Philosophy it seemed not inappropriate to allow him to recall us to these aims in his own words. The emphasis on the history of thought also seemed to me very timely; and the number of important works promised for the Library in the near future augur well for the continued fulfilment, in this and other ways, of the expectations of the original editor.

H. D. LEWIS

MUIRHEAD LIBRARY OF PHILOSOPHY

General Editor, Professor H. D. Lewis

Professor of History and Philosophy of Religion in the University of London

The Analysis of Mind. By BERTRAND RUSSELL. 8th Impression.

Analytic Psychology. By G. F. STOUT. 2 Vols. 5th Impression.

Coleridge as Philosopher. By J. H. MUIRHEAD. 2nd Impression.

Contemporary American Philosophy. Edited by GEORGE P. ADAMS and WM. PEPPERELL MONTAGUE.

Contemporary British Philosophy. By J. H. MUIRHEAD.

Contemporary Indian Philosophy. Edited by RADHAKRISHNAN and J. H. MUIRHEAD.

Contemporary British Philosophy. Third Series Edited by H. D. LEWIS.

Development of Theology Since Kant. By O. PFLEIDERER.

Dialogues in Metaphysics. By NICHOLAS MALEBRANCHE. Translated by MORRIS GINSBERG.

Elements of Constructive Philosophy. By J. S. MACKENZIE. 2nd Impression.

Ethics. By NICOLAI HARTMANN. Translated by STANTON COIT. 3 Vols.

The Good Will: A Study in the Coherence Theory of Goodness. By H. J. PATON.

Hegel: A Re-Examination. By J. N. FINDLAY.

Hegel's Science of Logic. Translated by W. H. JOHNSTON and L. G. STRUTHERS. 2 Vols. 2nd Impression.

History of Æsthetic. By DR. B. BOSANQUET. 4th Edition. 5th Impression.

History of English Utilitarianism. By E. ALBEE.

History of Psychology. By G. S. BRETT. Edited by R. S. PETERS. Abridged one-volume edition.

Human Knowledge. By BERTRAND RUSSELL. 3rd Impression.

A Hundred Years of British Philosophy. By DR. RUDOLF METZ. Translated by J. W. HARVEY, T. E. JESSOP, HENRY STURT. 2nd Impression.

Ideas: A General Introduction to Pure Phenomenology. By EDMUND HUSSERL. Translated by W. R. BOYCE GIBSON. 2nd Impression.

Imagination. By E. J. FURLONG.

Indian Philosophy. By RADHAKRISHNAN. 2 Vols. Rev. 2nd Edition.

The Intelligible World: Metaphysics and Value. By W. M. URBAN.

Introduction to Mathematical Philosophy By BERTRAND RUSSELL 2nd Edition. 8th Impression.

Kant's First Critique. By H. W. CASSIRER.

Kant's Metaphysic of Experience. By H. J. PATON. 2nd Impression.

Know Thyself. By BERNARDINO VARISCO. Translated by GUGLIELMO SALVADORI.

Language and Reality. By WILBUR MARSHALL URBAN.

Matter and Memory. By HENRI BERGSON. Translated by N. M. PAUL and W. S. PALMER. 6th Impression.

Modern Philosophy. By GUIDO DE RUGGIERO. Translated by A. HOWARD HANNAY and R. G. COLLINGWOOD.

The Modern Predicament. By H. J. PATON.

Moral Sense. By JAMES BONAR.

Natural Rights. By D. G. RITCHIE. 3rd Edition. 5th Impression

Nature, Mind and Modern Science. By E. HARRIS.

The Nature of Thought. By BRAND BLANSHARD. 2nd Impression.

On Selfhood and Godhood. By C. A. CAMPBELL.

Our Experience of God. By H. D. LEWIS.

Personality and Reality. By E. J. TURNER.

The Phenomenology of Mind. By G. W. F. HEGEL. Translated by SIR JAMES BAILLIE. Revised 2nd Edition 3rd Impression.

Philosophical Papers. By G. E. MOORE.

Philosophy and Political Economy by J. BONAR 4th Impression

Philosophy of Whitehead. by W. MAYS

The Platonic Tradition in Anglo-Saxon Philosophy. By J. H. MUIRHEAD.

The Principal Upanisads. By RADHAKRISHNAN.

The Problems of Perception. By R. J. HIRST.

Reason and Goodness. By BRAND BLANSHARD.

The Relevance of Whitehead. Edited by IVOR LECLERC.

Some Main Problems of Philosophy. by G. E. MOORE

The Theological Frontier of Ethics. By W. G. MACLAGAN.

Time and Free Will. By HENRI BERGSON. Translated by F. G. POGSON. 6th Impression.

The Ways of Knowing: or, The Methods of Philosophy. By W. P. MONTAGUE. 4th Impression.

THE WAYS OF KNOWING

THE WAYS OF
KNOWING
OR
THE METHODS OF PHILOSOPHY

WILLIAM PEPPERELL MONTAGUE

Professor of Philosphy, Columbia University

LONDON: GEORGE ALLEN & UNWIN LTD
NEW YORK: THE MACMILLAN COMPANY

First published in 1925
Second Impression, 1928
Third Impression, 1948
Fourth Impression, 1953
Fifth Impression, 1958
Sixth Impression, 1962

TO

MY WIFE

Printed in Great Britain by
COMPTON PRINTING WORKS (LONDON) LTD. N.1.

PREFACE

Since the time when, as a student of Professor Palmer at Harvard, I read Sidgwick's *Methods of Ethics*, I have had the ambition to follow in a small way the plan of that great work, and to set forth as best I could the methods of logic and epistemology disentangled from the more exciting problems of metaphysics.

Sidgwick's book still seems to me one of the greatest of philosophic essays, and the misunderstandings and cross-purposes of contemporary philosophic discussion appear to call now even more strenuously than before for a segregation of the dialectical and methodological problems of philosophy from problems concerning the nature of reality. In the general plan of treatment as well as in the subtitle of my book I have registered my obligation to Sidgwick.

It is my pleasant duty to acknowledge thankfully the many helpful suggestions which I have received from Dr. Muirhead, the Editor of the Library, in the preparation of this book for the press. To Miss May Sinclair I am grateful for the clearer appreciation of Idealism which I have gained from discussions with her and from her writings. Thanks are also due to Professor R. B. Perry of Harvard who read and criticised the MS. ; and to Professor John Dewey whose comments on the chapter on Pragmatism have cleared away some of the misconceptions which I had formerly entertained as to the relations of Instrumentalism to the logic and epistemology of Pragmatism as a whole.

To my friends Professors Lovejoy, Miller, Overstreet, and Sheldon I owe much in the way of encouragement and stimulus generously imparted through many years of delightful conversations and companionship.

Most of all I am indebted to my colleague Professor Helen

Parkhurst. She has not only revised and typed the entire MS., and prepared the index, but has for several years given unsparingly her time and her counsel in helping me to clarify and express the opinions which the book records.

In assigning to the several participants in the Dialogue the views which they are made to defend, I have had in mind as contributors to the composite personage of " Partridge," the Objectivist, the philosophic attitude of those British and American philosophers who might be classed as New Realists. " Lovelace," the Epistemological Dualist, is intended to represent the views of the more recent group calling themselves Critical Realists. While in the person of " Bryce," the Subjectivist, I have tried to present as fairly as I could, though doubtless inadequately, the point of view of several modern Idealists. These include my friends Professor Royce and Professor Creighton, who, I hope, would not feel their memory dishonoured by my use of their names in this connection. I hope also that no lack of respect for the great British Idealists who have died within the past year will be imputed to me for my venturing to associate their names in the index with the fictitious personage representing the viewpoint of the school to which they belong.

W. P. M.

New York,
March 24, 1925.

CONTENTS

INTRODUCTION

Philosophy and its three divisions : Methodology, Metaphysics and
Theory of Value—Methodology and its two subdivisions : Logic
and Epistemology—The possibility and desirability of segregating
the problems of method from one another and from the other problems of philosophy—Proposed use of the term epistemology—The
three methods of epistemology and their projected reconciliation
in Part II—Proposed use of the term logic—The six methods of
logic and their projected reconciliation in Part I.

PART I

WAYS OF ATTAINING KNOWLEDGE:
THE SIX METHODS OF LOGIC

CHAPTER I

THE METHOD OF AUTHORITARIANISM

The wide extent of authority in determining our beliefs—The limitations
of the individual outlook and the universal suggestibility of the
human mind make men dependent on the testimony of their neighbours—Authoritarianism weakened by the conflict between authorities and by the realization that testimony must sooner or later be
grounded upon some more direct source of knowledge—Difficulty
of appraising the rival claims of conflicting authorities without
going outside of the authoritarian method—Prestige, Number and
Age as criteria for evaluating authorities when in conflict—The
prestige gained by a man in one field of knowledge does not extend
to other fields—The *number* of adherents of a doctrine does not
strengthen its claim to be accepted except when the adherents have
reached their belief independently of one another and by some

7

CHAPTER II

THE METHOD OF MYSTICISM

CHAPTER III

THE METHODS OF RATIONALISM AND EMPIRICISM

The Psychological Genesis of Universals and the Logical Validation of Universal and Necessary Propositions.

PAGE

The joint discussion of Rationalism and Empiricism justified by the intimate inter-relationship of these two Methods of Logic—Question of the nature of universals in relation to the mind and in relation to the world 69–70

I

ORIGIN OF UNIVERSAL CONCEPTS.

Opposing attitudes of Rationalism and Empiricism—What is really given in experience—The six typical elements in any perceptual datum such as the appearance of a horse at a given time and place : H, h, S, s, T, t—The process of "abstraction" as consisting in *selection from the object* not in *creation by the subject*—How attention is successively restricted to fewer and fewer aspects of the datum so as to form the concepts (1) of the individual, (2) of the class, and (3) of the abstract essence—Other possible selections or restrictions of attention—How the problem has been obscured by confusing the psychological order (*ratio cognoscendi*) in which the individuals antedate the universals which inhere in them, with the logical order (*ratio essendi*) in which the universals antedate the individuals which exemplify them—The same confusion found in the Neo-Nominalistic preference of denotation to connotation shown by modern logicians—The traditional misconception of Induction—Misuse of the word "abstraction"—How universals are preserved in names—Contrast between the brute mind and the mind of man—No necessity for innate ideas—Universals not images but concepts—No necessity for composite photographs—Our view as a compromise between traditional rationalism and traditional empiricism . 70–78

II

ORIGIN AND VALIDATION OF UNIVERSAL AND NECESSARY JUDGMENTS.

Every proposition reducible to an identity-relation or copula uniting complex essences or terms—The universal symbol for any proposition : $S = Rn(P)$—Identity as meaning unity of denotation combined with duality of connotation—But what is denotation ? " Intrinsic " and " extrinsic " properties of every object—"Extrinsic" properties involve other objects—They are relational and constitute membership in a series—" Intrinsic " properties do not involve other objects, and they constitute only membership in a class—Significance of same word for *copula* and for *existence*—How denotation

CHAPTER IV

THE METHODS OF RATIONALISM AND EMPIRICISM (continued)

The Ontological Status of Universals and the Cosmological Significance of Universal and Necessary Propositions.

I

THE ONTOLOGICAL STATUS OF UNIVERSALS.

CONTENTS

II

THE COSMOLOGICAL SIGNIFICANCE OF UNIVERSAL AND NECESSARY PROPOSITIONS.

CHAPTER V

THE METHOD OF PRAGMATISM

Introductory and Historical.

The original Pragmatism of Charles Peirce—not concerned with the truth of propositions but with the meaning of ideas—Peirce's realism and anti-relativism—James's transformation of Peirce's principle—Professor Dewey's Instrumentalism—Its application to education—Professor Dewey's comments on certain misinterpretations of Instrumentalism—Dr. Schiller's revolt against Mr. Bradley's

CONTENTS

18

I

PRAGMATISM AS FUTURISM.

II

PRAGMATISM AS PRACTICALISM.

B

III

PRAGMATISM AS RELATIVISM.

CONTENTS

CHAPTER VI

THE METHOD OF SCEPTICISM

I

THE HISTORICAL ARGUMENT.

II

THE DIALECTICAL ARGUMENT.

Ultimate questions sometimes appear to require one or the other of two answers, each of which is incompatible with the other and neither of which is acceptable to the mind. Zeno's puzzles about motion are examples of such " antinomies," and are used by sceptics to show that ultimate reality is unknowable—Not only sceptics but mystics and pragmatists appeal to the antinomy in support of their respective theories—The world of sense, as involving motion and so conflicting with reason must be rejected as unreal, so speaks the mystic ; the pragmatist, on the other hand, claims that Reason and the laws of abstract logic must be rejected as invalid or inadequate because

III

The Physiological Argument.

According to the Sceptic, the objects outside us that compose the
material world are not directly open to our inspection, but must be
inferred as the ultimate causes of complex effects—We can have
certain and direct knowledge only of our mental states, and there is
no way of discovering the nature of their external causes or the
extent to which they resemble the effects produced upon our senses
—To this argument based on the indirectness of the process determining our perceptions there are three answers : (1) *The Phenomenalist's Answer.* The question as to what things are in themselves is
unanswerable, because it is meaningless—Things exist only in relation to us—They are what they appear to be or what they are
experienced as being—This answer is valid to the extent that appearances are real and important—But it is invalid to the extent
that the appearances of an object or the effects that it produces
on other objects cannot constitute its whole nature—Unless it
existed it could not produce effects—Unless it was in itself something it could not appear to be anything—The intrinsic nature of
a thing, however, need not be different in kind from its effects, nor
need it be as the sceptic assumes uninferrible from those effects.
(2) *The Scientist's Answer.* By comparing the various sense-data
with one another the physical scientist can eliminate progressively
those of their aspects which are peculiar to the positions and
conditions of the percipient subjects and with increasing accuracy
attain to a conception of the intrinsic nature of the single cause
which would be capable of producing the varied series of observed
effects—This is easier for the quantitative or so-called " primary "
qualities than for the specific and non-quantitative properties
called " secondary "—The scientist's procedure of inferring the
nature of the cause from the comparison of its various effects illustrated by the case of the sun—The problem of the objective reality
of the secondary qualities : the sense in which it is important and the
kind of data requisite for its solution. (3) *The Logician's Answer.*
The sceptic in his physiological argument assumes the validity of
certain propositions about the manner in which perceptual knowledge is produced as a basis for attacking the validity of all propositions and thus involves himself in something very like a logical
contradiction—This " logician's answer " applies against all argu-

CONTENTS

17

PAGE

IV

THE PSYCHOLOGICAL ARGUMENT.

18 THE WAYS OF KNOWING

CHAPTER VII

ENTENTES AND ALLIANCES—THE FEDERATION OF THE METHODS

I

ENTENTES AND ALLIANCES.

II

THE FEDERATION OF THE METHODS.

CONTENTS

PART II

WAYS OF INTERPRETING KNOWLEDGE :
THE THREE METHODS OF EPISTEMOLOGY

FOREWORD

CHAPTER VIII

THE METHOD OF OBJECTIVISM

I

EXTREME OR PRIMITIVE OBJECTIVISM.

This is the theory that every experienced object is real in itself exactly
as it is experienced and independently of whether it is experienced

CHAPTER IX

THE METHOD OF EPISTEMOLOGICAL DUALISM

CONTENTS

CHAPTER X

THE METHOD OF SUBJECTIVISM

I

THE FIRST STAGE OF SUBJECTIVISM : THE SUBJECTIVITY OF UNREAL OBJECTS.

II

THE SECOND STAGE OF SUBJECTIVISM : THE SUBJECTIVITY OF SENSE-DATA, OR IMMEDIATELY PERCEIVED OBJECTS.

III

THE THIRD STAGE OF SUBJECTIVISM : THE SUBJECTIVITY OF THE SECONDARY QUALITIES.

IV

THE FOURTH STAGE OF SUBJECTIVISM : THE SUBJECTIVITY OF THE PRIMARY QUALITIES.

At this stage the primary qualities as well as the secondary qualities
are removed from the external world and confined within the domain
of conscious experience—The universe, so far as its particular facts
are concerned, consists solely of minds and their states—But by
treating phenomena such as chairs and tables as public or shareable experiences in contrast with more obviously private phenomena,
such as pains and pleasures, the subjectivist is able even at this
stage of his development to preserve the ordinary working distinction between physical and psychical without violating his own
principles—The principal reason for the advance of the subjectivist

V

THE FIFTH STAGE OF SUBJECTIVISM: THE SUBJECTIVITY OF SPACE AND TIME AND OF THE CATEGORIES AND LAWS OF NATURE.

VI

THE SIXTH STAGE OF SUBJECTIVISM: THE SUBJECTIVITY OF THE GROUND OF OUR SENSATIONS, AND THE REDUCTION OF THE MANY TRANSCENDENTAL SELVES TO ONE ABSOLUTE SELF.

VII

CHAPTER XI

A REINTERPRETATION AND RECONCILIATION OF THE THREE METHODS OF EPISTEMOLOGY

I

The Re-interpretation of Objectivism.

II

THE RE-INTERPRETATION OF SUBJECTIVISM.

The two propositions in which Subjectivism is summed up :

III

THE RE-INTERPRETATION OF DUALISM.

IV

CONCLUSION.

POSTSCRIPT

THE KNOWER AND THE KNOWN

A DIALOGUE

Participants.
PARTRIDGE, an Objectivist.
BRYCE, a Subjectivist.
LOVELACE, a Dualist.
HYLANOUS, a Realist.

I

II

CONTENTS

III

c

INTRODUCTION

THE grand divisions of philosophy are: I. Methodology, II. Metaphysics, and III. Theory of Value.

The Theory of Value is concerned with the nature of ideals and with the ways in which they may be made actual. It may be subdivided into: (1) the study of the good and of the means of realizing it in conduct, which is Ethics; and (2) the study of the beautiful and of the means of realizing it in art, which is Æsthetics.

Metaphysics is concerned with all questions of a general and fundamental character as to the nature of the real. It may be subdivided into: (1) Analytical Metaphysics or Ontology, which is the study of the basic categories of the sciences; and (2) Synthetic Metaphysics or Cosmology, which is the study of the generic conclusions of the sciences, and which, by the inter-relating of these, produces a unified picture of the world as a whole.

Methodology may be subdivided into: (1) Logic, and (2) Epistemology, which deal respectively with the ways of attaining and with the ways of interpreting knowledge.

It is clear that these three main divisions of philosophy are partly, though only partly, independent of one another. What ought to be in the way of goodness and beauty is not necessarily determined by what actually exists. To that extent the ideals of ethics and æsthetics are independent of the conclusions of metaphysics. But the manner in which our ideals can be realized is obviously controlled by the kind of world we live in; hence, from the standpoint of the practical moralist and artist the philosophy of values is to some extent bound up with the theories of metaphysics. The same mixture of dependence and independence is to be found in the relation between metaphysics and methodology. What criteria we shall use to attain truth will depend largely upon the nature of the reality we are investigating ; and yet the same criteria may often be used to test the most diverse judgments. And as with logic so also with epistemology. The ways of interpreting truth as such, or the knowledge relation itself, will certainly depend in part upon what psychology and physics reveal as to the nature of the knowing subject and the known object. Yet here again the epistemological problem of whether realism or idealism is correct in its interpretation of the knowledge relation is a problem which at least in some of its aspects is independent of the particular nature of the terms of that relation. And finally, it would be easy to show that the relation between theories of method and theories of value contains a similar blend of dependence and independence.

In the philosophy of the last two centuries, however, the problems of method have been interwoven with those of metaphysics to such an extent that the issues distinctive of each have been lost sight of.⌐ For this reason it has seemed worth while to attempt a segregation of the two branches of methodology, which we have called logic and epistemology, from each other and from the other problems of philosophy.

As preparatory to this effort to isolate the methodological inquiry into the Ways of Knowing from the metaphysical inquiry into the Ways of Being, we must consider more specifically the two branches of methodology which we have referred to as logic and epistemology.

Epistemology, or the theory of knowledge, includes many problems and is consequently susceptible of many definitions. We prefer to treat under this title that phase of the knowledge relation which throughout the history of philosophy has generated the sharpest and most significant controversy. *To what extent, if any, are the things and qualities of the world dependent upon their being related as objects to a knower or subject ?*

On this question there are three classic theories which have contended with one another for acceptance. First, there is the theory of " objectivism " or epistemological *realism* which holds that objects exist exactly as they are apprehended, that things are in themselves and apart from us just what they seem to be when we experience them, and that consciousness reveals directly the nature of external reality. Secondly, there is the theory of "subjectivism" or epistemological *idealism* which holds that the nature and existence of an object is constituted by its relation to a mind or subject, and that consequently all reality in so far as it can be conceived at all must be conceived as conscious experience. Thirdly, there is the "representative" or "copy" theory of knowledge which we have called epistemological *dualism*. According to this theory objects are of two kinds, internal objects or "ideas," depending upon consciousness and directly revealed by it; and external or physical objects which are independent of consciousness and never directly experienced by it, but which can and must be inferred as the hypothetical causes of experience.[1]

It is these three theories which are discussed in Part II under the head of *The Methods of Epistemology*. We shall there try to show that the rival contentions of objectivism, subjectivism, and dualism can be restated from a realistic standpoint in such a way as to be made not only compatible with, but implicative of one another. To the extent that our effort is successful the epistemological problem will have been solved. And it will have been solved by the reduction of the three previously opposed *theories* to three diverse but mutually supplementary *methods* of interpreting the single set of facts involved in the relation of a knower to the object known.

Before discussing the methods of interpreting knowledge or truth, however, it seems appropriate to consider the methods by which knowledge or truth is attained. Hence Part I is concerned with what we have called logic. In traditional philosophy formal logic has been defined as the art and science of correct thinking. And correctness of thinking has been regarded as meaning only correctness of inference from premises to conclusion. It is obvious, however, that if, as logicians, we are seeking for principles of correct thinking, we cannot remain satisfied with the discovery of rules which do no more than make our conclusions accord with our premises. We must extend our search until we discover principles by which our

[1] There is indeed a fourth type of epistemological theory which can be called *relativism*. But this theory is so different in spirit and temper from the other epistemological theories, and is bound up so closely with the logic of pragmatism, that it has seemed best to treat of it in connection with the latter in Chapter V of Part I.

premises can themselves be made valid. This search for criteria of absolute validity and material truth as distinguished from relative validity and formal truth has sometimes been regarded as a branch of epistemology. We prefer, however, to regard it as the logical goal of logic itself. By logic, then, we shall mean *the search for the ultimate criteria by the use of which our beliefs can be validated and true knowledge be attained.*

As will be seen, the problem of validating beliefs is intimately associated with the problem of ascertaining the source of beliefs. Hence in connection with the logical problem of validity we shall treat to some extent the psychological problems of genesis.

Our ideas and beliefs can be traced to one or more of the following origins: (1) Testimony of others; (2) Intuition, which is at least partly grounded in instincts, feelings and desires; (3) Abstract reasoning from universal principles; (4) Sensory experience; (5) Practical activity having successful consequences. Each of these sources may be, and actually has been accepted as indicating a primary criterion for determining philosophic truth; and thus to the five sources of belief there correspond the following five types of logical theory: (1) Authoritarianism; (2) Mysticism; (3) Rationalism; (4) Empiricism; (5) Pragmatism.

For each of these types of logical theory there exists a type of belief for the validation of which it appears to be especially suited. To illustrate: any one of us, if asked whence we derived our belief in the existence of Napoleon Bonaparte and on what grounds we held it, would reply that the belief was derived from the testimony of historians and held on the ground of authority. Again, all of us hold certain beliefs which seem to have no basis of support other than that of intuition. The feeling that dark places and dead bodies are dangerous; that these persons are to be trusted and those distrusted; that certain ultimate evaluations of life and the universe must be accepted. All these are examples of the class of attitudes and beliefs of the second or mystical kind. The third or rationalistic criterion applies most naturally to mathematical propositions such as $7 + 5 = 12$, the truth of which is derived from and tested by deductive reasoning from certain universally accepted principles. Beliefs about particular things such as that grass will be green and that snow will be cold are derived from and tested by perceptual experience, and hence exemplify the use of the fourth criterion, that of empiricism. Beliefs that refer to the future and that are assumed primarily as bases for action illustrate the fifth or pragmatic criterion, which is not always easy to distinguish from empiricism. Such judgments as that an enterprise in which we are about to engage will be successful, that the future will resemble the past, are founded neither on direct perception nor on deduction from self-evident principles. They appear to be postulates which have been derived from the exigencies of practical conduct, and we are content to test them by their practical results. If they work badly, we reject them as false and seek others. Sixthly and finally, there are many propositions which we should all agree can be neither proved nor disproved by any of the above criteria, and which consequently furnish the grounds for a sixth and negative type of logical theory, that of Scepticism.

Thus we see that testimony, intuition, reason, perception and practice are all to some extent grounds of actual beliefs, and that as such they afford support for five diverse theories as to the method of attaining truth. The first part of our survey of methodology will be concerned with a critical analysis of each of the five positive methods of logic and of the one negative method, together with such of their general metaphysical and ethical affiliations as may seem appropriate. These six successive analyses will be followed by a synthetic program for the harmonious reconciliation of the rival theories through the assignment of each to that domain of experience for which it seems peculiarly fitted.

PART I
WAYS OF ATTAINING KNOWLEDGE:
THE SIX METHODS OF LOGIC

CHAPTER I

THE METHOD OF AUTHORITARIANISM

WE get more of our beliefs from the testimony of our fellows than from any other source. Little of our knowledge of the universe is directly tested by our own intuition, reason, experience, or practice. We accept on trust nine-tenths of what we hold to be true. Man is a suggestible animal and tends to believe what is said to him unless he has some positive reason for doubting the honesty or competence of his informant. In hypnotism this natural docility or credulity is well illustrated, for the channels are closed through which there could arise ideas that would conflict with those suggested ; and no matter how absurd the suggested statement might seem in normal life, it acts itself out uninterruptedly. To hear is to believe.

In the normal waking state some minds are more critical and suspicious than others, but in every mind suggestion tends in some degree to induce acceptance or belief. Young children whose minds are free from suspicion and whose experience has been too limited to conflict with what is said, are prone to believe what they hear from others as naturally as what they themselves perceive. We may say then that the prevalence of authoritarianism as a method of acquiring and testing truth depends first of all upon the limited nature of the individual and the consequent dependence of each on the testimony of others ; and secondly, upon the fact that authority makes its appeal to the suggestibility and credulity that is universal throughout the human species.

The weakness of the authoritarian method consists first in the fact that authorities conflict, and that there is consequently an internal discrepancy in the method which makes it difficult of application. This difficulty, however, is not peculiar to authoritarianism ; it is present, though to a less extent, in each of the other methods. The second and more serious source of weakness is due to the apparent impossibility of treating authority as an ultimate source of truth. When questioned as to why a given authority, say one of the writers of the Bible, should be accepted without question, the answer is almost inevitably a statement that the witness himself did not have to depend on authority, but possessed superior opportunities of acquiring the truth direct through some one of the other sources of belief, such as experience or intuition.

Let us consider first the difficulty due to the conflict of authorities. When witnesses disagree, there are two courses open to the authoritarian. He may seek for more and higher authorities, or he may invoke reason and experience to arbitrate the dispute. If he does the latter, he is abandoning his authoritarianism in favour of the empirical or rationalistic criterion. This is very often necessary. Consider, for example, the case of a Christian missionary who is attempting to convert a Mohammedan. He expounds the doctrines of the New Testament as inspired or revealed truths which are to be accepted on authority. The Mohammedan, however, replies by citing the Koran as also the product of inspiration and revelation, and hence to be accepted as an authority. Each regards his own as *the* authority, and if each were willing to go his own way that would be sufficient ; but if the missionary is to make a convert, he must cease appealing to the authority of his Bible, and must show that its teachings are more rational and more in accordance with experience than those of the Mohammedan Bible. When once an authority is challenged by some rival authority it becomes a mere futile begging of the question to demand that the genuineness of the document in question be accepted on its own testimony. The Bible may be inspired, but we can never prove that it is by showing that the doctrine of inspiration is affirmed by the Bible. When the veracity of a witness is questioned, the charge, however unjust, cannot be met by the witness himself affirming his veracity. As a matter of fact, the stanchest believers in authority are usually unwilling to argue in this circle, and will attempt to prove by an appeal to reason the super-rational nature of their authority. And yet, if once reason is admitted as qualified to pass judgment on the authenticity of rival authorities, it will be difficult to deny its competency to pass upon the merits of each particular doctrine ; and thus authoritarianism, in avoiding the Scylla of arguing in a circle, will have fallen a victim to the Charybdis of Rationalism. Suppose then that the authoritarian, to avoid this dilemma, refuses, when confronted with the conflict of authorities, to invoke the arbitrament of reason, and seeks to reconcile the conflict by the use of the authoritarian criterion itself. Is there any way of measuring the degree of authoritativeness of an authority without appealing to some other principle such as reason, experience, or intuition ? There would appear to be three possible ways of securing this measurement. An authority may be regarded as more weighty in proportion (1) to the *prestige* of its original exponents ; (2) to the *number* of its adherents ; (3) to the *time* through which it has lasted. Let us consider these in turn.

1. *The authoritarian criterion of prestige.* In the affairs of ordinary life our readiness to accept on faith the statements of others is at least in part proportioned to our regard for the persons making the statements. If I know an individual to have been honest and truthful in the past, I am the more willing to take his bare word on some new matter on which I have no other evidence. If I know that in addition to his honesty he has also proved himself an expert in a given field of knowledge, I will accept what he tells me concerning that field as true, even though it runs counter to what I should otherwise have believed. In short, the reputation which a man bears for honesty and insight—that is to say, his moral and intellectual prestige—is a real and proper criterion of the degree of faith to be given to his testimony. Now the principle on which the strength of this criterion depends in some cases is also the principle which determines its weakness in other cases. The reason why I should accept on faith the new statements of a witness whose former statements on the same subject have been found to be honest and competent, is because there is a fairly high *correlation* between the reliability of a man on a given subject at a given time and his reliability on the same subject at other times. Between statements of the same witness in different fields the correlation of reliability may be very small. It may in fact even be negative. I might,

for example, give implicit faith to the utterances of a zealous socialist concerning the details of socialist doctrine, while at the same time I might be justified in regarding his evaluation of an opponent's objection to socialism as more likely to be wrong than right. This would be a case in which the correlation would be negative. Or again, I might accept on authority the statements as to his science of a great experimental physicist, rejecting at the same time as unimportant his opinions as to the accomplishments of a spiritualistic medium. The habits of trustfulness developed in him by work with his colleagues in the laboratory might easily make him a worse than ordinary judge of the trickery of charlatans. The same man can be very wise and good in one field, and very foolish and bad in others. And it is always hazardous to assume that a justifiable prestige in a given department can be extended to other departments. There are, of course, many cases in which the degree of correlation between different types of expertness is in doubt. We should probably be justified in attaching more than ordinary credence to the otherwise unsupported opinions of a physicist in matters of biology or even of psychology. A degree of positive correlation might be expected in such allied fields. But as the homogeneity of the fields decreases there is a proportionate decrease in the probable degree of correlation. The authority of the great physicist would be quite trustworthy in chemistry, less so in biology, still less in psychology, and practically *nil* in literature or religion. In the same way we should realize that the opinion of Moses and other great personages of the Bible might be of the highest authority on the moral questions of their own day and at the same time be utterly worthless in such subjects as astronomy and geology, or even with regard to the moral problems of our own time. In short, the first of the authoritarian's three criteria, that of prestige, is strictly limited in its validity to the particular subject in which the prestige has been empirically established.

2. *The authoritarian criterion of number.* The number of those who accept a given authority is sometimes used as an index of excellence, though it is by no means acceptable to all authoritarians. Christians would never recognize the superiority of Buddhism simply because of the greater number of

Buddhists. Small religious sects are quite as loyal to their dogmas as those numerically larger ; and even the members of a large denomination would hesitate to vindicate what they believe to be the superior authority for their belief by the appeal to mere numbers. Strangely enough, the numerical criterion of the excellence of an authority is used more often by those who do not regard the principle of authority as ultimate. If, for example, there were two conflicting accounts of a certain incident, we should feel that the account given by the larger number of witnesses possessed the greater probability —always supposing that they had derived their knowledge independently of one another. But we should feel that this greater probability was due to the fact that errors are many while truth is one ; that there are many ways of seeing wrongly, but only one way of seeing rightly.   The greater the number of witnesses who agree in their accounts, the less likely are those accounts to be due to error. But this presupposes that the witnesses are accepted as authorities not blindly and on faith, but only because they were in a position to get knowledge directly through experience or reason. In brief, numbers add to the weight of an authority only when the *ultimate* source of knowledge is viewed as something other than authority.

3. *The authoritarian criterion of age.*—Age is more favoured than number as an index of reliability. Authoritarians are usually conservative, and look to the past and its institutions as preferable to those of the present. A church that has its foundations in the remote past claims a proportionately greater authority for its dogmas. There are, I believe, three causes for the strength which age lends to authority.

First, there is the perfectly justifiable appeal to our interest and sentiment. Any institution which has been used by many generations of human beings becomes enriched with a multitude of tender and beautiful associations which the new institutions, however excellent, must be without. A very old church calls to mind the hopes, fears, sorrows, and consolations which have been connected with it.   It is, as it were, a treasure-house of spiritual experiences, and he who can contemplate it without a thrill has a dull and meagre soul. It is natural but quite illegitimate that this feeling for the past should transform itself into an acceptance of the truth of the doctrines which such an institution has taught. The richness of historic interest which a creed may possess has in itself nothing whatever to do with its truth. To be convinced of this we need only visit a shrine of some religion hostile to our own, and associated with conflicts with it. The historic interest and sentiment will be there, but quite dissociated from the conviction of the truth of its dogmas.

The second reason for the supposition that the age of an authority is a mark of its reliability is embodied in a certain fallacy to which the conservative temperament is peculiarly prone. This fallacy is neatly expressed in the saying that, " As old age is wiser than youth we should revere the opinions of our ancestors." If our ancestors were now alive they would be very old, and their opinions, as the outcome of generations of experience, would indeed be worthy of reverence. But when our ancestors uttered the opinions which are now hoary with age and which we are asked to revere, they were as young in years as ourselves, and the world in which they lived was much younger in the matter of racial experience. Their opinions, however old they may be, express the childhood of the race, not its maturity. And the age of an opinion or dogma actually affords a presumption against its truth rather than in favour of it. The conservative tends to accord to old ideas and opinions, and especially to old customs and institutions, the same tenderness and respect which he pays to old persons. This is psychologically natural, for old persons and old institutions are associated ideas ; but it is logically absurd, inasmuch as the age of an opinion is only an indication of the immaturity of the generation which expressed it. In all that makes for wisdom we are not younger but older than our ancestors.

The third reason for regarding age as a strengthener of authority is more fundamental than either of the others. It rests on a theory which is itself very old : that the world, instead of evolving and progressing in wisdom, has been going backward, and that the customs, institutions, and beliefs of to-day are the degenerate survivals from a Golden Age in which men got their knowledge direct from the Creator. This primeval revelation of truth could from its very nature change only for the worse if it changed at all ; hence the farther back we can trace an institution or a dogma, the more likely it is to be true, for the nearer it is to the primeval fount of truth. This belief in a Golden Age, and a primeval, universal, and perfect revelation from God to man as the source of religious truth and authority, has had an incalculable influence upon the interpretation of history and upon history itself. Many men who would deny their belief in the myth when explicitly formulated are most strongly under its sway ; and it is only within recent years that the opposite conception of a world that is growing and progressing has really begun to take possession of men's minds. The older belief still remains as the mainspring of the method of authoritarianism, and of its accompanying emphasis on conformity, traditionalism, and all forms of conservatism. It is hardly necessary to say that the scientists and historians of to-day can find nothing whatever to justify this belief. Despite the great civilizations of ancient times, the farther back we go in time the less perfect on the whole do we find human institutions and human knowledge, and the more do we find of ignorance and cruelty. And when to the ordinary records of history we add the evidences of anthropology, we find in place of a single golden age a succession of ages in which stone, bronze, and iron are the characteristic materials by which man has painfully risen from the level of animal life.

We have seen that it is impossible for authoritarianism to justify itself as an ultimate method of deriving truth. The question that in one form or another has always proved fatal is the question : *Why should I accept your authority rather than his ?* The answer to this question must either be a senseless and question-begging demand that the validity of a given authority must itself be accepted on authority, or else an appeal to some other criterion such as reason or experience, or to a theory such as that of the Golden Age. The claim of blind faith or subservience to authority is in every case unable to meet the problem raised by the conflict of creeds. The essentially secondary nature of the authoritarian criterion might indeed have been exhibited simply and deductively, without the extended considerations which have been offered. We might have pointed out that a situation in which A holds a doctrine on the authority of B, B deriving it from C, who in turn has derived it from D, and so on, cannot be extended for ever. Sooner or later there must be a witness whose claim to truth does not rest on the say-so of any other witness, but on his own direct experience, reason, intuition, or practice. To dispense with this non-authoritarian basis for a chain of authorities would be as impossible as for a community of bankrupts to conduct a financial operation with what they borrowed from one another.

But, it may be asked, if authoritarianism is as indefensible as all this, why does it still persist so widely and maintain its hold upon so many minds ? For there are many even to-day who take pride in the fact that they accept their beliefs on faith, and who would regard it as arrogant if not sacrilegious to trust the free exercise of their mere reason or conscience in matters of religion.

I think that the prevalence of the authoritarian attitude is due to four principal causes :

(1) Many authoritarians combine their doctrine with the methodological theory of mysticism which we are to take up in our next chapter. They could freely admit all that we have said as to the impossibility of regarding authority or testimony as an ultimate source of knowledge, and could argue that those whom they accepted as authorities had derived their knowledge through inspiration, intuition, or divine revelation. If asked to state why they believed in this supernatural source of knowledge, they might appeal to the character and quality of the doctrines as being such that mere human experience and human reason could not have produced them. Thus the whole matter would have been removed from the domain of blind faith ; and the doctrine in question would have to be analysed and discussed on its merits, with a view to testing its claim to supernatural origin. It is conceivable that such a position could be successfully defended, but if it were, it would be by an appeal to reason and not by a demand for unquestioning and uncritical acceptance of authority.

(2) The sceptics as well as the mystics help to keep authoritarianism alive. Men who have tried the other methods of attaining truth in philosophy and have become befuddled and lost in a sea of doubt fall easy victims to the confident dogmatist who claims to have attained a truth which is so sacred and so

certain that it neither permits nor requires any proof. As to the validity of this alliance between scepticism and authoritarianism we must suspend judgment until we have considered the arguments in behalf of scepticism. There is in this connection, however, a rather common confusion against which we should be on our guard. It is due to a certain figurative sense in which the term " authority " is sometimes used. We may be told, for example, that all beliefs rest on authority of some kind ; and we may be challenged to explain why we should accept the " authority " of the senses or of reason or of intuition and reject the authority of testimony. The two kinds of authority are of course absolutely different. Sense, reason and intuition are all of them cases of a direct relation of the individual to the facts in which he is to believe, and they are " authorities " only in the sense of being sources or grounds of belief. But when testimony enters as the source of a belief the individual's relation to the truth is not direct but indirect, for it depends on the sense, reason, or intuition of a second individual. Whatever weakness may develop in the other methods of attaining truth, they are not subject to the indirectness of the authoritarian method.

(3) Sometimes an effort is made to link up authority with pragmatism by the claim that in order to live and act we must have faith in the testimony of others. Professor W. H. Sheldon eloquently defends this attitude in his book *The Strife of Systems*. In his chapter on Thomism (p. 397) he quotes with seeming approval from the article on Faith in the Catholic Encyclopedia the following passage :

" . . . the proposition [dogma] itself does not compel our assent, since it is not intrinsically evident, but there remains the fact that only on condition of our assent to it shall we know what the human soul naturally yearns for, viz. the possession of God Who is our ultimate end." And then Sheldon adds, expressing his own opinion (p. 398) : " It is not that practical needs urge us to believe certain things because we *wish* to believe them ; rather because we cannot, if we squarely face the practical situation—as the theorist does not —help believing them. . . . We must perforce appeal in the common conduct of life to some immediate authority. Men abide by commonsense in mundane matters ; and on the whole, in the ultimate questions, men accept some religious dogma or other, whether dictated by the heart's claims or by some potent personality ; and in neither realm have men stopped to demonstrate. The Catholic Church is simply the strictly logical conclusion in matters of religion, of the common human attitude ; and that is to say, of the inevitable human attitude. Faith we must have and do have. If life is a war upon evil and the church life's army, the soldiers must implicitly obey their commanders."

Against such a pragmatic justification of authoritarianism there are three objections that may be urged : (a) There is the objection to the pragmatist method itself, that the *end* (even when practically valuable) does not justify (in the sense of verifying) the *means* to its attainment, even if such means happens to be the holding of a certain theoretical belief. This objection, however, can only be dealt with properly when we come to the chapter on Pragmatism. (b) There is the objection that as a matter of psychological fact belief is not always necessary to action. I can try out a hypothesis without believing that it has more than a very slight probability of truth. (c) There is the objection based on the plurality of conflicting ends to the attainment of each of which some different faith may be necessary. How shall one choose between the kind of salvation for which faith in Mohammedan dogmas is a necessary means and other kinds of salvation for the attainment of which equally blind faith in quite other dogmas is demanded ? And what will the authoritarian say to those who prefer to preserve their intellectual integrity rather than purchase any one of these rival salvations at the cost of making a Pascal wager which would commit them to a made belief or make-belief unsupported by evidence ?

(4) The chief reason for the continuance of authoritarianism as a method lies not in its logical but in its psychological appeal. Men who are intellectually lazy or timid will always welcome the appeal to cease thinking for themselves and to believe what they are told to believe. Such men enjoy the freedom from responsibility which their conformity brings. So far from being ashamed of accepting a doctrine on the mere say-so of someone else, they actually make a virtue out of their weakness, and singing the praises of blind faith, they

proceed to persecute those who seek truth for themselves. These people are the natural and hereditary enemies of the philosophers. Between the two groups there can never be peace. The philosopher must regard reason as a sacred thing, and the using of it for the illumination of life as man's highest duty. He who repudiates this gift and the responsibilities which it brings, and binds himself over to the blind acceptance of authority, has exchanged his birthright for a mess of slave's pottage. He may be more comfortable, for the search after wisdom often brings sorrow and disillusionment, but his soul's comfort will have been purchased at the cost of his soul's honour. Better to raise one's eyes to the sky and seek humbly for the truth, even though the search result in failure and unhappiness, than to give our beliefs into the keeping of another.

We should, however, be on our guard against two possible misunderstandings of the position here set forth. First, the refusal to accept an authoritarian defence of a doctrine is by no means a refusal to accept the doctrine itself. The fact that the premises adduced in support of a conclusion are false is no indication that the conclusion is false. It is quite possible that the theological and ethical creeds which are usually based only on authority could be successfully vindicated in all their details by one of the other criteria. The battle for what is called the " higher criticism," or the right to study the Bible in the same honest and unbiased way in which we study other historical documents, has been won largely through the aid of those who believed so thoroughly in the reasonableness of the Biblical doctrines that they were ashamed to subject them longer to the suspicion of weakness which must attach to theories which are guarded from rational examination. The second possible misunderstanding against which we should guard is that in rejecting authority as a primary sanction we should by no means reject it as a secondary source of knowledge. As was said at the outset, by far the greater part of any individual's knowledge is derived from the testimony of others. And it is only when there is reason for doubting either the veracity or the competency of the witness that his authority should be impugned. Testimony that is to be accepted, in the manner of the authoritarian, on blind faith, regardless of the extent to which it may conflict with reason and experience, is one thing, and a bad thing, but testimony that is open to free and honest study remains as legitimate a source of knowledge as any other.

There is no doubt that in matters of theory the reign of authority has been growing steadily weaker from the time of the Protestant Reformation. The spirit of free inquiry and a recognition of the right to think for oneself has attained a strength in the Western world which seems to ensure its permanence against any possible wave of reaction. Even in the most conservative communities the appeal to reason in support of dogmas is more frequent than the appeal to authority. In ethics, however, the authoritarian is still largely in control. To the majority of people, righteousness means obedience to authority and its laws. The good child is obedient to the commands of his parent, and the good man is he who obeys the commands which have the sanction of religious authority. Thus conventional ethics is made to depend upon theology. It is, in fact, hardly more than theology applied to practice. And although our concern is with methodology rather than with the theory of values, yet in closing the discussion of authoritarianism we shall do well to note briefly some of its implications for ethics.

First to be mentioned is the negative character of a system of morals based on authority. Laws are essentially prohibitive. They tell us what we must not do rather than what we must do. A positive command cannot be made so definite and cannot be so easily enforced as one that is negative. Our code of morals, as usually taught, consists of a great number of prohibitions and taboos. " Thou shalt not " is the dominant note. We are warned at every turn not to yield to this, that, or the other impulse. The result of this is to make moral goodness appear either colourless and negative, or as something austere and repulsive to our nature. Now, there is a natural and primitive moral sense which protests instinctively against the authoritarian conception of the good. If we desired to express esteem and admiration for a friend, we should not be apt to describe him as one who obeyed every mandate of authority. We should characterize him as courageous, kindly, and fair-minded. These really cardinal virtues do not derive their value from the fact that they are commanded by anybody, human or divine, but from their own intrinsic worth and beauty.

A second consequence of authoritarianism for ethics is its tendency to block social progress. The environment of society is undergoing constant change, and a moral code that is suited to the needs and conditions of one generation may become highly disadvantageous for the generations of later days. Such institutions as slavery and polygamy, for example, may at one time have been morally justifiable institutions, making for the highest well-being of the community. To the society of the present day, however, they rightly seem abhorrent. Now, just in so far as such practices are regarded as owing their moral value to mere authority it must appear wrong to change them, no matter how much the environment may have changed, while in so far as they are viewed as deriving their moral value from their adaptation to specific conditions, there will, when those conditions change, be no motive for continuing practices which have been outgrown. In a loosely organized agricultural society, like that of the pioneering days in America, many rights and duties were recognized which in the present highly organized and industrial society would work for evil rather than good. I refer to such rights as that of unrestricted freedom of contract, of doing what one would with one's property, of always buying labour at the lowest market rate, etc., etc. ; and such duties as that of punishing with firearms injuries to one's self or one's family. It is the tendency of authoritarian ethics to take principles and rules of conduct such as these, and raise them above the realm of change by making them sacrosanct, supernaturally commanded, and immune to criticism. This results in the living present being oppressed by the dead hand of the past. If our moral code is recognized as resting upon reason, we can criticize and improve it and adapt it to new conditions ; while so long as it is regarded as resting upon authority it must be obeyed to the letter, no matter how useless or harmful its consequences. In this connection there are, I think, two erroneous beliefs that are held by those who take the authoritarian attitude toward questions of social ethics.

There is first the belief that it is always desirable to have stability of social institutions ; and there is secondly the belief that any institutional stability is impossible apart from an authoritarian basis. The falsity of the first of these beliefs follows from the fact that an institution is not, as the authoritarian supposes, an end in itself, but rather a means by which a social group adjusts its environment to its needs. Consequently, any change either in the environment or in the character or ideals of the group will require a corresponding change in the institutional form of adjustment. Under such changing circumstances, to keep an institution stable or unchanged would be to bring about a maladjustment that would defeat the very purpose of the institution. In forgetting their purely instrumental nature, the authoritarian ascribes to his institutions a sacrosanctness and intrinsic value that could at best belong only to the ends which those institutions are designed to serve.

In the second place, as regards the belief that no institutional stability is possible apart from authority, it, too, is false. For in a society in which there is a rationalistic or anti-authoritarian attitude there will be the same motive for preserving old institutions so long as they are efficient as for changing them when they cease to be efficient. The fundamental need of society in its institutional life is not *stability* but *flexibility*. Flexibility based on free reason and social self-consciousness will allow and encourage change where changing conditions demand it, and at the same time will insist on stability when conditions remain stable.

A third consequence of an authoritarian ethics is a destruction of moral perspective, with the resulting danger to the whole moral life. A child or a youth will be taught that all acts, no matter how different from one another, are wrong, in so far as they violate the code. First of all, there will be the cases of intrinsically heinous deeds such as stealing and murdering; secondly, there will be practices such as card-playing and drinking, which at certain times and in certain conditions might lead to bad consequences; and thirdly, such authoritarian teachings will almost always prohibit sternly any departure from theological dogmas and ritualistic practices the truth and value of which are at least debatable. To urge obedience to these very different classes of rules solely on the ground of authority is a lamentable error. It levels all moral distinction and puts the unimportant and the debatable on a par with what is fundamental and vital. The youth so taught comes sooner or later to discover that there are many otherwise estimable persons who do not respect the taboos of his own village or the ritualistic practices of his own sect. This discovery will of necessity bring into question the validity of that authority which he has accepted and from which all his rules of conduct have derived their morally obligatory character. Whatever discredits an authority discredits all its teachings equally. The valid and the invalid, the important and the trivial, for the very reason that they were made to derive their moral credit from a single source, must now share in the discredit due to the discrediting of their source. All the eggs have been put in the one basket and the moral smash is complete. How different would have been the result if, instead of deadening the child's powers of appreciating and discerning moral values by resting all precepts upon authority, his teachers had justified those same precepts by demonstrating the ways in which they made for the protection and development of society. To the child thus rationalistically taught, morality will be a matter, not of rules and commands, but of principles and ideals. And if, as is almost inevitable, the pupil discovers later that some of our teachings have been mistaken, instead of " chucking the whole thing " and feeling at liberty to gratify every impulse, no matter how base or how selfish, he will feel an increased responsibility to solve for himself the problem in whose solution his teachers have failed. In short, a rationalistic method of teaching ethics secures the pupil's essential morality against the consequences of the teacher's possible errors, and it also quickens and develops the child's moral sensibility by making him feel responsible, not only for doing right, but for finding out what is right to do. While, on the other hand, the authoritarian method of teaching ethics not only endangers the essentials of morality by making them dependent on an external authority, the validity of which may be later brought in question, but it also debauches and deadens the child's moral sense, and especially his sense for moral perspective, by refusing to submit its teachings to inquiry and verification and by lumping together in a code of arbitrary rules principles that are important and permanent with precepts that are trivial and temporary.

CHAPTER II

THE METHOD OF MYSTICISM

We have seen that the method of authoritarianism is often combined with the doctrine that the primary authorities possessed a means of access to truth which was higher than either sense or reason. This theory that truth can be attained by a super-rational and super-sensuous faculty of *intuition* is Mysticism.

When the mystic experience comes to a person of philosophic temper and interests it usually takes the form of an intuition of the oneness of all things, and especially of the union of the finite self with the universe, or with God. God is often conceived by the mystics as a being whose nature is so ineffable as to transcend the distinctions not only of the senses but of Reason itself. They feel that to ascribe definite characteristics to the absolute being, to say that he is personal, or conscious, or powerful, would be to put him on a level with other beings. Just because he is the unity of all things he cannot have the attributes of any. He is above relations and above distinctions, and as it is only through relations and distinctions that the intellect can comprehend its objects, the mystic must gain his comprehension of this absolute unity through an experience more intimate and immediate than that of thought, and more nearly analogous to a pure feeling or emotion in which the distinction between the self and its objects is no longer present.

Before dealing with the problem which primarily concerns us, the validity of mysticism as a method of logic, we must consider the psychological problem as to the nature of the " intuition " from which originate the beliefs and experiences on which mysticism is founded.

The simplest hypothesis as to the nature of intuition is

54

that it is that capacity of the soul by which man comes into direct telepathic communication with disembodied spirits, with mysterious cosmic energies, or even with God himself. This hypothesis of supernatural inspiration is naturally favoured by the mystics themselves, and on evidence which appeals to them as incontrovertible. It is, however, the prime duty of science and philosophy to exhaust the possibilities of natural explanation before turning to the supernatural. And it is only by maintaining this attitude and refusing, except as a last resort, to invoke unseen spirits to help us out of our difficulties that we have succeeded in gaining any solutions of problems or mastery over nature. I believe that the recognized factors of instinct and imagination afford the promise of yielding a natural explanation for many of the mystics' apparently supernatural experiences. But the fact that as yet we know little about the mechanism of imagination and less about the basis of instinct, makes it possible to indicate only the general lines along which a solution might be sought.

Each of us begins life with a number of inherited tendencies, both mental and physical. Our capacities for eating, walking, and talking are innate, though the specific forms in which they are utilized are the product of experience. Many of our likes and dislikes and of our feelings of enjoyment, anger, jealousy, etc., are similarly the manifestations of inherited tendencies. And although the biologists will not countenance the doctrine that we inherit directly the experiences of our ancestors and possess, as it were, an ancestral memory, yet it can hardly be denied that in so far as our brains and minds are the result of a long process of evolution we do possess in the form of instincts an indirect and partial equivalent of a racial memory. Our individual experiences are moulded and coloured by this background of inherited tendencies, and many of the intuitions or direct insights that seem inexplicable as products of ordinary perception may well be the spontaneous expression of congenital tendencies. Just as our instincts represent the life habits of our ancestors, so our memories represent the experiences of our own past and constitute an additional background for the intuitive judgments of the moment. It is this joint system of tendencies derived from inheritance and memory which without coming themselves into consciousness largely control our conscious processes and occasionally contribute original ideas and happy inspirations.   When the stored-up traces of the past act in this way, we speak, not of memory or instinct, but of *imagination*.   We all have a certain amount of imagination ;   and a characteristic feature of the faculty is the suddenness and spontaneity of its action.   Often, after we have been working over some problem and have put it aside as unsolved, the solution will flash suddenly into our consciousness.   The movements of all creative art and creative thought, and especially all expressions of humour and wit, have their inception in these flashes of the imagination.   Although, as was said, we know little of the underlying mechanism of instinct and imagination, we can see enough to understand how either of these functions, or both combined, could account for many of the visions, intuitions, and ecstasies of the religious and philosophic mystics.   Moreover, when we recall the readiness with which the imagination can create for us in our dreams distinct personalities whose speech and behaviour are often surprisingly consistent with their character, we may realize the difficulty of proving that the mystic is inspired by any powers more mysterious than those of his inner and deeper self.   The chief difference between the mystic and the ordinary man may consist in this : that in the ordinary man, so long as he is awake, the power of imagination is weaker than the sense of perceptual reality, while in the mystic the reverse is true.

• In favour of mysticism as a method of acquiring knowledge, it may truly be said that not only in philosophy, but in art, and even in science, some of the most significant ideas and ideals have originated from the intuitions of the mystic. Moreover, the belief which lies at the heart of all religion, that the soul of man can somehow unite itself with the substance of the universe, be that substance personal or impersonal, and thereby attain to a vision of truth far surpassing in its depth and sublimity and in the peace, joy, and power that it brings, anything that mere reason or sense can afford is, as we have seen, a product of mystical experience.   The major part of every human life is concerned with adjustments to the material world, and the consciousness accompanying such adjustments is sensory and external.   It is well for us that this is not the whole story, and that part of our experience is derived from within ourselves.   The sentiments and aspirations that come from within the self give us our world of immediate values.   These values are the expressions of temperamental likes and dislikes; they cannot be derived from perception or proved by reason.   No interpretation of reality that neglects or violates the inner harmonies of feeling can gain a hold upon the heart.   The mystic is one to whom these inner experiences appeal as vital and real.   He pictures the world in terms of them, and the picture is precious in that it embodies and makes visible in objective form the hidden depths of the human spirit. Even ordinary perception and reasoning is largely based upon the subconscious stores of memory and instinct.   They furnish the meaning with which our sensations are clothed, and the motives by which our reasonings are driven.   The intuitions of creative imagination as expressed in the cosmic revelations of the philosophic and religious mystics, and even in the less generic visions of the great poets, owe their grandeur and uniqueness to the fact that in them the subconscious functions more spontaneously, more nearly as a unified whole.   In normal experience intuition is the servant of the specific, external situation, and there is evoked only that part of the subconscious which is relevant to that situation, while in the real mystic intuition the inner self in its entirety is the controlling factor.   Now when we reflect that man is the inheritor at least of the congenital characters of a line of ancestors extending backward and downward through millions of years, and consequently embodying the varied capacities of a whole series of organic forms, from those more simple than the amœba to those as complex as his human parents, we should seem to have in our hereditary endowment a microcosmic system which, if it could be made available, would amply suffice for the most comprehensive of mystic revelations.   It is of course a question as to how far a man can avail himself of this wealth of data, and to what extent intuition can afford a channel by which more than the individual's own past may express itself as content of his conscious experience.

Nor must we forget that however adequate for explaining mystic visions the subconscious part of the self may be, we cannot exclude the possibility that the human mind at its deeper levels may be susceptible to external influences other than those affecting the physical senses. And in favour of the super-individualist hypothesis, it should be remembered that William James, who was fully aware of the tremendous possibilities of the subconscious and of the hidden energies of men, was himself not content to explain all of the varieties of religious experience in terms of the subconscious alone.

It seems highly improbable that a single type of physico-chemical compound, such as protoplasm, should be the exclusive vehicle for an entire dimension of being such as consciousness. If the cosmos as a whole, or any integral part of it, such as the solar system or the earth, were possessed of a psychic concomitant or mind as much vaster than our minds, as the matter of which it is composed is vaster than the matter of our bodies, there would be the possibility of a *rapport* between that larger cosmic life and the lesser lives of the individuals contained within it. The intuitions and revelations of the mystics would then be grounded not only upon subconscious memory and instinct, but also upon the influx of energy from a larger self.

The life of the spirit owes to the mystics a debt which is immeasurable ; the few considerations which we have adduced suffice only to indicate something of its character. And yet we must remember that what illuminates the soul may darken the world ; and the mystic, in reading his own yearnings and feelings into nature, has often made poetry of what should be prose, and has prevented man from gaining that insight into material things on which even his spiritual progress is ultimately dependent. We should, moreover, keep in mind that the peculiar feeling of certainty which attends the mystic vision is not itself a criterion of objective truth. The asylums are full of persons who see visions and hear voices and have intuitions of unutterable truths which can easily be proved to be no truths at all by those in possession of their faculties.

Even in those cases in which there is no question of insanity, and in which the mystic beliefs cannot be disproved by experience because they transcend it, we must recognize that the mystics to some extent refute one another in that their visions of truth are often incompatible. Joseph Smith, Anne Lee, and Mrs. Eddy, to say nothing of Buddha and Mohammed, were each vouchsafed a mystic revelation suffi-

ciently distinctive and important to be the basis of a religious
cult.   Yet between these various revelations there is the
widest divergence.   This should teach us that an intuition
which lacks the prosaic sanctions of reason and experience,
and appears to the mystic as something divinely inspired, may
have no more truth than idle fancy, and no more reliability
than the instinct of the moth to seek the candle.

Furthermore, we must recognize that the profound transformations of habits and dispositions which are wrought in
the soul by such mystical experiences as those of *conversion*
are by no means proof of the exclusive validity of the particular
doctrines or the particular disciplines or techniques with
which they may be associated.   The medieval monks, the holy
men of India, the Mohammedan dervishes, and the Christian
Scientists of our own day are but a few of those whose souls
have been flooded with an inner light bringing conviction to
the mind and peace and courage to the heart.   The several
sets of dogmas may be incompatible with one another and as
varied in character as the ritual practices by which the different
devotees work themselves up to the pitch of enlightenment.
That each mystic should attribute the power of his mystical
experience to the peculiar technique by which his state of illumination is attained, or to the truth of his particular creed,
is natural enough, but of no logical significance.

Although the problem of logical method is fairly distinct
from the other types of philosophical problems and capable of
being discussed on its own merits, yet each type of methodological theory has a kind of natural affinity to certain
non-methodological theories.   In the examination of authoritarianism, it will be remembered that we had occasion to note
the connection of that doctrine with the legend of a Golden
Age and the resulting attitude of conservatism in all matters
of ethics, politics, and sociology.   Now, while all mystics
agree in their definitive emphasis upon intuition as the means
of acquiring truth, the philosophical conclusions as to the
world and its values which are derived from this method are
of two quite diverse types.   The one type of mysticism we
may term negative, the other positive.   Let us consider first
those attitudes generally recognized as affiliated with negative
mysticism.

Closely allied with that monistic tendency of all mysticism to which we have already referred is the tendency of negative mysticism toward what we may call " illusionism," the belief in the illusoriness or unreality of material things. Zeno, the Eleatic, attempted to discredit the reality of the world of sense by his attack upon motion, which is the most universal of the world's characteristics. Whatever the motive which actuated Zeno in formulating his puzzles, it is certain that by showing that motion is impossible and that the evidences of sense are false, he prepared men's minds to accept the belief of Parmenides in the sole reality of a changeless and homogeneous Being. Our modern Christian Science is another example of the negative mystic's love of illusionism. Matter, sickness, pain, and evil are all regarded as non-existent, or, in Mrs. Eddy's phraseology, as mere " errors of mortal mind." It is in the philosophies of India, however, that the doctrine of illusionism is worked out most consistently. According to those philosophies, the entire physical world is the result of *mâyâ*, or error, which in its turn is due to sin. The root of all sin being selfishness or a desire for personal existence, it follows that only to him who can rid himself of all concern for his own prosperity will come enlightenment. As the scales of sense drop from his eyes he will see the hollowness and unreality of all that to the uninitiated seems most real ; while in place of his feeling of personal and individual existence comes the experience of perfect union and identity with the absolute and universal self.

The standing objection to this curious theory of illusionism is based on its futility. What· does it mean to say that the world is unreal, as long as we have the experience of it as real ? How does it lessen or in any way change the experience of a pain to call the pain an error ? The having the illusion is not itself an illusion. Pain and the illusion of pain are identical. Moreover, how is either the origin or the continuance of this illusion of evil compatible with the absolute perfection which alone is real ? To these theoretical difficulties there must be added a practical or ethical difficulty. If evil is unreal, why should we seek to diminish it ? If my neighbour's suffering is illusory, why should I seek to alleviate it ? Illusionism, in so far as it affects our conduct at all, affects it negatively.

It destroys all motives for serious action. Why take life seriously, if life is a dream ?

Most of those mystics who regard the world as unreal regard it also as bad. There is, of course, a contradiction in this combination of attitudes, for if a thing did not really exist, it could not be really bad. The contradiction is partly avoided, however, by taking the position pointed out in the previous paragraph. The belief in an unreal world may itself be real, and belief in an unreal evil may itself be evil. It is these false beliefs which the mystic regards as things that must be fought against and exterminated. And inasmuch as they are the inevitable consequences of life in the material world and are indissolubly bound up with the conditions of sensory experience, the object of human endeavour should be an escape from life and its duties. Pessimism is the name for this theory that the world contains a preponderance of evil over good and that life itself is essentially and intrinsically bad. To the negative mystic, with his mind filled with the vision of a supersensuous and supernatural reality, the ordinary life with its insistent appeal to the body and its appetites can hardly fail to appear as evil.

An answer to this pessimism would take the form of a demonstration that material life, so far from being incompatible with the ideal of the spirit, affords the best means for its realization, and that it is not the use of the body, but its abuse, that conflicts with spiritual interests.

Asceticism is the application of pessimism to ethics. If life and all that makes for life is bad, then the good that we should aim at is not fulfilment of life's interests, but a negation of them. The soul appears to the ascetic like a ship which is being driven by a powerful wind straight upon rocks that mean destruction. To be delivered, to escape, she must fight against the natural forces which would wreck her. From the standpoint of asceticism the flesh and the spirit are hopelessly at war, and the triumph of one means the doom of the other. Hence, virtue consists in a systematic harassing of the body and in a starving and thwarting of its appetites until the soul, released from their grip, makes its escape from this world, and becomes united once more with the God from whom it has been alienated. The moral code

E

of the ascetic is largely negative, a code of prohibitions and taboos. As all life is evil, it behooves us to abstain as much as possible from the things that make life pleasant. To have a natural or instinctive desire for a thing is *prima facie* evidence that the thing is bad. Solitude and poverty are good because they are the denial of the powerful desires for society and for property. Fasting and celibacy are still better, for they deny the more powerful instincts of hunger and love. Woman's status in a society dominated by asceticism is peculiarly dismal. Regarded as the standing and principal temptation to evil, she may attain to a position of genuine dignity and honour only in so far as she abjures her natural aspiration for love and motherhood and consecrates herself to a perpetual virginity.

The answer to this ascetic attitude which has so frequently been associated with mysticism is the same as that given to the pessimistic view of earthly life on which it is based. The soul is no more opposed to the body than the flower is opposed to the stem on which it grows. The attempt to develop the flower by destroying its stem would only result in its deformity and destruction ; and the attempt to make the spirit prosper at the expense of the body and its needs produces souls as mean and withered as the bodies that bear them, and a social life and culture that is illiberal and cruel.

Another tendency of negative Mysticism is " Other-Worldliness." The negative mystic, as we have seen, tends too often to regard the world as a place to which the soul has been banished, and this means that his heart is set on escape from this world to another. When he is not actually fighting as an ascetic against material things, his sense of banishment leads him to be indifferent to them and to their improvement. A man forced to live in a foreign country can hardly have the same interest in its welfare as one who has voluntarily chosen it. The indifference of this other-worldly type of mystic to the needs of the world is often more dangerous than the open hostility of the ascetic. Throughout the long advance in knowledge and in social amelioration, reformers have had to contend with the tendency of mystical minds to belittle secular education and material prosperity.

The last of the important tendencies to be associated with mysticism of the negative type is the belief in the occult and in the superiority of magic to science as a means of controlling nature. If the entire material world is but the shadow of a supernatural reality, it is folly to use the methods of control that are based only on sense and reason. Invocations and incantations will be more effective than science, and the knowledge gained from dreams and from spirit mediums will be more reliable than that secured in the ordinary way. It has taken the civilized world a long time to emancipate itself from this faith in a short and easy way of getting results. The notion of wishing-caps and love-philters is intrinsically fascinating, and there are very few, even in civilized countries, who are entirely free from superstition of one sort or another. And yet, in most of the departments of experience, the steady advance of science has driven out magic practices; and it has done this, not by any general refutation of the possibility of the occult and supernatural, but rather by the demonstration, in case after case, of the uncertainty and futility of magic, and of the efficiency and reliability of science.

In view of the power of intuition in the lives of men and the power of the mystics in human history, it is fortunate that the negative mysticism whose evil consequences we have been considering is in part corrected by what may be called " positive mysticism." The positive mystic is one whose revelation of the invisible and transcendent serves not to blind him to the concrete details and duties of visible existence, but rather to illuminate and strengthen his earthly life. His outlook on the world is devoid of illusionism, pessimism, asceticism, and occultism. To mystics of this higher type nature seems more real rather than less real, and beautiful rather than ugly. And instead of devoting their lives to the negation of the will to live and to a repudiation of earthly existence and its duties, they use their inner light to supplement the outer light of common sense and of science, and strive to incarnate the kingdom of heaven in this world. Their love of God is a supplement to, rather than a substitute for, their love of humanity; and instead of preaching a gospel of salvation from original sin, they inspire their disciples to militant service and unending increase of the good.

It is perhaps only the naturally great and generous spirit that can stand the intoxication of the beatific vision and turn it to a healthy and beneficent purpose. Whatever the theoretical validity of the mystic's intuition, the ethical and practical consequences of it are of the two types which we have characterized as negative and positive. The one is evil and narrow, perpetual enemy to the life of reason and of love ; while the other enhances and perfects the things of earth with a more than earthly beauty. Perhaps we may best guard against the moral and intellectual dangers of negative mysticism and best avail ourselves of the values of the positive type by remembering that the ideas and beliefs which are yielded by intuition should neither be discarded as false nor accepted as true, but taken tentatively as hypotheses which need to be tested by further experience. They should, in short, be treated precisely like those ideas that are derived from the testimony of others—as suggestions which we are thankful to receive, but careful to substantiate.

The antithesis of positive and negative mysticism has its application in the field of logical method no less than in those more general domains which we have been considering. The intimate relation of intuition to imagination was noted at the beginning of our chapter, and there is at least one kind of intuition that is nothing but imagination touched with conviction. And imagination is the main source of all new ideas and of all variations, not only in the life of art but in the life of science. We have seen how the memories of falling apples and revolving planets simmering in the mind of a Newton did one day reach the boiling-point and emerge into consciousness fused into the new unity of a theory of universal gravitation. This fusing of old matters of memory into new forms of imagination is the same kind of process, whether it occurs in the scientist or the poet. The difference lies only in the kind of elements and in the kind of interest by which the fusion is wrought. And both in poetry and in science, the value of the imaginative act is measured not so much by the novelty of its product as by the extent of the domain to which it is pertinent. For the poet or artist the new unit must possess an *affective* congruity with a manifold of *sentiment*, while for the scientist it must have a *cognitive* congruity with a manifold of *fact*. But between the two types of imaginative product there is this further difference that the inspirations of the artist must be left intact to stand or fall on their intrinsic merits, while on the other hand the inspirations of the scientist must be most severely tested by their extrinsic harmonies with other and perhaps opposing conclusions.

It is this latter business of comparing the newly-born hypotheses of imagination with the established community of older principles which constitutes the work of reason. The function of reason is, in other words, not so much to originate as to prove. Reason is the censor of fancy, selecting from the wealth of new ideas those which can successfully stand comparison with the old and be made harmonious with them. From this standpoint, the difference between positive and negative mysticism in the field of logic will consist in this : The positive mystic will accept the fruits of creative imagination as material for proof, while the negative mystic will accept them as already proved. To the former, the intuition of a new principle will constitute an obligation to substantiate it, to the latter it will constitute an excuse for not substantiating it. Thus the positive mystic, protected by a sense of his duty to verify, can avail himself freely and safely of the wildest vagaries of fancy, while the negative mystic, lacking the protection of an intellectual conscience, will risk error in accepting any, even the most seemingly certain, of his intuitive convictions.

But after all has been granted as to the need of testing objectively our fancies and intuitions, there remains a problem in the logic of mysticism which is as unescapable as it is important.

What are we to do with those intuitions which for any reason are beyond or above all direct objective tests ? Are we justified in accepting them, at least tentatively ? Or should we reject them as utterly groundless ? Or can we find an indirect criterion which would help in their evaluation ?

I believe that there is such a criterion, and that it can be legitimately used as a supplement to, and even when necessary as a substitute for the direct and objective test which we should all prefer. The nature of this criterion is psychological or psycho-analytical. We should seek to discover the subconscious source of the intuition in question. If as a result of such examination we find that our conviction has sprung from logically irrelevant causes, such as fears and hopes or vanities and jealousies, we ought to regard our intuitive certainty as logically valueless. Suppose, for example, that I have a sudden strong feeling of distrust for an individual, a real intuition of his wickedness, which is neither supported by any past evidence nor capable of being tested by experiment. In default of the objective test, I use the subjective method of self-examination. I am led to recall an occasion which I had forgotten when the man in question was the unwitting means by which my self-esteem was hurt or my ambition thwarted. My mysterious intuition thus traced to its sources appears as the morally ignoble and logically worthless " defence mechanism " by which my ego has been kept from admitting its own defeat. Or again, perhaps my self-examination enables me to recall certain fears in early childhood of hunchbacks or red-headed men or what not, originating in the words of a superstitious nurse. The silly and long-forgotten suggestions have crystalized into mysteriously vivid and impressive antipathies—" instinctive " or " intuitive " convictions as to the evil nature of certain types of men. Or still again, my intuitive estimate of a man's worth may be favourable; and in this case self-examination may show incidents of a flattering nature directly or indirectly connected with the individual that would have inclined me to feel pleasantly toward him. In such a case, as in those just considered, the discovery of factitious causes for the intuition would reduce its logical value to zero.

But now, finally, if the most careful self-analysis reveals no cause for bias, then the intuition may be taken to mean that the proposition under consideration possesses a congruity with a mass of subconscious memories of past experiences, and as such may be accorded a certain positive logical value, akin to that belonging to a vague induction. Intuition might indeed be defined not only as imagination touched with conviction, but also as the outcome of subconscious induction or deduction. For it is from the subconscious stores of memory and instinct that the intuitive judgment is derived. Whether its value is positive or negative will depend on the adequacy and relevancy of the data which generate it. Relevant data will consist of prior conclusions that are logically congruous with the intuited proposition. Irrelevant data, on the other hand, will consist of likes and dislikes, vanities and fears, that are emotionally rather than logically congruous with the conclusions which they produce. For an illustration of relevant data we might take the spontaneous preference which a scientist might feel for one hypothesis rather than another in a field with which he was very familiar. There is such a thing as intellectual good taste, and we should not be illogical in granting a presumption of validity to the intuitions of experts in science as in art. Even the quite uncorroborated guesses of a Faraday or a Clerk-Maxwell should be treated with respect. And the same might be said of the metaphysical intuitions of the great philosophers, though in this more recondite domain the chances of inadequacy and irrelevance are far greater.

I should like to supplement this brief and desiccated discussion of a great form of philosophy with a quotation from a letter of William James, published by his son, Henry James, in the *Atlantic Monthly* of September 1920. In this letter James summarizes his own position as expressed in *The Varieties of Religious Experience*, and voices with characteristic force and beauty his sympathy with what we have called the " superindividual " hypothesis as to the basis of mystic intuition.

" The mother-sea and fountain-head of all religions lies in the mystical experiences of the individual, taking the word mystical in a very wide sense. All theologies and all ecclesiasticisms are secondary growths superimposed ; and the experiences make such flexible combinations with the intellectual prepossessions of their subjects, that one may almost say that they have no proper *intellectual* deliverance of their own, but belong to a region deeper, and more vital and practical, than that which the intellect inhabits. For this they are also indestructible by intellectual arguments and criticisms. I attach the mystical or religious consciousness to the possession of an extended subliminal self, with a thin partition through which messages make irruption. We are thus made convincingly aware of the presence of a sphere of life larger and more powerful than our usual consciousness, with which the latter is nevertheless continuous. The impressions and impulsions and emotions and excitements which we thence receive help us to live ; they found invincible assurance of a world beyond the sense ; they melt our hearts and communicate significance and value to everything and make us happy. They do this for the individual who has them, and other individuals follow him. Religion in this way is absolutely indestructible. Philosophy and theology give their conceptual interpretations of this experiential life. The farther margin of the subliminal field being unknown, it can be treated, as by Transcendental Idealism, as an Absolute mind with a part of which we coalesce, or by Christian theology, as a distinct deity acting on us. Something not our immediate self *does* act on our life ! "

CHAPTER III

THE METHODS OF RATIONALISM AND EMPIRICISM

The Psychological Genesis of Universals and the Logical Validation of Universal and Necessary Propositions.

THE two theories of method which we are now to consider are so closely related to one another that it will be profitable to discuss them together rather than in succession. Rationalism is the method of proving propositions by appealing to abstract and universal principles ; empiricism is the opposite method of proving propositions by appealing to concrete and particular occurrences. The ordinary person makes use of both these methods as a matter of course. If we wanted to prove the proposition that the sum of the angles of a particular triangle were equal to two right angles, we could either measure the angles, and so prove it empirically, or on the other hand we could prove it deductively by appealing to the familiar theorem of geometry in which the truth of the proposition is made to follow from the general properties of triangles. But although we undoubtedly use both methods of proof, and although our experience undoubtedly reveals to us both facts and principles, both particulars and universals, yet the problem arises as to which is the more fundamental. The empiricist, with his preference for proving his beliefs by appeal to specific cases, naturally holds that particulars are fundamental and that universal and abstract concepts and universal and necessary judgments are derived from them ; while the rationalist maintains the contrary. The problem before us is of course primarily methodological, i.e. a matter of evaluating these rival criteria of truth. But the nature of the contending schools and the historical development of their contentions combine to make it advisable to divide our discussion into two chapters. We shall in this chapter consider the relation of universals to the individual mind, discussing, first, the question of the origin of universal and abstract concepts ; and secondly, the question of the origin and validation of universal and necessary judgments. In the next chapter we shall consider the relation of universals to the objective world, discussing, first, the question of the ontological status of universals ; and secondly, the question of the extent to which the world is pervaded by universal law and rationalistic necessity.

I

THE ORIGIN OF UNIVERSAL CONCEPTS.

The rationalist contends that our knowledge of universals is far superior to our knowledge of particular objects and in no sense derived from that knowledge.

The empiricist, on the other hand, holds that universal concepts, in so far as they can be admitted as genuinely present to the mind, are derived from the concrete particulars of experience, and that their importance is secondary and instrumental.[1]

By universals are meant such objects of thought as are signified by class-names—e.g. " horse," " man," " triangle " ; and by abstract names—e.g. " humanity," " roundness," " redness." Now, although we speak of horses in general or as a class, and make assertions such as " all horses are animals " or " the horse is an animal," yet we have never seen " all horses " or " the horse," but only particular horses of a particular size and colour, existing at particular times and places. In the same way, although we talk about roundness in relation to squareness, and redness in relation to blueness,

---

[1] This question of the origin of universals must not be confused with that other phase of the historic controversy as to innate ideas which concerns the genesis of imaginary objects. The imaginary objects which figure in dreams and day-dreams as well as in works of literary art are most of them particulars like the real objects revealed in perception. They are derived from the latter through the mind's power to synthesize the elements of perception which have been retained in memory.

yet " roundness " and " redness " have never been experienced by themselves, but only as distinguishable aspects of round things and red things. Shall we then say that these general and abstract ideas are furnished by the mind and not derived from experience ? Before surrendering the empirical position thus easily, let us consider what is actually given in the experience of a particular object, such as a horse. There is in the first place a complex of qualities, some of which are common to other animals of his species, and others of which are peculiar to this particular individual. Then besides these qualities there are the characters of position in a particular part of space and at a particular moment of time. Let us represent these various distinguishable elements of the perception of an individual horse as follows :

H = the qualities common to this horse and to others.
h = the qualities peculiar to this individual horse.
S = the property of being in space.
s = the particular space where the horse is seen or heard as distinguished from other places.
T = the property of being in time.
t = the particular time when the horse is seen or heard.

The entire experience-complex of a particular horse seen at a particular time and place may thus be symbolized as H, h, S, s, T, t. Every other experienced object could be analysed in a similar way into generic and specific qualities and into the generic and individual space and time characters. In short, the psychologically primary and ultimate experiential unit is always some specific complex of qualities possessing a specific date and a specific place, and anything more general than this is, from the psychological point of view, an abstraction. Now, it is probably true that we never can perceive or even concretely imagine any of these properties in isolation. We cannot picture a horse that appears at no time and no place, and we certainly cannot form a mental picture of a horse that is of no particular colour and no particular size. The imagined horse must have his particular colour and size, just as truly as the imagined triangle must have its individual size and form—scalene, isoceles, or equilateral.

This inability to *imagine* anything except particulars has

led some thinkers to the notion that we could not conceive or think of anything but particulars, in spite of the self-evident fact that a general name, like triangle or horse, certainly does mean something and certainly does not mean a particular horse or a particular triangle. But though we may not be able to imagine one of the elements or aspects of a concrete object of experience apart from the other elements or aspects, we can attend to it more emphatically than to others, and in that way conceive it. In the case of the individual horse perceived at a given time and place which was symbolized as H, *h*, S, *s*, T, *t*, I can attend to, interest myself in, and talk about any of these elements in distinction from the others. The time at which the horse was seen, the place where he was, his qualities, generic and individual, may become in turn the exclusive object of my thoughts. If I attend to the part of the complex consisting of H, *h*, S, T, then I have formed the concept as an enduring *individual* whose existence is not bound up with the particular place and time at which I have perceived him. Such a concept as this is connoted by a proper name, like Bucephalus, Dobbin, Pegasus, etc. If I restrict my attention still further and consider only the elements, H, S, T, I shall have formed the concept of the *general class* of existent horses, which is connoted by the concrete common noun " horse." If, finally, I restrict my attention to the generic elements of the particular experience, apart from any occupancy of space or time—if in our chosen example I think simply of H—then I have formed the concept of the *abstract essence* " equinity " or " horseness." Thus we have (1) the percept, sense-datum, or event, H, *h*, S, *s*, T, *t*, which, as such, is never named because it never recurs ; (2) the proper noun or singular term, H, *h*, S, T ; (3) the common noun or "general term," H, S, T ; and (4) the abstract noun H, each representing successive degrees of restriction in attention, with corresponding increases in the universality of the object attended to.

The process of restricting attention to parts of the manifold of essences embodied in a concrete object of perception can of course be carried out in various ways according to the direction of one's interest. Instead of directing our attention to the common equine qualities which this particular horse of our illustration shared with other horses, and which we symbolized by H, we could have selected the quality of being owned by Farmer Smith, and so have attained the class concept of " domestic animals that are the property of Smith," or the still simpler and broader class concept " property of Smith." Or again, we could have fastened our attention on the animal's colour and thus arrived at the class-concept " brown," or the still broader universal of " colour " or " coloured thing." The only limit to the process of successively higher generalizations in any direction is the simplicity or unanalysableness of the essences to which we attend. Mere " being " or " thinghood " is perhaps the simplest, as it is certainly the broadest, of our concepts. But besides this *summum genus* there are universals that are, as it were, off on the side, in a dimension of their own. Examples of such universals are " temporality," " spaciality," and " consciousness." We call them *sui generis*, because of the difficulty of analysing them into further significant genera. We can, to be sure, class them under such genera as " ultimate concepts" or " philosophical abstractions "; but analyses of this kind are felt to be formal and in a sense accidental. For we are no longer attending to the intrinsic properties of the essence, but rather to its extrinsic relations to knowledge and language.

The real nature of the process of forming universals has been obscured by the fact that an important and perhaps even psychologically necessary motive for analysing a perceptual object into its constituent essences is a previous experience of them in other contexts. Cognition of new concepts results from recognition of old percepts ; and our selective attention is so unoriginal that it tends to pick out qualities that are already familiar. This unfortunate limitation in our psychological processes has generated the confused logic of nominalism according to which the class itself is thought of as constituting the universal, and " denotation " and " extension " are conceived as prior to " connotation " and " intension." As a matter of psychology this would be correct, but in logic the reverse is correct. In the psychological *order of knowing* the class of objects comes before the universal, as its *ratio cognoscendi*. But in the logical *order of being*, the universal is prior to its class of particulars, and constitutes their *ratio essendi*. The Frege-Russell definition of the number two as the class of all couples is a good example of the neo-nominalism of modern writers on logistic, and illustrates what I believe to be a mistaken tendency to treat denotation as prior to connotation. Psychologically, we should probably never arrive at the concept of *two* except for antecedent experiences of many perceptual couples. The varied material qualities of these concrete *twos* help our poor minds to discriminate their invariant formal quality of *twoness*. We can only reach the abstract universal by a bridge of concrete particulars. But when once we have reached it, we should realize that what is last in knowledge was first in nature, and that no one of these existential couples could have been a *two* unless there had subsisted from all eternity a *two* for it to be. In this respect the relation of the universal to the particular is like the relation of my friend to the hearing of his words and the seeing of his face. These latter experiences constitute the *ratio cognoscendi*. They are the antecedent conditions of my knowing him. But he himself is their *ratio essendi*, and hence is logically and ontologically prior to them. Although only a layman as regards the new logic, I dare say that many of its admitted awkwardnesses are due to the wanton nominalism of its procedure, and that many of its admitted achievements have come in spite of rather than because of its preference of an extensional to an intensional interpretation of universals.

When we come to induction, where not universal concepts but universal propositions are. to be derived from perceptual experience, we shall see that the traditional treatment of the subject suffers from the same mistake that we have just been considering. Denotation has usually been regarded as prior to connotation, and the establishing of a universal proposition has been made to appear as a mysterious leap from the perceptual *some* of the premises to the conceptual *all* of the conclusion—an illegitimate synthesis in " extension " instead of a legitimate analysis in " intension."

It is customary to designate the process of restriction or concentration of attention by which the mind arrives at its knowledge of universals by the word " abstraction." We are

told, for example, that " the universals of the intellect are
derived by abstraction from the particulars of sense." The
word " abstraction " is a natural name for the process in
question, but it has proved disastrous to clear thinking
because it has been often interpreted to mean the taking
away of one of its qualities from the concrete experience.
When the term is thus interpreted the question immediately
arises as to the relation between the system of concepts and
the system of percepts from which the concepts have been
abstracted, or as it were *stolen*. It cannot be too much
emphasized that the universal or concept is not another
particular existing alongside of the particulars of experience.
It is, rather, an attribute of the particular which is shared
by other particulars. The process of forming abstract notions
does not consist in the abstraction of anything from the object,
but rather in the abstraction of our attention from the complex of properties that, as a complex, is peculiar to a single
sense-datum, and the concentration of it upon separate properties that are common to many sense-objects. Consequently the forming of concepts by abstraction does not in
any way change the nature of the objects, but only the nature
of our consciousness of such objects. It is a great advantage
to be able to think of the qualities common to different objects
without having always to take account of all the qualities
possessed by each object. By object I mean here, of course,
anything that can be perceived or conceived—not only concrete objects like horses, men, etc., but also relations and
activities such as might pertain to them, and from whose
occurrence at particular times and places we can abstract our
attention.

To each of the universals which, through being selected
by our attention, becomes a concept, we attach a name which
preserves it from being lost in the flux. These verbal
symbols serve as counters by means of which we can compare
with one another the particular percepts of our experience,
however remotely separated they may be from one another in
space or in time. Things, events, and relations, quantitative
and qualitative, can, in virtue of their similarity or identity
of kind, be grasped in a single act of thought, even though
they have been experienced years apart. The mind thus

groups into classes the particulars of experience, and, by comparing these classes, forms concepts having still higher universality. Our concepts are, as James says, like the seven-league boots in the old fairy tale. By their aid the mind is enabled to travel with the swiftness of thought over the entire realm of its experiences. The mind of the brute, which appears to lack the faculty of forming concepts by fixation of attention, is submerged by each successive wave of experience. The human mind, on the other hand, through its power of discovering universals and preserving them in names, is set free from the bondage of the here and the now, and, rising above the flux of experience, is able to survey at a single glance the past and the future, the near and the remote.

What then must we say as to the bearing of this theory of the nature and origin of universals upon the dispute between empiricist and rationalist ?

The rationalist has usually defended the doctrine of innate ideas. Plato even went so far as to maintain that all knowledge was innate, and that the only function of sensory experience was to awaken the mind to a realization and memory of the universal ideas with which it had been endowed prior to its existence in this life. Other less radical rationalists have held that the mind possessed as its native endowment only the more abstract and exalted universals, such as those dealt with in logic and mathematics. Empiricists on their side have sometimes denied altogether the possibility of genuinely universal ideas on the ground that they could not be pictured or imagined. We cannot form an image of a colour apart from an extent, or of a triangle that is neither scalene nor isosceles, or of a relation such as contrast or distance apart from some terms between which such a relation obtains. But the fact that we may not be able to *imagine* a universal does not mean that we cannot *conceive* or think of it. For as we have seen, to conceive a universal it is not necessary to take it out of its context and dangle it before the mind's eye. To form a general concept it is necessary only to fix the attention upon the quality or relation as it exists *in situ* and to affix a name to that part of the complex which has been thus discriminated. Consequently, the objection to universals on the score that they cannot be imaged or pictured, we must regard as irrelevant.

When empiricists have not denied outright our possession of general concepts, they have conceived of the process by which they are formed as one in which given elements of experience which are regarded as particular and nothing but particular either get combined by association under one name or through a kind of alchemy become fused and transmuted into a composite image. Now with this position we must disagree, for if the given elements of experience were nothing but particulars, if each particular that we perceived were as separate from every other particular, as are the moments in which they occurred, then indeed it would be as impossible to derive from them universal concepts as to get gold out of lead. Both rationalists and empiricists commit the same error, for they regard the originally given elements in experience as particulars and nothing but particulars, and as lacking anything that can be called universality. The rationalists, however, meet the difficulty that arises by attributing to the mind a mysterious power of supplying from its own inner nature the element of universality, while the empiricists, by an equally unwarranted procedure, explain away our universal notions altogether, or else vainly attempt to conceive a process by which what is not universal can combine to produce what is. Our comment on the situation is simply this : the fundamental assumption made in common by the two parties to the quarrel is wrong. Experience is indeed originally of particulars, that is, of objects that are presented at particular times and places. But each of these experienced objects has a universal nature which is as indefeasibly its *inclusive* property as is its unique position in space and time its *exclusive* property. In other words, the given elements of experience are complexes of universals, each complex being associated with a particular position in the space and time series. It is this latter factor of position which constitutes particularity and makes each individual numerically different from every other individual. To form the concept of a universal, it is, as we have already seen, not necessary for the mind to manufacture or create anything different from what is given, but only to abstract the attention from the particular position of the given complex and concentrate it upon some one or more of its qualitative or non-positional elements. *In short, a particular is nothing but a complex of universals endowed with a position in space and time.*

II

ORIGIN AND VALIDATION OF UNIVERSAL AND NECESSARY JUDGMENTS.

Every judgment expresses a consciousness of the reality of a relation between two or more objects. All propositional relations may be resolved into the basic relation of *identity*, either alone or in combination with some secondary relation ; hence every judgment expresses an identity-relation. To illustrate : The judgment " John strikes James " expresses a consciousness of the reality of the relation of striking between the terms John and James ; but this relation of striking is complex, and the judgment " John strikes James " can be resolved into : " John = a striker of James," where the symbol " = " indicates identity. Again, the judgment " No man is perfect " reduces to the form : " man = an imperfect being." In general, any judgment is susceptible of being reduced to the form $S = Rn(P)$, where $Rn(P)$ means " a thing related in some way (denoted by n) to P." Of course, the secondary relation symbolized by Rn may be itself the relation of identity, as in the judgment, " Plato is the greatest philosopher," where if Plato is symbolized by S, and the greatest philosopher is symbolized by P, the judgment can be written : $S = Ri\, P$, or $S = P$.

What is this concept of identity which is always present as an element of the relation expressed in our judgments ? It is indeed a notion most difficult to define, not only because it is so ultimate and so nearly simple as to make analysis almost impossible, but also because its meaning is of necessity presupposed in any statement we can make concerning it. When we say : " This smooth thing is black," or " This black thing is smooth," or " This black thing and this smooth thing are identical," we mean that the diverse connotations

" smooth " and " black " have one denotation. They are
" different aspects of the same thing." Every judgment
expresses a duality of connotation in its subject and predicate
terms and a unity of denotation in its copula. The black
thing *is* the smooth thing. Now to say that the identity
expressed in a judgment refers to single denotation combined
with diverse connotations is good and true as far as it goes,
but it does not go far enough, for it is only a restatement of
the problem in clear and promising terms rather than a solution of it. Granted that identity means singleness of denotation, we have still to ask : What *is* this single denotation
which two or more connotations can " have " ? To answer
this question we must recognize that any object of thought
possesses two fundamentally distinct sets of properties, which
we will call " intrinsic " and " extrinsic." By " intrinsic "
properties we mean those which do not involve in their meaning other objects ; by " extrinsic " properties we mean those
which do involve other objects. To illustrate : In the judgment " This object is black and smooth," *smooth* and *black*
could be parts of the connotation of this object without
being parts of the connotation of any other object. But if I
say : " This object is the favourite possession of John Smith,"
then I am ascribing to " this object " a property which would
be without meaning unless there were another object, " John
Smith," in whom the relational property also " inhered."
" This object " in addition to whatever intrinsic properties it
possesses, possesses certain properties which define its relation
to other objects. These relational or extrinsic attributes are
possessed by it and by other beings, such as " John Smith "
jointly but differently. For the complex relational property
" most favoured by " is related to John Smith as " subject "
and to the black smooth thing as " object." There are many
other relational attributes in addition to " most favoured by "
which apply to " this object." And as many of them as are
necessary when taken collectively to differentiate it from any
other object suffice by the same token to give it *singleness of
denotation.* The intrinsic properties of a thing give the thing's
essence which other objects might also have and still be
different ; the extrinsic properties of a thing give its denotation which other things, no matter how similar, could not

have. The denotation of a thing is relative in the sense that
it depends on its relation to other things. Any object of
thought has its denotation and also its connotation. Which
means that any object of thought will be a *focus* of relations
to other objects, as well as a *congeries* of purely qualitative
characters. Tweedledum and Tweedledee are examples of
objects that differ in denotation but not in connotation.
They have the same cluster of qualitative attributes, but not
the same total of relations to other objects. With the
" black " and the " smooth " of " this table " the case is the
reverse. " This black table " has the same totality of relations to other objects as has " this smooth table." The
" two " aspects of the table have the same relational focus.
As regards unity and plurality, our emphasis is usually on
denotation rather than on connotation. Hence the connotative unity of Tweedledum and Tweedledee is overshadowed
by their denotative duality, and we say that there are two
beings though with the same qualities. And analogously,
the connotative duality of the black table and the smooth
table is over-ridden by their denotative unity, and we say
that there is only one table though with diverse qualities.
But from a sophisticated Platonic standpoint we might
reverse the emphasis in these numerical ascriptions, and
speak of " Tweedle " as one thing that happened to be
exemplified in the two denotations of " dum " and " dee "
respectively ; and analogously we could think of *black-
tableness* and *smooth-tableness* as two things that happened to
share a single denotation.

   This fact that normally we think of denotation as closer
to the being or reality of a thing than connotation is prettily
and conclusively shown in our language forms, for the verb
meaning to *exist* is also the word for the copula.

   To the extent that the relational properties give an object
denotation, they give it a place or position with respect to
other objects. To be a focus of relations is to have position
in a system of more or less well-ordered objects. Anything
that can be the subject of a sentence possesses *connotative
essence* or qualitative attributes, in virtue of which its similarity and dissimilarity to other actual and possible objects is
determined ; but it possesses also a *denotative position* in

virtue of which its distance, near or far, from other objects is determined. For example, light grey and dark grey are partly similar and partly dissimilar, in that they have both identical and non-identical elements. They have common membership in the class of greys, and diverse membership in the classes of light things and dark things respectively. But with regard to the complex relational property from-white-to-black, they each have it, but they have it differently, like two men who hold the same stick but from opposite ends. And by virtue of this relational property which inheres in both, they cease to be merely members of definite *classes*, and become also members of a *series*, *order*, or *system*. This black table *is* this smooth table just because the word " this " indicates a single position or relational focus with reference to the speaker. And conversely : This black smooth table is not that black smooth table, just because " this " and " that " indicate different relational foci with reference to the speaker.

Space and Time, whether taken in their old Newtonian separateness or in their new Einsteinian togetherness, are, of course, the most familiar, as they are the most fundamental, relational systems. But there are any number of other manifolds of objects of thought constituted by relations which give position or denotation to their relata. The series of the greys from white to black, the colours from red to violet, the series of pitches, the group of blood-relations, are just a few of these assemblages which are more than classes.

For two things to be members of a class they must possess the same attribute in the same way. For things to be members of an order or system, they must possess the same property in different ways.

From what we have said it should be clear that denotation and connotation have much the same sort of relativity as that possessed by species and genus. Any object of thought is a species of a genus or a member of a class in so far as its connotation is a composite of simpler elements. Thus *rationality* and *animality* are elements of the connotation of *man*, predicates of *man*, and therefore genera of which man is a species. But also and equally of course *man* is itself a *genus* of the species *earthly poets*, because the whole connotation of *man* forms part of the connotation of *earthly poet*. Any term is *genus* with respect to any connotation which contains it, and species with respect to any connotation that it contains. And analogously, we may say that any term has denotation, or rather *denotes* to the extent that it has position in a series or system ; while a term has connotation or *connotes* to the extent that it belongs as predicate to something else that has position in a series or system. Thus in the judgment *Most roses are red*, " red " is primarily connotative, but in the judgment *Red is the colour most frequent in roses*, the subject-term " red " is primarily denotative, because it is considered as having a position in the series of colours possessed with varying frequency by roses.

And now that we have seen that the identity referred to by the copula of a judgment means oneness of denotation possessed by diverse connotations, and that this denotation in its turn means position in a series rather than membership in a class, we must turn to consider a category very close to identity, namely, " partial identity," or " subsumption," or " implication." When we say, *This black table is this smooth table*, we have complete identity of denotation between subject and predicate ; but when we say, *This black table is smooth*, the relation expressed by the term " is " is not complete and reversible identity. Whether we take the predicate " smooth " as meaning the quality or universal " smoothness," or as meaning the class of things possessing that quality, in neither case do we have a complete identity. Smoothness is identical with only one element of the complex of characters possessed by " this black table," and " this black table " is identical with only one member of the class of smooth objects. When both terms are taken denotatively or in *extension*, the subject class is a part of the predicate class. When both are taken connotatively or in *intension*, the predicate-quality is a part of the subject-qualities. When the subject is taken denotatively and the predicate connotatively, then the latter *inheres* in the former, or " this black table " *has* smoothness as an attribute or property. When the relation is taken in this third sense it acquires a unique or *sui generis* character that is not adequately expressible in terms of our ordinary preposi-tions. Dr. G. E. Moore protests against our saying that the universal is " in " or " a part of " the particular, on the ground, I believe, that a universal like smoothness could not be a part of a particular black table without contradicting the independence and logical priority which in the opinion of Platonists are the inalienable properties of every universal. If smoothness was *in* this black table, how could it also be *in* that red table ? For the latter is outside of the former. If b is a part of p, and t is outside of p, then b cannot be part of t. Smoothness can be " in " or " a part of " the group of predicates *modifying* " this black table," but it cannot itself be in or a part of " this black table " itself. Such seeming difficulties vanish when we realize that a universal is related to the particulars of which it is a predicate, as a line or spatial dimension is related to the points of which it is a co-ordinate. Different points can be in or parts of the same line and different lines can be in or parts of the points through which they pass. So, different tables can be in a quality like that of smoothness, and the latter can be in each of them without losing its connotative oneness any more than a line of defined slope loses its oneness by passing through the various points on its course. And one and the same sense-datum can have a variety of qualitative attributes as easily as one and the same point can have the lines x_1, y_1, z_1 and t_1 as co-ordinates. Sense-data are " in " their universals or qualitative dimensions as much as they are " in " their spatio-temporal dimensions. And universals are in particulars not as apples are in boxes or small spaces in larger spaces, but as all time is in each spatial point or all space in each temporal instant.

In short, when we make the judgment " This black table is smooth," the " is " means a relation of partial identity or implication between a position and one of the co-ordinates of that position. Whether we express the asymmetrical relation of implication as partial identity or whether we express identity as reversible implication, is of no consequence. If $a > b$ then $a = b + n$, and if $a \gtreqless b$ and $b \lesseqgtr a$ then $a = b$.

I have undertaken this somewhat tedious analysis of the meaning of identity as expressed in the copula of a judgment because of two recent rebellions against the Aristotelian logic. The first of these rebellions is that of the Neo-Hegelian idealists who find fault with what they regard as the barren

" logic of identity " ; the second is that of the realistic symbolic logicians who seem to regard the logic of Aristotle as incompatible with a world containing relations other than that of inherence.

The objections of the idealists hinge apparently on the fact that a judgment, S is P, asserts an identity while implying diversity. If P is not different from S, then S is P means only S is S. If P is different from S, then S is P means S is not S. Now if S and P are identical in the same sense in which they are different, then to be sure we have on our hands a serious indictment of the Aristotelian judgment and a crying need to replace it with a logic quite different which shall be less " static " and more " dynamic " than the Logic of Identity. But if the analysis which we have attempted is valid, and if the diversity of S and P is connotative while their identity is denotative, then there is no more difficulty with the Aristotelian judgment and the Logic of Identity than with a geometry that recognizes the possibility of non-identical lines meeting at an identical point. The lump of sugar discussed by Mr. Bradley in the second chapter of his *Appearance and Reality* can be both sweet and hard without mitigation on the one hand of the eternal diversity of sweetness and hardness, or on the other hand of the complete denotative identity of the sugar itself. The solid singleness of the point P_n is in no way disrupted by having as co-ordinates the eternally diverse lines x_n and y_n.

The second revolt against Aristotelianism is made by a quite different group and for a quite different motive. The Aristotelian metaphysics is dominated by the concept of substance-accident ; the Aristotelian logic is dominated by the concept of subject-predicate. The sins imputed to the former are visited upon the latter, and the discoverer of the ten categories or basic forms of relation is represented as having promulgated a logic which provides for no relation but that of inherence. When a man writes an arithmetic, he cannot be criticized for not treating of algebra. And when a man writes a treatise on the relations common to all forms of statement, he should hardly be blamed for not treating of relations peculiar to some forms of statement. The fact that when A is west of B and B is west of C then A will be west of C is interesting and important, but it in no way conflicts with the fact that " west of B " is as much a predicate of A as " red " is a predicate of " rose." That the latter is a simple quality and the former a spatial relation does not affect their common similarity of inhering as predicates in their subject. The traditional formal logic as a calculus of the universal relation of predication seems in no way to be excluded or superseded by any supplementary and specific calculus dealing with relations of space or number. And whether or not the Aristotelian *metaphysics* is properly chargeable with neglecting the types of external quantitative relationship which modern science finds fruitful, it does not seem to me that the Aristotelian *logic* is impugned either in its intrinsic validity or in its status of logical priority to any more specific logic of relations.[1]

When every judgment is reduced to a relation of identity between a subject-term and a relationally complex predicate-term, a proposition will be particular or universal according to whether the subject-term is itself a particular or a universal. If I say " Some material bodies gravitate," or " Some triangles have the sum of their angles equal to two right angles," the subject terms " some material bodies " and " some triangles " are particular, and hence the judgment is particular. If, on the other hand, I say " All bodies gravitate," or " All triangles have the sum of their angles equal to two right angles," I am making universal judgments, because the subject-terms " all bodies " and " all triangles " are universal. Now we have certainly never perceived " all triangles " or " all material bodies," but only some particular members of each of these classes. How and by what warrant do we pass from *some* to *all* ?[2]

Let us consider first the statement as to triangles which is typical of mathematical propositions in which there is both

---

[1] In Appendix I to this chapter I have attempted to show how the traditional syllogistic form can be broadened in such a way as to provide a single schema or hyper-syllogism for expressing not only the generic relations of inclusion and exclusion of classes in which Aristotle was interested, but also the more specific relations which interest the logicians of to-day.

[2] Let us note that we are dealing here with two kinds of universal propositions. The proposition as to bodies gravitating may be true, but it does not seem to be necessary, while the proposition about triangles seems to be not only true but necessary.

universality and necessity. The familiar geometrical diagram in which the base of any triangle is extended from its terminus, and a line drawn from that terminus parallel to the opposite side, serves to show the equality of the three angles of the triangle to the three angles formed. And as the relation of equality between the angles of the triangle and the angles formed by the auxiliary lines seems to depend only upon the properties of Euclidean parallels and upon the three-sidedness of the figure, and not at all upon the relative or absolute length of sides, we get revealed to us a direct relation of equivalence (i.e. a denotative identity of diverse connotations) between the abstract or universal concept " sum of the angles of a triangle " and the abstract or universal concept " two right angles." To perceive the reality of this relation of denotative identity of universals is at once the source and the warrant of the universality and necessity of the proposition. In the simple generalizations of arithmetic, as well as in the more complex cases of arithmetical induction, we derive universal judgments in the same manner. The child is shown that a group of five beads and a group of seven beads when put together form a group of twelve beads, and when his attention is concentrated upon this single concrete instance he perceives that the relation of equality apparently depends not at all upon the concrete material of the illustration, beads, chalk-marks, or what not, but solely upon the numbers involved. He *sees*, in other words, the identity of $7 + 5$ as such with 12 as such. In arithmetical induction a higher level of the same kind of generalization is reached by taking a character n, which symbolizes any number, irrespective of value, and showing that if a certain proposition held true of n, it would hold true also of $n + 1$. If it appears that the proposition in question is found actually true of some given number, 5 for example, it follows that when 5 is replaced by n it will be valid for each and all of the infinity of succeeding numbers. In the sphere of mathematics, then, it may be said that we can derive universal propositions from particular cases by abstracting the relation of equivalence as it occurs in those cases, in exactly the same way as we derive universal terms from particular terms by abstracting the nature of a thing from the particular space and time in which it figures.

Let us now consider the question as to how in the non-mathematical sphere we derive from particular experiences such universal propositions as are typified by the judgment " All material bodies gravitate." We perceive, let us say, an apple fall to the ground. The apple possesses the power of inertia or resistance to any attempt to change its velocity. If its velocity is zero, that is to say, if the body is at rest, some force must be exerted or energy expended upon it to change its velocity from zero, i.e. to set it in motion. Or if it is moving at a uniform velocity other than zero, force must be exerted in order to increase or decrease that rate of motion. Suppose we select this property of inertia, i.e. resistance to change of velocity, as the definitive attribute of " material body," then when we see the apple in our orchard falling to the earth we are perceiving a particular case of a material body gravitating, i.e. moving with accelerated velocity towards another material body. Now, if we have already formed the general concepts of " material body " and " gravity," the single observation of the identity of a particular case of material body with a particular case of gravitation would be enough (if we possessed the genius of Sir Isaac Newton) to *suggest* that not only apples and stones and other terrestrial objects, but the moon, the sun, and the planets possessed gravity ; and that suggestion would be expressed by the universal judgment " All material bodies gravitate." For that is the same as the proposition " Materiality or inertia implies gravity or mutual attraction." From the *perceived* relation of an identity between *particulars* we should have formed by abstraction the *conceived* relation of an identity between *universals*. The process of forming this universal proposition would so far have been the same as the process of forming the universal propositions about the triangle. There is, however, one very notable difference. The universal judgments of mathematics appeal to us either as self-evident and necessary in themselves, or as deducible from propositions that are such. That the sum of the angles of a triangle equals two right angles is felt to be self-evident and necessary as soon as we see that it follows from the relations between angles formed by traversing any two parallel lines with any third line. It is the same with an arithmetical proposition like $7 + 5 = 12$. But there is nothing self-evident or necessary in the proposition " All bodies gravitate " or " All crows are black." We can quite easily imagine the contradictory of either of the last judgments to be true, as the relation between subject and predicate is not self-evident. We can see no necessary relation between inertia and attraction, or between the blackness of the crow's plumage and such morphological and physiological charac-teristics as zoology may select as definitive of " crowness." We believe these universal propositions, not because they are deducible from self-evident principles, but because they are rendered more or less probable by inductive reasoning from a number of particular experiences. We have not observed, and cannot hope to observe, all crows, but we have observed such large numbers, and found them all black, that it is exceedingly probable that the blackness of plumage is due either to one of the definitive characters of the species, or to something permanently connected with those characters. In the case of bodies gravitating our evidence is still stronger, for although here also we have not observed " all bodies " or anything approaching a majority of bodies, yet we have observed bodies which appear to differ in every relevant respect excepting in the generic or definitive character of materiality or inertia. It is, therefore, overwhelmingly probable that inertia and gravitation are related either as cause and effect or as co-effects of the same cause. If we knew more about the real nature of inertia and of gravity, we might be able to perceive this relation as necessary and self-evident, but in the light of our present knowledge the proposition is what is called " contingent," and as such is to be distinguished from the necessary propositions of mathe-matics.[1]

[1] Let us note that universal propositions of the contingent type can vary in respect to their probable truth all the way from zero to unity. I can, by abstracting from any real or imaginary experience, form a universal judg-ment which is unsupported, or even positively refuted, by experience. " All trees are inhabited by dryads," " All men are perfect," are examples of such judgments. The degree of probable truth which a contingent judgment possesses is measured by the extent to which the inductive proof approaches completeness. The deductive reasoning by which necessary universal

The distinction between necessary and contingent propositions is very important, and we must try to analyse it more fully. A necessary proposition may be defined as a proposition in which the denotative identity of its terms depends solely on their nature or essence. The traditional criterion for detecting a necessary truth consists in the unbelievability, or, as it is usually but wrongly called, the inconceivability of its denial. This criterion is not, however, ultimately satisfying, because it does not enable us to tell whether the inconceivability is based on a real incompatibility of the terms, or whether it is due simply to our subjective limitations. The impossibility of conceiving of people at the antipodes without thinking of them as tending constantly to fall off is an example of an apparent necessity which is actually due to a purely subjective association between the idea of pressure upon the earth and the idea of an absolute unchanging direction in space. We could not dissociate the geometrical up and down from the feeling of the earth's attraction, and yet we now know that the feeling of *downness*

judgments can be proved we saw to consist in the process of relating the two terms of the judgment to a third or middle term. The process of induction is more indirect. We prove by it that two terms S and P are causally or universally bound together by *successively eliminating or refuting the rival alternatives to the hypothesis.* Knowing that what is universally connected with a phenomenon P must be present with it in each particular situation in which it occurs, we enumerate in any one instance of it all its antecedents or concomitants (among which the S of our hypothesis must, of course, be found). We then proceed by experiment (which is preferable) or by passive observation (if the facts are beyond our power to manipulate) to find new situations in which the various rivals to our hypothesis shall be observed to be (1) absent where P is present (Method of Agreement) ; or (2) present where P is absent (Method of Difference) ; or (3) invariable where P is variable (Method of Concomitant Variation) ; or (4) incapacitated for producing P through having exhausted their energy in producing other phenomena (Method of Residues). By these various methods we disqualify from universal or causal connection with P all claimants except S. But the proposition " All S is P " established in this manner can never be more than probable. For, as Hobhouse has so clearly shown in *The Theory of Knowledge*, there must always remain a possibility that our analysis of the concomitants has not been complete, and that the true cause of P is not S, but some unobserved X. The inductive procedure just analysed can be symbolized by a disjunctive syllogism in the following way :
The cause or invariable associate of P is either S or A or B, or possibly X.
It is not A or B (for they are excluded by one or more of the four Methods).
∴ It is S or possibly X. And this is the same as the universal proposition All cases of S (or X) are cases of P.
For a systematic exposition of this view of the indirect or eliminative character of all inductive proof, see Appendix II.

is due purely to the pull of the earth, and has nothing to do with any fixed direction in space. Since a similar fallacy may lurk in any other proposition that seems to us necessarily true, it becomes advisable, whenever possible, to find a less subjective and more reliable criterion for discovering necessity than mere feeling. We find this new criterion in the notion of self-contradiction as applied in the following way : *The truth of a given proposition is proved to be necessary when its contradictory implies self-contradiction.* Now, the only case in which the contradictory of an isolated proposition having simple terms is self-contradictory is when the original proposition is of the form A is A. Its denial would mean that A was not A, and as this is self-contradictory, the original proposition is necessarily true. But it is a very barren satisfaction to learn that judgments of the type " A is A " can be proved to be necessarily true, and we must recognize that the only fruitful kind of necessary truth that is capable of being proved to be such is that embodied in a system of propositions. For example, if A is B and B is C, then the proposition " A is C " can be known with certainty to be a necessary truth because the contradictory of " A is C " would involve a contradiction of the premises. For if A were not C, then as A is B it would follow that some B was not C, and that would contradict the premise " B is C," which was already assumed. In other words, the complex proposition " A is B and B is C imply A is C " is known to be necessary, because the denial or falsity of it involves self-contradiction. This is very simple and easy to see, and yet it is not a mere tautology like " A is A."

Now, let us take a case not quite so simple. Immanuel Kant was very certain that the necessity of the propositions of mathematics could not be due to the mere principle of contradiction. As he expressed it, mathematical propositions are synthetic and not analytic. The predicate is not contained in the meaning of the subject, but is something new, which nevertheless is joined to it by necessity. It does not, however, seem to have occurred to Kant that between purely synthetic judgments in which the predicate is not at all a part of the subject, and purely analytic judgments in which it is nothing but a part of it, there is a third class of judgments such as we have been considering, in which a proposition owes its necessity to the fact that its falsity would contradict, either the propositions which define the meaning of its terms, or the axiomatic or postulative propositions which express the fundamental relations between the terms. We might call this third class of judgments "complex-analytic." Kant's favourite illustration of the necessary synthetic judgment was the arithmetical proposition $7 + 5 = 12$, and we will now show how the necessity of this judgment, when taken in conjunction with certain definitions and axioms, can be proved by the principle of contradiction.

I. We shall assume that the simple and indefinable ideas of unity (1) and of addition (+) are known.   II. We will define positive real integral numbers as the following series of elements: $1 =$ unity, $2 =$ unity added to 1, $3 =$ unity added to 2, $4 =$ unity added to 3, and so on indefinitely, each member meaning primarily nothing but unity added to the preceding number.   III. We will accept the following axioms known respectively as the commutative and the associative laws of addition: (1) $A + B = B + A$; (2) $(A + B) + C = A + B + C = A + (B + C)$, where A, B, C are any numbers as defined in terms of I, II, and III. We can now prove that $7 + 5 = 12$ as follows:

$$7 + 5 = 7 + 1 + 4 = 8 + 4 = 8 + 1 + 3 = 9 + 1 + 2 = 10 + 2 = 10 + 1 + 1 = 11 + 1 = 12.$$

Each step in this proof is a "necessary" proposition in the sense that a denial of it would involve the system as a whole in self-contradiction. In the same way the more complex theorems of algebra and of geometry and of any branch of mathematics can be proved. It is needful only: first, to enumerate the simple or indefinable notions, including terms and relations; second, to define the classes of complex objects in terms of the indefinables; third, to observe the axioms or indemonstrable propositions which are assumed to hold true of the classes defined.

The only remaining question which we wish to consider here in connection with the concept of necessity is the question of the nature of *axioms* which are synthetic *a priori* propositions that, by reason of their simplicity, are not reducible to the type that we have called complex-analytic. It is of course perfectly true that a demonstration of the " complex-analytic " nature of such an apparently *a priori* judgment as $7 + 5 = 12$ does not mean that every *a priori* synthetic judgment can be shown to be merely a complex-analytic proposition. Such a judgment, for example, as " Black is the opposite of white " does not appear to be resolvable into an implication of a propositional system. It is *a-priori* in the only proper sense of that term, because it seems to express an identity relation between the essences " black " and " opposite of white," that is independent of the exemplification of those essences at any particular spatio-temporal position. Genuine axioms, such as Kant believed mathematics and mechanics to rest upon, would be *a priori* in this same sense. They would be identity-relations that appeared to be independent of or irrelevant to the space-time setting in which they were found. We should discover them *a posteriori*; but when once we had discovered them we should assert *a priori* that they would hold true for any possible position in which we might experience them in the future. The *a priori* character of such propositions would not be due to their dependence upon the " mind," as Kant supposed, but to their apparent independence of any particular date or place.

Concerning axioms we may hold (1) that they are arbitrarily selected by us simply for the purpose of proving certain theorems, and that in themselves they need not be, and cannot be known with certainty to be, either true or false. This is the view that " axioms are postulates." (2) We may hold that they can be seen to express a relation between universals as such, that in no way depends upon any spatial or temporal existence. (3) We may hold that they are proved by induction from experience, and that they differ from other inductions only with regard to the extent of the experiences that suggest and corroborate them.

The first view is that held by Dr. Schiller and by most mathematicians at the present time. It allows great freedom in the building up of purely conceptual systems, but it does not furnish us with any conclusions about the existing world. The second view is the most natural and satisfying, but, as was said above, it is open to the objection that what may appear to be a necessary relation between universals may be purely subjective, and due to our inability to dissociate ideas that have been cemented together by custom. The third view does not by itself seem to explain the necessary character of the axioms, but it is a very safe view to hold, because the most important principles of knowledge are those that are applicable to the existing world ; and, moreover, no proposition claiming to be an axiom is so far beyond the possibility of error that it can afford to despise the support of experience. The three views are not, indeed, mutually exclusive. Without any inconsistency, we may hold that the genuine axioms are those ultimate or indemonstrable propositions which are presupposed by a body of doctrines ; that they do express relations based on the intrinsic natures of their terms, thus rendering it impossible to imagine them false ; and that they are always corroborated, and never contradicted by experience.

We have now seen how universal concepts originate, and how the necessary judgments that express their relations are derived and validated. It remains to discuss the second or more objective aspect of the conflict between rationalism and empiricism, which involves the question, not as to how we derive universal terms and judgments, but as to what kind of ontological status they possess, and the extent of their applicability to the world of existence.

APPENDIX I

The Hyper-Syllogism : a Reduction of the Syllogisms of Formal Logic to Special Cases of the General Logic of Relatives.

We have seen that if two classes imply each other they are identical ; and that whether we define implication as partial identity, or define identity as mutual or reversible implication, is merely a matter of convenience. I prefer the former, however, just because there are many cases in which relations other than those of implication are combined in reasoning. As, for example, when I say with De Morgan, " This is the head of an animal, because it is the head of a horse, and a horse is an animal " ; or, " John is the nephew of James,

for he is the son of Peter, and Peter is James's brother."
The form of reasoning employed in these cases, as in all
others in which two terms are related to one another by means
of their relation to a third, can be called a syllogism, and any
syllogism may be symbolized as follows :

$$M = R_2P$$
$$S = R_1M$$
$$\overline{S = R_1R_2P}$$

and when $\quad R_1R_2 = R_3$ then $S = R_3P$.

The conclusion is reached by substituting in the second or
minor premise the value of the middle term M, as given in
the first or major premise, and then simplifying the compound
relation R_1R_2 whenever possible into a new relation, R_3.

We shall now proceed to illustrate the manner in which
the Aristotelian syllogisms when reduced to our generalized
syllogistic form appear merely as one important species of
relational syllogisms.

Aristotle rightly discerned that any proposition always
embodies in addition to its other relations one or the other
of the following four primary relations between a subject
term and a predicate term :

S is totally included in (i.e. a case   or   A, All S is P.
or an implier or a species of) P.

S is ·at least partially included in   or   I, Some S is P.
(i.e. a genus or implicate of a
species of) P.

S is totally excluded from (i.e. a   or   E, No S is P.
species or implier of the nega-
tive of) P.

S is at least partially excluded   or   O, Some S is not P.
from (i.e. a genus or implicate of
a species of the negative of) P.

We shall use R_V as the symbol for *a species of*, and R_A as the
symbol for *a genus of*, so that the proposition A, All S is P,
can be written either $S = R_VP$ or $P = R_AS$, for if S is a
species of P, P is a genus of S.

We shall use $R_{A\vee}$ as the symbol for *partial inclusion in,* which is the same as *a genus of a species of.* This relation is reversible or symmetrical, so that the proposition I, Some S is P, can be written either $S = R_{A\vee}P$ or $P = R_{A\vee}S$.

We shall use $- P$ and $- S$ as symbols for *the negative of P* or *the negative of S.* We shall use $R_\vee -$ as the symbol for *a species of the negative of.* This symbol is reversible or symmetrical, so that the proposition E, No S is P, can be written either $S = R_\vee - P$ or $P = R_\vee - S$.

We shall use $R_{A\vee} -$ as the symbol for *partial inclusion in the negative of* or *a genus of a species of the negative of*; so that the proposition O, Some S is not P, can be written either $S = {}_{A\vee} - P$ or $- P = R_{A\vee}S$. The *dictum de omni et nullo* tells us that whatever can be affirmed or denied of a genus can be affirmed or denied of its species. This means :

(1) That the relations $R_\vee$ and R_A are transitive, and that consequently $R_{\vee\vee} = R_\vee$ and $R_{AA} = R_A$ (*a species of a species = a species of,* and *a genus of a genus = a genus of*).

And (2) that the relation $R - {}_A = R_\vee -$ (*the negative of a genus of = a species of the negative of*).

This implies a corollary, viz. $R - {}_\vee = R_A -$ (*the negative of a species of = a genus of the negative of*).

We accept as axioms: I. The *Dictum de Omni et Nullo* as just explained ; II. the *Law of Excluded Middle,* which we shall interpret as meaning that *the negative of the negative of* anything is that thing itself, or that $- - M = M$; III. the *Substitutibility of Equivalents,* by which we mean that whatever is related in any way to a thing will be related in the same way to the equivalent of that thing. That is to say, if $M = R_2P$ and if $S = R_1M$, then $S = R_1R_2P$. By following the above explanations of notation and principles of combination, it will be a simple matter to exhibit any Aristotelian syllogism as a special case of the hyper-syllogism or generalized relational syllogism which was stated in the form

$$M = R_2P$$
$$S = R_1M$$
$$\therefore \overline{S = R_1R_2P}$$
$$\therefore S = R_3P.$$

To illustrate :

FIGURE I.

Barbara

$$\frac{\begin{array}{l}\text{All M is P}\\ \text{All S is M}\end{array}}{\text{All S is P}} = \frac{\begin{array}{l}M = R_v P\\ S = R_v M\end{array}}{\begin{array}{l}S = R_{vv}P\\ S = R_v P\end{array}}$$

Celarent

$$\frac{\begin{array}{l}\text{No M is P}\\ \text{All S is M}\end{array}}{\text{No S is P}} = \frac{\begin{array}{l}M = R_v - P\\ S = R_v M\end{array}}{\begin{array}{l}S = R_{vv} - P\\ S = R_v - P\end{array}}$$

Darii

$$\frac{\begin{array}{l}\text{All M is P}\\ \text{Some S is M}\end{array}}{\text{Some S is P}} = \frac{\begin{array}{l}M = R_v P\\ S = R_{Av} M\end{array}}{\begin{array}{l}S = R_{Avv}P\\ S = R_{Av}P\end{array}}$$

Ferio

$$\frac{\begin{array}{l}\text{No M is P}\\ \text{Some S is M}\end{array}}{\text{Some S is not P}} = \frac{\begin{array}{l}M = R_v - P\\ S = R_{Av} M\end{array}}{\begin{array}{l}S = R_{Avv} - P\\ S = R_{Av} - P\end{array}}$$

FIGURE II.

Cesare

$$\frac{\begin{array}{l}\text{No P is M}\\ \text{All S is M}\end{array}}{\text{No S is P}} = \frac{\begin{array}{l}M = R_v - P\\ S = R_v M\end{array}}{\begin{array}{l}S = R_{vv} - P\\ S = R_v - P\end{array}}$$

Camestres

$$\frac{\begin{array}{l}\text{All P is M}\\ \text{No S is M}\end{array}}{\text{No S is P}} = \frac{\begin{array}{l}M = R_\Lambda P\\ S = R_v - M\end{array}}{\begin{array}{l}S = R_v - {}_\Lambda P\\ S = R_{vv} - P\\ S = R_v - P\end{array}}$$

Festino

$$\frac{\begin{array}{l}\text{No P is M}\\ \text{Some S is M}\end{array}}{\text{Some S is not P}} = \frac{\begin{array}{l}M = R_v - P\\ S = R_{Av} M\end{array}}{\begin{array}{l}S = R_{Avv} - P\\ S = R_{Av} - P\end{array}}$$

Baroko

All P is M	$M = R_\wedge P$
Some S is not M	$S = R_{\wedge V} - M$
—	—
Some S is not P	$S = R_{\wedge V} - {}_\wedge P$
	$S = R_{\wedge VV} - P$
	$S = R_{\wedge V} - P$

$$\text{All P is M} \quad\quad M = R_\wedge P$$
$$\underline{\text{Some S is not M}} \;=\; \underline{S = R_{\wedge V} - M}$$
$$\overline{\text{Some S is not P}} \quad\quad \overline{S = R_{\wedge V} - {}_\wedge P}$$
$$S = R_{\wedge VV} - P$$
$$S = R_{\wedge V} - P$$

FIGURE III.

Darapti
$$\text{All M is P} \quad\quad M = R_V P$$
$$\underline{\text{All M is S}} \;=\; \underline{S = R_\wedge M}$$
$$\overline{\text{Some S is P}} \quad\quad \overline{S = R_{\wedge V} P}$$

Datisi
$$\text{All M is P} \quad\quad M = R_V P$$
$$\underline{\text{Some M is S}} \;=\; \underline{S = R_{\wedge V} M}$$
$$\overline{\text{Some S is P}} \quad\quad \overline{S = R_{\wedge VV} P}$$
$$S = R_{\wedge V} P$$

Disamis
$$\text{Some M is P} \quad\quad M = R_{\wedge V} P$$
$$\underline{\text{All M is S}} \;=\; \underline{S = R_\wedge M}$$
$$\overline{\text{Some S is P}} \quad\quad \overline{S = R_{\wedge\wedge V} P}$$
$$S = R_{\wedge V} P$$

Felapton
$$\text{No M is P} \quad\quad M = R_V - P$$
$$\underline{\text{All M is S}} \;=\; \underline{S = R_\wedge M}$$
$$\overline{\text{Some S is not P}} \quad\quad \overline{S = R_{\wedge V} - P}$$

Bokardo
$$\text{Some M is not P} \quad\quad M = R_{\wedge V} - P$$
$$\underline{\text{All M is S}} \;=\; \underline{S \Rightarrow R_\wedge M}$$
$$\overline{\text{Some S is not P}} \quad\quad \overline{S = R_{\wedge\wedge V} - P}$$
$$S = R_{\wedge V} - P$$

Ferison
$$\text{No M is P} \quad\quad M = R_V - P$$
$$\underline{\text{Some M is S}} \;=\; \underline{S = R_{\wedge V} M}$$
$$\overline{\text{Some S is not P}} \quad\quad \overline{S = R_{\wedge VV} - P}$$
$$S = R_{\wedge V} - P$$

FIGURE IV.

Bramantip

$$
\frac{\begin{array}{l}\text{All P is M}\\\text{All M is S}\end{array}}{\text{Some S is P}} = \frac{\begin{array}{l}M = R_\Lambda P\\ S = R_\Lambda M\end{array}}{\begin{array}{l}S = R_{\Lambda\Lambda}P\\ S = R_\Lambda P\\ _vS = P\end{array}}
$$

Camenes

$$
\frac{\begin{array}{l}\text{All P is M}\\\text{No M is S}\end{array}}{\text{No S is P}} = \frac{\begin{array}{l}M = R_\Lambda P\\ S = R_v - M\end{array}}{\begin{array}{l}S = R_v - {}_\Lambda P\\ S = R_{vv} - P\\ S = R_v - P\end{array}}
$$

Dimaris

$$
\frac{\begin{array}{l}\text{Some P is M}\\\text{All M is S}\end{array}}{\text{Some S is P}} = \frac{\begin{array}{l}M = R_{\Lambda v}P\\ S = R_\Lambda M\end{array}}{\begin{array}{l}S = R_{\Lambda\Lambda v}P\\ S = R_{\Lambda v}P\end{array}}
$$

Fesapo

$$
\frac{\begin{array}{l}\text{No P is M}\\\text{All M is S}\end{array}}{\text{Some S is not P}} = \frac{\begin{array}{l}M = R_v - P\\ S = R_\Lambda M\end{array}}{S = R_{\Lambda v} - P}
$$

Fresison

$$
\frac{\begin{array}{l}\text{No P is M}\\\text{Some M is S}\end{array}}{\text{Some S is not P}} = \frac{\begin{array}{l}M = R_v - P\\ S = R_{\Lambda v}M\end{array}}{\begin{array}{l}S = R_{\Lambda vv} - P\\ S = R_{\Lambda v} - P\end{array}}
$$

It will be seen from the above reductions that the entire group of Aristotelian syllogisms, dealing with the relations of inclusion and exclusion, total and partial, constitute only one special case of the general logic of relatives, and that as such they can be expressed in terms of our Hyper-Syllogism, for deriving the relation of any two classes to one another from a knowledge of their respective relations of any kind whatever to a third or middle class.

There is but one general formal logic, but there are as many special formal logics as there are types of relation capable of fertile combination. The rules of the Aristotelian syllogism are rules empirically discovered for combining relations of a special kind. For combining relations of any other kind analogous rules would have to be discovered.

APPENDIX II

On the Nature of Induction.[1]

Any proposition is susceptible to two sorts of proof. We can adduce premises that directly imply it, or we can adduce premises that indirectly imply it because they imply the falsity of its contradictory alternatives. In inductive reasoning we prove universal propositions by adducing as premises the particular propositions furnished by experience. Formal logic tells us that the value of a particular proposition consists in its power to disprove its contradictory universal rather than to prove its subalternate universal. We might naturally suppose that the evidential function of experience as a knowledge of particulars was to disprove universal statements rather than to prove them, and that if a universal conclusion was proved true by appeal to experience, the proof would be based upon the disproof or elimination of alternatives. That induction is actually and always of this indirect type of inference, and that as such it is properly expressed by a disjunctive syllogism in the negative mood (*modus tollendo ponens*), is what I wish to show.

There is, of course, no novelty in the conception of induction as a process of elimination. Mill's canons are efficacious because they embody implicitly the eliminative principle. In Hobhouse and Aikins, to mention only two of the modern logicians, the principle is explicitly recognized, and the chief problems of induction are treated, especially by Hobhouse, from that point of view. Yet so far as I am aware there has been nowhere an attempt to identify induction in all its phases with the kind of indirect inference known as the *reductio ad absurdum*, and it has seemed to me worth while to make that attempt for two reasons : First, because the several inductive

[1] Read at the annual meeting of the American Philosophical Association, at Cambridge, December 1905, and reprinted by permission from *The Journal of Philosophy and Psychology*, Vol. III., No. 11.

methods when viewed from this standpoint appear not as a group of disconnected principles, but as an organic system and hierarchy which is applicable in its entirety to every inductive problem and in which each principle has its own function and virtue by which it supplements the defects of the principles that precede it ; second, on account of the new light thrown by the indirect theory of induction upon the general problem of deriving universals from particulars.

And now, by way of introduction to the more positive treatment of the subject, let us consider some of the difficulties involved in what is still, I think, the usual conception of induction. Induction when treated as a mode of direct inference is divided into two kinds—perfect and imperfect. In perfect induction, we reason that as these A's are B's and as these A's are all the A's, it must follow that all A's are B's. It is clear that what is called perfect induction is only possible when the total number of individuals making the class is limited. Thus we can prove by this method that all the months in the year have less than thirty-two days, or that all the flowers in the garden are fragrant, but not that all bodies gravitate or that all men are mortal. In these latter propositions, which are genuine universals, the classes contain an unlimited number of members, and experience can never supply us with more than an insignificant fraction of them. In imperfect induction, which is sometimes supposed to be a degenerate form of perfect induction, we boldly conclude that because an infinitesimal portion of a class has been observed to possess a certain property the whole class will have that property. The methods or canons of induction are the principles that inform us when we can and when we can not take the inductive leap.

Now there is one circumstance in particular which might lead us to suspect that there was something radically wrong with the notion that induction is a degenerate form of perfect induction. Neither the actual number of positive instances observed nor the ratio of that to the total number has anything whatever to do with the degree of validity possessed by the induction. Perfect induction is essentially quantitative, depending, as it does, upon observation of all the members of a given class. The canons that guide us in making the so-called imperfect induction are, on the other hand, essentially qualitative, and not, as we might suppose, imperfectly quantitative. That is to say, it is never a question of observing almost all, or a bare majority, or even an appreciable fraction of the whole number of material bodies, for example, as evidence for the inductive generalization that all bodies gravitate. We contrive in the few cases under our control to eliminate by the methods of difference and especially of agreement all the characteristics of bodies that could possibly cause their gravitation except those of extension and inertia, and on the strength of this elimination we unhesitatingly conclude that a material body, merely as such (and hence all material bodies), will gravitate.

And now that we have briefly considered the contradiction between inductive theory as exemplified in the supposedly archetypal syllogism of perfect induction, and inductive practice as exemplified in Mill's canons, we may look to see how this contradiction can be removed by treating induction as belonging essentially and exclusively to the indirect type of inference.

Every inductive problem indirectly, and the usual inductive problem directly, concerns the determination of a causal relation. A phenomenon occurs in which we are for some reason interested and we at once seek among its antecedents and consequents for phenomena which are related to it as cause and as effect. Defining a causal relation as the relation of universal concomitant presence, absence and variation of two phenomena, we must assume as the basal postulates of all induction (1) that every event has an antecedent and a consequent with which it is causally or universally related, and (2) that we can enumerate these possible causal relations, by the aid of perception and previous knowledge. Now let M be a phenomenon whose causal relations we are seeking to discover, and let A be an antecedent or consequent phenomenon which we suspect, or provisionally assume, to be, and which in reality is causally related to M ; we can then classify the possible causal relations of M with respect to A under five heads. This division may be briefly stated in the form of a disjunctive proposition which will constitute the major premise of a typical inductive syllogism. Thus we can say that

The cause or effect of M is either (1) a phenomenon symbo-

lized by X that is related to A only casually or by chance;
or (2) a phenomenon symbolized by B, C, or D, which is collocated with A but not indissolubly; or (3) a complex phenomenon symbolized by A B, A C, or A D, of which A is an
indispensable part; or (4) a phenomenon symbolized by α
which is an aspect, phase or degree of A; or (5) A itself.
The four inductive methods of simple enumeration, difference,
agreement, and concomitant variation express the types of
particular negative propositions furnished by experience, and
as such they constitute the complex minor premises of the
syllogism and serve to contradict or eliminate all but one of
the alternatives set forth in the major premise.   The conclusion
is, of course, the categorical affirmation of the only alternative
not eliminated.   I shall now try to show how each of the
inductive methods is especially suited to eliminate one of
these alternatives, and that the eliminative function is the
only function that they could or do perform : First, then,
to remove the possibility that A and M are connected merely
by chance, we use the method of simple enumeration. We
observe the frequency with which M occurs in conjunction
with A, and compare this with the frequency with which M
might be expected to occur with A if they were quite independent.   If the former frequency greatly exceeds the latter, we
consider the conjunction to be something more than casual.
The *number* of observations required to eliminate the hypothesis
of chance is thus strictly determined by the joint independent
probability of the events in question.

Having eliminated chance by the method of simple
enumeration, we next eliminate by the method of difference
the possibility that M is causally related, not to A, but to the
antecedents and consequents with which A is collocated.   We
find, let us say, cases in which B, C, and D are simultaneously
or successively present when the event M is absent. The
results of such observations may be stated in the form of a
particular negative proposition, as follows: Some cases of
B, C, and D are not cases of M, which means that the universal
affirmative proposition: All cases of B, C, or D are cases of
M—which expresses a possible causal relation—is eliminated.

Supposing, now, that the phenomenon A has not been
found present in the absence of M, and consequently has not

been eliminated, it becomes necessary to apply the method of agreement in order to decide whether M is not causally related to a complex phenomenon such as A B, A C, or A D, of which A is only a part, for the weak point in the method of difference lies in the fact that it can only prove that A is at least a part of the cause or effect of M, not that it is the whole. We observe by the method of agreement that B, C, and D can be simultaneously or successively absent when M and A are both present. This again eliminates B, C, and D, but it also eliminates the possibility that A needs to co-operate with B, C, and D in order to be causally related to M.

We have now proved that M is causally related either to A or to some phase of A which we called a. And to secure the elimination of this fourth alternative we use the last and most powerful of the inductive canons, viz., that of concomitant variation. If we find that M and A vary in perfect concomitance we know that every phase or degree of A, rather than some particular phase such as a, is causally related to every phase or degree of M. If, on the other hand, we had discovered that A did not vary with M in any manner, we should have proved that the true cause or effect of M was a and not A, as such. Or, again, if we had found that M did not vary directly with A, but with some function of A, we should conclude that the cause or effect of M was A in conjunction with a.

The universal affirmative conclusion of an inductive syllogism is thus in any case the result of successive eliminations —in the form of the particular negative propositions furnished by experience—of all but one of the alternative universals set forth in the disjunctive major premise as hypotheses. And each of the inductive methods is, as we have seen, adapted to the elimination of a certain type of alternative.

And now a word must be said in regard to the two methods which we have not mentioned—the method of residues and the joint method of agreement and difference. The method of residues is confessedly a method of elimination ; it is, however, hardly worthy of being ranked with the other methods, for it is applicable only when both the antecedents and consequents are quantities of matter or energy, for in no other case can we apply the conception of a cause exhausting its causality in the production of a given effect. As for the joint method, its continued existence in logical text-books affords a good illustration (1) of the fact that logicians have failed to recognize the exclusively eliminative nature of induction and (2) of the results of that failure. The joint method bids us supplement the method of agreement, by the collection of as many different instances as possible of the absence of a phenomenon along with the absence of its supposed cause. Now it can easily be shown that these cases of concurrent absence are as such quite worthless as evidence of causal connection. If we are considering whether a protective tariff causes national prosperity we do not adduce as evidence the generation of Röntgen rays or the constructing of a sonnet, and yet these are different cases of the concurrent absence of protection and prosperity, and as such perfectly conform to the requirements of the joint method as worded by Mill and as symbolized by Jevons. What we actually seek to find in such an investigation are always cases in which not merely the supposed cause is absent, but in which *the alternatives to the supposed cause are present* along with the absence of the effect, and hence are eliminated. In the method of difference as usually schematized this is done in a single pair of instances in which ABC followed by M is compared with BC followed by the absence of M ; but it can equally well be done piecemeal or by a succession of instances, one showing simply the presence of B, a second the presence of C, a third the presence of D, etc. ; along with the absence of M. Now as the so-called joint method is, when rightly understood, nothing whatever but a combination of the method of agreement and the method of difference where each is applied successively in several instances, rather than simultaneously in a single pair, it does not deserve to be classed as a separate canon.

The claim was made at the beginning of the paper that the identification of induction with the indirect type of argument, or *reductio ad absurdum*, possessed two advantages, (1) the unification of the inductive methods, (2) the exhibition in a new light of the general problem of deriving universals from particulars. I have said what I could in regard to the first of these advantages, but I should like in conclusion to speak further as to the second.

The attacks upon the possibility of reasoning from particulars, that have been made by the sceptics on the one hand and by the extreme apriorists on the other, are based in the main upon a quite proper realization of the gulf between a subaltern proposition and its subalternates. The number of cases exemplifying a genuine universal or law of nature is, as we have said, always infinite, and hence the direct inference from some to all is not only uncertain (which would be admitted by inductive logicians), but would seem to be not even probable —to be, in fact, infinitely improbable. For we can, of course, never observe even an appreciable fraction, to say nothing of a majority of the members of an infinite series. Now when we give up this attempt at direct inference and exorcise from inductive theory the spectre of a so-called perfect induction as an ideal to be approximated to, the whole problem appears in a less paradoxical and more hopeful light. For the experiential evidence in the form of particular propositions, which was worthless as a means of direct proof of the subalternate, is perfectly capable of disproving the contradictory and thus indirectly establishing a hypothesis as a survival of the fittest. Of course this does not mean that we have merely, by the substitution of the intensive for the extensive view of the subject, removed uncertainty from generalizations from experience, but only that from our point of view we may more clearly see why it is that the degree of probability of any inductive conclusion is measured by the number of antecedently possible alternative conclusions and by the ease with which they can be isolated, enumerated, and eliminated rather than by the mere number of instances observed.

CHAPTER IV

THE METHODS OF RATIONALISM AND EMPIRICISM (continued)

The Ontological Status of Universals and the Cosmological Significance of Universal and Necessary Propositions.

THE subjective phase of the controversy between rationalism and empiricism fell naturally into two parts : I. The question as to the psychological genesis of universal concepts. II. The question as to the logical validation of universal and necessary judgments, especially those that are necessary and self-evident as distinguished from those that are merely contingent. And as regards each problem there proved to be three distinguishable types of theory : (1) Extreme empiricism which holds that universal concepts are reducible to particular percepts, and necessary judgments reducible to contingent judgments. (2) Extreme rationalism which would regard the particular and contingent as reducible to the universal and necessary. (3) The dualistic or compromise doctrine which in the main we defended, and according to which both universals and particulars, and both necessity and—at least in the light of our present knowledge—contingency were recognized to be genuinely present in experience. The objective phase of the controversy between empiricism and rationalism which we are to consider in this chapter may be divided in the same way into : I. The problem of the ontological status of universals ; and II. the problem of the cosmological significance of universal and necessary propositions. And the solution of each of these problems will again be of the three types noted above : (1) The extreme empiricist will hold that the world is composed exclusively of particulars, and that all laws and relations are reducible to contingent propositions.

(2) The extreme rationalist will maintain on the contrary that particulars are nothing but complexes of universals, and that all laws and relations are (theoretically) reducible to self-evident and necessary propositions.   (3) The adherent of the compromise or dualistic position will admit the reality of both particulars and universals, and of both necessary and contingent laws of nature.

We shall begin with the problem of the ontological status of universals, and attempt to establish the following conclusions :

(1) Universals have objective subsistence prior to and independent of the particular objects and events whose attributes they are.   (2) This independent subsistence of universals does not imply that they must exist alongside of particulars in space and time.   (3) Nor does it imply that they exist merely as thoughts in a mind.   (4) A complex of universals is not sufficient in itself to constitute a particular existent object.

I

THE ONTOLOGICAL STATUS OF UNIVERSALS.

1. *The Independent and Objective Subsistence of Universals.*— The universal is logically prior to the particular because it is an element or part of that complex of qualities and position which constitutes the connotation and denotation, respectively, of the particular ; and parts are always prior to the whole which they constitute.   We describe a particular object such as a table as having the attributes of hardness, smoothness, roundness, etc. How could the table have these qualities unless they were there to be had ?   In the terminology of the scholastic philosophers, we may say that the existence of a thing presupposes its nature or " essence " ; or that the actuality of an object presupposes its possibility. This is proved by the fact that we can raise the question of whether or not a certain thing exists. When a man asks, " Is there a subterranean stream beneath the spot where I am digging a well ? " no one accuses him of asking a meaningless question. The question not only has a meaning, but a meaning that is

important. If the affirmative answer to the question is the true answer, that means that the complex of qualities connoted by the words " subterranean river " is actualized or exemplified in the space below where the well is being dug. If the negative answer to the question is true, that means that those qualities are not exemplified or actualized in that space. Thus, whichever answer to the question is true, the meaning of the question implies or presupposes the consideration of the designated complex of qualities as having an ontological status of *subsistence* in and for itself. In short, whatever is discussable is a *somewhat*, the merely possible is discussable, and therefore the merely possible is a *somewhat*, viz. a subsistent, object.

2. *The Non-Existence of Universals as such.*—Now there is a misunderstanding of this Platonic theory which we must be careful not to fall into. We must not imagine that the subsistence of universals, independently of the particulars which may or may not exemplify them, means that universals exist as another sort of particulars. We must not think that space is filled with abstract qualities and disembodied essences or possibilities which float about like ghosts, invisible to us, but capable perhaps of being apprehended as particulars by superhuman beings or by human souls when freed from the body. Plato himself is partly responsible for this misunderstanding of his theory, for, in his eagerness to emphasize the independence of universals, he sometimes used metaphors which, if taken literally, would seem to make of them merely a new kind of particulars.[1]

We might compare the relation between particulars and

---

[1] One of Aristotle's famous criticisms of Plato's theory is based upon this misunderstanding. He declares that, if in addition to the particular members of a class, the class of men, for example, we assume with Plato an abstract universal Man, the following question will be forced upon us : What are the qualities common to the concrete men and the abstract universal Man ? To answer this question we shall, he tells us, have to assume a third human entity, a " tritos anthropos," still more abstract, which will be composed only of the qualities possessed both by particulars and the universal. But this is like asking what it is that is common to " animal " and " black animal " or to A and to AB. The answer is not a third something, such as X, but simply A itself. The particular is not an entity separate from the universal, but merely the universal *joined to or exemplified in* a given position in time and space. Just as every AB is a case of A though not every A is a case of AB, so, using a term of Plato's, we can say that every particular " participates in " a universal, but not conversely that every universal participates in a particular existence.

universals to the relation between whirlpools and the water surrounding them. Every whirlpool is surrounded by water, but not every body of water surrounds a whirlpool. So every particular exemplifies a universal, though by no means every universal is exemplified in a particular. The things that actually exist in the spatio-temporal nexus are to the totality of conceivable things as a cluster of tiny islands to the vast ocean from which they have risen. To these islets of actual *existence* the mind of every animal below man is confined. To man alone is it given to contemplate and enjoy with the eye of reason the great ocean of ideal *subsistence*.

3. *The Non-Subjectivity of Universals.*—We have seen that the independent reality of universals should not be misinterpreted to mean that they exist as a new kind of particulars. But we must be equally on our guard against a misinterpretation of the opposite type which would treat universals as purely subjective states, dependent upon consciousness, and incapable of any meaning or reality apart from consciousness. The universal as a part or constituent of the particular is, as we have said, logically prior to the whole in which it figures, and this logical priority of the universal would not be in any way explained by locating the universal in the mind. The aspects of things are not created by the mind, but discovered through abstraction or discriminative attention. The universal nature present in particular objects could not be conceived unless it were there to be conceived. If universals were real only in the mind, particular objects would not be composed of them or possess them as attributes, but would exist separately from them. This, however, is inconceivable. A round object could not be objectively real if the attribute of roundness were only subjective. The only way to justify the view that universals are subjective or mental in their nature is to hold that the existent particulars which contain them are also subjective, and that whatever is perceived is real only in the mind of the perceiver. By the same reasoning it follows that we cannot regard the universal attributes of things as existing merely as states of an absolute or divine mind unless we are willing to admit that particular objects also are real only in the divine mind. In short, the universal and abstract entities which Plato called " Ideas,"

the knowledge of which is obtained by restricting attention to the connotative aspects of sensory objects, are quite as objective as the latter ; and though no one of them exists as a whole in space or time, yet they can intersect or pass through space and time, such points of intersection constituting the qualified particulars of existence.

4. *The Inadequacy of Universals to Constitute the Entire Being of Existential Particulars.*—So far we have been defending the right of the Platonic rationalist to believe in the objective reality of a realm of ideals which both pervades and transcends the world of particular existence. The question now presents itself : can we go farther still and treat the world of concrete existence as itself a part of this ideal world ? The extreme rationalist would answer this question in the affirmative. He would have us view a particular object such as a horse as *nothing but* a complex of universals.

The time and space factors of position which we took as differentiating the particular member of a class from the class concept are regarded by the extreme rationalist as additional universals. Just as the extreme empiricist does not content himself with affirming the reality of particulars, but goes on to affirm that what we call universals are themselves nothing but particulars, mere names or words, so the extreme rationalist asserts that universals are not only real but that they are the only reality, and that particulars are nothing but complexes of universals. Plato himself was very far from holding this view. He believed that the world of particular objects in which we live presupposes not only the universals or abstract qualities, but a power or will which exemplifies them in space and time. The additional something that differentiates the particular from the universal is position in space and time ; and as whatever has position in space and time has the capacity for interaction and change, we could have defined the world of particulars as a dynamic and changing system standing out in sharp contrast to the vast enveloping realm of changeless ideals and eternal truths. To put the matter in other words, existence is not a new *quality*, which when added to the other qualities of a possible object makes it actual. It is rather a thing's *relation* of

interaction or spatio-temporal connection with the totality
of other things. An actually existent dollar possesses no
quality not present in a merely possible or ideal dollar. The
difference between them is relational or extrinsic, not qualitative or intrinsic. The actual dollar can pay my debts
and wear a hole in my pocket. The imaginary dollar, no
matter how vividly it may be pictured by me or by others,
can do neither of these things. Moreover, the actual dollar
is at each moment of time in some particular part of space ;
the merely ideal dollar is not in space at all. To say that it
does not exist is the same as saying that it exists nowhere.
When we awake from a dream or finish a novel, we regard
the objects and events of the dream or the novel as non-
existent, not only or primarily because of any internal
inconsistency or fantasticalness, but because they will not
fit into the time and space of the larger totality of waking
experience. We can never learn whether a perceived object
really exists by studying its internal nature. An illusion or
hallucination may seem in itself to be as objective as any
true perception, and it is only by ascertaining its relations
to what is external to it that we can learn whether it is in
interaction with the totality of other things, and hence can
claim a genuine position in the spatio-temporal system. The
merely ideal object influences only the mind of him who
perceives it, and on this account it has come to be regarded
as subjective or mental. The actually existent object
influences not only the mind that is conscious of it, but all
other things as well. We must deny to the extreme rationalist
his claim to reduce particulars to universals and the actual
to the ideal.

Empiricism is as true as rationalism. Both universals and
particulars are real ; neither can be treated as a mere accident
or aspect of the other. Why, out of the totality of conceivable
or possible objects, there should be actualized those that make
up our world of existence we do not know. The fact that
through what we call Will we are able to select and make
actual in conduct and in art certain of the ideals that are
revealed to our reason or to our imagination, may tempt
us to think with Plato of the existing world as the outcome
of an analogous selection by one or more cosmic wills. But

whether this suggested analogy can develop any value as a hypothesis is a question that we must pass by, at least for the present.

II

THE COSMOLOGICAL SIGNIFICANCE OF UNIVERSAL AND NECESSARY PROPOSITIONS.

Are the laws of nature ultimately necessary or ultimately contingent?

At the close of the last chapter we pointed out that the connections between things as expressed in propositions appear to be of two kinds : (a) necessary or inevitable connections which are self-evident; and which we cannot even imagine to be false ; and (b) contingent or merely factual connections which can easily be imagined to be false. The apparently contingent relations are expressed by such propositions as " Some square things are red "; " All material bodies gravitate "; " The perception of a given colour or tone is caused by a given number of ether or air vibrations " ; " The circle has not been squared." The apparently necessary relations are expressed by such propositions as " $7 + 5 = 12$ "; " The sum of the angles of a plane triangle is equal to two right angles " ; " Black is the opposite of white " ; " If people lived on the other side of the earth they would fall off." We pointed out also that the necessary propositions, which cannot be imagined to be false, owe their necessity to the fact that the relation between the terms appears to depend either directly or indirectly upon the intrinsic nature of the qualities connoted by the terms, rather than upon anything combined or associated with them. And we noted furthermore that the appearance of necessity was sometimes deceptive (as for example in the seeming impossibility of people living at the antipodes), and hence that apparently necessary propositions can be proved with certainty to be really necessary only when their falsity can be shown to involve self-contradiction. Now the empiricist holds that all relations are in reality of the contingent type, that necessity is merely a subjective feeling, and that many of the apparently necessary propositions as, for example, the seeming impossibility of people living at the antipodes, have turned out in the light of further knowledge to be not only lacking in necessity, but actually untrue. The rationalist, on the other hand, tends to believe that propositions that appear to be merely contingent are in reality necessary, and that the further our knowledge progresses the more this necessity is revealed. And just as the empiricist cited the old belief about the antipodes as an example of the illusoriness of necessity, the rationalist cites the belief in the possibility of squaring the circle as an example of the illusoriness of contingency; for we now know that what is meant by the squaring of the circle is incompatible with self-evident mathematical laws. The empiricist pictures the world as an aggregate of brute facts which simply happen to be what they are, and to co-exist with one another in certain specific ways. And he attacks the claims of his opponent on the ground that all systems of seemingly necessary propositions are at best either asymmetrical or hypothetical and relative.

The rationalist pictures the universe, not as an aggregate of brute facts, but as an interlocking system, all the elements of which are what they are, and are related as they are, by absolute necessity. And he may argue for this theory in any one of three distinct ways which we shall characterize as the Mathematical, the Teleological, and the Dialectical.

In our survey of the controversy we shall consider in succession the three distinct types of cosmological rationalism, and the two special arguments used by empiricists in rebuttal of the claim of any form of rationalism to be ultimate. And finally we shall make some suggestions as to a general evaluation and adjustment of the rationalistic and the empirical methods of attaining truth.

1. *The Three Types or Methods of Cosmological Rationalism.*

A. Mathematical or Pythagorean Rationalism.

Mathematical knowledge is the most perfect that we possess, and it seems to exhibit a completely rationalistic or necessary character. The number-series, for example, constitutes a system whose members manifest a complete and mutual interdependence of such a character that each member can be unambiguously determined by its relation to any other member. Thus $9 = 7 + 2 = 3 \times 3 = 15 - 6 = \dfrac{45,000}{5,000}$.

Or to express the matter in the most general terms : if m and n represent any members of the number system, and f, represents a given type of arithmetical relation, then a propositional equation of the form $m = f, (n)$ will always be true.

With space and time it is much the same as with number. The different parts of space are so interrelated that any one part can be expressed in terms of its relationship to any other, and no part could exist unless there existed all the other parts. I cannot think of space as a whole existing without the parts, nor can I think of the various parts of space without presupposing space as a whole. I cannot but recognize that the totality of 3-dimensional Euclidean space is composed of an infinite multitude of cubic miles. Such cubic miles constitute its parts. The sum of such spaces is equal to the whole space. But on the other hand it is equally true that each cubic mile or other part of space must have its *position*, i.e. must be *somewhere* in the space which it composes. To say that it has position is to admit that it presupposes the whole of space.

That time and number belong with space in the class of necessary systems can be seen by realizing that every *portion of* time has also its *position in* time, thus implying time as a whole ; and every number in addition to its cardinal nature or quantity, by virtue of which it is a *part* of the number system, has also its ordinal nature or *position*, by virtue of which it implies the reality of the number system as a whole.

Now space, time, and number are not only nearly perfect material for the exercise of our intellectual faculties, they are also the most fundamental conditions of the world of things. All things, in so far as they are spatial or temporal or numerable, must conform to the rationalistic or logically necessary character of these several forms of being. Hence it is natural to think that the more concrete and complex types of relational system also possess the thoroughgoing rationality possessed by the simpler and more fundamental. The fact that in many cases we cannot discover this rationality does not prove its non-existence. The various properties of number and space which are now known were discovered only after long periods of labour on the part of arithmeticians and geometricians ; but once discovered, they were realized to have possessed their necessary and rationalistic character all along. Even to-day there are many properties of mathematical systems, the necessity of which is not apparent. Why prime numbers occur as they do is not yet explained, but nobody doubts that there is a reason for it which, if it could be ascertained, would make the distribution of primes appear as necessary and rational as the distribution of, say, the successive powers of 10. Again, as we have said above, it was formerly supposed that the circle could be squared, and it was only after the nature of the transcendental number $\pi = 3 \cdot 1416 \ldots$, was fully understood that it was found that what was meant by the " squaring of the circle" would involve a contradiction of the self-evident laws of number. What had formerly seemed a merely contingent truth, " The circle has not yet been squared," was replaced by the necessary truth, " The circle cannot be squared." Even such simple examples of necessary truth as " $7 + 5 = 12$ " are not necessarily self-evident to every mind. A young child who has learned the meaning of 5, of 7, of 12, of $+$, and of $=$, to the extent of being able to recognize these terms and relations when he meets them concretely embodied in experience, may still not see why $7 + 5$ must be 12. He may take it on the authority of his arithmetic teacher, or as a brute fact, like the whiteness of this paper.

Now the rationalist argues that in view of the perfect rationality of such fundamental forms of existence as space, time, and number, we are justified in believing that all other forms and relations would exhibit the same sort of clarity, necessity, and unity if our knowledge could be sufficiently extended. Take the colour series, for example. Here we can perceive far less rationality than in the forms we have been considering. We cannot think of the colours as functions of one another as we can of the numbers. Given an experience of black, we could not predict that there was such a colour as green. And yet even the colour series has certain elements of rationality. White and black have as self-evident and necessary a relation of opposition as $+ 2$ and $- 2$. Again, such facts as that red can most simply change continuously into white by way of the series of pinks, suggest the possibility that to eyes more perfect than ours the colour series might possess a logical unity and continuity equal to or even greater than that of the tone series. Finally, the rationalist may hope that relations of logical interdependence may not always be confined to the elements of a single system or continuum, but may be so extended as to show a necessary connection between different continua. The science of analytic geometry exhibits many such relations between space and number, and the interdependence of time and space is implied in the Einstein theory of relativity.

The thoroughgoing rationalist is not content with arguing for the necessary and self-evident character of general quantitative and qualitative relations, such as we have been considering. He appeals to the law of causality to show that the relations of co-existence and sequence between particular events are controlled by the same type of necessity. Whatever happens at any time or at any place is determined by something other than itself ; and as each particular happening is seen to be a special instance of a causal law, causal laws are themselves seen to be special cases of still higher or more general laws, until finally the hierarchy of causal laws would, according to the rationalist, be found to culminate in a single universal or necessary principle, the truth of which was self-evident and eternal. Many psychologists, for example, regard mental processes as a special type of vital process, and hope to reduce psychological to biological law ; many biologists are in turn endeavouring to explain vital processes in terms of the chemistry of colloids ; while the chemists themselves would welcome the reduction of their laws to the still broader laws of electro-physics. Physics, which is already permeated with mathematics, arouses in the enthusiastic rationalist the faith that the at present irreducible physical constants, such as the constants of gravitation and of the velocity of light, may be the resultants of geometric or even arithmetic principles. If they are, then the whole system of laws governing the world of concrete existence could be demonstrated to be a necessary or self-evident consequence of the non-existential or abstract and eternal truths of mathematics.

Some such ideal as this seems to have inspired the Pythagorean philosophers who founded the earliest and perhaps the greatest of the rationalistic schools. They expressed their doctrine in the curious saying that all things are at bottom numerical, that number is the sole reality, and that all laws or relations between things are reducible to numerical relations. The advancing march of science has substantiated this daring speculation to the extent of succeeding in many cases in correlating the irreducible and heterogeneous qualities of things with a series of mutually commensurable and homogeneous quantities. Radiant heat and light, for example, which, when considered simply as perceptual qualities, are quite heterogeneous, gain a vicarious homogeneity when correlated with quantitative rates of electro-magnetic vibration. The solid and liquid forms of matter, which to perception are irreducibly different qualities, are likewise made mutually commensurate by being correlated with assemblages of molecules differing in their structures only spatially or quantitatively. Quantity in some form is the magic thread on which, like so many beads, the various qualities of experience are strung. But beads strung in a necklace are still beads, and qualities retain all their uniqueness even when science succeeds in correlating them with forms of mass and motion. So, after all, the Pythagorean type of rationalism is still far from being realized.[1]

B. Teleological or Anselmian Rationalism.

What we have called Teleological Rationalism takes the principle of spiritual perfection or the Good as the ultimate source of all that is, and regards a thing as rationalistically intelligible, just in so far as its nature and existence can be shown to be derived from the nature of a supreme perfection. The most notable development of this type of rationalism was

[1] Plato was much influenced, especially in his later writings, by the Pythagorean ideal. And Spinoza seems to have believed that all laws are in reality a consequence of mathematical necessity and that every thing and every event, no matter how trivial or arbitrary it may appear, follows from the nature of the universe as a whole with the same kind and degree of necessity as that by which the specific properties of a circle follow from the nature of the circle as a whole.

the so-called Ontological Proof for the existence of God, which was originated by St. Anselm. The argument may be stated as follows : *By God, we mean a being possessing all possible perfections. Is such a being actual or merely ideal? Actual, because existence is a perfection; a non-existent Deity would not be so perfect as one who existed; the goodness of any object is increased by being made actual. To believe that God did not exist would be like believing in a round square, for a non-existent God is a contradiction in terms; it would mean a being who is all perfect (by definition), but who is at the same time imperfect (by not existing). Therefore, God exists, and his existence needs no empirical proof, but can be seen to follow necessarily from the very nature of the idea or meaning which we have before our mind when we use the name God.* The principal defect of this argument was discovered by Kant. It is the fallacy which we have already noted of treating existence as merely an additional *quality*. The premise which asserts that existence is a perfection is false. An existent Deity has no more perfection than one that is non-existent. A world which contained a God would indeed be more perfect than one which did not. But existence is a relation which a thing has to the totality of other things, and to make the argument valid it would be necessary to show: (1) that a perfect being would be more consistent or compossible than an imperfect being with the totality of other beings; (2) that such consistency or compossibility is equivalent to existence in space and time. Neither of these vague and recondite propositions has ever been proved, and the duality between the ideal and the actual which the teleological rationalist strives to annul by means of the Ontological Proof remains as real as ever.

C. Dialectical or Hegelian Rationalism.

The third distinct type of rationalistic cosmology is that originated by Hegel. The dominant conception in Hegel's system is the idea that each object of thought implies its own opposite as a true and inseparable aspect of itself. The real nature of a thing is always threefold. It is first what it appears to be, second the opposite of that, and third the result of the union of the first two in combination. This principle of the identity of opposites had been developed to some extent by Hegel's predecessors, Fichte and Schelling. It appears most plausible in connection with the experience of moral action, where the highest good seems to consist not in mere innocence, in which there is neither knowledge of evil nor any temptation to commit it, but rather in the heroic triumph of good in the face of temptation to evil. Thus, in a sense, good seems to be bound up with its opposite, and to realize its true meaning only in connection with it. Hegel called the principle of the union of opposites the principle of "negativität," and the method of developing complex objects of thought from simple notions by means of combining two opposite ideas in such a way as to get a third conception different from either and richer in meaning, he called the "dialectical process."

Starting with the most general and abstract of all our notions, that of pure being, the dialectic enables us, so Hegel claims, to achieve a succession of more and more concrete conceptions. First, the concepts and laws of logic will appear, secondly, those of matter, while thirdly, the laws and ideals of human life and human history will develop through this dialectical procedure. And it is only the limitation of our finite faculties that prevents us from carrying on the creative work of thought to the point of deducing the existence of the particular objects and events which are going on around us. Hegel is at once the most original and the most thoroughgoing of all the rationalists of history. He is most original in that his conception of everything real as being animated by a spirit of paradox and self-contradiction forced him to invent a new logic which was the antithesis of the ordinary logic of self-consistency. He is the most thoroughgoing of rationalists because he applied his principle of negativity and his dialectic process to every department of experience, thus uniting all branches of his philosophy into a single complete and perfectly rounded system.

The chief weakness of the Hegelian rationalism lies in the principle of *negativität*. The only terms that have definite opposites are terms that occupy the extreme positions in a series—like hot and cold, white and black, etc. But there are no definite opposites to such terms as luke-warm, grey, sky, paper, etc. The attempt to generate *a priori*, or by pure thought, a new notion through combining a thing with its negative is usually futile. When Hegel appears to be successful in deriving or deducing a new concept, we may follow William James in suspecting that he has in reality surreptitiously taken from experience an object or quality bearing some resemblance to the two opposites from the union of which it is alleged to be derived. For example, if we take the opposition of " Being " and " non-Being," we can find in the process of " change " or " becoming " a mixture of the positive and negative ideas. (A becoming involves a change from what is not to what is, and from what was to what is not.) But unless we had experienced independently what we call change, it is pretty safe to say that we should never have been able to discover it by uniting the .ideas of being and nothing. A final very grave difficulty with dialectical rationalism is its tendency to confuse the process of thinking with the process in the objects about which we think. My thought of white suggests my thought of black, my thought of a very good man suggests the thought of a very bad man ; but these instances of associating ideas by contrast have no bearing upon the objective question as to how far being a very good man involves being a very bad man, or being white involves being black.

2. *The Two Special Arguments for Cosmological Empiricism.* —In opposition to the monistic tendency of rationalism to consider all reality as one great system, all elements of which are interlocked by necessity, the empiricist inclines to a pluralistic conception of nature. The universe, he says, is not a system, but an *aggregate* or *assemblage* of diverse and independent elements. These elements are not related by any intrinsic necessity, either causal or logical. They simply happen to stand in certain relations of coexistence and sequence. The discovery of these connections and the description and classification of the elements is the whole task and the only task of science. Let us now consider the two special arguments offered by Empiricism in rebuttal of the claims of Rationalism to ultimacy even in its chosen domain of pure universals.

A. Empiricist Argument from the Contingency and Asymmetry of Relations between Universals.

Redness and roundness are abstract universals, yet there is no fixed or necessary relation either of implication or of exclusion between them, because the presence of one of these qualities in no way determines or precludes the presence of the other. They are, in mathematical language, independent variables, and any proposition expressing their identity or co-presence in one thing is contingent. Even within the realm of pure quantity it is easy to find cases of independent variables and resulting contingent relations. The three dimensions of space are such independent variables. The length of a thing does not determine its breadth, nor do the length and breadth together determine its depth. What values of the different dimensions are combined is a purely contingent matter, for any value of one dimension can be combined indifferently with any value of either or both of the others. Finally, argues the empiricist, many, if not most, of the propositions cited by the rationalist as necessary are non-reversible or asymmetric. That is to say, the necessity of the relation is only a one-way necessity. For example, an isosceles triangle is necessarily a figure having the sum of its angles equal to two right angles, but a figure having this property is not necessarily isosceles; the powers of 3 are necessarily odd numbers, but odd numbers are not necessarily powers of 3.

Let us observe that these arguments against rationalism are not based upon the mere failure to attain the rationalistic ideal—a failure which might well be due to our present ignorance—but upon our actual knowledge of diverse and ambiguous relations between universals, apparently proving that not every abstract quality stands in a determinate or necessary relation to every other, at least as regards spatio-temporal conjunction or co-inherence in one thing. The only way a rationalist could even partially meet this argument for a plurality of ultimate independent variables would be by supplementing the ordinary logic of analysis with a synthetic logic based on some such creative principle as Hegel's *negativität* which would reveal the seemingly independent universals to be functions of one another. But so far no such attempt has succeeded.

B. Empiricist Argument from the Relative or Hypothetical Character of the Relations between Universals.

In support of his counter-argument that even those propositions that have the appearance of necessity are always hypothetical or relative, the empiricist claims, first, that in so far as they apply to existence they are obviously and directly hypothetical; and secondly, that even when not applied to existence, they can be shown to be indirectly hypothetical, in that their validity depends upon certain postulates which we are free to assume or deny.

No judgment, certainly no universal judgment, implies the existence of its terms. When I say, " All triangles have the sum of their angles necessarily equal to two right angles," I mean that " if a triangle exists it must have the sum of its angles equal to two right angles." But whether "all triangles" or even any triangle exists or not may be left an open question. And as existence is always contingent and never necessary, the empiricist demands that we recognize the relative or hypothetical character of all so-called necessary truths.

Now, we may admit the validity of the positive part of this contention of the empiricist, but not of the negative. That is to say, it is certain that any necessary truth can be expressed in terms of a hypothetical proposition involving existence, but it is equally certain that every such hypothetical proposition derives its truth from a categorical or unconditional proposition involving universals. Unless the complex of universals connoted by the term triangle involved or implied the quality of equivalence to two right angles, it could never be true to say, " If a triangle exists, its angles are equal to two right angles." The proposition, " If 2 things be added to 3 things the result must be 5," presupposes the proposition " 2 + 3 = 5." Or in general, any necessary and concrete hypothetical proposition of the form, " If A were B, C would be D," implies a necessary and universal categorical proposition of the following form : " The implicatory relation between A and B implies the implicatory relation between C and D."

In short, the fact that existence is contingent does not prove that necessary relations between universals are contingent. The chief significance of this matter is expressed in the generally accepted doctrine that *Mathematics is not an existential science.* This means that mathematics as a science of necessary truth has the merit of possessing a validity that is independent of the existence of any one of the objects with which it deals, while at the same time and for the same reason it has the demerit of being unable to tell us anything categorical or *positive* about what exists. In other words, mathematics has the "defects of its qualities." It can tell us what does not exist, but not what does. It can assure us that there does not exist any Euclidean material circle whose circumference is commensurate with its diameter, but it neither knows nor needs to know whether such a thing as a material circle exists at all.

The empiricist is not content with showing that all necessary propositions about existence are merely hypothetical; he would show in the same way that propositions about subsistence are equally hypothetical. And he may, strangely enough, go to mathematics itself, the very citadel of necessity, to support him in this position. To understand this we must remember that the mathematician of to-day differs from his ancestors in his attitude towards axioms. The earlier mathematician regarded the principles on which he founded his geometry or his algebra as objectively true and self-evident laws of nature. The modern mathematician is inclined to the view that "axioms are postulates"; that, instead of being ultimate truths to which existence must conform, they are merely the rules of the mathematical game, and that, like the rules of any other game, they are made by the players and can be unmade or changed whenever the players so agree.[1]

---

[1] This point of view seems to have developed in the following way. Euclid's axiom to the effect that through any point only one line parallel to a given line can be drawn seemed to many geometers susceptible of deduction from the other axioms of Euclid's system. But all attempts at such deduction failed, and it was at length found that the reason for the failure lay in the fact that two new and perfectly self-consistent geometries could be built up without assuming the truth of the Euclidian axiom of parallels. One of these geometries (the Lobachevskian) substitutes for Euclid's axiom of a single parallel the axiom that an infinite number of parallels to a given line can be drawn through a given point, the other (the

From this standpoint, all mathematical theorems become hypothetical or contingent in the sense that their validity depends upon the acceptance of certain postulates which, in themselves, have neither truth nor falsity. Now, the answers which the rationalist can make to this second attempt of the empiricist to show that necessity is hypothetical is the same as that which he made to the first attempt. The hypothetical proposition : " If certain propositions are chosen as axioms, certain other propositions follow necessarily as theorems," presupposes the categorical proposition : " The axioms in question, taken collectively, necessarily imp' ' or involve the theorems in question." This is an objective truth, and its validity is quite independent of whether or not we chose to select those particular axioms. The apparent freedom of the moder mathematician to *create* systems of algebra and geometry, as an artist paints a picture, or as a dramatist writes a play, is in reality not a freedom to create but only a freedom to *select*. He allows hims 'lf to believe that when he concentrates his attention upon certain pro-

Riemannian) that not even one such parallel can be drawn. When the new geometers are charged with substituting a paradox for a self-evident truth, in that the space of our experience is Euclidian and not Lobachevskian or Riemannian, they reply with a polite shrug of the shoulders that their business as mathematicians is not to investigate the laws of what actually exists. They are concerned with developing the self-consistent systems of theorems which are logically deducible from any group of assumptions which they choose to make. Whether Riemann's or Lobachevski's or Euclid's geometry is *mathematically* " true " they regard as a meaningless question. The problem as to which of these ideal spaces most nearly agrees with the space of experience has a meaning to be sure, but it is a problem quite beyond the province of mathematics as such to investigate.

At about the same time that geometry was divesting itself of its hampering and irrelevant references to existence, a somewhat similar evolution was taking place in the realm of algebra. Two instances out of many may be taken for illustration. In the number system with which we are familiar $a \times b = b \times a$ and $a \times a = a^2$ where a and b symbolize any numbers. But by substituting for the first of these axioms the apparent paradox $a \times b = -b \times a$, Sir William Hamilton developed a self-consistent system of theorems, which he called " Quaternions " ; and by substituting for the second axiom the proposition $a \times a = a$, George Boole developed another equally self-consistent doctrine, known as " Algebra of Logic," because the elements of a system so determined happen to behave, when combined in equations, exactly as the general terms or classes of formal logic behave when combined in propositions and syllogisms. These two new doctrines are related to the ordinary algebra as the new geometries are related to the ordinary geometry. And allowing Pythagoras to play, in algebra, a rôle faintly ; analogous to Euclid's rôle in geometry, we might characterize the ideal constructions of Hamilton and of Boole as " non-Pythagorean algebras " in the same sense in which we characterize the ideal constructions of Riemann and Lobachevski as " non-Euclidian geometries."

positional relations and apprehends their consequences he has *made* a new truth. Just so, when we attend to one of the attributes of a perceived object, and think of it by itself in abstraction from its embodiment in existence, we are tempted to conclude that we have *created* a universal. But we could not have apprehended the quality unless it had been there to apprehend. Riemann and Lobachevski could no more have created their non-Euclidean geometries than Columbus could have created America. The realm of universals and the multiple systems of implication which that realm contains are in no sense arbitrary or indeterminate or plastic. They await the eye of the intellectual discoverer as the gold in the earth awaits the eye of the miner. All the geometries and all the algebras are among these systems, and if the mathematician wishes to leave the realm of concrete existence and journey up into that wider realm of abstract subsistence, then let us by all means wish him Godspeed. But when he returns with his discoveries, let us not flatter him by calling them creations. Truth is never created ; it is found, partly by the senses, partly by the intellect. A proposition that was not true before it was discovered could never become true by being discovered. Creation does not consist in making possibilities, but in actualizing them. Facts or existences can be both discovered and created, but meanings or subsistences can only be discovered. And yet, despite the cogency of this defence of the rationalist, we must admit that the new mathematics, though it does not do away with necessity, does confirm the empiricist's belief that there is a plurality of independent variables in the realm even of abstract universals. The very fact that different and mutually inconsistent systems of geometry and of algebra possess certain axioms in common, proves that those axioms are independent or non-implicative of one another—that their relation to one another is contingent rather than necessary. In other words, the necessity in a mathematical system is, so to speak, vertical but not horizontal. It holds between the group of axioms taken collectively and the theorems deduced from them ; it does not hold between the axioms themselves nor even between any one axiom and the theorems derived from the whole body of axioms. One axiom cannot imply a theorem any more than a genus can imply any given one of its species, or a complex of universals its exemplification in the spatio-temporal world of existence.

3. *A General Evaluation and Adjustment of the Claims of Empiricism and Rationalism.*—In this chapter and the chapter preceding it we have examined respectively the subjective and the objective phases of the controversy between the Rationalists and the Empiricists. As regards the subjective or psychological question, we have found that universal concepts and the necessary propositions which express their relations are as truly given in experience as are particular percepts and the contingent propositions by which they are related. And as regards the objective or ontological question, we have found that universals and the necessary relations between them have an objective reality independent alike of the mind that apprehends them, and of the particular situation in which they are exemplified. The relation between the two orders of reality might be expressed in the statement that the ideal system of universals is at once immanent and transcendent as respects the existential system of particulars. Rationalism is right in maintaining that every particular contains and presupposes universals, and that every contingent proposition contains and presupposes propositions that are necessary. But empiricism is right in denying that particulars can be completely reduced to universals and that contingent propositions can be completely reduced to propositions that are necessary. We might liken the world to a woven web in which the warp symbolizes necessity and the woof contingencies. Each thread of the warp represents a series of logically necessary implications that may be discovered deductively, but the number and kind of these threads, and the ways in which they are interwoven and entangled in actual existence by the threads of the woof, is purely contingent, and can be learned only by observation and induction. In short, rationalism and empiricism are complementary criteria for the discovery of truth ; neither can be substituted for the other ; neither can contradict the other. When there appears, as there often has appeared, to be a conflict between empirical experience and rational reflection, we may be assured that such conflict or antinomy is not due to a

defect in either criterion of truth, but only to our misuse of one or the other or of both. It is the function of empiricism to discover through induction the universal propositions that are implied by the analysis of any group of concrete facts. It is the function of rationalism to discover through deduction the particular consequences implied by the synthesis of any group of abstract propositions. Regarding things from the standpoint of " intension " rather then " extension," empiricism is analytic ; rationalism is synthetic. Empiricism proceeds from the concrete and particular to the abstract and universal ; rationalism proceeds from the abstract and universal to the concrete and particular. The inductions of the empiricist may or may not agree with the theories already established. The deductions of the rationalist may or may not agree with already observed facts.

Pure empiricism gives us unrelated groups of natural laws based upon whatever groups of facts happen to catch the observer's attention, and the gravest danger to which the pure empiricist is subject consists in the possibility of un-checked errors and undiscovered contradictions lurking in his various isolated doctrines. Pure rationalism gives us logical and mathematical systems of consequences which may be wholly irrelevant to the facts of existence ; and the gravest dangers to which the pure rationalist is subject are: (1) that he may mistake a mere subjective feeling of neces-sity for an objective truth (as was illustrated in the ration-alistic denial, because of its unthinkability, of life at the antipodes) ; and (2) that in his love of order he may sacrifice truth to symmetry and try to force the wild and infinite variety of nature into the procrustean beds or formulas of his own choosing (as was illustrated in the refusal to accept empirical evidence for the elliptical orbits of the planets on the ground that perfect circles are the only curves worthy to describe the motions of heavenly bodies). When the two methods are joined, the empiricist furnishes propositions implied by facts, and the rationalist, instead of arbitrarily selecting from the whole realm of possibilities whatever suits his fancy, takes the propositions newly discovered by the empiricist, combines them with propositions already estab-lished, and from this union of old and new, of general and specific, deduces concrete consequences. It is then the turn of the empiricist to verify by observation the hypothetical deductions of his partner. And instead of indulging in haphazard observation, uncontrolled by any systematized interest, he will be influenced by a sense of the relative importance of the facts to be investigated, and will concentrate his observation and experiment upon those portions of the jungle of experienced facts which seem likely to confirm or refute, extend or modify the laws previously established. Moreover, empiricism and rationalism not only aid one another positively, but serve as checks upon one another's errors. To understand this we must note that there are four stages in the complete inductive-deductive cycle : (1) the initial experiences that set the problem and the imagining of a hypothesis that seems promising ; (2) the combination of the new hypothesis with old or previously accepted principles ; (3) the deduction, from this combination, of its hypothetical consequences ; (4) the verification of those consequences by further experiences. Hence, whenever a rationalistic deduction from empirically derived premises is refuted by experience, it is due to one or more of the following four sources of error, which correspond respectively to the four stages just mentioned : (1) the experience furnishing the problem was illusory ; (2) one or more of the previously accepted theories, or the new hypothesis which, when combined with them, constituted the premises for the deduction, was false ; or, (3) the deductive reasoning was invalid ; or, (4) the final invalidity pertained to the supposed verification by further experience.

Usually the early stages of an existential science are predominantly inductive. If the field of facts is a new one, the hypotheses derived from it will not be sufficiently homogeneous with other knowledge already established. Such sciences as meteorology and psychology are almost entirely inductive, because of the heterogeneity of the material in each. But as the field is extended and the hypotheses gain in generality, they come into connection with one another and with the theories of other sciences, and the opportunities for deduction increase. Biology as connected with chemistry, and chemistry as connected with physics, are examples of this second stage in the growth of a science—the stage in which the sciences help one another through their interrelation. While finally, such a science as pure mechanics has become so interwoven with mathematics that its procedure is predominantly deductive. From this standpoint we might liken the different sciences in their initial separateness and ultimate connectedness to the trees of a forest. When the trees are very young they are separate from one another; but as they grow they put forth branches which approach one another, till finally, when the trees are full grown, the branches interlace and form an aerial web, making the trees appear united into a single system. Yet, just as the separate trees may in some instances have grown from seeds or slips taken from their neighbours, so also there are cases in which a new science does not originate independently, but springs from a neighbouring science, or from a union of two or more sciences.

We may now see more clearly the reason for the tremendous importance of mathematics in the development of scientific knowledge. The mathematical concepts of number, space, time, and of velocity which is the ratio of space to time, form homogeneous systems in which almost limitless deductions are possible. Hence each science strives naturally and instinctively to reduce its discontinuous and incommensurable qualities to the continuous and commensurable categories of quantity. In so far as a science can correlate its phenomena with modes of mass and energy, to that extent it becomes deductive and capable of fruitful union with other sciences. It would indeed be the gravest mistake to think that because of such imaginative flights as non-Euclidean geometry and non-Pythagorean algebra, mathematics was a mere playground for the irresponsible rationalist. The rôle of that mighty discipline in the development of science might rather be likened to the rôle of money in the development of economic institutions. When once a medium of exchange is in use, clumsy barter of goods gives way to buying and selling. Articles the most diverse may each be given a price in terms of currency, and all values reduced to a common denominator. Just so, quantity is the common denominator or currency to which the otherwise incommensurable objects of nature can be reduced, mathematical deduction itself being the clearing house for all sciences that are methodologically solvent.

And now that we have seen something of the manner and extent to which empiricism and rationalism combine to perfect the inductive-deductive cycle involved in the acquisition of truth, we must be careful not to allow the closeness of the alliance of the two methods to blur the distinction between them. So long as there remain fields of facts that have not been inductively analysed and reduced to law, there will be a demand for minds of the empiricist type to undertake the task. And so long as there remain laws that have not been assimilated to the general system of established principles, there will be a demand for minds of the rationalist type to undertake that task. Just as an animal organism needs two sets of organs, one set for acquiring food, and the other for digesting and assimilating it, so it is with the organism of science. The empiricists acquire the food of science, and the rationalists digest and assimilate it. Without food in the form of new facts and laws, science would die of hunger, but without the ability to assimilate its laws into its system, science would die of indigestion. If science is to avoid both starvation and dyspepsia she must see to it that she possesses both empiricists and rationalists, both observers and mathematicians.

It is due largely to the organic way in which these two methods unite to corroborate one another's truths and to check one another's errors that the system of the natural sciences has become the most impressive work of the human mind. Neither authoritarianism nor mysticism, alone or in combination, has produced any such solid, coherent, and extensive body of truth as has resulted from the joint method of empiricism and rationalism.

CHAPTER V

THE METHOD OF PRAGMATISM

Introductory and Historical.

IN the *Popular Science Monthly* of January 1878 there appeared a paper by Mr. Charles Peirce entitled "How to Make Our Ideas Clear." Mr. Peirce, distinguished for the originality of his contributions to symbolic logic and to general philosophy, in this paper set forth a new method for ascertaining the meaning of concepts and judgments which he later named "Pragmatism," and still later "Pragmaticism," to distinguish it from the newer forms of pragmatic philosophy. According to Mr. Peirce, the real meaning of an idea is to be found in its concrete results, and especially in its practical consequences for human action. In the article just mentioned Peirce expresses his principle as follows : "consider what effects which might conceivably have practical bearings we conceive the object of our conception to have. Then our conception of these effects is the whole of our conception of the object."

It is interesting to note that Mr. Peirce offers his pragmatic principle as a criterion for ascertaining, not the *truth* of an idea or proposition, but its *meaning*. He opposes his conception to the Leibnitzian conceptions of what constitutes clearness and distinctness of ideas. According to Peirce, in order to understand the meaning of a thought, it is not sufficient to mark it off from other ideas, nor is it necessary to analyse its logical essence. What is both necessary and sufficient is to discover all its consequences both actual and possible. One might question whether this identification of the meaning of a proposition with its effects did not leave the proposition itself rather devoid of meaning. But it is more relevant to our present purpose to point out the great

131

difference between Peirce's use of practical consequences as a way of defining and discovering *meanings* from the later pragmatists' use of the *satisfactoriness* of practical consequences as a way of defining and discovering *truths*. I think it was Professor Dewey who pointed out that the characteristic generosity of William James caused him to over-estimate his debt to Peirce, and to under-estimate the originality of his own pragmatism. Consequences do, to be sure, however used, imply a prospective attitude; and the prospective suggests the conative or voluntaristic interest in the good. This in turn might have suggested that the good consequences of holding a proposition were a sign of its truth, and even that truth consisted in satisfaction. But to Peirce himself the proper method of verifying a belief as set forth in other papers of his series of " Illustrations of the Logic of Science " had nothing to do with the goodness or badness of the consequences, but consisted entirely in the use of observation and experiment, supplemented by a use of the theory of probability. As explaining his epistemological theory of the meaning of truth, as well as his logical theory of how we should verify our beliefs, the following passage is of interest :

" The opinion which is fated to be ultimately agreed to by all who investigate is what we mean by truth and the object represented in this opinion is the real." This passage from the article above cited might appear to have a slightly subjective flavour, but if we interpret it in the light of a passage in a preceding article of the series on " Illustrations of the Logic of Science," we shall see that the " fated agreement " in belief was to be brought about by purely objective factors. The article to which I am referring was published in the *Popular Science Monthly* for November 1877, and the significant passage reads as follows : " To satisfy our doubts, therefore, it is necessary that a method should be found by which our beliefs may be caused by nothing human but by some external permanency, something upon which our thinking has no effect. . . . It must be something which affects or might affect every man. And though these effects are necessarily as various as are individual conditions, yet the method must be such that the ultimate conclusions of every man be the same. Such is the method of science. Its fundamental hypothesis restated in more familiar language is this : There are real things whose characters are entirely independent of our opinions about them ; those realities affect our senses according to regular laws. And though our sensations are as different as our relations to the objects, yet by taking advantage of the laws of perception we can ascertain by reasoning how things really are. And any man if he have sufficient experience and reason enough about it will be led to the one true conclusion. "

In view of the subjectivism and relativism with which pragmatism appears to many of us to be infected, it has seemed worth while to show by these somewhat extended quotations that the prophet of the movement at least was sufficiently committed to a realistic theory of knowledge.

The novel and interesting doctrine of Peirce seems to have attracted little notice until in 1898 it was expounded and developed in a new form by William James in an address to the Philosophical Union of the University of California. James followed this address with many articles in which he set forth various phases of the pragmatic theory ; and in 1907 he published his *Pragmatism*, which, together with its sequel *The Meaning of Truth*, constitutes a fairly complete presentation of the Pragmatic philosophy in the form in which James held it.

While William James was pondering the Principle of Peirce and developing it into a many-sided philosophic doctrine, Professor Dewey had been developing a conception of knowledge and indirectly of logical and scientific method which he called " Instrumentalism." Dewey's Instrumentalism, although motived by the logical rather than the biological interests of its author, treats the function of cognition from a genetic and evolutionary point of view. Just as the modern biologist regards purely physical organs such as the eyes and the stomach as the outcome of favourable variations which have been developed and preserved through the agency of natural selection, so the Instrumentalists viewed mental functions such as memory and imagination as having been evolved as instruments of adaptation to the environment. This evolutionary viewpoint has been applied systematically by Angell in his *Psychology*, and was stated earlier by James himself in the following passage from his *Psychology, Briefer Course*, p. 4 : " . . . mental life is primarily teleological ; that is to say, . . . our various ways of feeling and thinking have grown to be what they are because of their utility in shaping our *reactions* on the outer world. On the whole, few recent formulas have done more service in psychology than the Spencerian one, that the essence of mental life and bodily life are one, namely, ' the adjustment of inner to outer relations.' . . . *Primarily then, and fundamentally, the mental life is for the sake of action of a preservative sort.*" (Italics mine.)

In my opinion, the most interesting part of Professor Dewey's philosophy consists in the application of this standpoint of evolutionary biology, not only to psychology in the narrower sense, but to the broader problems of logic, ethics, and educational method. If the human intellect has come into being in response to practical and biological needs of the organism, the measure of value of an intellectual process will consist in its specific efficiency to satisfy the need from which it was generated. Instead of treating logic as a body of absolute and eternal laws, with which any judgment must conform on pain of being condemned as false, the Instrumentalist views logic as a group of changing and flexible rules which originate and terminate in the exigencies of life, and which have as their sole purpose the guidance of man in making his thought effective in meeting the varying problems which confront him. Instead of regarding truth as an end in itself, a purely theoretical and abstract agreement with changeless principles, the Instrumentalist treats truth as one form of successful adaptation to environment. And thus independently there was developed by Professor Dewey a methodology very similar to that which James reached through a development of the Principle of Peirce.[1]

---

[1] Professor Dewey himself has kindly read in manuscript this chapter on Pragmatism and has made a series of comments explaining his position on some of the doctrines which I analyse. These comments clear up certain misunderstandings of Instrumentalism which I, in common with others, have suffered from, and while I cannot see that they invalidate the brief summary which I have just given, they undoubtedly constitute an effective demurrer so far as concerns Professor Dewey's own position, to many of the criticisms which I bring against Pragmatism in the later portions of the

While James and Dewey were developing their respective forms of pragmatic philosophy, Dr. F. C. S. Schiller of Oxford, a friend and follower of James, was building up a doctrine which he called " Humanism," and which may be regarded as a third form of pragmatism. Dr. Schiller was one of a group of philosophers who were dissatisfied with the philosophy of absolute idealism which, under the leadership of F. H. Bradley, had come to be the dominant form of thought at Oxford.   According to the absolute idealists, the world as we see it is not the real world, but a world of appearance. The true reality, the Absolute, is an eternal and unitary system of experience in which our concepts and ideals are transcended and transmuted. Human life and human interests are from this standpoint but the distorted fragments of the one cosmic life.   Dr. Schiller's humanism is primarily a protest against this philosophy, and like most protests it is the direct antithesis of the view to which it is opposed.   It is interesting in this connection to note that the pragmatisms of both James and Dewey were also largely motivated by a feeling of revolt against absolute idealism.   Professor Royce had developed independently at Harvard a form of idealistic monism which

chapter under the captions of " Biological Practicalism " and " Relativism." The reader is therefore requested to regard those criticisms as directed not against Professor Dewey's Instrumentalism, but rather against certain general tendencies which I regard as implicit if not explicit in the logic and epistemology of Pragmatism.

The chief points which my colleague has emphasized in his comment on my treatment of Pragmatism are the following :

1. " The motive which actuated the philosophy of Instrumentalism as set forth in *Studies in Logical Theory* was a critical reaction to the work of such Post-Kantian logicians as Lotze, Bosanquet, and Bradley. The aim was to show that it is not necessary to assume *a priori* forms of thought to which subject-matter is accommodated, but that logical forms and structures are distinctions within the process of reflective and experimental inquiry."

2. " I have never taught that all needs are practical, but simply that no need could be satisfied without action. Our needs originate out of needs that at first were practical, but the development of intelligence transforms them so that there are now æsthetic, scientific, and moral needs."

3. " I have never said that thought exists for the sake of action. On the contrary, it exists for the sake of specific consequences, immediate values, etc. What I have insisted on is quite a different point, namely that action is involved in thinking and existential knowing, as part of the function of reaching immediate non-practical consequences."

4. " How can Instrumentalism which holds that intelligence is the only sure method of achieving the good in consequences be anti-intellectualistic in the sense you describe ? It is anti-intellectualistic only with reference to certain theories about intellect, theories which seem to me to isolate knowledge from its connections, empirical and metaphysical."

aroused a strenuous though always friendly opposition on the part of James, who was convinced that no monistic system could do justice to the rich variety and change in the world of our experience. And Professor Dewey had felt and expressed this same sort of dissatisfaction with the form of absolute idealism defended by the German philosopher, Herman Lotze. Absolutism belittles man and exalts the universe. Humanism belittles the universe and exalts man. The Absolute Life of which our lives are alleged by the idealists to be mere fragments is, according to Schiller, a chimera. The universe is not one, but many; not eternal, but temporal; not absolute, but relative. Reality is not above or beyond human experience. Things are in reality just what they are humanly experienced as being. But now, one may ask, what has the connection between Dr. Schiller's humanistic protest against absolutism to do with the pragmatic method for attaining and evaluating our knowledge? The answer is to be found in Schiller's account of the part played by volition and emotion in what seem to be purely intellectual processes. What we think about and what we believe is determined more largely than we realize by our interests and desires. Our interest determines even what we see and hear. If an object has many aspects, our attention emphasizes and makes real to us only those aspects which bear upon our weal and woe. Hence the forms and connections of the world of our experience are not to be regarded as imposed upon us from without, either by a non-human system of material forces or by a superhuman system of absolute and eternal ideals, but are rather to be viewed as the outcome of the enduring interests, preferences, and needs of ourselves and our ancestors. The world that human beings perceive is a humanized world, *i.e.* a world that has been coloured and moulded by human aspiration and will. Schiller bids us recognize this fact and rejoice in it. If a theory conforms to human needs, it is in so far a true theory. If the established laws of nature have been accepted and recognized because they have met human needs, then there is a probability that a new hypothesis which satisfies some need or aspiration will accord with those laws. We must, in short, judge the truth of a theory by the pragmatic criterion of its value in practical life.

Thus we see that James, Dewey, and Schiller, each approaching the problem of method from a different angle, arrive at a virtual agreement. For James and Schiller thought or cognition exists for the sake of action rather than as an end in itself ; and for all three the truth of a judgment should be measured not by an abstract criterion such as consistency or copying of fact, but by the concrete criterion of its practical efficiency to satisfy the need by which it was generated.   It is a question, however, whether in spite of this general agreement there are not differences that are even more fundamental, especially between the theories of Dewey and Schiller.   For while both of these pragmatists agree that human experience is the outcome of an adaptive interaction between human needs and an environment, for Dewey, the emphasis is more upon the environment as the factor controlling the interaction, while for Schiller it seems to be rather the human personality that moulds the environment in accordance with its needs. The general tendencies of Dewey's pragmatism are, therefore, naturalistic and biological, while Schiller's sympathies seem to be more with the idealistic philosophers and the so-called voluntarists who feel that the world is being moulded and guided by the teleological forces that operate in our own spiritual life.   The position of James on this question is hard to determine.   He appeared to sympathize both with the " left wing " naturalism of Dewey and with the " right wing " idealistic voluntarism of Schiller, without definitely committing himself to either.

In view of these conflicting metaphysical tendencies on the part of leading pragmatists it might seem appropriate to follow up our historical sketch with separate expositions of their writings ; but inasmuch as we are concerned with pragmatism as a theory of method rather than with the different pragmatic theories of nature, I prefer to pass at once to a consideration of certain fundamental standpoints which are, I think, common to most pragmatists, and which taken together seem to me to constitute the true meaning and significance of the pragmatic movement.   The standpoints to which I refer are three, and I shall designate them respectively " Futurism," " Practicalism," and " Relativism."

I

PRAGMATISM AS FUTURISM.

Rationalism and authoritarianism might be described as methods of justifying beliefs by making them conform either to testimony or to axioms already established in the *past*. Empiricism and mysticism could analogously be described as methods of testing beliefs by their agreement with immediate *present* experience, either external or internal. Pragmatism, however, tests beliefs by the consequences that flow from them in the *future*. What does a given belief or theory promise for the future ? What can it accomplish ? How can it aid us in the mastering of our environment ? These are the questions asked by the pragmatist when he is passing judgment upon a theory. If the future consequences of holding and using the theory are good, then we shall take that as an indication of its truth ; if, on the other hand, it is an assumption which yields harmful consequences, then by that token its falsity will be indicated ; and finally, if the theory nakes no difference in the life of those who hold it, it can be regarded as meaningless. No matter how much a theory may conform to the body of established truth, or may copy present reality, it cannot be properly regarded as true unless it yields actual concrete consequences that will be of value in the future to those who use it. Because of this emphasis on the prospective or forward-facing aspect of cognition, I think it appropriate to characterize pragmatism as Futurism in philosophy.

The futuristic attitude which pragmatism expresses is by no means confined to logical and metaphysical theory. It is the attitude of radicals and reformers and of all who are working for social progress. It is above all essential to democracy and to the life of a free people. For the past, however splendid, is limited and beyond our power to change, while the future, however uncertain, is without limit and is plastic to our will. When Benjamin Kidd a generation ago brought out his book *Evolution and Altruism*, the social gospel therein proclaimed sounded strange and fantastic. For Kidd believed that the rank of a species in the evolutionary scale should be measured by the concern for the future shown by its members ; and he preached as the lesson of evolution the increasing need and paramount duty of each generation to provide for the generations to come.   We had flattered ourselves that at least in the Occident we were emancipated from ancestor worship ; but the rollicking lusty present seemed pretty good to us, and we felt hardly ready for the responsibilities entailed by a " religion of posterity." And yet, since the appearance of Kidd's book, the growth of futurism has been tremendous.   The philosophy of Nietzsche has become familiar to us, and futurism is the soul of that philosophy.   More recently still, the philosophy of Henri Bergson with its stimulating emphasis upon the creative character of the evolutionary process has voiced the spirit of futurism.   And while Nietzsche was the pioneer of the movement and Kidd its chief American expositor, Bergson is its latest prophet, and shares with the pragmatists the leadership of futurism to-day.

The futurist attitude is exemplified not only in philosophical theories but in concrete social movements.   The eugenics movement is an obvious expression of it.   Remorse for the thoughtless waste of our natural resources and the resulting movement for conservation in all its forms is another.   The great interest in insurance and the dawning interest in preventive medicine might also be cited.   The agitation in favour of easier methods of amending our constitutions and of freeing ourselves from the laws laid down by our fathers is a further sign of increasing futurism.   Even the jurists who are the natural and inevitable defenders of precedent are beginning to consider the possibility of making the law and its administration more opportunistic.   In England, Mr. H. G. Wells has urged the duty of serious and systematized forecasts of the future, and we may almost suppose him to hope that the history courses in schools and colleges may be accompanied, if not supplanted by, courses in " prophecy."   Finally, to these specific manifestations of futurism may be added the growing indifference to old things and old ideas.

If we turn from these phenomena of social life to the field of theoretical science, we find more evidence of the futurist attitude. It has always been recognized that a scientific hypothesis must fulfil three criteria, *viz.* : (1) it must explain the present facts, the facts which have raised the problem ; (2) it must not conflict with past knowledge, and must, if possible, make use only of *veræ causæ*, *i.e.* principles or concepts which have already been vindicated independently of the present situation ; (3) it must open the way to further knowledge and permit of experimental verification and application in new situations.[1]

But although these three criteria have always been recognized in a general way, they have not always been equally emphasized. Just at present there is a growing tendency to emphasize the third or futuristic requirement—to demand of a hypothesis that it prove fruitful in giving results. Any theory can secure respectful attention if it promises an extension of knowledge. Just as the manager of a modern business bases his selection and promotion of employees, not so much on their ancestry or on their good looks, as on their capacity

---

[1] It sometimes happens that a hypothesis conforms to one or two, but not to all of these criteria, and then arise interesting problems of method. An example of failure to conform to the second criterion is afforded by Le Sage's hypothesis for explaining gravitation. He assumed the existence of hypermundane corpuscles or minute particles everywhere present in space and travelling in all directions with enormous velocities. Any material body would be subjected throughout its bulk to a perpetual bombardment by these corpuscles, and any two bodies would, to some extent, screen one another so that the corpuscular impacts forcing them apart would be less than those forcing them together, with the result that they would drift toward one another with a force proportional to their masses and inversely proportional to the square of their distance apart—which is the gravitation formula. The chief (though not the only) objection to this ingenious supposition is the complete lack of any independent evidence for the hypothetical corpuscles. They do not constitute a *vera causa*, but rather an *ens ex machina*, and there is, therefore, an overwhelming probability against the truth of the theory.

An example of a hypothesis which fails in the opposite way by violation of the third criterion is furnished by the theory of vitalism in biology—at least in its cruder form—which attempts to explain such a process as the development of an egg into a chick by postulating in the egg something analogous to a conscious intention to become a chick. Now, such a hypothesis conforms to the first two requirements, in that it in some sense explains the process, and in that it uses a *vera causa*, or recognized principle such as conscious intention. But it violates the third requirement for a good hypothesis, because the assumption of a quasi-consciousness on the part of an egg or a seed is not susceptible of further verification and leads to no further knowledge. Indeed, the vitalistic hypothesis has proved not only sterile, but positively harmful by reason of the fact that it seems to absolve the biologist from the obligation to search for the actual physical factors which are involved in every vital process ; and it is only by the discovery of such factors that real advance in biology is made.

to advance his interests, so the modern scientific man values a hypothesis, not in proportion to its conformity to scientific tradition, but in proportion to its promise of fertility. Curiously enough, this pragmatic attitude is, as has already been noted, most marked in mathematics, which, for a long time, was the most fixed and dogmatic of sciences. The modern mathematician no longer asks of a new principle that it shall conform to established truth or even that it shall agree with any aspect of experience. His interest in it is measured by its promise of significant results. As illustrations, we may refer to the paradoxical " axioms " of the non-Euclidian geometries and of some of the newer algebras to which we referred in the preceding chapter. Again, in physics and chemistry we can find interesting indications of the pragmatic attitude. A physicist may say, " I do not believe there is any such thing as the ether, but I recognize that it is a good working hypothesis, a good instrument for extending our knowledge of physical phenomena, and I accept it as true in that sense." Many chemists have taken the same position with regard to the atomic theory. They regard it, not as a copy of anything actually existing, but as a useful means of extending our knowledge of actual chemical phenomena. Even in theology the pragmatic or futuristic influence is felt. Dogmas and ritual are increasingly viewed as having their principal, if not their only, significance in the consequences which they produce.

Many more illustrations could be used, but these will suffice to give an idea of the way in which pragmatism as futurism permeates both the social and the intellectual life of our time. The greatness of a philosophy is in some degree proportioned to the extent to which it expresses the spirit of its age ; and pragmatism, as measured by this criterion, is a really great and significant movement. There are, however, certain rather obvious limitations to an exclusively futurist attitude in life and in science, and these we must now consider.

In the first place, as regards the spirit of futurism in the social movements of to-day, it may be said at once that even the most novel and revolutionary of these movements are profoundly and confessedly motivated and guided by history.

Marxian Socialism itself is based upon a philosophy of history —the so-called materialistic or economic interpretation—and, irrespective of the truth or falsity of that interpretation, it calls for and implies as great a devotion to the study of the past as any conservative could desire. All intelligent planning. for the future must be based on a knowledge of the past. An attempt to cut loose and create a future out of nothing would be as absurd as an attempt to use imagination apart from memory. The only future for which we can plan must consist of a new arrangement and a new emphasis of factors and elements already given. A new social institution has as a rule a better chance of success if based upon a modification of already existing customs and institutions rather than upon revolution and destruction. There is a very real analogy between social growth and the growth of a living organism. There are cases when a "folkway" or social habit becomes actively evil or malignant and analogous to a cancerous or gangrenous member of the body politic. It is then that the revolutionist or social surgeon must be called in. But in the majority of cases a diseased institution like a diseased body can be treated more successfully by medicine than by surgery.

An example of an over-emphasis of futurism is found, it seems to me, in the tendency to carry to an extreme the elective system in education. To leave a child free to study any subject or none is simply to deprive him of his social inheritance. He cannot choose intelligently until he knows what there is to choose *from*. If we wished to make a civilized man out of a savage, we should not take him direct from his forest and put him naked in a department store, bidding him choose whatever clothing caught his fancy. The child is intellectually and culturally naked, and the only life he knows independent of our teaching is the forest life of his instincts. Why should we expect him in the name of "individuality" and "self-realization" to repeat all that the race has learned by generations of trial and error? To abstain from all compulsion and all prescription in the teaching of children is, we repeat, merely to rob them of their rightful social heritage.

Let us turn now to the objections to futurism as a method of testing scientific hypotheses. The pragmatic futurist tells us that the truth of a hypothesis is primarily dependent upon the consequences to which it leads rather than upon the extent to which it copies present reality or harmonizes with principles established in the past ; and he cites numerous cases of scientific procedure to justify his contention.   The two principal objections to this phase of futurism may be taken as setting forth respectively the claim of the past and the claim of the present.   In spite of the undoubted freedom of the scientific investigator to depart from the methods of his predecessors and adopt any concept or theory which will yield fruitful consequences, it remains true that by far the greater number of such theories are adaptations of principles established in the past.   Just as a program of social reform which is without any historical sanction is almost, though not quite, certain to fail, so a hypothesis which is opposed to or even unconnected with the great body of scientific laws already in our possession is doomed to an almost certain sterility.   Of course, the greater the novelty of the problem, the greater may be the justification for a theory that breaks with the past.   But, in general, the steady advance of science has been due to the utilizing and extending of its past achievements.   Here, as in the case of the elective system in education, it is largely a question of economy.   Why disregard the lesson already learned ?   A man presents a scheme for a perpetual motion machine, and feels that it is very unfair for the orthodox scientists to reject it without any pragmatic test of what it can accomplish.   But to do otherwise would be a waste of time, a doing over again that which has been done in the past.   When a principle, like that of the conservation of energy, has been vindicated again and again and has been used with success in many different fields of inquiry, the probability that it is false, and that a new principle that contradicts it is true, is so small as to be hardly worth testing.   Of course, in science as in social matters confidence in the rightness of the established order may be mistaken.   A genuinely revolutionary theory or movement may be needed.   But other things being equal, there is always a presumption in favour of principles that have been tested by past experience.

The second objection to the futurist criterion for evaluating a hypothesis rests upon a truth often overlooked by the pragmatist. *There is always a reason why a good hypothesis yields fruitful results for the future and that reason is its agreement with the present structure of reality.* Pragmatists often speak as though they had told the whole story when they point out that a hypothesis gives good results. They do not feel the need of asking why the results are good. A theory, to them, is like a key. It unlocks the door of the future and reveals to us facts that were hidden. As a key is good when it will unlock a door, so a theory is good or true when it will help us to a future discovery. But when a key unlocks a door it does so, not by chance, but because its structure is such as to conform to the structure of the lock ; and quite analogously when a theory yields new discoveries it is because it conforms to the facts as they are. This does not mean that we must wait until we discover whether a theory is a statement of present facts before trying it. It would be inconvenient and sometimes impossible to test either a theory or a key in any other way than by its results. Only, when we get the results we should recognize the reason. Our enthusiasm for the future should not blind us to the fact that it is and must be based upon the present. The pragmatist may attempt to meet this objection by citing such cases as that of the Ptolemaic theory in astronomy and the atomic theory in chemistry. The former theory we now know to be in disagreement with the facts, but it proved useful in the past, and would still be useful if we were deprived of the more adequate theory of Copernicus. As for the atomic theory, is it not sufficient to recognize that while there may be chemists who believe that it is false in the sense of not being a copy of what actually exists, yet there are few, if any, who would deny its truth in the pragmatic sense of utility in yielding valuable consequences ? To this suggested defence of the pragmatist we may answer as follows : The extent to which a theory agrees with or copies reality depends not on the resemblance of its *terms* or *qualities* to those of reality, but on the resemblance of its *relations* to the *relations* between facts. To illustrate : suppose the real facts to be symbolized by X, Y, Z, W, and their relations by R_1, R_2, R_3. Suppose a theory about these real facts to contain terms A, B, C, D, and relations R_1, R_2, R_3, then no matter how great the difference between the intrinsic natures of A and X, B and Y, C and Z, D and W, the theory will be true, provided A, B, C, D are related in the same way as X, Y, Z, and W. That is, if XR_1Y, XR_2Z, XR_3W represent the objective reality, then AR_1B, AR_2C, AR_3D will represent a true theory or copy of that reality. In other words, it is relational and not qualitative resemblance or identity that constitutes significant truth. Now, between the Ptolemaic theory which describes the motions of the planets as they appear to an observer on the earth, and the Copernican theory which describes them as they are (or, if you prefer, as they would appear to an observer on one of the fixed stars), there is a large measure of one-to-one correspondence or relational resemblance. And we may say that the Ptolemaic theory owed its utility to the aspect in which it resembled the Copernican theory, and agreed with the facts.

As regards the atomic theory, we may confidently assert that whether or not such things as material atoms actually exist, yet just to the extent that the theory of atoms proves useful to us in dealing with facts, to that same extent the relations holding in reality are the same as those represented as holding between atoms. In general, when theories that are apparently contradictory prove useful in dealing with reality, it does not follow that reality is arbitrary or indeterminate, and that an account of it can be true only in a pragmatic sense and false in every other sense. The utility of such theories will always be due not to their qualitative difference from one another and from the facts, but to their relational resemblance, or correspondence to one another and to the facts.

We have now stated the case for pragmatism as futurism and also the case against it. How much of importance and permanent value remains in the theory after the critics have exposed its shortcomings? It seems to me that a very great deal remains; that philosophy has received a permanent modification and addition at the hands of the pragmatists; and that the spirit of futurism, both in social movements and in abstract theory, has come to stay.

The exhortation of the social conservative to remember

that plans for the future must be based upon knowledge of the past, that social institutions grow slowly, and that evolution is generally preferable to revolution and construction to destruction—all these admonitions are merely samples of the platitudinous wisdom of common sense, and need give the pragmatist no real alarm. Study the past by all means, he will say, but study it not so much in the spirit of the antiquarian who loves it for its own sake, but rather from the view-point of its lessons for the future. Futurism would not destroy history, but would revivify it by giving it that prospective and selective emphasis which comes from a desire to utilize it in shaping the future. Again, the futurist can take proper account of the established order and pay proper respect to long-standing customs and institutions, but his respect will be reasoned and self-conscious, not blind and automatic. The mere fact of age as such will be no more a recommendation than novelty as such. As long as the conditions under which an institution has grown up and endured remain unchanged, the conservative is right in holding that its age is a presumption in its favour, and that the burden of proof is upon the radicals who would overthrow it. But when conditions change and become, it may, be, the reverse of those which shaped the origin of a custom, the tables are turned. The burden of proof now rests upon the conservative, who must show cause why new social conditions should not be met by new social adjustments. Consider, for example, the feudal system in Japan. This institution developed and endured for centuries in a peculiar Oriental environment ; but when Japan became Occidentalized the very points which had justified feudalism under the old environment now called for and achieved its destruction. Take again the question of disestablishing the Church in Great Britain. As long as the great majority of the people of the nation were of the same religious belief it seemed right enough that the Church should be subsidized and administered by the Government ; but when, as in Wales, conditions changed and the great majority of the people dissented from the established religion, it became preposterous to use the public taxes any longer in its support. Disestablishment was demanded and achieved.

As applied to education, we criticized futurism for its over-emphasis on the elective system and its tendency to advocate, in the name of individuality, a policy of complete *laissez faire*; yet, after all, the futurist might well regard our arraignment as unjust. He might admit the desirability of compelling the child to become acquainted with the most important achievements of culture and of science and still insist that such teaching was to be undertaken in a pragmatic spirit : that it was to be given not as an end in itself, but as the best and most obvious means of enabling the pupil to elect with intelligence the subjects suited to his individual needs. Again, as to the criticisms advanced against futurism as a scientific method, it seems to me that while the objections here are serious, they are by no means fatal. The obligation which the scientist feels towards long-established principles and theories, and the duty he is under to make his new hypotheses to accord with them, is measured, not by the age of the older theories, but by the extent to which the evidence on which the older theories were based is recognized as authentic. If new evidence is discovered which conflicts with the old, then new departures in the way of hypotheses are justified, for the same reason that new social adjustments are justified when the conditions which generated the old customs have ceased to exist. Phenomena such as those of X-rays and radium may call for hypotheses which differ from or even conflict with theories that, prior to these novel discoveries, were rightfully regarded as authoritative. When once the new discoveries are made, the presumption in favour of the theories already established ceases to exist. Lastly, the objection that the futurist neglects to realize that the reason why a theory yields good results in the future is because it agrees with the hard facts of the present, seems to me valid. But even to this criticism it may be answered that in many cases the only test of such agreement of a theory with present fact is to be sought in the future consequences to which the theory gives rise. In short, futurism as a method of logic is valid to the extent that the consequences of a belief, though they cannot constitute its truth, can reveal it.   They are its *ratio cognoscendi*, though never its *ratio essendi*.

II

PRAGMATISM AS PRACTICALISM.

The pragmatic principle is embodied, as we have said, in the statement that the truth of a theory depends upon the practical value of its consequences. Now, if the word " consequences " is emphasized in this statement, pragmatism becomes that general and widely diffused tendency or attitude which we have been discussing under the name of *futurism* ; but if the emphasis is on the word " practical," the pragmatic doctrine takes on a somewhat different colour and character and may be designated as *practicalism*. And in this form it applies more specifically to the problems of logical method. Although it is worth while in the interest of clearness to give separate consideration to these two phases of pragmatism, yet in distinguishing between them we must not lose sight of their close connection with one another. The future is the only part of time which we can influence by our action, and hence all practical interests imply the future-facing rather than the retrospective attitude.

The analysis of pragmatism as *practicalism* necessitates our taking account of three quite different meanings which are attached by pragmatism to the term practical. These three meanings are the following : 1. Practical in the sense of specific, concrete, particular, as opposed to universal and abstract. 2. Practical in the sense of what satisfies our personal needs and human aspirations as distinguished from what merely conforms to a supposed impersonal and purely intellectual ideal of truth. 3. Practical in the sense of biologically efficient mastery of environment and control over circumstances, as distinguished from what affords mere enlightenment or satisfies purely theoretical curiosity. The three doctrinal tendencies corresponding to these three senses of the term " practical " may be called " Empirical Practicalism," " Humanistic Practicalism," and " Biological Practicalism." Let us consider them successively.

1. *Empirical Practicalism.*—The primary importance to philosophy of the concrete, specific, and particular has been

emphasized by all the leaders of pragmatism, but more particularly by Professor James and Professor Dewey. In the work of Professor James it may be regarded as a sort of connecting link between the methodological doctrine of pragmatism and the ontological doctrine of phenomenalism which James formulated in the last years of his life and termed *Radical Empiricism*. Practicalism in this sense is indeed virtually identical with nominalistic empiricism, for it is an appeal to us to base truth upon specific and particular facts of perception rather than upon abstract and universal principles of reason. We have sufficiently examined the logic of empiricism and its great rival, rationalism, in the preceding chapters ; hence, with this mere mention of the sense in which pragmatism claims to include the older theory as one phase of its own method, we may pass to a consideration of the more novel and distinctive meanings of practicalism.

2. *Humanistic Practicalism.*—The second of the three meanings of the term practical is present to some extent in the many-sided pragmatism of Professor James ; it is, I believe, the dominant tendency in the pragmatism of Dr. Schiller ; while in the instrumentalistic pragmatism of Professor Dewey it is hardly to be found at all. One source of the doctrine is to be found in James's famous essay on *The Will to Believe*. In that essay the following theory is defended : When there are two incompatible propositions between which it is impossible to decide on grounds of ordinary evidence, it is right to believe in the truth of that one of them which would best harmonize with our wishes and our happiness. Now the pragmatic humanism of Dr. Schiller seems to me to be very largely an extension and generalization of this theory. The truth of a proposition is to depend on the practical value of its consequences, and " practical value " means that which satisfies our personal needs. There are, it seems to me, three principal arguments in support of this second or humanistic form of practicalism, and we must consider them in turn.

The first argument is based on the doctrine of " The Will to Believe," where it is maintained that in cases in which the ordinary evidence in favour of two incompatible propositions is just balanced, we are confronted with the dilemma of accepting one of the propositions as true or of remaining sceptically inactive. Inaction is very often worse than wrong action, therefore it will often be right to accept as certain a proposition which is uncertain. Now, as we had occasion to note above, Mr. Bertrand Russell has pointed out in his criticism of pragmatism that this dilemma is unreal. A scientific man can act upon a hypothesis to test its truth without making believe or making himself believe that the hypothesis has any greater probability than the data warrant. All of us have been in situations where we were obliged to take a long shot or a desperate chance, *i.e.* to act upon premises which we frankly recognized to have only a slender probability of truth. An honestly sceptical attitude does not by any means bring about a paralysis of action.

The second argument in support of humanistic practicalism is based upon our actual procedure in arriving at conclusions. All the pragmatists, and most emphatically Dr. Schiller, remind us of the extent to which our emotions and desires, our deeper interests and our inherited temperaments, operate to determine our beliefs. No conclusion is ever sought, and certainly it is never attained, without the aid of something beyond mere abstract and impersonal curiosity. Since it cannot be denied that bias or interest enters into and permeates the search for truth, why not recognize the fact frankly and without regret ? Make a virtue of necessity and admit that the older logicians in their quest for a logic independent of psychology, and for canons of proof that should be independent of individual preference, were pursuing an *ignis fatuus* ?

Now, it is interesting to compare this brand of pragmatic appeal with other noteworthy reminders of the extent to which reason is coloured by personal bias. The Greek philosopher Xenophanes declared that if dogs or oxen were capable of conceiving the gods they would assuredly depict them as glorified dogs or glorified oxen. He wished by this comparison both to recognize and to protest against the tendency of his contemporaries to make the gods in their own image and to ascribe to them the weaknesses and vices of human beings. About two thousand years after Xenophanes, Francis Bacon, actuated by the same motives, made his

famous classification of " idols " or types of bias which influence men in seeking truth. We are hampered, says Bacon,
not only by our tendency to view the world anthropomor-
phically (the idol of the tribe), but by the idiosyncracies of
our individual temperament (the idol of the cave), by the
tradition of the past (idol of the theatre), and finally by our
too great susceptibility to the opinions of the crowd and the
language in which those opinions are expressed (idol of the
market place). To these testimonies by philosophers as to
the extent to which reasoning is influenced by the personal
sympathies and antipathies of the reasoner, we may add the
acceptance by legal custom and by common sense of the principle that a judge is disqualified to decide a dispute in accord
with truth and justice if he has a personal interest in the
triumph of one of the litigants. It will be seen from these
illustrations that the novel feature of this second argument
for humanism is not its premise but its conclusion. Everybody admits that our beliefs are coloured by our interests,
but the humanist alone regards this condition as an aid rather
than a drawback to the attainment of truth. For him truth
is something human and personal, and he will recognize
neither the desirability nor the possibility of getting rid of
the anthropomorphic bias and eliminating the personal equation. That his position is false, and that freedom from bias
is generally desired, seems to me sufficiently proved by the
above-mentioned efforts which men make to secure freedom
from bias on the part of whoever is to pass judgment upon
evidence. That these efforts are in many cases successful,
and that freedom from emotional bias is possible as well as
desirable, is shown by the numerous cases in which men have
had the honesty to reach a decision that is actually opposed
to their interests and to their preconceptions. We are indeed
rarely able to rid ourselves of the impulse to believe that
which we desire ; but by recognizing our prejudices we can
make them innocuous. It is with prejudices as with illusions
of the senses—they may continue to exist after they are
understood, but they no longer have power to deceive. I
cannot prevent a stick partly immersed in water from appearing bent, but when once the nature of the illusion is understood I can allow for the false appearance. If I have a strong

prejudice in favour of a particular doctrine in religion or in politics, I can rob that prejudice of its power to mislead me by recognizing its existence and taking pains to give extra attention to evidence offered by my opponent. For any honourably minded person, the clear recognition of his own bias is all that is needed to make him scrupulously fair. It is only when unrecognized that our sympathies and antipathies can exercise a sinister control over our conclusions.

The third argument for humanistic pragmatism is based upon the fact that intellectual or cognitive processes are as truly active and purposive as the so-called volitional processes. And as the success of the latter is measured by the feelings of satisfaction which accompany the attainment of the desired end, it is claimed that the measure of truth is the extent to which the conclusion affords us satisfaction; and thus the distinction between the true and the good may be regarded as artificial. Here again we may accept the premises of the argument without accepting the conclusion. We may cheerfully grant that intelligence is dynamic, not static; that a large part of truth is not born with us, or thrust upon us, but achieved by us. We must fish for truth in the stream of consciousness and hunt it out from the jungle of sensory experience. The seeking and attaining of truth, like the seeking and attaining of what we desire, can be regarded as the passage from a state of instability to a state of equilibrium between the individual and his environment. But I contend that the equilibrium which we seek as the " true " is the opposite type to that which we seek as the " good."

These two opposed ways in which we can seek to attain an equilibrium with the environment are in fact analogous to the two ways in which a man can adjust a glove : he can strive to keep the glove unchanged, and if necessary cramp his hand until it fits into the glove (which is the analogue of the search for the truth) ; or without changing the shape of his hand he can stretch the glove until it fits (which is the analogue of the search for the good).

Good is the attribute which we ascribe to objects in so far as they satisfy our desires and needs. *Truth* is the attribute which we ascribe to our ideas and judgments in so far as they agree with reality, *i.e.* in so far as what they assert is a fact.

When we seek to realize the good we strive to change the real into the ideal and make the environment conform to our desires; but when we seek truth we have the contrary aim, that of making our ideas and judgments conform to the real. The truth-seeker strives to make of his mind a colourless mirror in which facts are seen exactly as they are, undistorted by hopes or fears. It is perfectly true that the search for knowledge may involve the most aggressive activity. The worker in experimental science will not be content passively to observe nature, he will alter and manipulate the environment in order to discover the truth that he seeks. But all such alteration is strictly subsidiary and instrumental to his primary undertaking. His practical activity is only a means to the better gratification of his intellectual curiosity. And irrespective of the activity which upon occasion is necessary to attain truth, or the passivity which upon occasion suffices for the attainment of the good, the kinds of adjustment or equilibrium between the individual and his environment are different and opposite in the two cases.

In short, the humanist is not justified in breaking down the distinction between the satisfaction of reason and curiosity (which is truth) and the satisfaction of sentiment and desire (which is goodness) by urging that they are both " satisfactions," that " intellect is as dynamic as will," and that the true (conceived as only " the good in the way of belief ") is a type of that equilibrium or harmony of the individual with his environment, the attainment of which in some form is the goal of all conscious activity.

We can, to some extent, determine reality by our desires and shape the course of nature to our needs. But the overwhelming majority of the things in the world are beyond our power to change, though not beyond our power to know. The things that we know to be true, but cannot and should not regard as good, are equalled in number only by the things which we can and should regard as good, but which we know are not true. To close our eyes to this tragic aspect of existence, and to insist with the humanistic pragmatists that there must be a correlation of the true and the desirable, is as vicious and futile as it is false. Our main hope of improving the human world lies in a clear, unflinching recognition of the difference between facts and ideals, between what we find to be true and what we wish to be true. No good can come of flattering ourselves into an anthropomorphic or humanistic optimism which would allow us to *make believe* or *will to believe* that a theory that satisfies the aspirations of our hearts is more likely to be true than one which does not.

Pragmatism as Practicalism, it will be remembered, was subdivided into three doctrines: Empirical Practicalism, Humanistic Practicalism, and Biological Practicalism. It remains for us now to consider the third of these doctrines.[1]

3. *Biological Practicalism.*—Biological practicalism is itself a two-fold doctrine. First, it maintains the purely psychological theory that thought, both phylogenetically or in the human species as a whole, and ontogenetically in each individual of the species, has evolved from the needs and exigencies of practical life. Secondly, it maintains the theory, partly logical and partly ethical, that the criterion and goal of thought consists in its utility for the preservation and extension of practical life. The second part of the doctrine which deals with the validity and value of thought is in large measure based upon the first part which deals with its genesis.

In Schopenhauer's *The World as Will and Idea* (Haldane and Kemp, Fourth Edition, p. 199) occurs the following passage: " Thus Knowledge generally, rational as well as merely sensuous, proceeds originally from the will itself, belongs to the inner being of the higher grades of its objectification as a mere μηχανή, a means of supporting the individual and the species, and just like any organ of the body, originally destined for the service of the will, for the accomplishment of its aims, it remains almost throughout entirely subject to its service ; it is so in all brutes and in almost all men." If we substitute for Schopenhauer's single cosmic Will with its tragically mistaken aim at self-realization, the concrete organisms in situations in which their needs and desires are

---

[1] Before proceeding to the following exposition and criticism of that phase of the pragmatist philosophy which I have called Biological Practicalism, I would request the reader to return to the footnote on page 134, containing Professor Dewey's explicit disclaimers of the positions which I discuss.

Biological Practicalism is not Instrumentalism, though I cannot help thinking that it could claim a natural if illegitimate descent from the teachings of Professor Dewey in somewhat the same way as Russian Bolshevism could claim descent from the teachings of the early socialists.

for the moment in conflict with one another and with their environment, we could take the above passage as a tolerable formulation of the theory of genetic psychology embodied in the third or biological form of practicalism. When desires, by reason of their complexity, are no longer able to secure immediate and automatic satisfaction, knowledge and thinking are evolved—and, by natural selection, preserved—as new and useful instruments of adaptation to environment.[1]

Does this theory of the origin and evolution of thought afford any new criterion for estimating the truth or falsity of thought ? I confess I am unable to see how the knowledge that an instrument is useful can in itself throw any light on the problem of how to use it. The way in which an axe should be used is determined not by the fact that the axe was made for use, but by the properties of the wood which we desire to chop. Again, the way in which an optical instrument should be used, whether it be the eye itself or a telescope, is determined entirely by the laws of light. Our needs and desires do indeed tell us *where* and *when* to use our instruments, but the *how* is always determined by the nature of the objects upon which the instrument is to be used. Admitting that thought originates as a means of removing the obstacles that balk our desires, the way in which thought does this is thought's own business. To say that the criterion of truth is the satisfaction of a cognitive need would be like saying that the most useful way to use an axe was to use it " axily." Thought is useful because we can adjust ourselves better to the present immediate situation if we know something about other situations. We can satisfy the needs of future situations more surely if we think out what those situations will be ; and we can do this only by recalling and analysing past situations. But the objective nature of what we desire to think about always has constituted and always will constitute the sole clue to determine how we should think about it. If

---

[1] This view of the origin of thought seems to me to have much truth, but it overlooks the part which the environment plays in forcing itself and its specific qualities upon our notice, oftentimes independently of or even in direct antagonism to our needs and desires. Truths are sometimes achieved by us, but at other times they are thrust upon us. The theory also overlooks the instinctive nature of curiosity as it exists in man and in some animals, and the possibility that even from the beginning it may have functioned independently, and not entirely as a servant of, practical needs.

the situation which I need to think out is a conflict of my own desires and hopes, why then the efficiency of my thinking is measured by the extent of my knowledge of the nature of those desires and hopes. If I am thinking about concrete situations, the truth of my judgments will be determined by the extent to which they conform to the nature ᴐf those concrete situations. If I wish to think about something abstract, such as the properties of space or number, the truth of my ideas will be entirely determined by the nature of space or number.

There has been much said in the name of pragmatism about the " abstractness " of intellectualistic logic, by which is meant, I suppose, the tendency to forget that any given thought activity is always directed to a given situation and controlled in its procedure by the nature of that situation ; and that, consequently, there is no such thing as thinking *überhaupt*. But the same sort of caution might be given, with at least equal justice, to anyone who, in the name of pragmatism, should treat desire or need or activity *überhaupt*. Our beliefs and judgments considered as instruments possess the peculiar kind of value called *truth*, not by satisfying " needs in general," but only by satisfying the peculiar kind of need called *cognitive*. And this latter need is, as we have seen, a need to get an unbiased adaptation of the relatively variant thought of the individual to the relatively invariant structure of his environment. That it is a very specific need or interest rather than needs in general that is relevant to the attainment of truth is recognized by the pragmatists themselves when they come to apply their practicalistic criterion of validity to concrete cases. This is shown both negatively and positively. It is shown negatively by the fact that they would refuse to measure the truth of a parent's belief in the nobility of his offspring by the degree of comfort which such a belief might bring. They would say that the kind of efficiency which ideas must have in order to be true must be an efficiency that is *relevant to their meaning* rather than one which merely results in happiness.

The same aspect of their theory is shown positively in such a book as *How We Think*. In that brief exposition of the methodology of instrumentalism, Professor Dewey sets forth the steps taken by the individual in solving a cognitive problem, or in reacting to a situation by using thought as an instrument. The process is "practical" only in the sense that it is tentative and experimental—an affair of trial and error. But the *end* to which the activity is directed is not practical, for what is sought is a clarified vision of objective facts. The thinker is not practical in the sense in which the moralist is practical. He aims to see things as they are, rather than to change them into what they are not but ought to be. But if I am right in ascribing to practicalists of the biological type the view that thought is practical only in the sense of ministering to specific cognitive needs, the theory cannot be credited with having furnished a new criterion for estimating truth. My criticisms can in short be summed up in the following dilemma: The claim that a new logical criterion results from interpreting truth as the satisfaction of needs is either an innocuous truism or a dangerous paradox. For the needs to be satisfied are either cognitive or non-cognitive; if the former, it is obvious but not enlightening to say that their satisfaction constitutes the attainment of truth; if on the other hand the satisfaction of non-cognitive needs is asserted to constitute the attainment of truth, the assertion is important but palpably false.

This failure of biological practicalism to contribute new criteria to logic does not mean that the theory lacks either value or originality. The emphasis which it has placed upon the experimental character of the thinking process and its warning against invoking high-sounding generalities as substitutes for the specific answers demanded by the specific situations which have called forth the cognitive reaction constitute a doctrine that is both new and true.

Let us turn now from the consideration of biological practicalism as a theory of the method of thought to a consideration of its claim to determine the field of thought's interest.

If thought has originated from practical needs, why should not practical needs select its subject matter and control its application?

Against this proposal to restrict the scope of the cognitive interest, we can argue that all evolution is rich in cases in which organs or instruments outgrow their original uses and functions. Almost every organ that satisfies a previously existing need calls into being new needs whose satisfaction is to be got by new uses of the organ. In social evolution the institutions which man has created end by, in large measure, creating him. If art and religion, for example, could be shown to have had a purely practical origin, it would be no indication that their later functions either are or should be primarily practical. The advent of the thinking habit makes of man a new being, a thinking being, and no longer merely a practical being. Theoretical curiosity as to the nature of the world becomes emancipated from the practical needs in which it was originally submerged. Human beings no longer have merely the need to live, they have also the need to know. Man began to think in order that he might eat ; he has evolved to ·the point where he eats in order that he may think. By which I mean that what is most distinctive of human life is the subordination of the physical needs of the animal organism to the fulfilment of the entire system of intellectual, æsthetic, and spiritual aspirations. To assume that the use and purpose of a function are limited by the motives which originally called it forth is opposed to the trend and meaning of evolution. To deny the legitimacy of abstract problems or problems about the nature of the universe on the ground that thought made its first appearance in racial and individual life as an instrument for solving very concrete and very practical problems of conduct, is like denying that' we should use our fingers to manage a pen or to play a musical instrument on the ground that fingers originated from the peculiarly arboreal needs of our animal ancestors. .

The practicalist theory on its psychological side is in large measure true ; it is, at any rate, interesting ; and it illuminates in a remarkable manner the historical development of our categories. It emphasizes the experimental character of the thought process ; and it has served as a much-needed corrective of the over-intellectualistic psychology which conceived all forms of human experience as confused or degenerate products of a primordial mind or transcendental ego capable of functioning *überhaupt.*

And not only as a theory of genetic psychology, but even

as a theory of logical procedure, the doctrine of biological practicalism is of value to the extent that it is used *positively* as a *supplement* to the interest in truth as such rather than *negatively* as a *substitute* for that interest. The Baconian exhortation to utilize knowledge should be obeyed, but not at the cost of forgetting to love and enjoy it for its own sake.

III

PRAGMATISM AS RELATIVISM.

The third of the major phases or tendencies of pragmatism I have called, for want of a better name, Relativism. Like Futurism and Practicalism, it is to be found in some form and to a greater or less extent in all who call themselves pragmatists. But while futurism is mainly significant for ethics, education, and social philosophy, and while practicalism in all of its three phases is mainly significant for genetic psychology and for the problem as to the proper criteria for attaining truth, relativism, in distinction from the other parts of the philosophy of pragmatism, is concerned primarily with epistemology, *i.e.* the branch of methodology that addresses itself to the problem, not of how knowledge is and should be attained, but of how the meaning of knowledge or truth when once attained should be interpreted. And as was pointed out in the Introduction, the question as to the meaning of truth turns upon the question as to the manner in which the objects of knowledge are related to the minds that know them. The systematic treatment of the problems of epistemology is reserved for Part II ; but because of the intimate manner in which the practicalist logic of pragmatism is bound up with its relativistic epistemology, it seems best to discuss them together. This somewhat irregular procedure is further justified by the arrogant claim of the epistemological relativist that his interpretation of the meaning of truth is so superior as to render meaningless and artificial all of the traditional answers to the epistemological problem. And this attitude of arrogance is carried so far by the relativist that he does not even like to call his particular species of epistemology by the generic name. He prefers to regard his doctrine as a substitute for epistemology rather than as a form of it, and as a means of escaping the whole set of puzzles involved in the relation of the knowing subject to the objects known.

This relativistic epistemology of pragmatism can be best understood if we treat it as an outgrowth of its practicalistic logic. Hence, before criticizing the relativistic conception of the meaning of truth, I should like to say something about the manner in which it has developed from the practicalist conception of the method of attaining and testing truth. At the outset, let us remember that at least one of the beginnings of pragmatism was the attempt to apply evolutionary biology to the domain of psychology.[1] This results in what James called a " teleological " interpretation of mental processes. And if every phase of mental life is interpreted teleologically, as a dynamic process aimed at the satisfaction of individual needs, it is natural to take the further step of subsuming the logical interest in attaining cognitive satisfaction under the ethical interest in attaining practical satisfaction.

Now, the empirically-minded founders of pragmatism were naturally in strong sympathy with the ethical Utilitarianism of Mill ; hence their affiliation of logic with ethics meant that logical value or truth was to be interpreted by the utilitarian principle of expediency. If the morally good is the expedient or satisfactory in the way of conduct, then also the logically true is the expedient or satisfactory in the way of belief. And as utilitarianism in ethics means a relativistic conception of the good, the pragmatic extension of Utilitarianism to logic will mean a relativistic conception of the true. William James's dedication of his *Pragmatism* to the memory of John Stuart Mill voiced with beautiful precision the mission of the new philosophy. The Utilitarians had abolished the notion of a Good that was absolute and independent of the changing desires of individuals. The pragmatists were to abolish the conception of a Truth that was absolute and independent of the changing beliefs of individuals. The utilitarians had substituted for the absolutistic conception of an independent good the relativistic theory that whatever satisfied desires was in so far forth good. The pragmatists

[1] *Cf.* the passage in James's *Psychology* quoted above, p. 134.

would substitute for the absolutistic conception of the true the relativistic theory that whatever satisfies individual beliefs is in so far forth true. And as the utilitarians had answered the charge that their theory meant mere anarchy in ethics, by declaring that the highest good was what was most satisfactory to the desires of the greatest number, so the pragmatists can answer the charge that their theory means mere anarchy in logic by declaring that the highest truth is what proves most satisfactory to the beliefs of the greatest number. *It is the essence of each theory to deny that the good and the true, respectively, possesses any absolute content apart from the interests of individuals.*

It has been customary in recent years for various groups of philosophers to criticize the utilitarians for their somewhat artificial hedonistic psychology ; but at least among the empirically-minded of such critics there can be found few if any who will deny the tremendous service which utilitarianism rendered to the whole vast domain of the moral sciences. So much of the spiritual energies of men had been spent in devotion to abstract rules and principles of conduct which had lost their relevance to actual human wants, that there was need for a new ethical gospel which should sweep away antiquated taboos and fine-sounding slogans and call on all lovers of the good for a single-hearted devotion to such measures and only such measures as would increase human well-being. These advocates of the new dispensation appraised any and all codes of morality by the sole criterion of their efficacy to satisfy human needs ; and to the service of that supreme ideal they unhesitatingly conscripted the resources of organized knowledge, physical and psychological. Their aim in brief was to make ethics a science, and to substitute the co-operative and experimental methods of intelligence for the sterile competitions of sentiment and dialectic.

Now, the inheritors of this great and clarifying movement of utilitarianism are the pragmatists of to-day. And we cannot properly estimate the strength and weakness of their doctrine of epistemological relativism unless we keep in mind their inheritance of ethical relativism from Bentham and Mill. All pragmatists are in a broad sense utilitarians, and because their relativism in the theory of values is useful

and valid they and their friends have assumed that their relativism in the theory of knowledge must be equally useful and
valid. I feel sure that it is this extension of relativity from
the field of the good to the field of the true that constitutes
the principal cause for the success of pragmatism to-day.
And I feel equally sure that this contention of pragmatism,
that relativity of value implies relativity of truth, is as false
in reality as it is plausible in appearance. It is plausible in
appearance because the methods applicable to the moral and
social sciences seem to be and in many cases actually are the
same as those applicable to the other branches of science.
The leaders of pragmatism deserve much credit in the fields
of law, education, and political and economic reform, for
making the methods of procedure more flexible and efficient
and more relevant to the concrete questions at issue. Hence
it is natural enough to suppose that their principles. will be
equally sound in other fields. If it has proved beneficial to
conceive the ethically desirable or good as relative to individuals, why should it not prove equally beneficial to conceive the cognitively desirable or true as equally relative to
individuals ? But this identification, though plausible in
appearance, is false in reality because of that profound contrast between the good and the true which we have noted
above. We can only express once more our conviction that
the adjustment between the individual and his environment,
which is the goal of the cognitive interest in truth, is an
adjustment in which the environment is the primary and
independent variable, the individual's ideas and judgments
being secondary and dependent for their validity upon their
agreement with objective facts. On the other hand, the goal
of the conative interest in the good is an adjustment between
the individual and the environment in which individual
desires and sentiments constitute the primary and independent
variables, the environment being secondary and dependent
for its goodness on its agreement with individual needs. The
cognitive equilibrium of truth is cosmocentric and absolute,
while the conative equilibrium of goodness is anthropocentric
and relative. Because of this contrast, to recognize that what
is really and not merely apparently good for one may be
really and not merely apparently bad for another is very

sound ethics ; while for the same reason, to claim that what is really and not merely apparently true for one may be really and not merely apparently false for another is very unsound logic. Ideas are *true* only when they conform to objective facts ; but facts are *good* only when they conform to subjective needs.

In explaining the manner in which the relativism of the pragmatists has developed from their practicalism we were led to a statement and criticism of the first and principal argument in support of that relativism, *viz.* the apparent similarity between the cognitive satisfaction of human beliefs and the conative satisfaction of human needs. The latter being relative to individuals, it was falsely argued that the former was equally relative ; and that consequently pragmatism could clarify the concept of *truth* in the same fashion that utilitarianism had clarified the concept of *good*.

In addition to its supposed agreement with utilitarianism, there are, I believe, three further reasons for the growth of pragmatic relativism : (1) its apparent connection with the doctrine of evolution ; (2) its apparent connection with the attitude of scepticism ; (3) an ambiguity of the term " truth." Let us consider these reasons in turn.

The theory of evolution has made us familiar with the extent to which the universe is pervaded by change ; even the things that appear to be most permanent, such as the heavenly bodies, the seas and mountains, and the species of plants and animals, are in a process of change. Human institutions and human beliefs that at one time seemed eternal are now being revised. It is natural for us to suppose that this evolutionary process to which all existing things are subject should extend to the realm of logical meaning ; and consequently we tend to regard the notion of an unchangeable system of truth as a relic of the pre-Darwinian age. Yet while the extension of the notion of change from the things of physics to the things of logic may be natural, it is absolutely unjustifiable and leads only to confusion. In the first place, change itself has no meaning unless the terms of the process remain fixed. I cannot speak of a man changing from youth to age, or of a species changing from simian to human, unless the terms " youth," " age," " simian,"

" human," are supposed to preserve their meanings un-changed. What holds true of logical terms holds true equally of propositions which are relations between terms. If the proposition that the earth has been spherical for the ten billion years prior to the year 1900 is true at this moment, then that proposition will always be true on pain of losing its meaning as a proposition. The earth might change to-morrow from a globe to a disc without changing the truth of the above proposition. In short, the maxims : *True for one, true for all*, and *once true, always true*, apply not only to all abstract or non-existential propositions, but to all other propositions in so far as they are made thoroughly unambiguous with respect to the time and space of the facts asserted. Change resides only in physical processes and in the psychological processes by which we become aware of physical processes. But between those processes and the logical relations which they reveal there is fixed a gulf which no change can cross.

Let us turn now to the second of the three causes for the spread of the doctrine of relativism, *viz.* its connection with scepticism. And here the relativistic pragmatist can make out a somewhat better case. We may imagine him to speak to us as follows : " You talk about an absolute truth, independent of anyone's belief in it or knowledge of it. Well, supposing that there were such a thing, we could never attain it ; or at least if we did attain it, we could never recognize it for what it was. All that we can know in the way of truth is something that is believed. Each man calls his own belief by the eulogistic name of *truth*, and with respect to this as an absolute standard, he describes his neighbour's opinions by such uncomplimentary names as ' apparent truths ' or ' subjective beliefs.' Consequently, we pragmatists, recognizing this universal shortcoming of human nature, are frank enough to say that there is no truth with a capital T ; no absolute impersonal objective reality, not even our own, and that whether we like it or not we have to put up with *the best in the way of belief.* We may still use the word truth in this semi-subjective sense, and it is in this sense that truth is relative to different persons and subject to change."

Now, the only trouble with this reply of the pragmatist is that it is a virtual confession that the relativistic feature of his doctrine, when freed from ambiguities, reduces to pure scepticism. For scepticism is the theory that truth in its objective sense is unattainable by any means within our power. The only difference between pragmatic relativism and scepticism is that the former doctrine uses the word " truth " in a purely subjective sense that is different from the sense in which it is used by the other methodological theories. The thoroughgoing sceptic believes with the relativist that we possess beliefs which we prefer to those of our neighbours, but he gives himself no false verbal comfort by calling these preferred beliefs " truth." He reserves that word for the objective reality which he thinks lies beyond the reach of our knowledge. But whether he is right or wrong in holding to his pessimistic and negative attitude towards the methodological problem, we cannot discuss until the next chapter.

The third of the reasons for the popularity of Epistemological relativism may be stated as follows : *All truth depends upon or is in part created by individuals. It is, therefore, inseparable from them and relative to them ; and as such, it changes as they change.* Now there are two meanings involved in this statement of relativism which depend upon the two meanings that can be given to the word truth. By " truth " may be meant (1) whatever is believed, or (2) whatever is real or is a fact. If the word is taken in the first or subjective sense, then the relativistic principle that truth changes becomes a truism, for it means only that *people's beliefs change as people's minds change.* If truth is taken in the second or objective sense, the relativistic principle ceases to be a truism and becomes a paradox, for it then means that *the facts or realities of the world change as people's minds change.* We may illustrate the difference by the following example : " ' That the earth is flat ' was for the ancients an obvious truth ; ' that the earth is round ' is for us an established truth. Their truth was not our truth. Truth, therefore, is relative and changing, and what is true for one may be false for another." These statements sound pretty well, and we should probably pass them over unchallenged, because we should take for granted that the word " truth " was being used in its subjective sense as a synonym of belief. It is a truism that people's beliefs can differ, that one can believe what another disbelieves; and it is a commonplace that a change in beliefs took place with regard to the shape of the earth. The ancients believed it to be flat, and we believe it to be round. But if we were told that the author of the statements cited meant " truth " to be taken in the objective sense, we should suppose that he had been indulging in either a geological or a logical paradox. If he meant that the flatness of the earth was a truth (fact) in ancient times and also that its roundness was a truth (fact) in modern times, we should assume that he believed that the earth's shape had undergone a marvellous geological change from a disc to a globe. If in still adhering to the objective meaning of the term " truth " he denied that he intended any such geological absurdity as the above, we should have to assume that he was committing the still greater logical absurdity of supposing that the shape of the earth could be both flat and spherical at once.

The pragmatic doctrine of the relativity of truth is thus seen to owe some of its plausibility to an ambiguity. Before the ambiguity is revealed, the truism and the paradox conceal one another and unite to produce the appearance of a novel and important discovery. In exactly the same way a black cardboard seen through white tissue paper appears to be a single surface of grey. When we look at the thing edgewise, however, the effect of grey disappears and we see only the black and the white. So, when once we recognize the ambiguity of the term " truth," and insist upon the relativistic pragmatist using the word in one sense or the other, we find only an ill-looking juxtaposition of the paradox that facts depend upon people believing them, and the truism that our beliefs about facts change and vary. In case the illustration chosen fails to satisfy the reader, I would suggest that he make up for himself examples of statements which can loosely be regarded as cases of " truth changing " or of " true for one but false for another," and see for himself whether a little analysis of the meanings involved in all such statements will not disclose the above-mentioned ambiguity or duplicity of the " truth " in question.

In concluding this analysis of the relativistic epistemology of pragmatism I should like to call attention to a very real disaster which threatens the study and teaching of philosophy, and which is likely to be brought nearer by the spread of the doctrine we have been considering.

There is a certain type of "up-to-date" student to whom the humility involved in honourable scepticism is intolerable. These students, eager, earnest, and not consciously insincere, will study for a time the problems of Being and Knowing which have been raised by the great philosophers. They do their best, but they become confused. They disagree with the idealistic conclusions of Berkeley and Kant, but cannot refute the reasoning on which those conclusions are based. They are piqued and stirred by such vitalistic criticisms of the current scientific naturalism as are made by Driesch and Bergson, but they lack the knowledge of the elements of natural science that would make possible even a tentative appraisal of those criticisms. It is inevitable that the less scrupulous and more confused of these students, when placed in such a situation, will seize with avidity upon any device, no matter how hollow, which will serve to conceal their failure even from themselves, and enable them to gain a sense of superiority over the great philosophers of the past. There is grave danger that the relativistic form of pragmatism will be adopted to meet such needs. For to the relativist with his covert suggestion that "truth" is only the best that we attain in the way of belief, all questions about the nature of objective reality will appear as "artificial." And if there is no objective reality apart from human interests and beliefs, it may seem unnecessary to bother oneself about the problems of traditional philosophy. Philistine minds will be tempted to mask their incompetency with the boast that the puzzles that they have failed to solve were "unreal," "old-fashioned," "dialectical" subtleties with which a practical man in a practical age need not concern himself. Like the fox in the fable, if we fail to get the grapes we can save our face by calling them sour.

We have now completed our survey of Pragmatism as a methodological theory. We have sketched briefly its origin in the Principle of Peirce, and its development at the hands of James, Dewey, and Schiller, and we have discussed

separately its three principal aspects : I. Futurism ; II. Practicalism in its three senses : (1) empirical, (2) humanistic,
(3) biological ; and III. Relativism. Of these three aspects
of Pragmatism, Futurism seems by far the most valuable.
Indeed, it is difficult to estimate the revolutionary changes in
human society which may result from a substitution of a
prospective for a retrospective attitude in science and culture.
We cannot, of course, give exclusive credit to pragmatism
for this interest in the future. Futurism existed before
pragmatism in the philosophy of Nietzsche, and, independently of pragmatism, in the philosophy of Bergson.
Moreover, it has touched with its influence fields of activity
which are indifferent to the utterances of official philosophers.
As has been said, the broader spirit of futurism is, like pragmatism itself, the outcome of the doctrine of evolution.
Evolution taught us to think of all things as in process of
change and growth. The first realization of this view was
touched with sadness. We could see in evolution only its
negative side. It robbed us of our golden age, of our god-like
ancestors, and of the various mythical glories which in one
form or another have been attributed by all races and nations
to their own past. The primordial aristocrat in each of us
grieved at the evolutionist's debasement of human origins.
It is only lately that this aristocrat's shame in the fact of
having sub-men for ancestors has given way to a democrat's
pride in the possibility of having supermen for descendants.
Moreover, this modern effort to attain emancipation from the
past differs in its spirit from the spirit of previous revolutionary movements, and especially from that of the great
revolution in France, in that it is permeated with a biological
and historical spirit. It is voluntaristic rather than rationalistic, and is constructive as well as destructive. Futurism
is not mere opposition to the past. It is not even an
eighteenth-century attempt to put the Goddess of Reason in
the place of all lesser idols and to impose upon future generations a Utopia of our own. It is a more positive but less
dogmatic, a more experimental and less metaphysical attempt
to prepare the world for whatever may turn up. And while
pragmatism has not created this movement, it has expressed in
technical philosophical form the character and the essence of it

As for pragmatism as practicalism, here too we find in all three of its phases an expression of modern tendencies, especially as they are at work in America. Practicalism as empiricism is voiced in the popular demand for concrete facts rather than for abstract laws, for the expert knowledge of the specialist rather than for the old-fashioned general culture. Practicalistic humanism, too (though often in partial conflict with practicalistic empiricism), is expressed in the familiar demands for a more ample recognition of personal needs and human sentiment in such subjects as economics, and for a view of physical nature more intuitive and impassioned than that which the cold-blooded pronouncements of natural science would seem to warrant. As for pragmatic practicalism in its third or biological sense, the best examples of it are to be found in the movement for functional rather than formal education, and in the growing feeling that for the old contemplative ideal of truth for truth's sake should be substituted the Baconian ideal of knowledge as a means to the practical control of material conditions.

In addition to these manifestations of futurism and practicalism, the pragmatic doctrine of relativism is also embodied in current movements. The notion that truth is changeable and relative to individuals is, as we have already seen, congenial to a society that is imbued with the spirit of utilitarianism and that feels itself to be in a stage of transition. Moreover, the practicalist's relegation of theoretical learning to the status of an instrument for obtaining practical results fits in well with the view that the essence of all truth is relative.

In conclusion we may note a certain congruity of pragmatism, particularly of pragmatic relativism, with the general attitude of anti-intellectualism which is so prevalent in social philosophy to-day. It was a long time ago that Thrasymachus proclaimed that justice was only the interest of the stronger. But from Thrasymachus down to the latest disciples of Nietzsche, Marx, or Freud, there has existed a sort of Macchiavellian tradition of political "realism" and anti-liberalism. The upholders of this tradition are characterized by two attitudes: (1) a negative attitude of disillusionment as to the capacity of the human mind for a disinterested pursuit of ethical ideals ; (2) a positive attitude of a somewhat cynical but wholesome curiosity as to the concrete and interested motives which are the real causes of man's actions. That the practice of hypocrisy is an acknowledgment of the efficacy of virtue is not admitted by these political realists. Nor do they perceive that unless there were a genuine and effective sensitiveness to ideals on the part of the herd, it would be impossible for the herd's leaders to mask their selfish interests by proclaiming high ideals. How could the profession of justice be to the interest of the stronger unless real justice were actually operative as an ideal in the minds of men generally ?

Having discarded the validity of the professed ideals for social action on the ground that they are abused, our political " realist " feels that he has reached a standpoint that is " beyond good and evil "—terms which to him as to Nietzsche are merely names, complimentary or the reverse, for selfish interests. And since there are no logical or ethical *reasons* for human actions, but only physical and psychological *causes,* he sets to work to discover just what these causes are. The cynically motivated search for the non-rational factors in social evolution has proved painfully rich. Hobbes, Buckle, Marx, Nietzsche, and Freud, with the aid of troops of investigators in the field of natural science, have unearthed case after case in which man figures not as a rational animal ordering his life according to principles, but only as a complicated animal driven this way and that by the reflexes which constitute what he eulogistically calls his " will." As for his " reason," it fills the otiose and epi-phenomenal rôle of apologist and ratifier of action after the fact.

Knowledge of the psychological mechanisms of logical and ethical processes is bitter and hard to digest. To keep one's faith in the reasons for an action when one understands its causes is difficult at best. And in the face of the present-day onset of the anti-intellectualists it is helpful to recall two earlier and classic protests against misinterpreting man's discovery of his own mechanism.

The first of these protests was the clarion call of Huxley in his *Evolution and Ethics,* warning us not to enthrone nature in place of the old supernature as a source of moral authority.

The meaning of ideal right is unaffected by existential might, and we are to hold fast our faith in the values of the human spirit even in the very teeth of nature. For no matter how blind or cruel we may discover nature to be, she and her laws are morally irrelevant except as instruments to be used by us in pursuit of our own ends. This proclamation that moral values do not depend for their sanctions upon physical existence, though it came from a mechanist, was thoroughly Platonic in its wisdom and beauty.

A second warning of similar significance is to be found in the essay by William James entitled *Reflex Action and Theism*. James protested against the then current tendency to belittle intense spiritual experiences merely because they were found to possess certain regular physiological correlates. That a derangement of the digestive or reproductive system occurs in connection with an experience of religious emotion must not be interpreted as a reduction of the religious to the digestive or reproductive. In other words, the value of an experience is to be judged on its intrinsic merits regardless of its bodily correlates. The anti-intellectualism of the present day is not, as in the time of Huxley's essay, based on the discovery of the physical origin of man ; nor, as in the time of James's essay, on a realization of the physiological correlates of human emotion. It derives its new strength from the advance in history, anthropology, and social science generally. The discovery of the humble origins of many of the most cherished elements in our culture, such as art, religion, etc., engenders in the mind of the anti-intellectualist the modern fallacy of *geneticism* which consists in evaluating ethical ideals in terms of their historical origins, or even in depriving them of value altogether merely because they have origins. It is the same naturalistic and pragmatistic irrelevance, though in a new form, as that which called forth the protest of Huxley the naturalist and James the pragmatist. That nature shows no preferences for courage or love is no reason for us to lessen our regard for these virtues. That our highest emotions are conditioned by changes in our blood and sweat in no-wise diminishes their value. And no more should the deluge of new historical discoveries concerning the practical and interested origins of our theoretical and disinterested attitudes cause distrust of *their* value. Our values are what they are irrespective of their physical environment, physiological conditions, or historic origins.

Now, pragmatic relativism in its repudiation of logical validity and in its substitution of the new interest in psychological genesis for the old interest in objective truth and falsity voices accurately and in the language of technical philosophy the anti-intellectualism that dominates the new school of political and social science. This confusion of the genesis of a belief with its truth and of the genesis of a virtue with its value is as morally dangerous as it is intellectually fallacious. In theory it means the deliberate and systematic repudiation of that disinterested faith in ideals which, however imperfectly practised in the past, has been the inspiration of human greatness. In its political program it means the interest of the stronger, the repudiation of democracy, and the adoption of class-dictatorship, whether " red " or " white," as the goal to be sought. In its tactic it means the substitution of bullets for ballots ; " direct action," and the unashamed use of force replacing the painfully acquired devices of parliamentary procedure. If the new knowledge of the origins of man's culture is to be purchased at the price of abandoning that for which his culture is most significant, it will turn out to be the worst bargain in history.

The need to-day is for a return to the revolutionary idealism of the eighteenth century. But in returning to the Age of Reason, we need not abandon what the age of intelligence has taught us.

Now, it is the self-appointed task of Pragmatism to make articulate in philosophy these world-wide modern interests in cultural origins and human mechanisms. If it uses them as a substitute for the old devotion to objective truth, it will prove a curse and a blight ; but if, on the other hand, it makes of them a new instrument for the realization of human ideals, it will rank among the greatest of philosophies.

CHAPTER VI

THE METHOD OF SCEPTICISM

SCEPTICISM is the negative member of the group of logical theories. It is itself a method of logic only in the sense that anarchism is a theory of government, or atheism a kind of theology. The sceptic, in short, denies that any or all of the five methods of deriving ideas and justifying beliefs can give genuine knowledge.

The four principal arguments which have been urged in support of scepticism may be called (after Weber) : I. The Historical Argument; II. The Dialectical Argument; III. The Physiological Argument; and IV. The Psychological Argument. Let us consider them in order.

I

THE HISTORICAL ARGUMENT.

The *historical argument* for scepticism rests on the fact that there are few opinions that have been advanced on any subject that have not been doubted or rejected by someone at sometime, and that in all questions of philosophical or fundamental importance history shows a hopeless diversity of beliefs among those who are regarded as experts no less than among men in general. It is indeed true that there is a fundamental opposition in philosophy between the materialistic or naturalistic, and the idealistic or spiritualistic world views ; and this primary opposition of philosophical attitudes includes most of the lesser divergencies, and applies in some degree to each of the principal types of philosophical inquiry which were enumerated in our introductory chapter. It is likewise true that these opposite tendencies, together with the various types of compromise doctrines, have persisted throughout the history of philosophy.   Materialism and idealism were exemplified in the beginnings of speculative thought by the theories of Democritus and Plato ; they are exemplified to-day by the theories respectively of Haeckel and of Royce.   The sceptics, then, point to this interminable warfare among philosophers as a historical justification of their claim that the world riddle is insoluble.   Whether matter and its mechanistic laws are to be regarded as primary ; or whether, on the other hand, the primacy in all fields is to be accorded to the group of teleological experiences which we call spiritual ; or whether both or neither should be taken as metaphysically ultimate, remains, they say, and will ever remain an insoluble problem.

There are two replies which may be made to this first or historical argument for scepticism.

1. Although the opposition between the materialistic and the idealistic attitudes persists through the generations, yet with the passing of time the opposing theories gain on the whole both in intrinsic force and in appreciation of one another. There is, too, a great deal in each theory that is positive and not incompatible with the other.   The modern materialist (or " naturalist," as he prefers to be called) knows more about the material aspects of reality and can do justice to them better than ever before ; and though the final issue remains in doubt, a large part of his doctrine is established as true.   He is also better qualified to do justice to his opponents.   And the same may be said of the modern idealist and of the various compromise schools.   The history of philosophy could be symbolized by a spiral, broad at the base and converging towards a point as it ascends, the various types of world view being represented around the circumference of each coil and the historical sequence being indicated by the upward direction of the spiral as a whole.[1]

2. The historical argument for scepticism may be answered not only by referring to the lessening of hostility that results

[1] There are, indeed, in addition to the antithetic attitudes of materialism and idealism, two principal types of intermediate theories : (1) Dualism, according to which matter and spirit are both real ; and (2) Phenomenalism, according to which only the stream of given experience exists, matter and spirit as entities being regarded as merely useless and invalid constructs of the imagination.

from the increasingly synthetic character of the opposing types
of theory, but also by pointing to the number of once hopeless
problems that have actually been solved.   This progress gives
us the right to hope that the problems which are still unsolved
may yield to the investigations of a later time.   Indeed, the
plight of philosophy is really not nearly so bad as it seems,
because, as William James has remarked, when a philosophic
problem gets solved, it ceases to be called philosophic and
passes over into the realm of science.   In short, the course of
history would seem to justify the sceptic in saying only
ignoramus, not *ignorabimus*.

II

THE DIALECTICAL ARGUMENT.

The *dialectical argument* in favour of scepticism is based on
the alleged fact that although it is logically necessary that
one member of a pair of contradictory propositions must be
true, yet, in many, if not all of the problems as to the ultimate
nature of reality, we seem restricted to a choice between two
theories which, though they contradict one another, must
both be called false.   In these cases, which are called " antinomies," the mind, after a survey of the entire situation, seems
forced to admit that a solution of the problem is logically
impossible.   From the many puzzles or antinomies that have
been formulated, I select for detailed examination that one
which is perhaps best known and which can fairly serve as
representing the entire class.

Nothing seems more real than *motion*, yet it is claimed
that the movement of a body can be shown to be impossible,
because the path of the motion consists of an endless number
of intervals, and we cannot conceive of an infinite series of steps
being completed in a finite time.   Therefore, while Sense tells
us that motion is real, Reason tells us that it is unreal :   to
reject sense is nonsensical, while to reject reason is unreasonable,
yet no third possibility suggests itself.

This puzzle was presented by the ancient Greek philosopher
Zeno.   Although Zeno did not use his puzzles to prove scep-

ticism, yet they could be, and as a matter of fact actually have been, so used by other philosophers. The sophist Gorgias based his scepticism on the puzzles of Zeno, and the British philosopher, Sir William Hamilton, based his agnosticism on what were essentially the antinomies of Kant. By both Gorgias and Hamilton, the absolute or unconditioned nature of the reality which expresses itself in our experience was believed to be essentially and demonstrably unknowable.

There are, in fact, four points of view which logically may be and which actually have been taken towards such an antinomic situation as is involved in the Zenonian puzzles about motion. There is first of all the Sceptic's view that the conflict between reason and sense is irreconcilable, and consequently the nature of reality is proved to be unknowable. This negative attitude is merely a counsel of despair, and is only justifiable if the positive solutions of the problem have all been discredited. These positive solutions are : (1) the Mystic's solution, adopted by Zeno himself, according to which reason is defended at the expense of sense; (2) the pragmatist's solution, adopted by Bergson, according to which sense is defended at the expense of reason ; (3) the common-sense solution, one variety of which we shall defend, and according to which the seeming conflict between logic and experience is shown to be removable by a new analysis of the situation in which the conflict arises. It is only after considering each of these positive solutions in turn that we shall be able to appraise properly the Sceptic's negation of all of them.

1. *The Mystic's Solution.*—Zeno feels that the phenomenon of motion affords a clean-cut conflict between logical reason and sensory experience. Now, to the ordinary man, reason and experience are two equally reliable and mutually harmonious sources of knowledge. For Zeno, however, they are neither harmonious with one another nor of equal reliability. They are not harmonious, because experience reveals motion as a fact while reason reveals it as an impossibility. And they are not of equal reliability because, according to Zeno, the authority of reason is self-evident, while sensory experience merits nothing but contempt. It follows that whenever sense-experience is so unfortunate as to conflict with reason, it must give way at once. In Zeno's opinion this happens not only

in the case of motion, but in the case of variety or plurality ; hence, plurality as well as motion must be regarded as illusory or unreal. And as all that we call nature is permeated with movement and variety, it follows that all of it is unreal or " non-being." True reality is for Zeno a Being one and eternal, without change or variety of any kind, and therefore ineffable or transcendent of all experience. Thus Zeno's solution of the contradictions which he believes he has found in the fact of motion is the simple one of dismissing motion and with it the whole world of sense as an unreality.

2. *The Pragmatist's Solution.*—The opposite horn of the apparent dilemma is taken by the French philosopher Henri Bergson. When sense and reason clash, it is reason that must go to the wall. Instead of rejecting motion as unreal, Bergson rejects logic as invalid. Reason, according to this philosopher, is an instrument evolved by the life-force for the purpose of controlling the relatively inanimate and static aspect of nature. In so far as it is used for this purpose it is admirable, but when we attempt to express by its means the nature of life itself, or even of the dynamic aspect of matter, it proves inadequate. Motion can be experienced, but it defies and transcends logical analysis, and the fact that it does so is proof of its ultimate and irreducible reality.

Now, to the ordinary mind there is little to choose between the opposing solutions of Zeno and Bergson. To deny with Zeno the reality of sense, or to deny with Bergson the validity of reason, is almost equally distressing. As said above, the one is nonsensical, the other unreasonable. At first sight the Bergsonian horn of the dilemma might appear preferable, for logic is less familiar than sense, and could be abandoned with less of a shock. Yet the popular preference of irrationality to nonsense, is, I think, only apparent. If the " plain man " were beset with this puzzle about motion, and compelled to choose between Bergson and Zeno, he might say that he would admit the invalidity of logic, but he would probably mean that there was a fault which he could not discover in this particular application of logic, rather than that logic itself was faulty. And if you were to put the dilemma in a more obvious form by asking him whether, if he had to choose between denying the reality of sensible squares and circles, and admitting the reality of irrational square-circles and round-squares, I think the latter alternative would be fully as repugnant to him as the former.   It is small wonder that the sceptic should exclaim in cases like this that the only sound attitude is the attitude of doubt, and the only certainty the certainty of the unknowable nature of reality.

3. *The Common-sense Solution.*—It is undeniable that any space through which a body moves is divisible into an endless number of parts ; and that consequently the motion itself involves the completion of an infinite series of steps.   Nor can we, as is sometimes suggested, regard the perfect continuity of the motion as any mitigation of the infinity of intervals that must be traversed.   A mile is a linear space made up of the sum of a half-mile, a quarter-mile, an eighth-mile, a sixteenth-mile, etc., without end.   And an inch is as bad as a mile.   In fact any distance, however small, teems with this infinity of parts, every one of which must be passed over by whoever or whatever would move through it.   Now, if a body were to move uniformly at the rate, say, of a foot a second, then at the end of any finite number of seconds it would have moved over an equal number of feet.   And in order to move through an infinite number of feet it would require an infinite number of seconds.   There must be, in short, as many intervals of time as there are intervals of space, in order to have motion accomplished.   In other words, motion seems to consist of a one-to-one correspondence or numerical equality of spatial distances and temporal durations.   From this it follows that to answer Zeno's question as to how the fleet-footed Achilles can traverse in a finite period of time the infinite series of distances that intervene between him and the slow-moving tortoise that he pursues, it would be only necessary to show that the finite time at Achilles' disposal contains an infinity of durational parts equal in number to the spatial intervals that he must traverse.   When the puzzle is stated in this way, a moment's inspection yields us the answer.   For, as Aristotle pointed out in his *Physics*, the so-called finite period of time which elapses during the pursuit is in reality quite as infinitely divisible as is the space through which the motion extends.   A century, an hour, or a second is divisible into, and therefore composed of, a half, a quarter, an eighth,

a sixteenth part, and so on without end, of whatever period of time, no matter how small, we may choose to consider. If the senses reveal a body moving a distance of one mile in a time of one minute, we shall be able to submit the minute of duration to precisely the same infinite series of divisions as that to which we submit the mile of extension. And for any of the troublous infinities of finite space, we can find adequate antidotes in the equally potent infinities of finite time. The situation derives its poignancy from our remembering the infinity of infinitesimal distances to be traversed, and our forgetting the equal infinity of infinitesimal durations which by their *elapse* are placed at the disposal of all that moves.

To this simple solution of the puzzle, however, it may be objected that the question has merely been shifted from the possibility of a movement *in* time to the possibility of a movement *of* time. Such phrases as " an infinity of durations *at the disposal of* the moving body," and " the *lapse* of time," beg the whole point, because, it will be claimed, it is as difficult to conceive how an infinite number of moments can elapse as it is to understand how the infinity of distances can be traversed.

To this objection I should answer that there is no more difficulty in conceiving of the infinite divisibility of a temporal period than of a spatial distance , while as to the alleged difficulty of understanding how or why time can elapse, it is no more significant than the question as to how or why space can extend. It is the self-evident nature of space to be infinitely divisible into parts that *extend*. It is the equally self-evident nature of time to be infinitely divisible into parts that *elapse*. The former is admitted as obvious, so why should the latter be objected to ? When the objector speaks of time itself as *moving*, and thus involving a recurrence of the puzzle about motion, he speaks improperly. The lapse of time is not a motion, but rather the condition of motion. To conceive of time as moving, it would be necessary to conceive of another more basic time in which or through which it moved ; and that would be as nonsensical and futile as to demand another and more basic space to provide a place in which space might extend.

In short, we must repeat that the motion of bodies revealed to the senses owes its apparent irrationality to the careless claim that you cannot traverse an infinite number of distances in a finite time. The Zenonian antinomy ceases to be formidable, and rational analysis is restored to its normal harmony with sensory experience as soon as we realize that finite time is as infinitely divisible as finite space ; and that consequently the one-to-one correspondence between a spatial and a temporal series of intervals which all motion demands is adequately provided for by the very nature of time itself.

In the analysis here given no mention has been made of the *points* and *instants* in terms of whose correlation it is now customary to define motion. The infinity of points which are present in every space do not constitute extension. It is not the infinity of points or instants, but rather the infinity of side-by-side relations or extension-intervals between the points, and the infinity of lapses or succession-intervals between the instants, which are the really significant and adequate constituents of distance and of duration. And motion consists in the one-to-one correlation of those *intervals* rather than, as is usually alleged, of the points and instants by which the intervals are bounded.

The advantage of taking intervals rather than their punctiform boundaries as elements of the continua of space and time lies in the fact that while they are equal in their infinite number to the points and instants (between each respective pair of which they obtain), they also possess what the latter lack, viz. *proportionality to the whole of which they are the parts.* A gamma infinity of points is no nearer to constituting an inch than a mile, but the gamma infinity of " infinitieths " of a mile is as adequate to make up a mile as is a gamma infinity of " infinitieths " of an inch to make up an inch. *The limit approached by a process of infinite division of a mile or an hour is not a point or an instant but the " infinitieth " of a mile or the " infinitieth " of an hour.* The limiting elements of a mile or an hour are as wholesomely different from the limiting elements of an inch or a second as are the concrete wholes which they respectively compose. Points and instants are on the other hand not only hopelessly inadequate to make up any extension or duration, but they are still more inadequate to differentiate one concrete magnitude from another. The points in a mile, for example, are the same in kind and the same in number as the points in an inch. If, *per impossibile*, the punctiform elements were the only elements, there would be no difference between one concrete space or time and another.[1]

The hypothesis here set forth as to the relational character of the elements of space and time has the advantage, so to speak, of killing three birds with one stone. In the first place, it provides elements which, unlike points and instants, are really adequate to constitute our concretely perceivable magnitudes of distance and duration. In the second place, the theory provides elements which are adequate (as points and instants are *not*) to differentiate larger and smaller magnitudes from one another. In the third place, the conception of motion as a one-to-one correlation of elemental extension-relations and succession-relations (rather than of points and instants) restores to motion its inalienable character of transition *from* one place *to* another ; whereas the orthodox mathematicians of our day oppose to our common sense a Neo-Eleatic conception of motion as a mere succession of static occupancies of positions by bodies which themselves never really change *from* one position *to* another.

Zeno's puzzle as to how the swift-moving Achilles could overtake the slow-moving tortoise, or, stated in its less picturesque but more generic form, the puzzle as to how any moving body can traverse an infinite series of steps in a finite time, is of historic and intrinsic interest, but our excuse for treating it at such length rests upon the fact that it is perfectly typical of the whole series of puzzles and antinomies which have been used by mystics and pragmatists, but most of all by sceptics, to justify their respective methodological theories. It best represents what we have termed the dialectical argument for scepticism, for it seems to exhibit a hopeless conflict between reason and experience, between what it is logically necessary to believe and what our senses compel us to believe. If this conflict were as irreconcilable as it appears, the sceptic would be correct in his view that the true nature of things is unknowable. For the whole system of human knowledge rests upon the assumption that the conceptual laws of logic apply to the perceptual world of fact. And if that assumption,

[1] For a more detailed defence of the relational character of spatial and temporal elements as applied to the general problem of antinomies, and to Zeno's arrow-puzzle in particular, *cf.* the author's article, " The Antinomy," in *Studies in the History of Ideas*, Columbia University Press, 1918.

which is held in common by both groups of intellectualists, *i.e.* by empiricists no less than by rationalists, were to be proven false, we should have to choose either *mysticism*, which is what rationalism becomes when it opposes itself to experience; or *pragmatism*, which is what empiricism becomes when it opposes itself to logic; or *scepticism*, which repudiates all methods, whether intellectualistic or anti-intellectualistic, because it recognizes that a failure of either reason or experience would be the failure of both. And in such a crisis, the sceptic, on account of his more neutral and negative position, would come out best. It is then of the utmost importance to show that motion does not involve a conflict between sense and reason, and that in this typical case the dialectical argument for scepticism breaks down.

And, finally, if the reader is dissatisfied with our solution of the puzzle, or if he doubts whether solutions could be found for the other puzzles and antinomies, the consideration of which we are compelled to omit, let him remember that a failure to solve a problem is not a proof of its insolubility, and that even if those aspects of reality involved in the puzzles of Zeno and in the antinomies of Kant still remain unknown, it by no means follows that the sceptic is right in believing that reality itself is unknowable.

III

The Physiological Argument.

The sceptic, as we have seen, defends his position by appealing to the disagreements between philosophers, which from the earliest times down to the present day have prevailed in all departments of speculative thought. And to this historical argument he adds the dialectical argument based upon the seemingly hopeless contradictions and paradoxes which confront the mind when it endeavours to penetrate to the heart of things and to explain such basic concepts as motion and infinity. But stronger and more familiar than either the appeal to history or the appeal to dialectic is the argument which we are now to consider. This argument is based upon what we know of the physical and physiological conditions of perception, and it derives its strength from the hopelessly indirect character of the process by which things and events spatially external to the percipient organism come to figure as objects of its experience. This indirection of the perceptual process is by no means evident at first sight. Our primary and natural attitude is one of implicit trust in the validity of perception and in the truth of our senses. " Things are just what they seem," and for an object to be perceived by me, it seems sufficient that the thing shall exist and that my eyes or other organs of perception shall be open and directed towards it. The actual facts of the situation are, however, quite otherwise, and the naïve confidence in the directness of perception and in the validity of immediate or perceptual judgments can be proved false so convincingly that no one who will take the trouble to attend to the evidence can remain unpersuaded.

Let us consider a typical and familiar case of the perception of an object at a distance from the organism by means of the sense of sight. The object, we will suppose, is the sun. The entire act of seeing the sun reveals nothing of the conditions of its occurrence ; but we know that the sun is approximately ninety million miles distant, and that it gives off from its superheated surface a complex system of electro-magnetic waves which travel through space to our eyes in about eight minutes. These waves are refracted by the lens of the eye and brought to a focus on the retina. The retinal image then produces upon the sensitive terminals of the optic nerve some sort of mechanical, chemical, or electrical effect, which is transmitted along the nerve to the brain, and ultimately to those parts of the brain which are called the occipital lobes. The disturbance thus produced in the visual region of the cerebral cortex is in turn modified by other processes in the brain, and then, and only then, does there occur what we call the *perception of the sun*. The occurrence of this conscious perceptual experience is either accompanied or immediately followed by various currents of neural energy along the motor nerve-fibres leading from the brain to the muscles and glands. These efferent currents produce certain movements of the body, notable among which are adaptive movements of the sense-organ through which the stimulus has originally entered the body, movements which result in perpetuating or enhancing the stimulation, if pleasant, and in shutting it off or diminishing it if unpleasant. Now, of the various physical and physiological processes which constitute the conditions for our seeing the sun, there is one which, though it is to be sure but a single term in a continuous and normally uninterrupted process, is nevertheless in itself the necessary and sufficient determiner of our experience of the sun. The condition to which I refer is the sensori-motor state of the brain. That brain-state, though normally produced by the sunlight stimulating the eye, would nevertheless give us a perception of the sun even if it were produced by a cause wholly within the organism as is approximately the case in the dreams of sleep and of delirium. In such circumstances, objects that have no existence outside the organism are nevertheless experienced as though they did so exist. And when, on the other hand, this requisite brain-state is not produced, the other factors may be present without effect, so far as experience is concerned. Finally, not only is the given cerebral state universally present when the perception is present, and universally absent when the perception is absent, but whenever the brain-state varies in character or intensity, the perception varies concomitantly in character and intensity.

Let us now examine more carefully the relation of the sensori-motor brain-state (which is the one necessary and sufficient condition for perceiving the sun) and the actually existing sun which starts the series of effects that lead up to the brain-state. If we represent the external object, in this case the sun, by Oe, and the objective brain-state that is finally produced by it and through which we perceive it as Ob, then we may indeed say that Ob depends upon or is a function of Oe. In symbols $Ob = f(Oe)$; but we must also realize that the brain state Ob depends upon or is a function, first, of the medium (m) through which the light waves pass; second, of the eye or sense-organ (s) which is affected by the light-waves; third, of the nerve fibres and brain (b) through which the sensory current must pass. We can then express the dependence of the final brain-state upon all these conditions by the equation $Ob = f(Oe, m, s, b)$, where the terms m, s, and b are independent variables, any one of which may change without the others changing, but no one of which can change without affecting the last stage of the process which is the dependent variable O*b*. Now, the sceptic argues from these facts that we can never be sure as to whether the experience determined by O*b* resembles the external object which is one, but only one of its causes. *The sun appears to me to be yellow and round and in a certain position in the sky. What guarantee have I that the yellowness and roundness and the position assigned are really characters of the external cause rather than products of the medium* (m), *through which the sun's light must pass, or of the sense-organ* (s) *and brain* (b) *which must be affected before we can have the perception ? In short, the sun as it is in itself, may be entirely different in colour, shape, and position from what it appears to be.*

To this physiological argument for scepticism there are three answers. Let us consider them in turn.

1. *The phenomenalist's answer.* With phenomenalistic relativism as a form of pragmatism we were made familiar in the preceding chapter. We saw there that the relativist tended to identify the true with the believed, or at least with the best in the way of belief. From the identification of the true with the believed to the identification of the real with the experienced is but a short step. It is from the point of view of this second identification that the phenomenalist makes his answer to the sceptic's argument. To the challenge to explain how we can know the nature of things in themselves when we experience them only in relation to the complex media and organs of perception, the phenomenalist boldly answers : *There are no things in themselves, but only things in relation to our experience.* There is no " reality " hidden behind the veil of sensory appearance ; the appearances of things are their reality. And for the sceptic to bewail the fact that we can know nothing but appearances is as silly as it would be to bewail the fact that we have nothing to wear but clothes, and nothing to eat but food. Suppose you know just how an object would look and sound and smell in any relation or situation in which you might be confronted with it. Would you want to know anything more about it ? Would there indeed be anything more about it to know ?

To what extent can the sceptic meet this reply of the phenomenalist ? In my opinion he can meet it half-way. He will have to admit that appearances are real, but he need not admit that they are the whole of reality. Granted that things have a nature of their own that is what it is independently of whether or not there is produced that complex series of their effects upon which our perception of them depends, it would, nevertheless, be of comparatively little value to attain a knowledge of that nature *an sich* unless we could couple with it a knowledge of its appearances *für uns*. Knowledge of appearance is revealed to us immediately in the sensory experience of how things look, how they feel, how they sound and smell and taste. There are, to be sure, certain contemporary pragmatists who do not regard this immediate revelation of the qualities of things as knowledge at all. They speak of it as merely *data*, and claim that knowledge begins only when one goes beyond the circle of his present perceptions and begins to anticipate and reconstruct. These philosophers say that every case of knowledge is a case of judgment, which may be either true or false ; and that a sense-perception is a natural event like a thunder-storm, and not a judgment at all. Now, as a matter of fact, I think it could easily be shown that every perception, besides revealing a certain group of qualities, does also point beyond itself and contain an anticipatory judgment which would make it cognitive, even in the sense required. (The perception of a straight stick which appears bent because partly immersed in water carries with it the anticipation that the tactual and other qualities of the stick would appear at later moments in the position which they are now seen to occupy. The expectation would be disappointed, and therein consists the error. So it was with the dog in Æsop's fable, who saw the reflection in the water of the bone he was carrying, snatched at the shadow and lost the reality.) We can keep ourselves from acting upon these false appearances, and so make them practically innocuous ; but usually we cannot eradicate them. Thus, when someone says that perception itself never deceives and that it is only inference based upon perception that can be in error, we may assent, with the proviso, however, that there never was and never will be a perception that does not carry with it some degree of inference beyond the present moment. From this standpoint the question as to whether we speak of " errors of sense " or of " errors of inference inseparable from sense " becomes a purely verbal matter not worthy of further discussion. In either case we must recognize that these errors of immediate or unconscious perceptual inference are a class quite distinct from those of conscious or indirect inference.

But quite apart from this inferential aspect of perception (which is subject to error) I think the phenomenalist is quite right in holding that sensation, as such, is reality, and that the immediate appearance of the qualities of things in perception is knowledge. It is perhaps the only kind of knowledge that can never be in error. That a pain from which I am suffering is caused by my tooth may be an error, but that I am suffering from a pain that appears like a toothache cannot possibly be an error. That what I dream is real is in all probability false, but that my dreaming itself is real cannot possibly be false. The phenomenalist, then, can always answer to the sceptic that there is at least something that is known and known with absolute certainty, viz. the qualities that appear at each present moment of our waking life. (The refusal to apply the name " knowledge " to that which is the most certain of all knowledge is hardly more than a passing terminological vagary.) And that this knowledge of the momentary and relative appearance of things is a knowledge that is worth having can be seen by considering a case in which it is lacking. A person born blind can learn the science of optics and can know that the sun gives forth waves of visible light that vary in frequency from 400 trillions per second to 760 trillions per second. He may learn further that these vibration rates, when they stimulate a normal eye, produce experiences of specific qualities which are as different from tones and odours as tones and odours are from one another, and that these specific qualities are given the names, *red, yellow, green, blue, violet* ; and all such knowledge acquired by the man born blind is worth having, and is by no means possessed by all men, even by all who can see ; but it does not and cannot console him for his ignorance of what the specific qualities are. With the colours themselves he has no *acquaintance*. And in addition to his conceptual

knowledge of their physical nature he would give much to
know how they *appear*, and to realize just what kind of sensory
experience it was that a normal man called by the name
" red." I think that all of us have the craving for the irre-
placeably intimate knowledge of reality that comes only
through perception ; and that while we recognize fully the
worth of indirect and conceptual knowledge, we would not
willingly rest content with it alone.

In short, the phenomenalist is right in emphasizing our
knowledge of appearances, and the sceptic is wrong in dis-
regarding it. But, on the other hand, the phenomenalist goes
too far when he claims not only that appearances are real,
but that they make up the whole of reality, and that in knowing
them we know all that there is to be known. The sceptic
can still claim that there is a valid meaning in the question
as to the nature of things in themselves, independently of
their appearances, and that we should all of us desire to know
what that inner nature of things is. The nature of a thing in
itself is real, but it is not something incommensurably different
from its appearances, and, therefore, hopelessly unattainable
to our knowledge. We can think of it as simply the most
central and most privileged of its appearances, *i.e.* as the
appearance of the thing to itself. For example : if I have in
my mind a thought which I am trying to convey to others by
various actions—as in playing charades—to one of my com-
panions my actions will suggest one thing, to a second another,
to a third still another, and so on. But behind these more or
less accurate impressions of my meaning there will be the
meaning itself, that is the meaning as it is for me. It follows
from the nature of the thing in itself as thus conceived that
there are two possible ways of learning its nature in any given
case : (1) directly and absolutely by *being* it (each knows his
own states, and only his own states, in this intimate way) ;
(2) indirectly and approximately by calculating the single
and invariant element in the changing variety of appearances.
For the appearance of a thing is nothing but the effect that is
produced by the action of the thing upon a recipient. And as
the effect would always be a repetition of the cause, except
in so far as modified by the medium through which the thing
acts, it will be possible, by comparing diverse effects (due

to diversity of media) of the same cause, to eliminate the influence of the media and approximate the nature of the cause : The more complete the diversity of its appearances or extrinsic nature, the closer will be our approximation to its intrinsic nature. The manner of making this advance beyond a knowledge of mere appearance can best be understood by considering the scientist's answer to the physiological argument for scepticism.

2. *The scientist's answer.* When the sceptic argues that an object, such as the sun, may be different in colour, in shape, in position, and in size from what it is perceived as being, the scientist assents ; but he subscribes neither to the sceptic's pessimistic despair at these possibilities, nor to the phenomenalist's optimistic disregard of them. He undertakes to study the appearances with a view to distinguishing the qualities due to the physical and physiological media through which the object appears, from the qualities of the object itself. He finds that the apparent size of the sun or of any other object is a function of its real size and of its distance, and having ascertained its distance by the parallax method, and having measured the size of the sun's image, he then uses his knowledge of optics to calculate the actual size of an object which at a given distance projects an image of a given size. Having thus learned the real size of the sun, he no longer cares whether it appears in perception as small as a saucer or as large as a washtub. The scientist then proceeds to determine the angular position of the sun. As in the case of the apparent size, he finds that the apparent position is a function of several variables : (*a*) the refraction of the air ; (*b*) the distance of the observer from the sun ; (*c*) the velocity of light ; (*d*) the earth's velocity of rotation ; and (*e*) another factor which is independent of the observer's relation to the sun, and which may be called the sun's objective position or its position with reference to the fixed stars.

The refractive power of the air can be empirically determined and allowed for ; the velocity of light has been measured ; the distance from the sun to the earth is known, as is also the angular velocity of the earth's rotation, which is responsible for the apparent diurnal motion of the sun around the earth. Suppose the slight effect of the air's refraction upon the sun's apparent position to have been allowed for, we should then calculate in terms of the sun's distance and the velocity of light, the time taken by the light to pass from the sun to the earth. This time is approximately eight minutes. The news of the sun that we get by means of our eyes is then known to be eight minutes old, and what we perceive as the sun at any moment is really not the sun as it is at the moment of perception, but the sun as it was eight minutes ago. Now, eight minutes ago the sun was east of its present position just the amount of angular distance which the earth has rotated in eight minutes. As the earth rotates through 360 degrees in twenty-four hours, it rotates in eight minutes $\frac{1}{180}$th of 360 degrees, which is 2 degrees. Therefore, apart from the aberration due to refraction, the sun's true position at any moment is 2 degrees west of its apparent position at that moment.[1]

We come next to the determination of the objective shape of the sun. In direct perception, and also when viewed indirectly through its image upon a reflecting surface or photographic plate, the sun appears as a circular disc. Now, there are various shapes which will project circular images upon flat surfaces. A circular disc itself will project such an image, if the direction of the light is perpendicular to it ; an elliptical disc will also produce a circular shadow if inclined at a suitable angle to the direction of the light ; so would an ellipsoid ; so,

[1] Inasmuch as the sun affects the earth by gravity (noticeably in the phenomenon of the tides), as well as by light, and as gravity is (or has been) supposed to be instantaneous in its transmission, it should be possible to calculate the true position of the sun with respect to the earth at any moment, by observing the state of the tide at the moment and eliminating the effect of the moon's participation. The gravitating effect of the near-by earth upon the fluids in the semi-circular canals and in other parts of our body is so much greater than that of the far-off sun that our senses are not sufficiently delicate to perceive directly the internal tidal strains due to the latter ; but were it not for this purely practical obstacle there would be no theoretical difficulty in our perceiving instantaneously through a " sense of gravity " events upon the sun which would only be perceived by the eyes eight minutes after they had occurred. The relation between visual perception and this hypothetical perception through gravity would then be analogous to the familiar relation between the visual and auditory perception of events a few hundred yards distant, as when we see the axe of the woodchopper across the valley strike the wood several seconds before we hear it strike.

Whether the ability to use gravity to ascertain the positions of the heavenly bodies would or would not put a quietus upon any of the paradoxes of the " Theory of Relativity " in physics, must be left to the physicists themselves to say. See footnote on p. 210.

finally, would a sphere. The mere appearance in perception of circularity leaves open all of these possibilities as to the sun's actual shape. But the fact that the earth is found to go around the sun in the course of the year, and that its axis is inclined to the plane of its orbit, and that, nevertheless, the sun's image is always circular, is incompatible with any of the possible shapes of the sun, except only that of the sphere. The sun's real shape is thus inferred to be spherical, *as the only means of bringing consistency into the system of its appearances*.

There remains to be determined only the colour. To us, in perception it appears yellow ; what is it in itself, independently of its relation to us ? The first thing that the scientist discovers with respect to this problem is that the wave motions, or electro-magnetic vibrations that cause us to perceive light, are of different frequencies, and that to each colour there corresponds a given frequency. These vibration rates are independent of the surface upon which the light falls and of the distance which they have traversed ; they are a function only of the vibrations of the atoms on the surface of the luminous object from which they proceed. There is then no doubt that the vibratory basis of colour-quality is an objective or intrinsic property of the things which appear coloured. In our chosen instance of the sun, the situation is complicated by the fact that the sun's rays contain all of the vibration rates, and that in passing through the air these rates are affected by the nature and density of that medium. To clear the issue of this complication, let us consider the case of an approximately monochromatic or single-coloured object, such as grass, which can be seen from a distance so short that the intervening air has no appreciable effect upon the luminous vibrations. Knowing, as we do, that the surface of the grass has the same vibration-rate as the light that falls upon our retina, can we infer that the green quality itself is also a property of the grass, or must we believe that the quality of greenness is, in reality, a property only of the energy of the stimulus after it has been modified by the optic nerve and brain ? Between these two alternative answers it is not easy to decide, and the sceptic can enjoy a measure of triumph. For with respect to colour, and also with respect to sound and the other non-quantitative or so-called secondary qualities, he can declare that we really do not know to what extent the qualities of the objects themselves are the same as what they are experienced as being.   But this triumph of the physiological argument is mitigated by two considerations : First, whether or not the secondary qualities are properties of objects apart from their relation to the sentient organism is a problem that is unimportant from the standpoint of practical common sense. Second, it is also unimportant from the standpoint of physical science.

First : The problem is unimportant from the standpoint of common sense, because from that standpoint we are interested only in the appearance of things, *i.e.* in the way they will affect us from different points of view.   We do not care, for example, whether there is in a dish of ice-cream a quality similar to the quality of pleasantness which we experience in tasting it.   That it produces that quality in us is sufficient to justify us in calling it pleasant, and to demand more than this would be to pry into the private character of the delicacy, with which, as an article of diet, we have no interest whatever.   As it is with the pleasantness or unpleasantness of a food, so it is with the colour of an object like grass or the sun.   We ascribe to an object the quality of green or of yellow on the sole and sufficient ground that at ordinary distances, and with ordinary eyes, it produces the experience of green or of yellow.

Secondly : The problem of the objective reality of the secondary qualities apart from their relations to our sense-organs is unimportant for ordinary physical science because, so far as we can discover, the behaviour of physical objects is entirely determined by the purely quantitative properties of size, shape, distance, mass, velocity, etc., and any qualities, such as colour, sound, and odour, which they might conceivably possess, are totally ineffective or " epi-phenomenal."

This problem, although unimportant from the standpoints of science and of common sense, does possess a certain metaphysical interest, and it is not insoluble, but only unsolved from the lack of certain empirical data which may at any time be furnished to us.   If, for example, we knew precisely the alteration undergone by the energy of a stimulus in passing from the physical medium of ether or air to the physiological media of sensory nerve and brain, we could form an estimate as to the degree of difference between the specific qualities of colour and sound residing in the objects themselves, and the specific qualities which appear in perception. Were the energies in our brain, which immediately condition the experience of green, identical in nature with the light-vibrations emitted from a luminous body, there would be no reason for doubting that greenness itself was an intrinsic quality of that which appeared green. At first thought, it seems highly improbable that this is the case, for the optic nerve is a very different medium from the ether which carries the stimulus from the object to the eye. And yet it may be that the difference which the stimulus undergoes in passing from the extra-organic to the intra-organic medium is not so great as is usually thought. Though the velocity of propagation in the nerve is enormously slower than that of light, there is some evidence that the vibration-rate with which the colour is correlated undergoes no change in passing from the object to the brain.[1]

But whether this is so or not, the problem is in no sense transcendental, for the degree to which the secondary qualities of objects resemble the qualities which they appear to have would be learned by an extension of the same empirical methods which science already uses to tell us of the degree to which the primary or quantitative properties of objects resemble those which appear in perception.

To sum up : the answer which the physical scientist makes to the sceptic's doubt about the truth of perception is to proceed, by a comparison of perceptual data, to measure the errors and aberrations due to the perceptual mechanism, and thus attain to a conception of the objective order of nature which, at least on the quantitative side, possesses a probability approaching certainty.

3. *The logician's answer.* The last of the three typical answers that may be made to the physiological argument for scepticism is of a purely logical character. We may point

---

[1] For some interesting evidence in support of this possibility the reader is referred to Dr. Sumner's account of his experiments on the flatfish ("The Adjustment of Flatfishes to Various Backgrounds," *Journal of Experimental Zoology,* 10, No. 4) and to Professor Pitkin's comments thereon (*The New Realism,* pp. 397 ff.). The ability of the flatfish to reproduce on his skin the pattern presented to his eye would seem to indicate that the energy-complex was not much distorted by its passage through the labyrinth of the central nervous system.

out to the sceptic that his argument is stultified by the fact that his conclusion contradicts the premises by which it was proved. The conclusion is that knowledge is invalid; the premises assert the validity of that branch of knowledge which discloses the indirect and complicated mechanism of perception. That is to say, the sceptic, who uses the physiological argument, begins by assuming the existence of ether, and air, and nerves, and brain; using these media to show that any given perception may misinterpret its objects, he finally concludes that all knowledge that is founded on perception is doubtful. He should go on to say that, therefore, the physical and physiological conceptions on which his argument rested are equally doubtful, thus cutting away the ground from under his feet. This flaw in the logic of the sceptic is not confined to the physiological argument for scepticism, although it is more flagrant and obvious there than elsewhere. If we generalize the situation, it amounts to this: The only way to prove one proposition doubtful is by assuming other propositions which are not doubtful, from which it follows that any attempt to prove the sceptic's doctrine that all propositions are doubtful is bound to be self-contradictory. This " Logician's Answer " is not a refutation of the sceptic's conclusion, but only of his positive arguments in support of that conclusion. It leaves his contention not disproven, but only unproven. And it remains conceivable that the sceptic's assertion that *nothing can be known* is really true even though all arguments in its favour are false.

Our examination has shown that the sceptic's conclusion from the Physiological Argument is not warranted by the premises, and that there are three specific ways of attacking it, which we have termed the answer of the Phenomenalist, the answer of the Scientist, and the answer of the Logician.

The phenomenalist's answer showed that even if our knowledge of objects were limited to a knowledge of their appearances or effects, it would still be decidedly worth while; the scientist's answer revealed the way in which the good knowledge of effects can be used to give us the still better knowledge of the causes that produce the effects, the collective data of many perceptions being employed to eliminate the error or distortion in any given perception; and finally the logician's answer disclosed the fact that no proposition can be regarded as proved false except by assuming some other proposition to be true, and that, therefore, the physiological argument for scepticism commits a contradiction when it calmly appeals to the truth of the physical and physiological laws of perception in order to prove that all truth is unattainable.

We must now turn to the last of the four proofs of scepticism, that which we named " the psychological argument."

IV

THE PSYCHOLOGICAL ARGUMENT.

The argument for scepticism which we are now to consider is more radical and far-reaching in its claims than any of the three already examined.   It resembles the physiological argument in denying our right to be certain of things beyond the data of immediate experience, but it emphasizes the temporal rather than the spatial difficulties of self-transcendence. Whereas the former argument was content to point out the difficulty of learning what is the real nature of bodies *outside us in space,* the present argument challenges our right to believe in anything that lies *beyond the moment of time* in which the perception takes place.   Our own experience of an hour hence or an hour since are, it is claimed, as much beyond our knowledge as is the nature of the Milky Way.   The psychological sceptic impugns the validity of *memory* and the validity of *anticipation,* and leaves us prisoners of the present instant, cut off from all knowledge of the future.

In analysing the grounds for this most sweeping attack upon the possibility of knowledge, we shall do well to begin by considering whether there is any essential difference between the validity of memory and the validity of anticipation.

At first sight there would appear to be a marked difference between the inaccessibility of the past and that of the future. Memory at its best gives us what is apparently a direct experience of our own past, and the feeling of certainty accompanying it may be as great as that accompanying the apprehension of present sensations. Anticipation of the future never presents itself with this determinateness or directness. It possesses always an inferential rather than an immediate character. A mistake in memory is like a hallucination ; whereas a mistake in anticipation is counted as error of calculation. Despite this difference, however, mistakes in memory do certainly occur. Events that we have frequently heard about or imagined often come to have that peculiarly intimate and familiar character that makes us rank them as " remembered," even though they may never have happened. And even in what is called primary memory, or the experience of the just past, error is possible, as when in listening to a clock we are conscious of its having struck a certain number of times, though in fact it may have struck either one more or one less times than our present consciousness registers. In short, anything that we assert about a time other than the time when we make the assertion may be erroneous.

The psychological sceptic, however, does not as a rule base his main argument on the occasional fallibility of the memory experiences. He prefers rather to deal with the vastly broader field of inference to the future.

We shall, therefore, consider this phase of the argument first, and return later to the questions raised by the errors of memory.

Let us suppose, then, that the sceptic concedes to us the correctness of our memories of the past, but challenges our claim to go beyond what has been experienced and assert anything of the future. How shall we answer him ? We believe, for example, that water will continue to quench fire, and that bodies will continue to gravitate, and we hold these beliefs on the strength of experience. The sceptic reminds us that we have only experienced the fire and water of yesterday, and that consequently an assertion about the fire and water of to-morrow cannot be based upon experience. We may reply that past experience has shown that certain sequences of phenomena are constant, and that the attraction of bodies and the quenching of fire by water are examples of these invariable relations. We call them laws of nature, and all our plans and actions, the most immediate and trivial, as well as the most remote and far-seeing, are based on the assumption of their validity for the future. This assumption that relations which have been found constant in the past will be equally constant in the future is the assumption of *the uniformity of nature*. We must be careful not to interpret it as a denial of change. It does not tell us that the future will resemble the past in all respects. It does, in fact, explicitly provide for change, for it tells us not only that relations that have been found permanent or causal will continue permanent or causal, but also that relations that have been found variable or casual will continue variable or casual. Thus, my expectation that my future hands at whist will be different from those held in the past, is as truly based upon my belief in the " uniformity of nature " as my belief that the gravitative behaviour of bodies will not be different in the future from what it has been in the past.

This is perhaps a sufficient statement as to the meaning and importance of the Uniformity of Nature, but it is not a sufficient answer to the sceptic. For he has not denied the importance of this principle as the basis of all induction and all intelligent behaviour. On the contrary, he has admitted it and even emphasized it as the one and only basis of our assertions about the future. His challenge is addressed, not to its importance, but to its validity. What reason have we for supposing that it will continue to be true ? Granting that nature's laws have exhibited constancy in the past, why may they not change and cease to be constant to morrow ?

There are two answers that have been made to this final attack of the sceptic, and to my mind they are neither of them satisfactory. The first is the answer of the logician and philosopher, John Stuart Mill. Mill declared that the uniformity of nature was itself proved by past experience. He pointed out that all that is now the past had once been the future, that consequently futures are not new things, but have often been experienced and their resemblance to their pasts been noted, and that when we now make statements about futurity, we are making statements about something that is familiar. The short answer to the argument of Mill is the sceptic's reminder that it begs the question. Mill assumes that because the future has resembled the past in the past, it will continue to do so.

If nature is uniform, then its uniformity will continue; but whether it is uniform is the very point to be proved. The futures that we have experienced do not include the future that now confronts us, and we cannot argue from old futures to new, or from the fact that the uniformity of nature has been found true up to the present to the conclusion that it will be found true in the future.

The second attempt to meet the sceptic's doubt as to whether nature's laws will continue to hold is based upon a consideration that we have already mentioned, namely the importance and even the necessity of belief, if we are to act at all. The argument can be stated as follows : Whatever belief is necessary for action must be true. The belief in the uniformity of nature is necessary for action, therefore it must be true. We may grant the second or minor premise ; but the major premise is doubtful, if not false. There are many cases in which an action presupposes a belief that is not true. For example : a prisoner would never plan for his escape, except on the belief that he had a chance to succeed. His guardians, however, may all the time have been cognizant of his efforts with the result that he has had at no time any chance to succeed. Or again, prior to an earthquake, the actions of the unsuspecting inhabitants are based upon the belief that the earth will remain quiet. The existence of this belief in no way obstructs the catastrophe that falsifies it. I should not start writing this sentence unless I believed that I should live to finish it, yet I may be stricken at any moment. This is enough to show that the fact that a belief is necessary to action does not make the belief true, and that the principle of the uniformity of nature cannot be theoretically justified by its indispensability for practice. If at this point we turn sulky and ask the sceptic whether he seriously expects us to give up our belief in the uniformity of nature because of his arguments, or whether he himself permits his logic to weaken his belief, he will retort that we have missed the point. He neither desires nor hopes to weaken our belief in the future ; he wishes only to show that that belief (which he shares with us) is a pure act of faith, *biologically and psychologically necessary*, but without a shadow of *logical justification*. Let us believe, by all means, he would say, only let us as philosophers be frank enough and humble enough to admit that the entire system of common-sense expectation and scientific prediction, in so far as it is based upon the assumption of the uniformity of nature, is based not upon reason, but upon will and faith. And there are many who will feel, after the first shock to their pride, that faith or instinct is not, after all, such a bad foundation for living. But is what is good enough for mere living really good enough for science and philosophy ?

There is, however, one line of defence against the psychological argument for scepticism which we have not yet tried, and before surrendering unconditionally, it may be worth while to examine it. It rests upon a certain interpretation of causality and of the law of probability, and we may approach it through the following considerations :

There are two conceivable kinds of conjunctions between things : Dependent or causal conjunctions and independent or casual conjunctions. A causal conjunction would be a relation in which one thing " influences," " enforces," or " determines " another thing. Such a relation, if it existed, would be entirely independent of the particular times and places in which the things related were located. It would concern the natures of the things and not their specific positions in the spatio-temporal system.

It is important to note that no claim is made here to assert the reality of this kind of relation, but only to assert its meaning. Causality may have no more reality than a dragon or a mermaid, it may be a pure product of the human imagination ; but just as we have a perfectly clear knowledge of the meaning of centaurs and mermaids, so we have a perfectly clear notion of causality or enforcement. David Hume, the philosopher who most successfully attacked the reality or validity of the notion of cause, was himself quite clear as to its meaning. Had he not been, his attack would itself have been meaningless. Now, besides the causal relation, we conceive of relations that are casual. Casual relations are the negative of causal. If two events are such that there is nothing in the nature of one to necessitate or enforce the presence of the other, we call them independent, and when they occur together we say that their conjunction is casual. And so long as we continued to believe that they *were* independent, we should continue to call their conjunction casual, even though we always experienced them together. The relations in our world undoubtedly appear to be both causal and casual. They may be as they appear, or they may be all causal, or all casual. There are, undoubtedly, many relations which first appear to be causal and are afterwards judged to be casual. Thus to many primitive and primitively minded folk, things and the names by which they are called appear to have an intrinsic and quasi-causal affinity. This is comically illustrated by the saying : " The swine is rightly so called," and by the classic query as to how the astronomers discovered the names of the stars. Again, many people who are called superstitious get a striking feeling of causal connection between any two events which are surprising or strongly exciting, as when a death follows upon the breaking of a mirror or upon the sitting down of thirteen at the table. On reflection we become convinced that such conjunctions are casual, and we call the inference from mere sequence to consequence the fallacy of *Post hoc ergo propter hoc.* Now, these feelings of necessary connection are so untrustworthy and have been so often discredited, that even in the cases in which they are felt strongly by all of us (as for example when motion follows the application of muscular effort or force) it is unsafe to trust them. We should be willing to admit that all of them *may* be illusory. We should, however, be equally willing to recognize the alternative possibility ; and if the feeling or appearance of necessity were all we had as evidence, we should have to leave the question undecided.

We have, however, an indirect way of testing the matter. If the conjunction of the events A and B were really causal, the second event would follow the first, except when some counter-acting cause was present. And if, in order to avoid this complication of counter-acting causes, we define a cause as *an unopposed tendency to produce* an event, we may say that every cause would be followed at all times by its effect. Keeping this in mind, let us consider what would be the case if the conjunction were casual instead of causal. Here the average frequency of the happening together of the two events would be measured by the product of the average frequencies of the events taken separately. Thus, if the average frequency of a penny's falling heads up is $\frac{1}{2}$, then the

average frequencies with which two independent but similar pennies will fall heads up is $\frac{1}{2} \times \frac{1}{2} = \frac{1}{4}$. And if the average frequency of a die falling six up is $\frac{1}{6}$, and the average frequency of drawing a heart from a pack of cards is $\frac{1}{4}$, the average frequency of drawing a heart and throwing a six together would be $\frac{1}{4} \times \frac{1}{6} = \frac{1}{24}$. And the average frequency with which this casual conjunction would occur twice consecutively would be $(\frac{1}{24})^2$; three times consecutively, $(\frac{1}{24})^3$; n times consecutively $(\frac{1}{24})^n$. Now the reason why the average frequency of a die falling six up is $\frac{1}{6}$ is that there are five possible ways in which a die can fall without falling six up, and one possible way in which it can fall six up. *The ratio of the number of ways in which an event can happen in a given situation to the number of ways in which it both can happen and fail to happen, is called the probability of the event.* This fraction might be symbolized as $\dfrac{h}{h + \bar{h}}$ where $h =$ the number of ways the event could happen and $\bar{h}$ the number of ways it could fail to happen. It is obvious that the probability-fraction for any event will always lie between o and 1, for the positive integer forming the numerator cannot be less than 1 and the positive integer forming the denominator cannot be less than the numerator. Of course, it is assumed in this definition that the units themselves are all equal, and that there is no reason for preferring any one way of happening (or failing to happen) to any other.

From the meaning of probability as above defined it is evident that if the probability of a given event happening is $\dfrac{1}{m}$, the probability of its not happening is $1 - \dfrac{1}{m}$. And as any conjunction of events must be either causal or casual, the probability of its being causal will be one minus the probability of its being casual. Thus the principle of probability which is primarily a law for measuring casual conjunctions, *i.e.* conjunctions of independent events, has the peculiar virtue of enabling us to measure the probability that a series of conjunctions is causal rather than casual. In other words, *the law of chances contains a measure of its own applicability to a given material.* Before showing how this feature of the principle of probability enables us to answer the sceptic's

attack upon the uniformity of nature, I wish to make the point
clear by considering one or two simple illustrations of its
working.

We are, let us say, playing cards with an acquaintance of
whose honesty we know very little. We observe that when
he deals the cards he holds the winning hand. The question
would suggest itself: Is the conjunction of dealing and
winning casual or causal? As the probability decreased of the
repetition of conjunctions being casual—an honest run of
luck—the probability of a causal or dishonest relationship
would increase. If the coincidences were sufficiently numerous,
we should infer a causal connection, even in the face of a reputation for honesty. Again, suppose we are asked to examine
the claims of a mind-reader by thinking of some object, say
a certain card, and then requesting him to name it. There is
one chance in fifty-two that without any causal relation between
our minds he would think of the same card that we thought of.
If instead of a single card we thought of a sequence of ten,
twenty, thirty, the probability of his guesses being successful
apart from some causal connection would be $(\frac{1}{52})^{10}$, $(\frac{1}{52})^{20}$,
$(\frac{1}{52})^{30}$, and the most sceptical observer would soon be forced
to admit the probability of a causal connection. The precise
point at which the admission would be made would depend
on the individual's pre-existing prejudice against the existence
of a causal connection of the type under investigation. Thus
in the case of telepathy, the disbelief among the great majority
of psychologists is so strong that if they had to assign it a
measure they would very likely say that there is not one
chance in a trillion of there being any such thing as a causal
influence through non-sensory channels of one mind upon
another. To a person holding such a belief, a train of apparently
telepathic happenings, the antecedent probability of which,
as mere casual conjunctions, would be less than a trillionth,
would be necessary in order to produce conviction.

Of course, we must remember that inasmuch as the antecedent improbability of any specific combination of events is
great in proportion to its complexity, the combination that
is to be evidence of causal connection must not only be of
great antecedent improbability, but must also be such as
would be inevitable if the causal connection held. Thus, the

improbability of dealing yourself thirteen trumps at whist is no greater than the antecedent improbability of any specific hand that is actually held.   It is the improbable that always happens.   Yet, as there is a motive, and so a possible cause for dealing a hand that would have a special significance, because of its value or because it was prophesied or designated beforehand, we should be pretty certain that if any such hand were dealt it would not be a mere coincidence.   The ordinary hand, though equally improbable, is accepted as mere luck, because it has no precise correspondence to any pre-existing expectation or desire which might act as its cause.

Let us now apply our principle to those recurring sequences of events which are termed natural laws and which give rise to that belief in a uniformity of nature which is challenged by the sceptic.   Water quenches fire ; fire melts ice ; bodies gravitate toward one another.   Are these conjunctions casual or causal ?   The sceptic declares that they are casual, and that therefore there can be no rational ground for the belief that they will continue to be repeated in the future.   We admit that he may be right ; that it is perfectly conceivable that the sequences which nature deals to us so regularly and repeatedly may be honest runs of luck and hence likely at any moment to change.   While admitting this to be possible, we claim, however, the right to entertain as equally possible the opposite hypothesis, viz. that nature may play with marked cards and loaded dice, and that each of her events (independently of the time and space of its occurrence) may possess as " cause " a power to produce or enforce another event as " effect."   Both hypotheses are consistent with the facts as we know them.   Neither hypothesis can be proved with absolute finality.   The only way and a sufficient way to decide between them is to ascertain which is the more probable ; and we claim the right to do this by the same means that we should use in any other case in which the question at issue is whether a repeated conjunction of events is casual or causal.   The probability that a conjunction is causal increases as the probability that it is casual decreases. Let us take the case of water quenching fire.   What is the probability that a fire would happen to go out at the moment when water was thrown upon it in a world in which there was no such thing as causal enforcement ?   Let us assume that the probability of such a conjunction would be one-half, that the chances for and against its happening are even. (This is a very generous assumption, for it means that fire is as likely to go out at any moment as to continue, and that consequently the water that is thrown upon it is as likely as not to find it in its going-out phase.) The probability then of a casual conjunction of the event water-thrown-on-fire and the event fire-going-out is $\frac{1}{2}$. The probability that this conjunction, if casual, will occur twice in succession is $\frac{1}{4}$; the probability of its occurring three times consecutively would be $(\frac{1}{2})^3$ and of n times consecutively, $(\frac{1}{2})^n$. Now, the facts are that the number of occasions on which the going-out-of-fire (in whole or in part) has been observed to follow the throwing-on-of-water are thousands of millions, and the number of cases of a failure of the second event to follow on the first is zero. It follows, therefore, that the probability that these oft-repeated sequences could be casual (i.e. a mere run of luck comparable to that by which a penny would come up " heads " a billion times in succession) is so small as to be negligible ; and that consequently the counter-probability that the regularly repeated conjunction is the expression of a genuinely causal relationship between events that are not intrinsically independent of one another is so high as to be equivalent, for practical purposes, to certainty. And as it is with the law that water quenches fire, so is it with the countless hosts of other laws. That the unvaryingly recurrent sequences which those laws express are casual conjunctions between intrinsically independent events is infinitely improbable. The prevalence of true causality and the accompanying guarantee that the uniformity of nature will hold in the future as in the past is proved against the sceptic, not indeed with certainty, but with overwhelming probability.

There are, however, two objections which the sceptic might offer to this attempt to use the law of chances to determine whether or no the world is permeated by chance.

He may claim that the law of probability is derived from our experience of particular parts of nature, and hence cannot be used to determine the constitution of other parts not yet experienced, still less the constitution of the world as a whole. To this we reply that the law of probability is as much and as little dependent upon the particular facts of experience as are any of the laws of logic and mathematics. For let there be conceived any two things or events whose probabilities are absolutely unknown. Let $\frac{1}{x}$ be the probability of one of them and $\frac{1}{y}$ the probability of the other ; then the probability that both of those imagined events are real is $\frac{1}{x} \times \frac{1}{y}$, which is less than either $\frac{1}{x}$ or $\frac{1}{y}$, no matter what the value of the integers x and y. For example, we have no idea what the probability is that the star Vega has a planet that is inhabited, but we are none the less certain that the probability that that star has two planets both of which are inhabited is less than the probability that at least one is inhabited. And in the same way it can be shown that of two events concerning which nothing is known except that one is more complex than the other, the more complex is the less probable. That is to say, an event (A) containing the elements X, Y, and Z is less probable than an event (B) containing only the element X.

The second objection which the sceptic may urge against our argument is based on the fact that " it is the improbable that is always happening " ; that the antecedent improbability of any situation in the concrete fullness of its relations to all other situations is infinitely great. From which it follows that any possible combination of the world's events is as improbable or as probable as any other, so that in the last analysis a Nature or World that was so constituted as to simulate perfectly the appearance of uniformity and causal law up to a certain time, e.g. the present, and then reverse itself and turn chaotic (which is the situation in the possibility of which the sceptic believes), would be as intrinsically probable as any other one of the infinity of conceivable arrangements of events. This objection to our argument would be valid except for one thing : it fails to consider that in addition to the totality of casual arrangements of events no one of which is more probable than another there is also the alternative possibility which is intrinsically as probable as the reign of chance : a *causal* order. And that one overlooked possibility is made overwhelmingly probable by the fact that the world, so far as observed, is just what it would be if the causal order were the real order.   The case is precisely analogous to the whist game in which the acquaintance concerning whose honesty we were in complete ignorance invariably dealt himself all the trumps.   We should accuse him of cheating, and he might reply by pointing out that the improbability of thirteen trumps in one hand was no greater than that of any other designated set of thirteen cards.   We should be unconvinced just because his reply took no note of the fact that in addition to the trillions of equally probable casual combinations there was the sinister alternative of a causal relation between his interest in having a trump hand and his manipulations of the cards.   And this overlooked alternative, however small the probability which we should ordinarily assign to it, would assume overwhelming proportions in such a contingency as an unvaried succession of all-trump hands.   We could only accept the defence as valid on the supposition that a causal relation was absolutely impossible. Such a supposition could never be justified in a card game, for there would be the possibility, no matter how small its probability, of a causal connection.   And the same is true in the case of the appearance of uniformity in nature.   *In short, our whole argument in refutation of scepticism stands or falls with our claim that a causal order in nature with its guarantee of a continuance of uniformity in the future, is at least possible, and therefore admissible as a hypothesis.*   For if you are willing to admit that it is possible at all, you can be compelled to admit that it is infinitely probable, by reason of the regularly repeated conjunctions of the events of experience.

It will be remembered that at the outset of our exposition of the Psychological Argument for scepticism we stated the sceptic's attack upon the validity of our memory of the past, but postponed any attempt to answer it until we had considered his graver challenge of our right to expect nature's uniformity to continue into the future.   We are now in a position to return to the problem of memory, and we shall treat it in the light of the principle of probability which we have just been defending in connection with the problem of prediction.

We start by conceding to the sceptic that memory has sometimes been found to be in error, and that as nothing beyond the experience of the moment is absolutely certain it is at least possible, or abstractly conceivable, that all our memories may be in error, and that what appears as our own past life together with everything that is related to it—in other words, the entire world—may be a dream from which at any moment we may awake. Granted that this is a *possibility*, what is its *probability*?

The sceptic must believe that the chances in favour of this wholesale deception are even, or at least that they cannot be proved to be other than even ; we shall try to show that on the contrary they can be proved to have only an infinitesimal or negligible degree of probability. Let us consider the following case : A judge hears a number of witnesses testify from memory to the effect that they observed a given event. We will suppose that these witnesses are *unbiased, i.e.* without any motive to deceive, and (which is more important) that they are *independent* in the sense that not one of them has communicated with, or been in any way influenced by, any other, either in giving their testimony or in forming the belief to which they testify. Let us, in generosity to the sceptic, assume that, despite the unbiased and independent character of the testimony, there are three chances out of four that each witness is at fault, either through wilful deception or through an honest error of memory. If the number of witnesses is ten, the probability that they are all of them independently and simultaneously testifying to something that never happened will be $\left(\frac{3}{4}\right)^{10} = \frac{58949}{1048576} =$ approximately $\frac{1}{17}$; hence the counter probability that at least one of the ten witnesses is telling the truth will be $1 - \frac{1}{17}$ or $\frac{16}{17}$, which is tolerably near certainty. If the number of witnesses were twenty instead of ten, the probability would be much greater that their independent agreement was explained by their memories *being based on objective fact*. And if, instead of witnesses, there were a number of circumstances that independently corroborated one another by pointing to the same fact, the probable truth would be determined in the same way. If the witnesses or circumstances are very numerous, it does not matter much how weak or unreliable are the individual elements, because the formula expressing the probability that the event pointed to really happened is $1 - \left(\dfrac{1}{m}\right)^n$ where $\dfrac{1}{m}$ measures the probable deceptiveness of any element, and n denotes the number of elements.   It is plain that, regardless of the value of m, if n is very large, the fraction $\left(\dfrac{1}{m}\right)^n$ will be near zero, and hence the formula as a whole will be near unity, which means certainty. Now if, instead of the court-room situation with its witnesses or circumstances, we take the total contents of our experience at any moment, we find a condition in which the reality of the world beyond the moment as built upon memory is implied by millions of elements.   If the remembered world is real, all these experienced data are given meaning and significance. If on the contrary it is unreal, we must suppose an almost unbelievable combination of circumstances which, though independent of one another, miraculously conspire to form a perfect counterfeit of what *would* have happened if the remembered world *were* real.

A final and very simple illustration of the principle with which we are fighting the sceptic may be given to show its application, not only to the psychological but to the physiological argument.   I have, we will suppose, a visual impression of a material object, such as a serpent ; it is possible that this experienced object has no objective reality : that it is a hallucination.   To test this possibility I supplement my visual experience by tactual, auditory, and olfactory impressions ; in other words, I touch, hear, and smell the serpent.   It is still possible, however, that there is no objective basis for these experiences, and that I am the victim of hallucinations in all four senses at once.   To test the possibility of this I call in my friends, and we will suppose that their experience corroborates mine.   Again, however, the doubt may be expressed that we are all of us independently quadruply hallucinated at the same time.   We might attempt to dispel this doubt either by calling in more witnesses or by indirect means, such as trying whether the serpent would eat food or affect a camera plate, or in other respects behave like a real external serpent.   No matter how many of these tests were put, it would always remain abstractly conceivable that the various corroborative experiences were independently caused, and that the supposed serpent existed

only in our experience.   But long before the half of the tests
had been carried out the probability of our being in error
would have become infinitely small, and we should accept as
virtually proved the existence of a real serpent as the single
adequate explanation of our various experiences.   In quite the
same way we prove beyond a reasonable doubt the existence
of other persons.   We cannot directly experience the existence
of their minds, and we cannot be absolutely certain of them,
but the totality of their acts of behaviour form a convergent
system quite of the type we have been discussing, and the
alternatives that confront us are :   (1) the real existence of
other minds similar to our minds to the extent that their
behaviour is similar to our behaviour ; and (2) a miraculous
combination of independent or chance factors which perfectly
counterfeit the effects of such minds.   Between these two
alternatives the probabilities in favour of the first are overwhelming.

CONCLUSION.

We have now surveyed the four principal arguments
that have been brought forward by sceptics in support of their
negative contention that none of the five sources of knowledge
is adequate to provide a reasonable basis for human beliefs.
Our conclusion is that the historical, the dialectical, the
physiological, and the psychological arguments do indeed show
that the human mind is unable to attain absolute certainty in
any field of inquiry.   But between this *certainty* maintained
by the extreme anti-sceptics, or, as Kant called them, the
" dogmatists," and the blank indifference of *complete doubt*
maintained by the sceptics, there exists the intermediate
realm of the *probable*.   And as our position with respect to the
historical and dialectical arguments was the modestly optimistic claim of *ignoramus* as against the sceptic's despairing
ignorabimus, so with respect to the physiological and psychological arguments our claim has been that the main systems
of belief, such as those resting on the Uniformity of Nature,
and on the reality of a single set of physical objects underlying the varying perceptions of individuals—maintained by
common sense and by natural science—possess a very high

degree of probability. Just how great is the probable truth of any given system depends upon the number of its elements and the extent of their convergence or mutual corroboration.[1]

[1] For a more detailed discussion of the methods of testing the probable reliability of a system of inference from experience, the reader should consult Hobhouse's *The Theory of Knowledge*, Part II, which contains a treatment of the problem of eliminating error to which the present writer owes much.

Footnote to p. 190.

Two friends have called my attention to the fact that the validity of my argument for a difference of two degrees between the sun's true position and its apparent position, at the moment of perception, depends upon the questionable assumption that the earth's rotation on its axis is identical in its optical effects with a Ptolemaic rotation of the sun around the earth.

CHAPTER VII

ENTENTES AND ALLIANCES — THE FEDERATION OF THE METHODS

THE six methods or theories of logic which we have severally examined are by no means mutually exclusive, yet our treatment of them, so far, has mainly emphasized their differences and contrasts. It therefore seems worth while to devote a chapter to considering some of the ways in which the methods have been combined with one another. By this discussion of ententes and alliances we may be led to conceive of a genuine federation of logical methods, whereby each contending theory, in exchange for its claim to monopolize all truth, would be assigned a unique function and permanent value in no way irreconcilable with that of its rivals. This would mean an arrangement according to which the methods, instead of warring upon one another's merits, would peacefully supplement one another's defects. To exhibit the manner in which any method can be combined with all the others it will be sufficient to take them up two at a time.

I

ENTENTES AND ALLIANCES.

1. *Authoritarianism and Mysticism.*—In the chapter on authoritarianism we have already spoken of the way in which that method may be combined with mysticism. Most authoritarians, in so far as they attempt any philosophical justification of their doctrine, feel the need of putting a term to the otherwise endless regress according to which the authority of each

witness is .nade to depend upon the authority of another, who in turn has derived his knowledge from a third, and so on. And that final term or ultimate foundation of the chain of authorities was usually, as we saw, a supposed revelation, inspiration, or supersensuous intuition of the truth which is testified to.

2. *Authoritarianism and Rationalism.*—In the writings of Christian theologians, both Catholic and Protestant, it is usual, and one might say almost universal, to find certain primary propositions accepted on authority as dogmas from which as premises long chains of consequences are deduced in purely rationalistic fashion. Indeed, it often seems as if the Schoolmen had attempted by an over-refinement and scrupulosity of ratiocination in secondary matters to atone to their intellectual conscience for the violation done to it in the acceptance of their primary premises on mere faith.

3. *Authoritarianism and Empiricism.*—The possibility of combining empiricism with authoritarianism is so obvious as to require merely a word or two of comment. None of the methods disdains the use of the senses in gaining information as to specific, material facts. And one often finds that those who are most scrupulous in accepting their religious dogmas on authority are, in all other matters, of the hard-headed type who scorn intuition and abstract reasoning and demand concrete empirical proofs for their beliefs.

4. *Authoritarianism and Pragmatism.*—The combination of pragmatism with authoritarianism is congenial to the practical type of person who has little use for intellectual analysis. Certain fundamental propositions will be accepted on authority, while more specific and subsidiary beliefs will be held on the ground of their practical utility. Indeed, the acceptance of authority is itself often justified pragmatically. It is easier and more satisfactory for the unintellectual person to take his philosophy of life ready made from the great men of the past than to work out a scheme for himself.

Then, too, we must remember that authoritarianism and pragmatism are both of them anti-intellectualistic in character, and hence can combine naturally with one another. Both the authoritarian and the pragmatist look with suspicion upon the mere intellect as an instrument for arriving at truth. They regard thought, not as an end in itself, but as a means to life.

Another factor that makes possible the combination of these methods is the prevailingly authoritarian character of the rules for the conduct of practical life. These rules, which make up the greater part of our ethics, are not worked out by the individual, but are taught to him in his childhood. His acceptance of them on the authority of his parents and teachers is associated with his efficiency in managing his affairs. And it often happens that what tends to upset this trust in authority tends equally to upset habits of action, and to decrease efficiency.

In addition to these general reasons that make for the combination of authoritarianism and pragmatism, there are certain special considerations with respect to religious beliefs which bring about the same result. To most people, for example, the beliefs in the existence of God and in the immortality of the soul are acceptable not only on grounds of authority, but on the pragmatic ground that they increase the happiness and the courage of those who hold them. They appear more easily demonstrable by the methods of authoritarianism and pragmatism than by those of reason and experience.

5. *Authoritarianism and Scepticism.*—Although scepticism opposes itself to all the methodological theories, yet, inasmuch as it is usually the result of an unsuccessful attempt to work out the solution of philosophical problems by intellectual analysis, it follows that the sceptic often feels himself less opposed to the non-intellectualistic methods than to either rationalism or empiricism. Belief of some kind is usually necessary for action. The paralysing doubt involved in a total scepticism cannot be carried beyond the philosopher's closet. The sceptic having failed to earn a system of belief, may be tempted to steal it or beg it from others in order to be able to live at all. It is, therefore, a very natural and very frequent phenomenon to find a philosopher passing suddenly from extreme scepticism to extreme dogmatism, from a critical distrust of all reasoned conclusions to an uncritical acceptance of doctrines which disdain the justification of reason. Notable examples of this combination of scepticism and authoritarianism

are St. Augustine, Cardinal Newman, and Lord Balfour. In each of these philosophers religious authoritarianism seems to have been accepted as a necessary and justifiable refuge from a scepticism which is felt to be unendurable. This transition is made the more easy and natural by the sense of failure which usually attends sceptical conclusions. Having failed himself to work out by his own powers a positive system of belief, the philosophic sceptic may feel sufficiently humbled to be willing to accept gratefully the beliefs of those who claim to have been more successful.

6. *Mysticism and Rationalism.*—This combination is less frequent than those that we have so far considered. The mystic with his love of intuition and emotion is usually hostile to those processes of abstract deductive reasoning upon which the rationalist relies. The meeting-ground for the two methods when it exists at all is to be found in the attitude which the rationalist takes toward his first principles. It is only occasionally that these latter are self-proving, that is, demonstrated to be true by the very attempt to show that they are false. (It was by this means, for example, that Descartes proved his basic principle : *cogito ergo sum*—the very attempt to doubt one's existence proves that one exists.) Usually the axioms of the rationalist are accepted on the strength of something resembling intuition. They are vouched for by their own clarity and by the feeling that it is impossible to imagine them false. This similarity of attitude is, however, diminished by the fact that whereas the propositions accepted by the mystic on the strength of intuition are usually of a concrete and specific nature, the first principles of the rationalist are abstract relations between universals.

A second point of community between mysticism and rationalism lies in their joint opposition to empiricism. In discussing the paradoxes of Zeno in their bearing upon the dialectical argument for scepticism, we had occasion to observe the manner in which a rationalistic argument, pursued in extreme opposition to the testimony of sense-experience, tended to yield a view of the world not unlike that of the mystic. Zeno rejected the reality of motion solely on the ground of its apparently illogical and self-contradictory character ; but in giving up the reality of motion he gave up also the reality of

the entire world of sense, and took refuge in a realm of changeless and unitary Being.   This realm of pure Being, although
arrived at by a rationalistic process, possessed much the same
character as the world revealed to the mystic in intuition.
In divesting Being of all the qualities of sense-experience the
Eleatic philosopher had left nothing to which the categories of
reason could apply.   Reality, in being made supersensuous,
had become superrational.

Another form of alliance between these two methods is
exemplified in a philosophical system such as that of Neo-
Platonism, in which the mystical method of intuition is made
to *supervene* upon the method of rationalistic deduction.   The
world is not regarded by the Neo-Platonists as anti-rational ;
on the contrary, the rationality of the major part of reality is
insisted upon.   It is only the innermost core of absolute being
that possesses a nature that is beyond even the power of reason
to comprehend, and that therefore requires intuition for its
appreciation.   In the ultra-intellectualistic philosophy of
Spinoza, and some would say even in that of Plato himself,
there is this tendency to supplement rationalistic analysis with
mystical intuition.

7. *Mysticism and Empiricism.*—Feeling and emotion possess
the same kind of concreteness as that belonging to sense-
perception, and hence the mystic often insists upon the vivid
and semi-perceptual character of such deliverances and visions
as those of Joan of Arc and of some of the medieval saints.
The only difference between an empiricist and the mystic of
this type lies in the fact that the mystic's visions are experienced
only by himself, while the perceptions of the empiricist are
common to many observers.   In other words, a mystical
experience whose objectivity could be vouched for by others
would possess the certainty of an empirical observation, and
conversely an ordinary perceptual experience of an external
object, if it were accessible to one mind alone, would lose its
empirical character and be classed as a mystical intuition or
as a mere hallucination, according to whether it was regarded
as valid or invalid.

In addition to the above-named positive resemblance there
is a negative affinity often to be found between the empiricist
and the non-rationalist type of mystic.   For while it is true

that mystics of the type of the Neo-Platonists combine their mysticism with the rationalistic method, the majority of mystics are inclined to be impatient of rationalistic procedure. The popular belief that intuition and reason are opposite faculties has a sound basis of fact. People who base their action on intuition and inspiration are apt to be interested in the concrete and impatient of abstract calculation. In what is known as the " artistic temperament " we often find the power of reaching conclusions by flashes of intuition combined with the power of accurate and extensive observation of empirical facts. This last resemblance of empiricism to mysticism may be expressed in technical philosophical terms as a mutual liking for the *immediate* aspect of experience, and a mutual dislike and distrust of the *mediate* or indirect categories of the intellect.

8. *Mysticism and Pragmatism.*—Mystics and Pragmatists are, as a rule, radically opposed to one another in their attitudes towards the world ; for the mystic derives his conclusions from an inner and, as he claims, a spiritual source, while the pragmatist derives his from external action and behaviour. Despite this apparently irreconcilable opposition, we have recently had a very striking and interesting example of an almost perfect blending of mysticism and pragmatism. I refer to the philosophy of M. Henri Bergson. In his account of the origin and growth of science, and indeed of all intellectual categories, Bergson shows himself a thoroughgoing pragmatist. The life force, according to him, evolves thought as an instrument for the practical control of environment. We think in order that we may eat ; theory exists for the sake of practice ; intellect exists for the sake of will ; intelligence is defined as the tool-making faculty, the faculty by means of which life fashions inanimate matter into instruments for the extension of its own powers. This alleged utilitarian origin and utilitarian purpose of men's intellect is regarded by the ordinary pragmatist as a mark of its validity. Indeed, truth and utility are thought of as virtually identical. For Bergson, however, it is quite otherwise. The pragmatic value of thought is for him a bar to, rather than a confirmation of, its truthfulness. In order to know the inner nature of reality, we must abandon intellect and resort to intuition. For the essence of the real consists of

movement, change, novelty, all of which are categories repugnant to intellect.   Logic is successful just because it neglects
the living flux of reality and puts in its place a system of static
forms or concepts.   Bergson himself sees nothing anomalous
in this combination of pragmatism and mysticism.   Logic
is useful, but not true ; intuition is true, but not useful.   Each
is justified in its own right, and neither conflicts with the other.

Although Bergson's theory of method is the most picturesque
example of a combination of mysticism and pragmatism, there
are other philosophers who take somewhat the same attitude.
Mr. F. H. Bradley, for instance, believes that all intellectual
analysis is a falsification of the real to the extent that it breaks
up its unity into a system of separate terms and relations.
The primary form of the intellect is the judgment, and every
judgment consists of a subject and a predicate held in relation
by a copula.   The concatenation of judgments constituting
a science furnishes a useful and indeed inevitable substitute
for the reality which it describes, but the very discreteness to
which its utility is due does violence to the true nature of its
subject-matter.   It is in the attitude of feeling rather than
that of thought that the unified structure of reality is most
nearly revealed.   We must bear in mind, however, that while
Bradley and Bergson agree that it is in intuition rather than
in thought that reality appears as it is in itself, they differ in
their beliefs as to the nature of the real.   For Bradley, change
is an appearance, while for Bergson change constitutes the very
heart and core of reality.

Another example of a pragmatic conception of science
combined with a belief that it falsifies what it so usefully
describes is afforded by the philosophy of the late Professor
Muensterberg.   That writer believed that the scientific analysis,
not only of physical, but also of psychical existence, should
proceed along atomistic lines if it is to be successful ; but he
believed even more emphatically that the true nature of both
types of existence consists in a non-atomistic unity.

To the present writer these beliefs that the practical utility
of a scientific description is compatible with its theoretical
falsity seem untenable.   The usefulness of a theory or of a
set of ideas normally depends upon the extent to which the
relations between the ideas correspond to the relations between

the facts. The hypothesis that oil or gold lies buried in a certain portion of the earth will be a useful hypothesis provided that it is true ; but if the facts in the case do not correspond to the hypothesis about them, the latter can possess no utility except irrelevantly and by accident. Is it not equally plain that such an assumption as that matter is atomic in structure owes its measure of utility to the measure of truth that it possesses ? How would it be possible for a false representation of a thing to enable us to gain control over it ? Intellectual control depends upon the mind's adjustment to its environment, and such adjustment must consist always in a correspondence between the relations among the mind's ideas and the relations among the environing objects. Hence, although Bergson may be right as to the essentially dynamic nature of reality, there must nevertheless be an aspect of the real corresponding in its structure to the system of static terms and relations which constitute a science. In like manner we may say of the positions of Mr. Bradley and Professor Muensterberg that however intimately the qualities of the real may be united, yet any such super-relational unity must be capable of corresponding to the relations expressed by a system of judgments, at least to the extent that such a system enables an individual to adjust himself successfully to his world.

But apart from the soundness or unsoundness of these objections of the author, the positions which we have been discussing illustrate the possibility, if not the legitimacy, of supplementing a purely pragmatic theory of the function of the intellect by a belief that the nature of reality is such that it can be appreciated only by a more or less mystical act of intuition.

9. *Mysticism and Scepticism.*—The attitudes of the mystic and the sceptic are generally opposed to one another, and the opposition is mainly due to the fact that a principal characteristic of intuition is the feeling of certainty which attends it, while the attitude of the sceptic is by definition one of doubt or uncertainty. In spite of this divergence, however, there are cases in which the two attitudes are combined in one individual. With Cardinal Newman, for example, not only his authoritarianism but also his mysticism served in part as a refuge from intellectual scepticism. The same propositions

which appear certain to intuition may seem to warrant nothing but scepticism from the standpoint of mere reason. Then, too, the attitudes of mysticism and scepticism, when not addressed to the same propositions, are, of course, often present in the same individual with reference to different propositions. The mystic may, for example, possess an intuitive conviction that God exists or that the soul is immortal, and may yet be quite sceptical as to the concrete implications of such beliefs. His intuition may fail to inform him on such matters as God's relation to the world or the soul's relation to the body or the manner of its continuance after death. Such admitted scepticism as to details is by no means incompatible with a mystical feeling of certainty regarding the truth of general propositions. To put the matter in a more commonplace way, mystical assurance in one domain of reality does not preclude sceptical uncertainty in other domains.

10. *Rationalism* and *Empiricism*.—The logical methods of rationalism and empiricism resemble each other in that neither of them is anti-intellectualistic ; and our previous treatment of them will have sufficed to show that not only can they be combined, but that if they are to be productive of any value they must be combined, and combined in such a way as to supplement one another. As Kant put it, " concepts without percepts are empty, and percepts without concepts are blind." Deductive reason needs the concrete particulars of experience as material to work upon ; and conversely, the data revealed by sense would make up a merely disjointed and chaotic manifold unless they were unified and integrated by the relations revealed to reason. A science is perfect in proportion, on the one hand, to the multitude of empirical facts contained under it, and on the other hand, to the degree to which those facts are rationally related and interrelated.

11. *Rationalism and Pragmatism*.—The pragmatist and rationalist are usually enemies. Pragmatism arose largely as a protest against a certain type of rationalism. Fixed rules and laws, which are the breath of life to the rationalist, are anathema to the pragmatist. As we tried to show in our treatment of the latter method, pragmatism in each of its three aspects, as practicalism, as relativism, and as futurism, insists on the concrete as against the abstract ; on the particular as against

the universal; on the temporarily expedient as against the fixed and eternal; on the dynamic as against the static; on novelties of the future as against the fixed custom of the past. Despite these very real and far-reaching oppositions, a union of the two methods has not been found impossible. It is perhaps best exemplified among mathematicians of the type of Poincaré. Poincaré and his school believe that for any given body of facts there exists an indefinitely great multitude of theoretical explanations and unifications, no one of which can claim validity at the expense of the others ; which of them is to be chosen will depend solely upon the pragmatic factor of *convenience*. Shall the scientist, for example, follow Ostwald in dispensing with the atomic theory and in ascribing to a number of irreducibly specific types of energy the same objective reality as to motion, and in ascribing to a number of irreducibly specific or " secondary " qualities the same physical reality as to inertia and shape (which is, as I understand it, the program of the physicists and chemists of the school of *Energetiker*) ? Or shall he, on the other hand, follow the time-honoured custom of treating the world (for purposes of physical and chemical explanation) as composed of a multitude of particles or atoms of matter possessing no qualities other than those of mass and shape, and no other energy than that of actual and potential motion, the other qualities of matter and the other forms of change being regarded, not as objective or physical, but merely as subjective manifestations in consciousness ? To this and to similar questions the rationalist-pragmatist follower of Poincaré would answer that the choice between the two scientific procedures should be determined entirely by considerations of practical convenience. Both theories might conceivably enable us to explain the facts as at present known, and also to predict and therefore control the facts of future experience. In that sense and to that degree both of these rationalizations could without prejudice to one another claim equal objective validity. But it may perfectly well turn out that one system will possess a far greater simplicity and elegance or a far greater practical utility and convenience than the other, and thus prove to be pragmatically superior. This way of treating the methodological problem accords full sway *within* any system to the method of rationalism, while at the same time it allows to the pragmatist full power to choose *which* system is to be employed. In pure mathematics, even more frequently perhaps than in physics and chemistry, do we find this union of the pragmatic and rationalistic methods. It is generally recognized that in such subjects as geometry or algebra or algebra of logic, there are many systems of postulates capable of affording a rationalistic and deductive explanation of the subject-matter under treatment ; and when one set of postulates is preferred to another, the preference is accorded on no higher ground than that of pragmatic convenience.

12. *Rationalism and Scepticism.*—There are two ways in which the methods of rationalism and scepticism may enter into partnership. The first is somewhat similar to the combination of rationalism and pragmatism discussed in the foregoing section. A rationalist may recognize that there are a number of different hypotheses about the world, or about some portion of it, from each of which he can deduce a self-consistent system of propositions that will accord fairly well with the facts. These hypotheses may be such as to preclude the truth of one another, and the sceptical attitude will then be expressed in the inability to choose between them. A student of philosophy, for example, after studying a materialistic system such as that of Herbert Spencer and an idealistic system such as that of Hegel, may feel that each system explains many of the facts of nature ; and that so far as he can see there are no facts that are positively incompatible with either. Yet at the same time he may recognize that both of these systems cannot be true together, and as to which is to be preferred he may feel a complete scepticism.

The second way in which rationalism and scepticism may be combined is exemplified in the systems of those philosophers who call themselves Agnostics as distinguished from Sceptics. Herbert Spencer, for example, expressed complete scepticism as to the nature of that absolute power which he believed to underlie all physical and mental phenomena. But as to the nature of the phenomena themselves and the laws which connect them, he was in no wise a sceptic. He worked out a system which, though it claimed to be empirical, was in fact largely rationalistic, and in which all classes of facts were

P

explained naturalistically and to his own satisfaction. In somewhat the same manner the idealist Kant divided the universe into two realms. One of these was knowable and susceptible of rationalistic explanation. This was the realm of *phenomena*, the realm of actual and possible experience. The other realm consisted of *noumena*, that is, things as they are in themselves apart from their appearance to our senses. Truth in this latter domain is not to be discovered by the intellect ; like the unconditioned and absolute reality of Herbert Spencer's system, noumenal reality is to be classed as unknowable. It is hardly necessary to say that this method of combining a belief in the possibility of explaining the relative,' phenomenal, and superficial aspects of the world, with a disbelief in the possibility of knowing the absolute and fundamental nature of reality, is by no means confined to Spencer and Kant, but is a very natural and customary attitude among philosophers, and one which was made popular in England by Hamilton and Mansell.

13. *Empiricism and Pragmatism.*—In discussing that phase of pragmatism which we named practicalism, we saw that there was one meaning given by the pragmatists to the term " practical " which made their doctrine virtually identical with ordinary empiricism. When the *practical* means only the *concrete and specific* as opposed to the abstract and unexperienceable, then the pragmatist's theory that the truth of a judgment is to be determined by its results for practice means no more than the empiricist's theory that the truth of a judgment is to be determined by its agreement with sense-perception ; the two methods of logic then become virtually identical, and such slight difference as may still separate them will lie in the fact that the pragmatist takes a more prospective attitude than the old-fashioned empiricist, putting more emphasis upon the validation of judgments by their agreement with future experience than by their agreement with the experience of the present and past. I think that those natural scientists who have welcomed the advent of pragmatism in philosophy, and who have hailed it as the method of science itself, understand by it no more than a futuristic and utilitarian empiricism. And the philosophical pragmatists on their side, even when they do not interpret the term practical in the

narrow sense which we have been discussing, feel that their theory of method is nothing more than a reformed empiricism ; an empiricism, that is, in which more justice is done to the practical and purposive function of human judgment, and in which more recognition is accorded to the evolutionary nature of the mind and the world. Then, too, in addition to this quasi-identification of pragmatism and empiricism, there is always possible that combination which is based upon the differentiation of domains of experience which we have noted in the previously treated combinations of methods. That is to say, a man may use the method of humanistic pragmatism to decide questions in the domain of social and individual ethics and at the same time employ the method of ordinary empiricism in the domain of natural science.

14. *Empiricism and Scepticism.*—What was said regarding the combination of rationalism and scepticism will apply equally to the combination of scepticism and empiricism. One may believe that the method of empiricism is adequate to give satisfactory knowledge of the nature of the world up to a certain point and remain a sceptic as regards what lies beyond. Indeed, it is quite customary for empiricists to hold that while we can attain adequate knowledge of the particular facts of nature and of the relations of sequence and co-existence between them, it is for ever impossible to discover the *why* and the *wherefore* of these facts, and that consequently the reality underlying the phenomena of sense-perception is unknowable. Some empiricists would indeed go so far as to maintain that the validity of the empirical method in matters within the field of sense-experience implied the invalidity of that method or of any other to reveal to us the nature of things in themselves.

15. *Pragmatism and Scepticism.*—The possibility of combining pragmatism and scepticism is obvious. To the pragmatist even more than to the empiricist the problems susceptible of solution are felt to be confined to the realm of the concrete and the practical. The questions that lie outside of this realm are often characterized by the pragmatist as artificial or meaningless. The nature of God, the nature of the soul, the origin and destiny of the world, are without interest for the pragmatic philosopher in so far as the different answers that

might be given to such questions could not produce concrete differences in our actions ; and any proposition which is without effect upon human action is regarded by him as lacking a genuine meaning. .Nevertheless, if the pragmatist is pressed sufficiently on such questions as the above, he will usually confess that what he calls the artificiality of the problem is in its turn derived from the impossibility of reaching a solution of it in terms of experience, and in this way he can be forced to admit (though grudgingly and with a good deal of surliness) that his attitude toward the ultimate questions of metaphysics is that of the sceptic. He holds, as we have seen, that the intellect and its categories have arisen out of the exigencies of practical life, and that they have interest and value not in themselves, but as tools or instruments for the furtherance of our interests and for the more efficient control of our environment. But despite this utilitarian theory of the origin and purpose of reason, the pragmatist cannot deny that it is possible for the human mind to formulate questions, the answers to which would not be utilitarian or practical ; and as to such trans-experiential answers he must remain in the same state of doubt as the ordinary sceptic.

We have now considered all the combinations of the theories of logical method taken two at a time, and it may be hoped that the somewhat tediously complete survey will have convinced the reader that the possibility of co-operation between the methods is no less genuine than the differences and antagonisms which were emphasized in the chapters which dealt separately with each. It only remains to be shown how all the methods together are capable of being combined in a synthesis in which their distinctive principles and functions can be preserved intact, but in such a way as to supplement and complete one another.

II

THE FEDERATION OF THE METHODS.

The objects of the universe are usually classified on the basis of their intrinsic properties. Our present interest is, however, not in things as they are in themselves, but rather in things as related to a mind that would know them. From this purely methodological standpoint we shall be justified in making what may seem to be the somewhat arbitrary division of knowable objects into the following five classes or domains :

1. The domain of objects and events that can be experienced only by other minds than our own. 2. The dual domain (A) of ultimate and non-instrumental values, (B) of a supposed ultimate and ineffable truth. 3. The domain of commensurable and abstract relations. 4. The domain of particular facts and concrete relations. 5. The domain of individual and social conduct.

It will be my contention that while all of the logical methods are applicable in some measure to the investigation of each of the above-mentioned domains of reality, there is over and above this general applicability a special applicability of each of the five positive methods (taken in the order in which they have been treated) to each of the five domains (taken in the order just listed) : *viz.*, to the first domain, *authoritarianism* ; to the second domain, *mysticism* ; to the third domain, *rationalism* ; to the fourth domain, *empiricism* ; and to the fifth domain, *pragmatism*. As for the negative method of scepticism, its function is to temper with modesty the otherwise dogmatic confidence of each method in its assigned domain.

1. *Authoritarianism and the first domain.*—It is necessary for an individual to trust other individuals in matters which he cannot investigate for himself ; and unless there is reason to suppose that the witnesses are biased or incompetent, their testimony should be put on a par with his own. The major part of the first domain consists of the past, and in that field the method of authoritarianism must hold a dominant position. It will, to be sure, usually be possible to confirm or refute by the methods of rationalism and empiricism the direct testimony of witnesses—even in the matter of things past and gone—by the indirect evidences contained in facts that are accessible to present observation. And the great monuments of historical scholarship could never have been erected without the use of the strictest scientific procedure. The ultimate premises of the historian must nevertheless rest upon the testimony of

other minds than his own, and it is both justifiable and inevitable that we should give at least provisional credence to all disinterested authorities. Viewed in this manner, the method of authoritarianism can be assigned a permanent and honourable place in the federation of methods.

2. *Mysticism and the second domain.*—The second domain, as we have said, comprises two quite distinct regions. The first of these regions consists of the objects of those evaluative interests and judgments which are *elemental* as distinguished from those which are *composite*. In this region, intuition in the sense of immediate feeling would seem to be not merely the most appropriate faculty, but the only faculty for affording information. We might take as an example of an elemental interest romantic love and the judgment of faith on which it is based. It would surely be a vain and preposterous undertaking to discover one's true sweetheart by accepting the authority of others, by using deductive reasoning and calculation, by cold-blooded empirical analysis of her perceivable qualities, or by considering the extent to which she might be a practical utility. All of these non-mystical methods would doubtless be appropriate in the selection of a business partner, a housekeeper, or even in making a marriage of convenience. But no one either could or would fall in love for any other reason than that the beloved appealed in a direct and unanalysable manner to his heart or his feelings. In other words, the lover as such is and must always remain a mystic. And even in forming the belief on which one bases his choice of a friend, intuition is almost as indispensable as in choosing a sweetheart. True friendship is certainly not based upon either calculation or utility, but upon the direct appeal to our sympathies and affections. The same might be said of objects of art, the primary enjoyment of which is not based upon considerations that are rationally analysable. We do not, it is true, always acknowledge this to ourselves. If someone asks us why we believe Dante to be superior to Shakespeare, or Shaw to George Eliot, we may undertake with a show of sincerity to justify our preference by enumerating the merits of the favoured authors. Such justifications have no more real relevance to our choice, and are no more convincing to others than the ridiculous attempts of the lover to prove by argumentation

the superlative superiority of his mistress's eyebrows. As it is with these higher objects of interest, so is it also with humbler and more material things, such as clothes, games, and food. Why a certain fashion appeals to us ; why certain games are liked and others not ; why shad is so much better than custard— these are things that we know by intuition and by no other method.

The other region of this domain is far more problematic than the one just considered. We described it as the hypothetical realm consisting of the ineffable realities which are regarded as both supersensuous and superrational. It is difficult to discuss the ineffable, because those who have not had the true mystic's experience can know little as to its nature. The mystics themselves claim that their intuitions of the higher truth possess at least as much clearness and certainty as the revelations of reason and sense. How are we, who have not been vouchsafed this nobler sort of intuition, to decide whether the alleged revelations are genuine, or whether they are mere delusions and hallucinations produced by the same kind of purely internal mechanism as that which creates our ordinary dreams ? Our only recourse seems to be to compare with one another the deliverances of the various mystics, and ascertain to what extent they accord with one another and with what we know of reality by non-mystical methods ; but this is a task for which the writer has neither the time nor the ability. One curious and possibly significant point on which almost all of the great mystics seem to agree is that the things of the world, including human minds, are united with one another and with the heart of all things in a kind of unity more intimate and complete than any that is afforded by perception or thought ; and that the experience of appreciating and participating in this transcendent unity is attended by a feeling of peace and joy and illumination that passes all understanding. Yet, with regard to this highest and most characteristic revelation of the mystic, no less than with regard to more concrete and specific experiences of the sort reported by Joan of Arc and John Bunyan, we have no basis for knowing whether they are genuine revelations or whether they are characteristic results of a definite type of mental disease. We may hazard the safe commonplace that " where there is so much smoke there is probably some fire." And with more confidence we may say that although mystical revelations, when they are confined to things which have no bearing upon the world of experience and practical life, are at least harmless, yet, when they are made to yield theoretical deductions and practical consequences which conflict with our ordinary knowledge of life and nature, they may prove exceedingly dangerous checks, both to our intellectual and to our ethical progress. We may make this somewhat vague evaluation of mysticism more concrete by applying it to Christian Science, which is perhaps the most notable contemporary expression of the mystical method.

Christian Science has a positive and a negative teaching. In its positive teaching it instructs us how to improve our mental and physical health by assuming a quasi-mystical attitude of contemplation in which the dominant thought is the primary reality of the ideal good.   In its negative teaching, it bids us abandon scientific methods of restoring health.   Not satisfied with having discovered a new way of combating disease, it insists that we give up the old ways.   The positive part of the doctrine can do no harm and seems in many cases to be definitely productive of a measure of good; but these good results are more than balanced by the stupidity and danger of refusing to avail ourselves of the means of alleviating pain and restoring health which scientific medicine places at our disposal.   In the light of the distinction between " positive " and " negative " mysticism (which we stressed in the chapter dealing with this method) it should be possible to accept the constructive doctrines of any or all of the mind-healers without accepting their destructive and mischievous attacks on other therapeutic methods.

To conclude : Mysticism is and must be pre-eminent in the dual domain of elemental interests and of supersensuous revelation, but the fact that it is the only method primarily applicable to these realms must not be taken to imply that the results attained by it are always valid.   Evaluations based upon sympathy and intuition are often proved to be mistaken, and revelations of the supernatural are by no means a guarantee of their own validity.   The gravest danger of mysticism is, as we have stated, its tendency to transcend the limits of the domain proper to it and thereby place itself in competition with the other methods in matters in which they should have a predominant, if not an exclusive sway. If, however, these qualifications are borne in mind, mysticism may legitimately be assigned a place in the methodological federation.

3. *Rationalism and the third domain.*—The applicability of the method of rationalism to the domain of abstract commensurable relationships was discussed at length in the chapters dealing with rationalism and empiricism. Some relations, notably those of quantity, are capable of being combined in such a way as to yield new relations of the same general type. These chains and systems of relations comprise the science of mathematics, a science whose procedure is governed primarily by rationalistic deduction. The method of rationalism, however, is applicable not only to abstract relationships in isolation, but also to bodies of particular facts in so far as commensurable relations hold between them. In other words, deductive reasoning is of use in applied mathematics and in all concrete sciences to the extent that the material under investigation is susceptible of quantitative treatment.

Yet, like the other methods, rationalism can prove dangerous to the cause of truth when it is applied beyond its own domain ; and for that matter even within its own domain when it refuses the corroborations of empiricism. The chief abuse of this method, as manifested in the history of thought, has consisted in the attempt to substitute *a priori* reasoning for empirical observation ; as when it was argued that the orbits of the planets must be circular rather than elliptical because planetary motions are heavenly motions, and heavenly motions are perfect motions, and perfect motions are circular. The same abuse would be committed if one should wait to investigate empirically the relation between gravitating bodies, or the relation between brain and mind, until one had first reasoned out deductively a satisfactory explanation for such relations. The search for *explanations* is praiseworthy and should be encouraged, but it should never be allowed to stand in the way of the search for *descriptions*. With these provisos, the rationalistic method may be assigned its permanent place in the federation of methods.

4. *Empiricism and the fourth domain.*—The method of empiricism may rightly be regarded as the most widely applicable and reliable of all.   It is the only suitable method for the domain of particular facts and relations, and it is usually susceptible of being applied at least indirectly and as a check in the other domains.   The authoritarian, the mystic, the pragmatist, and above all the rationalist, can well afford to permit their somewhat precarious procedures to be reinforced and corroborated by the superior tests of sense-perception. To empiricism, therefore, belongs the honour of the highest place in the federation.

5. *Pragmatism and the fifth domain.*—It may be remembered that the general outcome of our examination of pragmatism was to the effect that each of the three forms of the pragmatic method, namely, practicalism, relativism, and futurism, is of doubtful validity when applied to inquiries into the nature of the objective facts and relations of the material environment, but that when, as in the Utilitarian ethics, pragmatism is applied to the domain of human action, it is both valid and pre-eminently valuable.   This dual verdict was justified by the contrasting natures of the search for the good and the search for the true.   It was shown that in the search for the true we are concerned with the adjustment and subordination of our ideas and beliefs to the structure of physical nature ; and that to permit our decisions of scientific problems to be controlled by our practical interests or by our emotional fears and aspirations would be fundamentally subversive of scientific truth.   But when, on the other hand, we are interested, not in the theoretical search for the truth, but in the practical achievement of the good, our personal interests are no longer distorting and irrelevant factors, but controlling and essential guides.   For the " good " means that which fulfils any tendency, desire, or capacity ; and its attainment means an aggressive alteration of the environment which should continue until the extra-individual reality has been completely adapted to intra-individual needs.   We have argued that while the attitude of the truth-seeker is and should be cosmo-centric, the attitude of the seeker for good is and should be bio-centric.   The realization of either truth or goodness means the attainment of an equilibrium between the individual and

his environment, but that equilibrium in the case of truth is attained by subordination of the individual to the environment, while in the case of the good it is attained in the converse manner by the subordination of the environment to the individual. Thus, the fixed laws of nature, knowledge of which from the point of view of theoretical inquiry constitutes an end in itself, are from the point of view of moral and practical endeavour to be regarded as instruments to be used by us for the achievement of human good. To repeat what was said above, the pragmatic method is justifiable only in so far as it expresses the attitude of ethical utilitarianism ; the attitude, that is, which looks upon all moral codes from the standpoint of pure expediency, and which recognizes only one unchanging moral law, the law that every person should strive at every moment of his life so to act as to produce an intensive and extensive maximum of well-being for all. This is the categorical imperative of ethical pragmatism. It applies, of course, not only to the control of individual living, but also to the control of the social customs and institutions, political, economic, educational, and religious, which make up the conditions under which our individual lives must be passed. When thus restricted to its own domain, pragmatism may claim a high and permanent place in the final federation of logical methods.

6. *Scepticism in relation to the other methods.*—We can hardly do more in this section than to repeat what was said at the end of the previous chapter. The function of the sceptic is to make us realize that no knowledge attainable by the human mind is absolutely certain. Systems of belief in all of the five domains which we have considered are and must always be open to revision. Even if one and the same judgment could claim the support of the five positive methods, it would acquire thereby, not certainty, but only a high degree of probability.

To retain toward all problems a measure of open-mindedness is as difficult as it is important. We have an almost unconquerable temptation to shun uncertainty, and to commit ourselves definitely either for or against a given proposition, yet it shows at least as much wisdom to suspend judgment when the evidence is insufficient as to hold a definite con-

clusion when the evidence justifies it.   And the former attitude
requires the greater courage.   Most of us would prefer to
decide even a theoretical question by tossing up a penny
rather than to confess our inability to reach a decision.   This
intellectual vanity which fights against scepticism, even when
scepticism is called for by the situation, is reinforced by a
confused identification of theoretical doubt and practical
inaction.   It is often better to run the risk of acting wrongly
than not to act at all ; and people are apt to feel that every
action must presuppose an attitude of certainty.   Such a
feeling is, however, quite erroneous.   As was said above, Mr.
Russell has shown in his criticism of *The Will to Believe* that
we do not need to will ourselves to accept the truth of a theory
in order to try it out.   It is possible to act upon a hypothesis
while clearly realizing that the probabilities against its truth
are even stronger than those in its favour.

There is a further reason why scepticism should be treated
with special respect by the philosopher.   Philosophy itself is
the most uncertain and least successful of all the sciences ;
that is the price it must pay for its lofty and comprehensive
ideal.   And philosophy in the past has often exhibited an
unwillingness to admit the tentative character of its conclusions,
and has attempted to conceal its shortcomings by making the
most extravagant claims for the superiority of its procedure
over the procedure of science.   As men are often humble in
matters where they truly excel, and proud of virtues in which
they are conspicuously lacking, so likewise are they most
prone to take refuge in revelations and claim supernatural
certainty in those of their beliefs which are most open to
honest doubt.   Scepticism is most needed in philosophy just
because philosophers have often shown themselves willing to
court absurdity by boasting of their strength on the very
point in which they are weakest—the point, namely, of the
certainty of their conclusions.   " *A priori* validity " and
" transcendental necessity " are eulogistic descriptions which
philosophers are fond of applying to their own methods.   The
obvious discrepancy between their claim and their accomplishment has resulted in making the layman even more distrustful
of the philosopher than the circumstances need warrant.   If
for the " revealed dogmas " of the theologian and the " trans-

cendental certainties " of the philosophers we could substitute the modest phrase " working hypotheses," a great deal of needless criticism would be obviated ; and even the more extravagant conclusions of those who speculate about the universe would receive a patient and sympathetic hearing.

To sum up : the negative method of scepticism should have a place in the federation along with the five positive methods as a necessary prophylactic for each of them, and as a constant reminder of the limitations of human faculty and the need of tolerance and open-mindedness, especially on the part of philosophers.

Conclusion.

We have now completed the first half of our undertaking, *viz.*, a survey of the branch of methodology comprising the problems of the philosophy of logic. Treating logic, not in the restricted sense of a science consisting of rules for getting valid conclusions by deduction and induction from premises already accepted, but in the broader sense of a philosophical inquiry as to the sources of human belief and the consequent criteria for determining its truth, we outlined six distinct attitudes or theories which have been held with regard to the problem. These theories which we named Authoritarianism, Mysticism, Rationalism, Empiricism, Pragmatism, and Scepticism, were each of them based upon an attempt to extend a definitely given source of knowledge into a controlling method for the determination of truth. These definitely given sources from which the methods severally take their origin are *testimony, intuition, reason, sense-perception, practice,* and *doubt.* We began by considering the theories separately in a manner designed to emphasize their divergencies. And in connection with each we devoted some time to a consideration of both the ontological and the ethical beliefs which were usually affiliated with them. These separate expositions and criticisms were followed by the more comparative and eirenical treatment of the present chapter, in which we have endeavoured to show, I. that, in spite of the divergencies of the various logical theories, they are nevertheless capable, with certain modifications, of being combined with one another in various fields of inquiry; and, II. that the true solution of the methodological problem of logic consists in the federation of all six methods in a harmonious synthesis, in which each of the positive methods is assigned a pre-eminent, though not exclusive, rôle in a given domain of the objects of actual and possible philosophical inquiry.

PART II

WAYS OF INTERPRETING
KNOWLEDGE :
THE THREE METHODS OF
EPISTEMOLOGY

FOREWORD

THE problem to be discussed in Part II under the name of Epistemology originates in the situation that is presented whenever any sort of individual apprehends any sort of object. The chief philosophic question that arises in such a situation is as to *whether or not the object thus apprehended can retain its existence and character apart from its relation to the apprehending subject*. It is obvious that this is a question which cannot be answered by direct experience; for to suppose that the nature and existential status of an unobserved object could be determined by observing it would be self-contradictory. We can only infer the fate of things at times when they are not experienced by studying their character and behaviour at times when they are experienced.

There are four fairly distinct positions that can be taken towards this problem, and they amount to four methods of interpreting the meaning of truth or knowledge. They are: I. The epistemological method of *objectivism* or "naïve realism"; II. the epistemological method of *dualism*, sometimes called "the copy theory of knowledge"; III. the epistemological method of *subjectivism*, sometimes called "idealism"; IV. the epistemological method of *relativism*, regarded by those who accept it as being not so much a positive solution of the episte-mological problem as rather a negative means of evading it altogether. The last-named of these methods of epistemology has been discussed already in our chapter on pragmatism. As was there explained, the close connection between the pragmatist logic with its practicalistic method of attaining and evaluating truth and the pragmatist epistemology with its relativistic method of interpreting the meaning of truth, justified our treating them together. Consequently, in what follows we shall treat the epistemology of relativism only

Q

incidently, and to the extent that it figures in a modified form in the other theories.

The three primary and positive methods of interpreting the relation of objects known to the subject that knows them will be discussed in turn. We shall show that the position of extreme objectivism or realism leads through a succession of seemingly inevitable steps to the position of extreme subjectivism or idealism. And we shall find that the arguments in each case for passing from a more realistic to a more idealistic position are mainly based upon a single great assumption— the assumption, namely, that " (selective) relativity " implies dependence, and that because every known object is (selectively) relative to the knowing subject, therefore it is dependent upon the knowing subject and incapable of existing apart from consciousness.

These separate treatments will be followed by a comparison of the three types of epistemological theory in which the principle of (selective) relativity will be given a new interpretation. And in the light of that new interpretation it will be shown that each of the methods of epistemology can be amended and restated in such a way as to preserve its essential and positive significance, and yet bring it into complete harmony with its rivals.

CHAPTER VIII

THE METHOD OF OBJECTIVISM

THERE are three forms of objectivism or naïve realism which are sufficiently distinct and significant to warrant separate expositions. We may name them :

> I. Extreme or Primitive Objectivism.
> II. Moderate or Common-sense Objectivism.
> III. Relativistic or New Objectivism.

I

EXTREME OR PRIMITIVE OBJECTIVISM.

The method of interpreting the epistemological situation which is the most natural, simple, and primitive is to conceive of every experienced object as existing, and as existing independently of the fact that it is experienced. Just as a chair can stand in the relation of *nearness to* a table without in any way depending for its existence upon that relation, so from this most extreme of realistic standpoints, any object can stand in the relation of *being known by* someone without being in any way affected thereby. " Things are (apart from us) just what they seem (when experienced by us)." This appears to be the standpoint of the child and the savage. The conception that some of the things that we apprehend exist only as and when we apprehend them is a conception that results from a relatively high degree of reflection. And yet long before that reflection is reached, a distinction is made between such manifestly peculiar events as those that appear in dreams and illusions, and the events that figure in waking life as common to many individuals. But the illusory objects, instead of being regarded as *mental* or *subjective*, are considered by primitive realism to be merely queer and unreliable physical existents. The child does not think of dreamland as a place within his head, but as a remote and fantastic realm, somehow cut off from the world of waking life. And as it is with the dreamland of the child, so it is with the ghostland of the savage, which is populated in large measure with the products of his dreams, fancies, and tribal legends.

There comes a time, however, in the life both of the race and of the individual when a more mature and careful comparison of illusory objects with objects of the ordinary kind makes the position of the extreme or primitive form of naïve realism too difficult to retain. The contents of illusory experience are gradually discovered to lack that consistency with one another which is characteristic of non-illusory things, and to change and vary concomitantly with the individuals who experience them.

It is this observed relativity of the unreal object to the conscious subject that leads to the conclusion that the creatures of illusion and error differ from other things in being located exclusively within the mind. This is the second or moderate form of naïve realism, and it constitutes the epistemology of common sense.

II

MODERATE OR COMMON-SENSE OBJECTIVISM.

The common-sense attitude toward the epistemological question seems at first sight to avoid the fantasticalness of savagery and the sophistication of dualistic and subjectivistic philosophy. It regards as merely subjective and exclusively inside the mind all that is unreal, while at the same time all that is physically real is regarded as independent of, or external to, the mind, although directly and immediately present to it.

The all but universal popularity that this theory enjoys is due to the fact that the (selective) relativity to the observer of *unreal* or illusory objects is of great practical importance, and is noted by everybody, while the (selective) relativity to the observer of *real* objects is not practically important, **and** is hardly noted at all. The technical weakness of the common-sense realism consists in the fact that the admittedly real objects of our experience can be shown to be (selectively) relative to the minds that know them, to exactly the same extent as the objects of the most fantastic dreams ; and if (selective) relativity implies subjectivity in the one case it should imply it equally in the other.

The difficulty in maintaining the modified realism of the common-sense epistemology can be perhaps more clearly seen if we take the standpoint of a bystander or external observer who views the knowledge-situation as it appears in relation to a mind other than his own. From this standpoint we find that another person's report of what he experiences does not depend merely or primarily upon the nature of the objects themselves (as we experience them), but upon the position and general condition of the person who makes the report.

To illustrate : If my neighbour and I are both looking at some common physical object, such as a chair or a mountain, and if my neighbour presses his eyeball and reports resulting movements in the object (which to me continues to appear motionless), then I seem forced to believe that the object which he experiences somehow depends upon his action, and therein differs from the object which I experience, and which I assume to be independently real. In short, when my neighbour's experiences of such things as chairs and tables differ from my own (by varying with his position and behaviour), I explain the discrepancy by assuming that the objects of his experiences exist only in his mind and not in the space that surrounds us. Thus there comes to be formed the notion of a realm of " mere ideas " or " states of consciousness " dependent upon the knower and separate from the real objects to which they more or less accurately correspond. These secondary or subjective objects are at first conceived of as residing only in the minds of *others*. We continue to think of ourselves as apprehending the external world directly and truly, even after we discover that our neighbours can apprehend it only indirectly in the form of the subjective effects or images which it produces in them. This naïvely egotistic attitude, however, cannot long endure. The same reasons that made us believe that our neighbours perceived internal reflections or copies of things rather than things themselves will be advanced by *them* as proof that we, too, are cut off from a direct consciousness of anything other than our own mental states.

In this way there arises the second of the main types of epistemology, which we have called " dualism," or " the copy theory of knowledge." According to this theory the things of the world are divided into two mutually exclusive classes : on the one hand, internal or subjective states of mind, directly apprehended ; and on the other hand, external objects, indirectly inferred as the causes of the first class.

But before examining this second epistemological method of interpreting knowledge, we must consider a third form of naïve realism which has been recently proposed as a desperate means of preserving our common sense from the artificialities of dualism and subjectivism.

III

RELATIVISTIC OR NEW OBJECTIVISM.

The theory which we are now to consider is a variant of a general doctrine which we have twice before had occasion to discuss. In the chapter on Scepticism we found the " Physiological Argument " for the sceptic's conclusion opposed by the claim of the " phenomenalist " that reality consists solely of " phenomena," or contents of experience, and that to know how things will *look* and *feel* under all circumstances is to know all that there is to know about them. And again, in considering Pragmatism we discussed under the title of *Relativism* the negative form of epistemology according to which the *true* is identical with the *believed*, and as such is regarded as relative to the apprehending agent, and as consisting of his adjustment to the concrete situation in which he finds himself. Relativistic Objectivism differs from Pragmatic Relativism in restricting the principle of relativity to the domain of perceptual phenomena and refusing to extend it to conceptual relations between those phenomena. Thus it does not, like pragmatism, deny that there is an absolute and objective truth independent of any belief or judgment. It contents itself with holding that the concrete objects of perception owe their nature to the relations in which they stand to the individuals who perceive them.

As to the connection between Relativistic Objectivism and Phenomenalism, it is fair to say that while both theories accept the principle of relativity in the restricted sense just mentioned, *the new objectivism differs from traditional phenomenalism in explaining the relativity of perceptual experience in physical rather than psychical terms.*

In order to make clear this point (which gives relativistic objectivism its chief claim to distinction) let us consider the case of the apparent convergence of the parallel rails of the track as viewed from the rear platform of a train. The primitive or extreme realist would regard this convergence as externally real independently of the observer; the moderate or common-sense realist would not regard the convergence as externally real at all, but as a distorted mental image caused by external parallel rails; the relativistic objectivist, however, would contend that the converging rails were as " physical," " external," and " objective " as the parallel rails themselves; but that each pair of rails is relative to a context rather than independent and absolute. The same rails may in one context be parallel; in another, convergent; in another, perhaps, divergent. The whole situation can, moreover, be explained in terms of purely physical (optical) laws, without invoking any psychic factor or mind. Were a photographic plate put in place of the human eye the result would be analogous, if not identical.

If the opponent of the new objectivism appeals from cases of distorted perspective to cases of dreams and outright hallucinations to prove the unreality (except as conscious states) of the objects of such experiences, the relativist will reply that the situation is still quite within the realm of the physically objective. The brain of a person suffering from a hallucination must be considered in relation not only to the present, but also to those past events of the material world with which it has interacted and which constitute what we call its " memories " or " apperception mass." The unreal objects which appeal to the diseased imagination as external *are* external in that particular and highly complicated system that includes past events together with the present abnormal condition of the patient's blood and nerves. To express the whole view in technical terms we may characterize relativistic objectivism as the theory that relations between two phenomena of experience are never merely *dyadic*, but are always at least *triadic* ; that what appears to be a simple case of A R B [A related in a given way to B] is in reality a case of (A-R-B)-R-C [A related to B with reference to a given context C] ; and an important element in the context C will be the brain of the percipient.

The first difficulty with this position consists in the fact that the diverse appearances of the same thing in different contexts always presuppose a single primary system of events, each of which occupies a single unequivocal position in objective space-time ; and it is by means of this single public and physical system that the variety of private and subjective perspectives can be explained and harmonized. Thus, to return to our illustration of the parallel train-tracks : there are as many degrees of *apparent* or *perspective* convergences of the rails as there are points of observation in a straight line. But despite these variations of perspective, the rails *behave* as if they were parallel, and the whole series of merely perspective convergences can be explained as the simple optical effects upon differently situated recipients which would be produced by a single pair of really parallel rails.

A second objection to the relativistic objectivist is based upon the fact that whether or not we always *ought* to be content with apprehending facts and relations with the qualifying phrase " real for us," or " true in this context," we never are thus content. Unless we are conscious of being deceived, every one of our cognitive assertions—the most immediate perception no less than the most reflective judgment—claims to transcend the context in which it occurs and to confer upon its objects a status of universal and absolute existence. Suppose, for example, that a starving man is suffering added pangs by having the hallucination of a plate of food within his reach, and that a relativistic objectivist tries to comfort him by explaining that the food is perfectly " real " and " objective," and by no means a mere " subjective " conscious state. Our comforter will conclude with the admission that the hallucinatory food exists, to be sure, only in the visual and not in the gustatory or tactual system of physical phenomena. The reply of the starving man to such attempted consolation would, I should imagine, run somewhat as follows : " It is not the mere content as such of my hallucination that plagues me, it is the claim that the visual content makes to be more than merely visually objective that is the cause of my torment. Food that is ' real ' only in the sense of figuring in a hallucinatory context is not *real* at all ; I do not deny that the visual appearance can be explained in physical terms, but that does not in any way alleviate my disappointment in finding that the meaning which it carries with it of being real in the sense of eatable, is invalid or false. In short, the object which I apprehended was not simply *visual food*, but *visual eatable food* ; and *that* object was unreal." [1]

CONCLUSION.

Our exposition and preliminary criticism of the first of the three positive methods of epistemology has included a consideration of each of its three varieties.

We have seen that the extreme or primitive form of the doctrine has the merit of being in accord with our instinctive immediate conviction of the independent reality of every experienced object. It ascribes a status of external existence equally and consistently to the objects of erroneous and of veridical experience. Its weakness lies in its failure to estimate the degree to which and the manner in which the real differs from the unreal, and in its failure to take account of the relativity to the apprehending subject of the contents of dreams and hallucinations and of all illusions and delusions.

The moderate or common-sense form of objectivism was

---

[1] The popular method of disposing of *unreal objects* and of evading their crucial significance for the epistemological problem is to characterize them as "only real objects misplaced," or as " composed of real elements ' only ' wrongly related." This device is, however, misleading and quite without merit. The unreality of a hallucinatory serpent or of a centaur has nothing to do with the sensory elements themselves, but only with their relations, external and internal. The difference between a Shakespearian sonnet and any other combination of the letters of the alphabet, or between a lion and a mouse, is "only " a difference of relation between the same elements. But it is just this *relational ensemble* as such that is in question as real or unreal.

found to be strong where the first form of the theory was weak. Common-sense epistemology clearly recognizes that the objects of illusory experience are (selectively) relative to the knowing subject, and because of this recognition it denies to those objects any locus outside of mind or consciousness. This clears the physical world of the rubbish of dreams and fancies, and marks the difference between maturity and childhood, and between civilization and savagery. The weakness of common sense is, as we might expect, a weakness of theory rather than of practice. If the moderate realist is right in assuming that (selective) relativity to a percipient is in itself a sufficient ground for condemning to a subjective or intra-mental status the unreal objects that are found to be infected with it, then there is no ground left for refuting the epistemologies of either dualism or subjectivism. For the upholders of these methods of interpreting the knowledge relation have no difficulty in demonstrating that the so-called real objects of veridical perception suffer from the same kind of relativity as that which pervades the unreal objects of illusory perception. The plain man is disconcerted and rebellious at the claim that we can never directly experience anything except our own mental states, but he is helpless to combat that claim intellectually.

The third and very recent variety of objectivism attempts to rescue and revive the epistemology of naïve realism first by frankly admitting the relativity to the percipient individual of all perceivable objects, and second by boldly claiming that this relativity, although implying dependence upon the individual, is nevertheless quite compatible with our according a physically objective status to real and unreal objects alike. The new theory is strong in its recognition of the possibility of explaining all error in physical terms, as the result of the relation of objects to a brain rather than to a mere mind or consciousness. But it is weak in that on the one hand it neglects the tremendously important difference between the single inferrible over-individual system of events in which each existent element occupies a determinate position in the spatio-temporal order, while, on the other hand, it fails to note that the plurality of individual perspective-systems of sense-data can be harmonized and explained only by reference to the one primary and public system which they presuppose. Neo-objectivism displays, moreover, a second weakness in failing to recognize that no matter in what sense the private perspective-system of sense-data of a deluded individual may be called " physical " and " externally existent," it is not physical or externally existent in the meaning which the individual has in mind. For, as we have lately pointed out, the erroneousness of an error consists in the fact that the contents of the experience *mean* or *claim* membership not only in the private system of the individual's momentary consciousness, but also in what is felt to be the one real system that is independent of and implied by each and every one of the individual perspectives of sense-data.

The weaknesses successively displayed by the three varieties of Objectivism justify our postponing further discussion of this method of epistemology until we have considered its two great rivals, Dualism and Subjectivism.

CHAPTER IX

THE METHOD OF EPISTEMOLOGICAL DUALISM

THE theory which we are about to discuss is called dualism because it recognizes two separate and distinct orders of existence : (1) the sense-data which are directly and immediately present in our consciousness ; and (2) the external things which can be inferred from those data as their causes. The theory is termed *epistemological* dualism in order to distinguish it from psycho-physical dualism, which is the theory that the body and mind of an individual are different from one another either in essence or in existence, or in both essence and existence. Epistemological dualism has no bearing whatever upon the truth or falsity of psycho-physical dualism. It is concerned not with the relation of mind to body or of ideas to brain processes, but only with the relation of the data of experience to the external objects which are believed to cause those data. Moreover, it asserts nothing one way or the other as to the intrinsic character of either the sense-data or their causes. It contents itself with maintaining that the thing that we perceive is numerically or existentially other than the cause of our perceiving it. As to the intrinsic nature of these percepts and their causes, it is open to the epistemological dualist to believe (1) that both are physical or material in character, in other words, that percepts are nothing more nor less than states of the sense-organs or brain, and hence as truly physical as the air waves or ether waves which cause them—the view maintained by Dr. Thomas Case in his *Physical Realism* ; or (2) he may believe that both percepts and their causes are mental or spiritual in their nature (which is the view set forth by Professor C. A. Strong in the book *Why the Mind Has a Body*) ; or (3) he may believe that the sense-data are mental or spiritual in their nature, and that their causes are material or physical (which is the view usually, though not necessarily held by epistemological dualists) ; or (4) he might believe that *percepts* are physical and their *causes* spiritual or mental. But whichever of these four views is accepted as to the qualitative nature of the immediately given appearances and the mediately inferred agents, the theory of epistemological dualism itself means, we repeat, only that sense-data and their causes, irrespective of their intrinsic natures, are numerically separate, that is, capable of existing independently and varying independently, each of the other.[1]

I

THE ARGUMENTS IN SUPPORT OF EPISTEMOLOGICAL DUALISM.

The theory of epistemological dualism has had a long and honourable history, and though, as we shall see, it is open to certain grave and perhaps unanswerable objections, it still remains the ordinary working attitude both of natural science and of reflective common sense. The triumphant sway of the theory has been due to the same causes to which it owed its origin : 1. The convenient manner in which it deals with the problem of illusion and error. 2. The equally convenient manner in which it deals with the problem of perceptual relativity, that is, the problem that arises from the seeming dependence of sense-data upon the position and general condition of the percipient of those data. 3. The convenient means which it provides for explaining the objective world in terms of pure quantity, thus relegating the whole troublesome mass of specific and incommensurable qualities, such as colours, tones, and odours, to a secondary realm of

---

[1] The reason why I have treated these distinctions at such length is because many writers on the epistemological problem have shown a tendency to treat epistemological dualism as though it were identical with the doctrine that percepts and their causes are qualitatively rather than numerically different, and to assume that a refutation of the theory of a qualitative difference would be equivalent to a refutation of epistemological dualism itself. I have in mind, as particularly open to this charge of mistaking the point at issue, my friends E. B. Holt and W. B. Pitkin in their articles in *The New Realism.*

sense-data or consciousness. Let us consider these matters in turn.

1. *The dualistic explanation of error.*—To the epistemological dualist, sensory consciousness is analogous to a photographic plate or to a mirror, on which is represented or reflected in the form of images the objects and events outside the organism. A mirror and a photographic plate do not always represent accurately the objects which impress them, for the images are the joint product of the objects and the reflecting agent, and as such they may (1) possess qualities which the objects themselves do not possess ; (2) lack qualities which the objects do possess ; (3) embody a spatial and temporal arrangement of relations (that is to say, a perspective) which is different from that possessed by the objects themselves. The dualistic or copy theory of perception thus provides for an explanation of error as due to the distorting influence either of the perceiving mind, or of the medium which intervenes between it and the external causes of its ideas. In other words, our ideas are true when and in so far as they agree with their objective causes. They are false or erroneous when and in so far as they disagree with their objective causes. Columbus believed that land lay to the west of Europe ; the truth of this idea consisted in the fact that it agreed with reality outside his mind. The belief that the earth is flat was an idea that existed in the minds of many persons, and its falsity consisted in the fact that it did not agree with the reality outside their minds. From the point of view of the dualistic theory, all thinkable things can be divided into four classes. First, things that exist both outside and inside the mind : this is the class of *known truths*. Second, things that exist outside individual minds, but are not represented in those minds by ideas : this is the class of *unknown or potential truths*. Third, things that exist only as ideas in the minds of individuals with nothing corresponding to them in external nature : this is the class of *actual errors*. Fourth, things that do not exist either as ideas or as external objects : this is the class of *unknown or potential errors*.

The dualistic theory recognizes two distinct types of error —errors of sense and errors of intellect. An error of sense occurs when the primary effect produced upon the mind fails to correspond with its cause.   For example, when a straight stick is partly immersed in water it produces the appearance of a bent or broken stick.   But the quality of bentness is present only in the percept and not in the stick itself, for it is the composite effect of the waves of light coming to the eye through the media of water and air, combined with those which come through the medium of air alone.

Errors of the second or intellectual type are due to false interpretations and inferences from sense-data which, in themselves, may correspond exactly to their objective causes. If, for example, a person should show me a straight stick and declare that he was about to thrust it partly into the water, and then very quickly, unobserved by me, substitute for it a bent stick that was supposed to be immersed in water, but really was not, I should infer that the cause of my perception was a straight stick, which would be an error.   It often happens, however, that the intellect corrects the errors of sense. Consider once more the case of the bent stick.   Most of us understand the cause of this false sensory appearance, and hence, although the error persists, its power for harm is counteracted by our knowledge of the truth.   Sometimes the habit of correcting false appearances by intelligent reactions becomes so ingrained as to enter into perception itself.   This is illustrated by our acquired, or perhaps congenital, capacity to allow for *perspective*.   If we look at a square table obliquely, although the primary impression is of a rhomboidal form, the table itself appears not rhomboidal, but square.   Or, again, when a person walks away from us, the primary visual impression is of an object decreasing in size, but here, as in the case of perspective, the false sensory appearance is corrected by a kind of inference that enters into the perceptual experience itself, and we perceive, not an object of changing size with constant distance, but an object of constant size with changing distance—which is as it should be.   Thus, we see that the dualistic theory offers a clear and simple explanation of error in its various forms.

2. *The dualistic explanation of the relativity of perception.* —In that portion of Chapter VI in which we discussed the physiological argument for scepticism, we had occasion to analyse the mechanism of the perceptual process, and we saw

that an object, in order to be perceived, must emit some form of energy or motion which traverses the physical medium (ether or air), and arouses a specific type of change in the sense organ. This change is followed by a characteristic neural current, which is transmitted to the higher centres of the brain (where it undergoes more or less modification due to other cerebral conditions), and there produces as its final result a conscious perception, together with an appropriate motor reaction. The mechanism of perception being of this character, it follows that the external object which emits the stimulus is not the proximate determiner of what appears in perception. The only direct and proximate determiner of the perception is the condition finally produced in the brain. What this condition will be is thus determined partly by the nature of the external object from which energy is emitted, and partly by the position and nature of the perceiving brain. We should then expect that our perceptions of a given object would vary not only with the nature of the object, but with our relation to that object. As we approach a mountain from a distance, its changing colour does not correspond to any physical change in the mountain itself. It is determined by changes in the distance between us and the mountain.

The epistemological dualist declares that because of this relativity of perception, we should recognize that the perceived object is inside the organism of the percipient, and that as such it is numerically different from its external cause. *If two things can vary independently of one another, they cannot be numerically identical.* The locus of one is not the locus of the other. We have seen in the case of approaching a mountain that the perceptual distance can vary independently of the mountain itself. It is equally possible to find cases in which objects outside the body can in their turn vary without any corresponding variation in the perception of them. Of the multitude of stars, for example, which we perceive on any clear night, there may well be some that have undergone radical changes, or even ceased to exist several years previous to our perceiving them. And there is nothing in our perception that corresponds to the changes that may have taken place in the stars themselves during the years that have elapsed since the light-waves that are now impressing our eyes started upon their long journey through the ether. Thus, despite the fact that our perceptions are caused by objects outside our bodies, that causal relation is of so indirect a nature as to allow of variation in one of its terms without corresponding variation in the other.

So we see that it is in the matter of relativity as it was in the matter of illusions. The necessity for taking account of the errors of perception and the relativity of perception lead to the formation of the dualistic theory.

3. *The dualistic theory of " secondary qualities."*—The physical objects that figure in our experience possess two distinct kinds of qualities or properties—the quantitative and the non-quantitative. The quantitative qualities comprise number, position, size, shape, duration, mobility, and inertia or mass—in other words, all the forms of spatial, temporal, and spatio-temporal relations. The non-quantitative qualities comprise colour, sound, smell, taste, and the various modes of tactual sensation (with the possible exception of the quality of resistance or force). Between these two sets of qualities there exist three important contrasts, which it is necessary to understand.

In the first place we may remind ourselves of some of the aspects of number and figure which were discussed above in Chapter IV. The quantitative qualities form a continuous and homogeneous series, any one of whose terms can be expressed as a function of any other. For example, the number 10 can be expressed as $7 + 3$, as $\frac{20}{2}$, as the square root of 100, etc. And as with numbers, so with spatial and temporal relations ; each quantity is capable of precise determination by comparison with other quantities of the same kind. The non-quantitative qualities, on the other hand, are discontinuous, heterogeneous, and incommensurable, and therefore no one of them can be expressed as a function of any other. To illustrate : if a child knew the meaning of 3 and of 7, and of the operation of addition, I could make him understand the meaning of 10 by explaining to him that it was $7 + 3$; but if he knew only the colours blue and yellow, I could never, by a comparison of those colours, make him understand the nature of green. Or, again, a person might be perfectly familiar

R

with the fact that heat-qualities and light-qualities give rise to one another, but he would not in the least be able to imagine how or why this transformation took place. But if instead of being concerned with heat and light qualities, he is concerned with long waves and short waves, he is easily able to understand how and why each system can be transformed into the other. In the second place, the quantitative qualities of an object are revealed through many different senses, but most clearly through those of sight and touch, while the non-quantitative qualities of a given kind are revealed only through a single sense. Thus number is revealed through all five of the senses ; position through sight and touch, and to a slight extent through hearing and smell ; shape and motion through sight and touch. But colour is revealed only through sight ; sound only through hearing ; taste, smell, and hardness only through their respective sense-organs of palate, nose, and skin. In the third place, the quantitative qualities of a given object, besides being directly observable, are also capable of being indirectly and experimentally proved to exist by their effect upon other objects ; while the non-quantitative qualities are without ascertainable effects, and their existence can be known only by direct observation.

The three contrasts just described between the two sets of qualities have had an interesting and important influence on the development of scientific methods. During the Middle Ages, when the Aristotelian conception of nature was current, the non-quantitative qualities were regarded as more important than the quantitative. This was probably due to the fact that in our own conscious life they figure more prominently ; and Nature's processes were then regarded as more or less analogous to conscious processes. But with the coming of Galileo, Descartes, and the other founders of modern physics, medieval anthropomorphism gave way to a view of nature which was mechanistic rather than teleological, and quantitative rather than qualitative. From this new stand-point the nature and behaviour of physical objects were conceived as determined, not by internal powers, but by the external or spatial relations obtaining between bodies. Consequently the quantitative properties came to be regarded as all-important or " primary," while the non-quantitative properties were regarded as without effect upon the movements of bodies, and hence as " secondary." The principal justification for this change of attitude consists in the first of the three above-mentioned contrasts between the two kinds of qualities. It is enormously more useful to describe physical facts in terms of commensurable, continuous, and homogeneous quantity than to describe them in terms of the incommensurable, discontinuous, and heterogeneous qualities of the special senses. We have already spoken of the gain in intelligibility that results from a reduction of the change from heat qualities to light qualities to a change from long vibrations to short vibrations. And the same principle is involved in reducing the changes from solid to liquid and liquid to gas, to changes in the spatial structure of a molecular system. To reduce all differences of material condition to differences in mode of motion, or in spatial structure, is analogous to reducing fractions to a common denominator. What was hitherto incommensurable and heterogeneous has become commensurable and homogeneous. Or, to use another figure, we might compare the reduction of quality to quantity in the fields of matter and energy to the introduction of a monetary system in a community which had hitherto conducted the exchange of its goods by methods of direct barter. Various articles of merchandise, such as food, clothes, building materials, etc., become admirably commensurable if a price in currency is attached to each article. The value of each in terms of the others can then be easily ascertained and expressed. The quantitative relations, in terms of which modern science seems to describe all the facts of the physical world, thus fill the rôle of a common denominator or universal medium of exchange. With reference to the second of the differences between primary and secondary qualities, it is easy to see that those properties of a body which are capable of being observed and verified by several senses would furnish an instrument of description greatly superior to any that was based upon a single sense. And thirdly, the possibility of discovering the quantitative properties of bodies indirectly by their effects upon other bodies, makes them definitely preferable, as an instrument of description, to the non-quantitative qualities, which, as we have seen, are without discoverable effects, except those directly produced upon the special sense-organs of the observer.

And now, the reader may ask, admitting that these are three good and valid reasons for the scientist's insistence upon a purely quantitative description of his world, what bearing has all this upon the dualistic theory of knowledge? The answer may be given very simply. From the belief that the non-quantitative qualities of objects are ineffective and useless, it is but a short and tempting step to the belief that they are not really objective attributes at all, but merely subjective effects which are produced upon the mind of the observer, and which exist only therein. The dualistic theory makes this step possible, for, according to that theory, the objects presented in direct perception have their locus within the percipient, and are in no sense numerically identical with their extra-organic causes. Then, too, if the secondary or non-quantitative qualities have ceased to be welcome in the realm of physical causes, they have to be, out of mere decency, as it were, provided for in an asylum, and what more natural than to regard the mind itself as that refuge? Since the secondary qualities are restricted in their effects to the perceiver's own processes, it seems appropriate to think of them as essentially and exclusively mental in their nature, and hence as of interest to psychology rather than to physics.[1]

---

[1] Consider as an illustration of this point the way in which we determine the temperature of a thing. I put my hand in a bowl of water and it feels hot. The hotness, of course, appears as an attribute of the water, but I have no way of expressing accurately the degree of its intensity. I may call it " a little hot," " pretty hot," " very hot," " unbearably hot," etc. This lack of precision is bad enough, but there is another defect in this direct method of measuring temperature which, from the point of view of science, is still worse. If I ask a friend to test the water, he will, as likely as not, give a different estimate of its degree of hotness. There is no way to tell which of us is " right." We cannot even be sure that our words mean the same thing ; for the sensation which he might describe as " very hot," I might, if I experienced it, describe as " pretty hot," and as long as we consider the specific and non-quantitative quality of " hotness," we can do nothing to overcome these difficulties. But suppose that instead of attempting to test the heat of the water by its direct effect upon our sense-organs, we recognize that inasmuch as the secondary quality of hotness can be correlated with, or reduced to, the primary quality of motion (on the part of the molecules of a substance), and thus measured by its effect upon other bodies, it would be both possible and desirable to ascertain the degree of heat by its effect upon the expansion of mercury ; we then put a thermometer in the water and, noting the height at which the column of mercury stands, we secure a perfectly satisfactory measure of the water's temperature. This indirect method of measurement is satisfactory, first because it is

Thus it is that the theory of epistemological dualism comes to be acceptable to the student of natural science because it seems to accord better than either of the other epistemological theories with his well-grounded desire to reduce nature to a purely quantitative system of masses and motions.

II

THE OBJECTIONS TO DUALISM.

There are three principal objections to the dualistic theory of knowledge which, taken together, have sufficed to convince the majority of philosophers of its falsity and of the need of supplanting it by the theory of subjectivism or epistemological idealism. These objections differ in their nature and in their degree of cogency, but their aim is the same, namely, to show that *the assumption of extra-experiential causes for intra-experiential sense-data is both useless and untenable.*

In the opinion of the author, the first of the three objections is quite without weight, the second valid only as against a special form of epistemological dualism, while the third does constitute a complete refutation of the theory, at least as ordinarily presented. Let us consider the three objections in turn.

1. *The objection based on the supposed difficulty of comparing sense-data with their causes.*—The dualist defines truth as a relation of agreement between the terms and relations of his experience and the terms and relations of the causes of his experience. When our ideas copy facts they are true. When they fail to copy facts, or when they are bad copies, they are false. As soon, however, as we ask the natural and inevitable question as to how we are to discover the agreement or disagreement of experienced facts and their unexperienced causes, we are puzzled to find an answer. We can tell whether a photograph is good or bad when and only when we can compare

quantitatively precise, and second, because it is objectively and experimentally verifiable in the sense of being independent of such variable factors as the sensitiveness of the skin of the observer. We are to bear in mind that these advantages are due entirely to *the capacity of the primary or quantitative properties of bodies to produce effects upon other bodies and not merely upon a particular sense-organ.*

it with the original. Seeing them both together, we can judge of their likeness. To use this method for comparing an experience with its cause would, from the dualistic standpoint, be impossible, for the cause of an experience, according to the dualist, lies outside experience.

This objection, however, is not so deadly as it seems. The dualist's contention that the data of his experience are the effects of something beyond his experience is based on the fact that the data of experience do not themselves afford an explanation for their own occurrence and behaviour. Each new sensation is an intruder into the circle of pre-existent sense-data. I am, we will suppose, contemplating a peaceful country scene when an angry shout bursts upon my ears, and a blow falls upon my head. My experience of the moment before contains nothing to account for these rude interruptions, and I am irresistibly reminded that I live in a world that is wider than my experience of it. This wider realm of existence is continuously forcing upon me new experiences, and it is from these new experiences that I infer both the existence and the nature of their causes. For example, when I stand near to a woodchopper I experience the sound of his blows at the same time that I see them. If I walk steadily away from him, the interval of time between the sight of the axe striking the wood and the sound that it makes steadily increases. There is absolutely nothing *in* the perceptual situation to explain this variation *of* it. If, however, I assume that my hearing of the sound is caused by an invisible motion in the air that is transmitted at a fixed rate to my ears from the object heard, and that this rate is very much slower than the rate at which the equally invisible light waves are transmitted, the variation becomes perfectly explained, and explained in such a manner that I am able by means of my conceptual hypotheses of unexperienced air waves and light waves to know exactly what will be the interval between the seeing and the hearing of the same event at any given distance from the place of its occurrence. In short, our conceptual hypotheses can be tested as to their truth or falsity by their success or failure in confirming expectations that are based upon them. Let us take another illustration. It used to be supposed that certain material objects possessed an intrinsic tendency to fly up from the earth into the sky, regardless of the medium of air in which their movement took place. This assumption of positive lightness or anti-gravity was, of course, a pure inference—something conceived and not perceived. It was natural and reasonable to explain our perceptions of the behaviour of experienced objects, such as smoke, by inferring a cause, such as anti-gravity ; and for a limited number of sense-data, and to a limited degree, the hypothesis was confirmed by experience. But when it became possible to observe the behaviour of objects left unsupported in a vacuum, the old hypothesis was proved false because expectations based upon it were not fulfilled ; and the new hypothesis (that all material bodies without exception tend to fall toward the earth unless interfered with by some external force, such as the pressure of air, or water, or other medium) was confirmed. And because the experiential expectations founded upon the new hypothesis of universal gravity are confirmed, we may conclude with a high degree of probability that our ideas on the subject are true ; or, in other words, that they correspond to a reality that causes our sense-impressions. A final illustration of this possibility of testing the agreement of ideas with reality without the latter entering directly into our experience is afforded by the judgments which we make about the thoughts and intentions existing in minds other than our own. I give to a person a letter to be posted. A little later the person assures me that he has posted the letter. From his words and his honest manner of uttering them I infer that there is in his mind a consciousness of having spoken the truth. My idea of what is going on in his mind is an inference, not a perception. There are few who would claim that the existence of the thoughts and feelings of our neighbours can be directly experienced by us as sense-data. We can experience our neighbour's behaviour, but the existence of a consciousness that animates or actuates it can only be inferred. To return to our illustration. If I receive an answer to my letter, my inference as to the consciousness of truth-speaking on the part of the man to whom I entrusted it will be confirmed ; if, on the contrary, I receive no answer to my letter, and discover it lying unposted in the pocket of my faithless messenger, I am justified in concluding that he had in his mind when he told me that he had posted it a thought different from that which his words and behaviour expressed. In either case, the truth of my inference as to the cause of my sense-data is adequately tested without my having had to accomplish the impossible task of directly observing that cause through a telepathic vision of another person's consciousness.

We may conclude that the dualistic theory of knowledge, whatever other defects it may turn out to possess, is not affected by the specious objection that it is impossible for us to discover agreements or disagreements between experiential effects and the extra-experiential causes of those effects. What we cannot directly observe we can indirectly infer.

2. *The objection to the* QUALITATIVE *duality of perceptions and their causes.*—It should be noted that this objection is not properly addressed to the theory of epistemological dualism itself, but rather to that particular form of the theory which natural science adopted when it relegated the secondary qualities of objects to a realm distinct from that of the primary qualities. If all the physical causes of perception are regarded as consisting exclusively of primary qualities, it follows that the secondary qualities, and with them all the objects of sense-perception, must be regarded as non-physical in character ; and hence what began as a mere assumption of numerical duality between sense-data and inferred objects has evolved (or degenerated) into the quite different assumption of a qualitative duality. That this second assumption is not necessarily involved in the first, and that as such it is no essential part of the theory of epistemological dualism, was sufficiently set forth in the opening paragraph of this chapter ; but inasmuch as both assumptions have been adopted by natural scientists in dealing with the problems of secondary qualities, I deem it justifiable to discuss them together.

The crux of the objection consists in the fact that we have no material in terms of which to conceive a physical world supposed to differ in kind from our sense-data, except the material furnished by the sense-data themselves.

So far as I can sée, the only way in which our dualistic scientist can meet this objection is by abandoning his assumption that sense-data are composed of different kinds of stuff from the physical causes of our perception. Would this mean that the secondary qualities would have to be put back into the physical world ? I think that it would. That would not, however, imply any abandonment of the ideal of a purely quantitative and mechanistic explanation of physical processes. When a merchant assigns a monetary value to the various articles which he has for sale, it does not mean that the goods themselves cease to exist as physical and become merely subjective; the prices do not replace the goods, but may merely indicate their positions, as it were, in a common medium of exchange. But though the goods retain all their specific reality, their *movements* in the commercial medium are determined by their *prices*. It is, or should be, much the same with the objects of science. When the physicist expresses red light in terms of a certain number of ether vibrations, violet light in terms of a different number of ether vibrations, and explains the relations and transformations of the two kinds of light in terms of the vibration-rates respectively associated with them, he does not need to assume that the qualities themselves have ceased to be physical and become merely subjective or mental. They can be conveniently ineffective or epiphenomenal without forfeiting their objective status.

By way of conclusion, we may declare that the form of epistemological dualism which asserts that the immediate data of sense differ qualitatively as well as numerically from their inferred causes is by no means necessarily implied by the sound scientific method of *correlating* the secondary or non-quantitative with the primary or quantitative qualities of objects ; and we may further conclude that the assumption of two qualitatively distinct realms—psychical sense-data and physical causes—would seem to be incompatible with the necessity for conceiving the latter in terms of the former.

3. *The objection to the numerical duality of the space and time that is inferred and the space and time that is perceived.* —The objection which we are now to consider applies to the doctrine of epistemological dualism itself, rather than to the extreme form of that doctrine which, as we have just seen, the scientists were tempted to adopt as a means of attaining a purely quantitative explanation of physical nature.

The crux of this third objection consists in the fact that

the only space and time in which the physical causes of sense-data can be located is the space and time of the sense-data themselves. To illustrate : I perceive before me a table. On the basis of the theory of epistemological objectivism, which is the theory of naïve common sense, I would hold that the table that I perceive is numerically one and the same with the physical cause of my perception, in other words, that the sense-data are themselves physical objects enjoying an existence that is independent of their occasional presence in our consciousness ; but on the basis of epistemological dualism, my attitude towards the perceived table is quite different. I recognize that, as an immediate sense-datum, it exists only as a state of myself (regardless of whether I think of " myself " as an immortal soul, or as a merely material organism), and that as such it is incapable of existing independently of my process of perceiving it. But the manner in which this sense-datum intrudes itself upon me makes me realize that it is the effect of a cause external to me. This cause I am tempted to name " the real table " to distinguish it from the internal or perceived table. This " real table " can of course only be inferred, never experienced, because, according to this theory, the self can experience only its own states. The inferred table, then, exists in a space other than the space of the perceived table ; for numerical difference means nothing more than difference of spatio-temporal position. But where can this " real " space be ? The only space I can possibly *conceive* is the space which I *perceive*—the space, that is, in which the perceived table and the other sense-data are located. This perceptual space is, of course, too internal and too subjective for real physical objects to exist in, and so I must look beyond it for a suitable place in which to conceive my inferred table as located. The trouble is, however, that I cannot look beyond perceptual space ; I cannot possibly *conceive* of any space external to (in the. sense of discontinuous with) the space that I perceive. The space that I experience contains my body, the earth on which I stand, and the farthest stars revealed by the telescope. The epistemological dualist tells me that it is pre-empted by mere sense-data, and hence not good enough, *i.e.* not external enough, for a real table to exist in. But be it good or bad, it is the only space that I can attach any possible meaning to, and if the physical table does not exist there, there is no conceivable "where" for it to be in ; in short, the dualist's conception of an inferred space lying beyond perceived space has turned out to be utterly meaningless.

Exactly the same fatal difficulty will be found with the epistemological dualist's conception of real time. To illustrate : I remember that five minutes ago I sharpened my pencil. My memory is a present fact. It has for its object or content certain of the vague and flickering visual qualities which were more vividly and definitely present in the original perceptual experience, and in addition to these sensory characters the memory-content possesses a group of relational and meaningful elements which are hard to describe more specifically, but which constitute the object before my mind when I have the memory-experience of sharpening the pencil. This content that is present to my mind is the sense-datum. According to the dualistic theory, it is a present state of myself, numerically separated by a five-minute interval of time from the real event of the sharpening of the pencil. That is to say, my memory image exists now ; the sharpening of the pencil existed five minutes ago, and the latter is not known to me directly, but is inferred as the (temporally) external cause of the present sense-datum. This real external event must exist in a time other than that of the memory image or percept, according to the dualistic theory ; but the question arises as to what time is conceivable other than the time in which my sense-data are located. I have a vague but unmistakable apprehension of the five-minute interval of time (if it were a five-second interval, it would figure quite clearly in my consciousness), and I cannot possibly attach any meaning to a real five minutes or to a real time that is outside of or disconnected with the time which I perceive. Even if instead of five minutes ago I should think of five thousand years ago, the concept would have no possible meaning unless it were regarded as a member of the same temporal series as that of my present perceptions. In short, the dualistic notion of an inferred time outside of or beyond perceived time turns out to be without meaning, and we are driven to admit that *the time as well as the space in which the physical causes of our sense-data are supposed to exist can be no other than the time and space of the sense-data themselves.* And as the only way in which the causes of what we remember could be numerically different from the sense-data of memory, would be by their location in a time other than that of perception, it follows that the attempt of epistemological dualism to maintain a numerical separateness of sense-data and their causes fails completely.

The three objections to epistemological dualism which we have discussed have led to the abandonment of that theory, at least on the part of some philosophers, and to the adoption of a third interpretation of the knowledge relation which is usually known as " idealism," but which we shall call by the less eulogistic and less ambiguous name of " subjectivism." To the examination of this theory we must now proceed.

CHAPTER X

THE METHOD OF SUBJECTIVISM

THE theory of Subjectivism or Epistemological Idealism can be defined as the belief that objects, particularly material objects, cannot exist independently of a consciousness of them, and that therefore all reality consists exclusively of conscious being and its states. Before considering the strong and weak points of the principal forms of subjectivism, the whole subject may be brought into a clearer light if we trace in a manner partly logical and partly historical the successive applications of the subjectivistic principle from that first stage in which only the unreal and illusory objects are made dependent upon consciousness to the culminating stage of solipsism, according to which the entire universe is unreal apart from one's own experience.

I

THE FIRST STAGE OF SUBJECTIVISM: THE SUBJECTIVITY OF UNREAL OBJECTS.

The manner in which the first stage of subjectivism arose has already been set forth in the chapter on objectivism. Of the various objects of experience, all of which, to the naïve mind, appear to exist independently of the observing consciousness, the first to be deprived by philosophic reflection of their independence and assigned a purely subjective status are those which occur in perceptual and conceptual *error*. We see, for example, a person approaching us who at a distance appears to be an acquaintance. Upon a nearer view our supposed acquaintance turns out to be a stranger. The object of our earlier experience was our friend John Smith, in a given place at a given time ; the object of our later experience is another person, occupying the place and time which we falsely had assigned to Smith. The later experience is regarded as more reliable than the earlier, and there appears no way in which to make the earlier and less reliable experience compatible with the other, except to regard the object of the earlier experience as existent only in our consciousness. Or again, while suffering from a fever I perceive a serpent coiled on the foot of my bed. My nurse assures me that no such object is there, my friends confirm her statement, and I myself, by placing my hand in the space in which the serpent appears, fail to receive those tactual sensations which are the usual result of handling serpents. The easy and natural way to reconcile the visual serpent of my earlier experience with the absence of anything serpentine in the broader experience of my friends and in my own more reliable tactual experience, is to regard the serpent, in spite of its objective appearance, as a thing having no existence in the space outside my organism—as being, in short, nothing more than a subjective state of my own consciousness.

As it is with the perceptual errors of waking life, so also is it with the more thoroughgoing illusions of sleep. For the very primitive epistemology of the child and the savage Dreamland is objectively existent. But the fact that different dreams conflict with one another as well as with the experiences of waking life soon makes it necessary to abandon the interpretation of dreams as excursions into a mystic and shadowy realm that is somehow sundered from the everyday world. And because the objects of the dream, like those of an ordinary illusion, seem to vary directly with, and therefore to depend upon, the self that perceives them, we soon find ourselves compelled to regard them as existing only in our consciousness.

The objects of conceptual error share the same fate as those of perceptual error. The gods inhabiting Mount Olympus and all the other hypothetical objects with which man in his ignorance supplements and explains the experienced world are, as soon as their unreality is realized, relegated to the purely subjective realm of conscious states. And thus the mind in addition to its own proper activities of thinking, feeling, and willing, comes to be credited with the function of serving as a vast dumping ground for all the unrealities of life. The self is no longer thought of as merely the perceiving agent, the focus and centre of the system of real relations between the organism and its environment, but also as the mysterious container of all such objects as are incapable of finding a place in the self-consistent world of reality.

II

THE SECOND STAGE OF SUBJECTIVISM : THE SUBJECTIVITY OF SENSE-DATA, OR IMMEDIATELY PERCEIVED OBJECTS.

The nature of the second stage in the process of transferring externally existent objects to the internal realm of subjective states of consciousness has been sufficiently discussed in the chapter dealing with the theory of epistemological dualism. We need only repeat here that the principal reason for regarding sense-data as subjective, and for leaving to the world of external existence only such objects as can be inferred as the extra-experiential causes of experience is the same as that which led to the subjectivizing of dreams—the reason, namely, that *which objects we are at any moment to perceive* is found to depend directly and primarily upon the conditions of our own organism, and only indirectly and secondarily upon the things outside of our organism. Thus, from our present standpoint, the theory of epistemological dualism in its purest and simplest form appears as the second stage in the evolution of subjectivism.

III

THE THIRD STAGE OF SUBJECTIVISM : THE SUBJECTIVITY OF THE SECONDARY QUALITIES.

The matter here under consideration, like that of the preceding section, was discussed in the chapter on epistemological dualism. We saw there that the scientists, in their natural enthusiasm for building up a purely quantitative explanation of the physical world, had yielded to the temptation of reducing all the non-quantitative qualities of objects to conscious states which are produced in the perceiver by outside causes in no way resembling them. We need repeat here neither the reasons which made this step appear advisable, nor the objections which can be brought against it. It will be sufficient to recall that as the second stage of subjectivism characterized the earlier and purer form of epistemological dualism, so this third stage of subjectivism characterizes the more radical and thoroughgoing form of the dualistic theory.

IV

THE FOURTH STAGE OF SUBJECTIVISM : THE SUBJECTIVITY OF
THE PRIMARY QUALITIES.

It is at the fourth stage in its development that subjectivism becomes acute and distinctive. The world of the epistemological dualist is left behind and in place of the two realms—subjective sense-data on the one hand, and their physical and objective causes on the other—we now have *all* the facts of existence reduced to a single domain composed solely of conscious beings and their states or ideas. This is subjectivism proper : a theory which recognizes no reality outside of experience. What the dualistic scientist describes as a system of independent material objects is conceived by the subjectivist as a system of more or less fixed and regular relations between certain states of consciousness. The states of consciousness which the subjectivist puts in the place of physical objects form a special class, more or less clearly marked off from the rest of our conscious states. These "physical" states or experiences are differentiated from the others by being apparently common to many minds, by being, that is to say, public or shareable experiences. Thus the tables and chairs, the mountains and stars which I *perceive*, together with the atoms, electrons, and ether which I *conceive*, appear to be possessed in common by my own mind and by the minds of my neighbours. And though they may have **no**

existence outside of conscious experience, they can be clearly
distinguished from such things as pains and pleasures, hatreds
and ambitions, which are the private and exclusive possession
of each individual.   These latter private experiences are called
" psychical," to distinguish them from those that are public
or physical ; though of course, strictly speaking, the subjectivist must regard all experiences, or at least all perceptual
experiences, as private.   In the view of the subjectivist, the
table that I experience is not and cannot be numerically
identical with the table that you experience, just because his
central contention is that no one can experience any other
objects than his own states.   The states of different persons
could no more be identical with one another than could the
persons themselves.   But although the table that I see cannot
from the standpoint of subjectivism be numerically identical
with the table that you see, yet the two tables, because they
occupy analogous positions and fulfil analogous functions in
their respective systems of experience, will be regarded as
identical, and can be treated as such.   With things like toothaches and aspirations, however, it is quite different.   You
and I may chance to suffer simultaneously from toothaches
of equal intensity, but we should never think of regarding
these contents of experience as identical.   My toothache will
not occupy a position in my field of experience analogous to
the position which your toothache occupies in yours ; the
two toothaches will exhibit dissimilar concomitant variations.
Your toothache may suddenly take a turn for the worse,
mine remaining unchanged ; whereas, if we are both experiencing what we call the " same " table, any change in the
content of my experience, such as the overturning of the table,
will be accompanied by a quite analogous and corresponding
change in the content of your experience.   It is by considerations such as these that the subjectivist justifies his claim that
without transgressing his self-imposed limitation of a world
consisting exclusively of conscious beings and their experiences,
he may yet adequately distinguish between the two realms of
physical and psychical objects.

   And now that we have seen something of the general
characteristics of this fourth or definitive stage of subjectivism,
we may consider the reasons which have led many philosophers

s

to adopt this theory in place of the epistemological dualism which was its parent.

The principal reason for the adoption of the new theory was indeed no other than that which had led to the substitution of epistemological dualism for objectivism. That reason, it will be remembered, lay in the increasing awareness of the (selective) relativity of experienced objects to the person experiencing them. Illusions and hallucinations were relegated to the subjective realm because they appeared to depend upon the self or subject, rather than upon objects external to him. While again the motive for relegating sense-data or perceptual objects to a subjective status lay in the fact that the more we knew about the physical and physiological mechanism of perception, the more we recognized that what we are to perceive at any moment will be determined directly and primarily by the processes occurring in our organisms. And it was this same factor of (selective) relativity that influenced scientists to regard the secondary qualities as merely subjective states of consciousness. Whether an object is to appear green or red, hot or cold, deep-toned or shrill-toned, may depend indirectly upon causes outside the percipient organism, but the direct and proximate determiners of such experiences consist entirely of the brain-states of the perceiver. In view of all these considerations, it was small wonder that the brilliant Bishop Berkeley should have conceived the idea of applying the test of relativity to the primary or quantitative properties of objects which made up all that Locke had left of the external material world. He showed quite conclusively that our perceptions of the sizes, shapes, and distances of objects, together with their hardness and softness, their heaviness and lightness, depended primarily upon the conditions of the perceiving self. *The quantitative properties of things are as truly (selectively) relative to the subject as are the non-quantitative properties, and if Berkeley's predecessors had reasoned correctly in concluding that (selective) relativity implied subjectivity, they would have been logically bound to extend their principle to all the contents of experience.* The conclusion seemed unavoidable, but it was none the less disconcerting and startling in the extreme, for it carried with it a denial of the independent existence of the material world. Henceforth, all material objects, such as atoms and ether, and even the brain itself, would on this basis be relegated to the same kind of purely subjective existence as that of the secondary qualities. When confronted with the objection that such a view is preposterous in that it would reduce the solid earth to the stuff that dreams are made of, Berkeley has a ready answer. Our ideas or states of consciousness are, he tells us, of two classes. The first of these, caused by something beyond ourselves, constitutes the physical order of nature ; the members of the second, which not only exist within our minds, but also originate from our mental activity, are what we call psychical. These latter ideas are the private and exclusive possession of each self and lack the regularity and community which are characteristic of the first or "physical" set of ideas. Inasmuch as the only kind of causal agency of which we have any experience is the power of our own conscious wills, we must assume that the cause of our physical ideas is a conscious will like our own, but infinitely wiser and more powerful. This all-wise and omnipotent Being is God ; and for Berkeley the world consists of a system of finite conscious beings, together with one infinite conscious being who continuously, according to his own immutable Laws, creates those " physical " experiences which we describe as the material world, and which we wrongly suppose to have an existence independent of consciousness. So much for the answer which Berkeley made to those who objected that his theory of subjectivism failed to do justice to the obvious distinction between physical objects and human dreams and fancies.

There is, however, a second objection to Berkeley's subjectivism which cannot be answered so easily. The epistemological dualist claims that the simplest and most probable causes of our sense-data are objects which resemble the sense data at least with respect to the primary qualities. He holds that it is far simpler to infer an independent material chair as the cause of our experience of a chair than to infer an infinite spirit as its cause. In general, causes are found to resemble their effects except in so far as the medium through which they have worked may have modified their influence. Why then should we not suppose that there is the same degree of similarity between our sense-data and their causes as there is between the reflections in a glass or a pool and the objects which cause those reflections ?   To this objection of the dualist Berkeley gives three answers.

In the first place, as we have already noted, he claims that the only cause known to us is conscious will, and hence that it is a conscious will other than our own rather than an independent world of matter which must be assumed as the cause of our sense-data.   The difficulty with this answer is that it is, at best, only partly borne out by the facts.   Granted that in every case of our own activity we can discover an element which we call " will " or " effort," yet it is equally true that along with this factor of effort there is a second factor of quality or form that is required to determine the character of the effect.   Mere will or conscious force by itself would be indeterminate.   The most that the dualist would need to grant to Berkeley would be the assumption that some power analogous to that of our own will must be assumed to be present in the material bodies from which our sense-data are derived.

In the second place, the Berkeleyan answers the dualist's objection to his position by the claim that since all sensory qualities are immediately perceived states of our consciousness as the dualist himself admits, those same qualities are thereby debarred from being also present in objects outside our consciousness.   The claim is, in other words, that if a quality modifies a state of consciousness it cannot modify anything that is not a state of consciousness, which is as though one were to say that if an image in a pool is admitted to have a certain colour and shape, it will be impossible that the object which causes that image should have the same or a similar colour and shape.   But nothing is more common than to find the same qualities existing in objects which are numerically different.   Why then should one hold that if the quality of yellow, for example, is admitted to be at the moment when we perceive it a state of our consciousness, it thereby becomes disqualified to be a quality of an object outside our consciousness ?   When put in these terms, the fallacy is obvious.   It has been well named by Professor Perry of Harvard the " fallacy of exclusive particularity."   We may say then that the second answer of the subjectivist to the dualist's objection is entirely sophistic and wholly lacking in validity. There is no reason at all why the same set of qualities should not be exemplified in subjective states of consciousness and also in an independent material world inferred as the most probable cause of those states of consciousness. A sensation, like anything else, can have a cause which resembles it in quality.

In the third place, Berkeley gives an answer to the dualist's objection which, in the opinion of the writer, is far more forceful than either of the two answers already discussed. Berkeley and his followers appear to believe that the alleged independent material objects of the dualist would at best be meaningless, because there would be, so to speak, *no place to put them*. In this they would seem to be right, since, as we have already said in our criticism of dualism, the space and time of our sense-data are the only space and time to which we can attach definite meaning.[1] The subjectivist is then on firm ground when he insists, in opposition to the dualist, that the only spatial and temporal world in which either common sense or science can have an interest is that in which experienced objects have their locus. Beyond that world we cannot go. Inference and conception can amplify and re-arrange the realm of sense-data, but they can never transcend it. Such conceptual objects as atoms and ether are either mere formulæ for the shorthand description of the course of experience, or else potential sense-data having the same kind and degree of existence as the percepts which they are assumed to explain. In other words, the atoms and electrons, if they exist at all, must exist in the same space and time as the colours, sounds, tables, chairs, and stars which figure as objects of our perceptual experience.

This last and successful answer of the subjectivist to the dualist appears to justify the former in his claim to have finally disposed of the notion of a material world existing

---

[1] Of course, this should not be understood as precluding the possibility of conceptual constructions such as the non-Euclidian spaces, or spaces of four or more dimensions. We are under no obligation to conceive of the relation of unreal spaces to the space of our own sense-data. If they have no existential status, internal self-consistency is their only requirement. In this respect they resemble the space and time in which the events of a novel or drama are imagined to have occurred, and are in no sense comparable to that space beyond the space of our sense-data in which the epistemological dualist locates his hypothetical causes of the objects which we perceive.

beyond and behind the world which we experience. And
inasmuch as both subjectivist and dualist are already in
agreement (as against the objectivist) that the objects of
direct experience are states of consciousness, and therefore
incapable of existing apart from consciousness, the outcome
of the discussion may be said to be a vindication of the claim
of subjectivism that the entire world consists only of conscious
beings and their ideas.

V

THE FIFTH STAGE OF SUBJECTIVISM : THE SUBJECTIVITY OF
SPACE AND TIME AND OF THE CATEGORIES AND LAWS
OF NATURE.

From the discussion in the preceding section of the degree
of subjectivism represented by Berkeley and his followers,
it might seem as though there were no further steps possible
in the process of transforming the supposedly independent
and objective world into a world that is subjective and
dependent upon consciousness.   Such a conclusion, however,
would be quite erroneous.   Berkeley and the British subjectivists were careful to insist that their doctrine of *esse est
percipi* applied only to the individual *facts* or *terms* of experience, and not to the *laws* or *relations* that unite them.   The
order of nature, that is to say, the sequences, co-existences,
and causal and logical relations of the facts of experience to
one another, they regarded as independent of the minds which
experience them.   For example, the event described as
putting-wood-in-fire and the event described as smoke-and-
ashes are each of them states of consciousness, but the relation
of invariable sequence, according to which the second event
follows upon the first, is not a mere state of consciousness,
and its existence is in no way dependent upon its being
experienced.   According to Berkeley, the *routine* in which our
ideas are given to us by God is not itself an idea.   If an
individual should by any chance, through shortness of memory
or other disability, fail to notice the relation of sequence
between his experience of a piece of wood being put in the

fire and his experience of the smoke and ashes which follow, the fact of sequence would be none the less real. In order to make clear the nature of this exception to his theory of subjectivism, Berkeley advocated the use of the word " notion " as a name for that kind of knowing which did not involve the reduction of the object known to a state of the subject knowing it. Every cognition of particular physical objects Berkeley called an *idea*, meaning that the object as cognized exists only as a state of mind. But the cognition or knowledge which I may have of minds other than my own, or of the relations between my ideas, constitutes a *notion* ; and such notional knowledge, as we have just said, is held by Berkeley to be compatible with the independent existence of the things known.

If we omit from consideration the somewhat peculiar position of David Hume with regard to this problem, it is to the philosophy of Immanuel Kant and his followers that we must look to find the next advance in the evolution of subjectivism. Kant begins where Berkeley leaves off. He undertakes to show, in his famous work, *The Critique of Pure Reason*, that not only the terms and elements of our world are subjective, but that all the forms and relations of those elements, or at least all which are susceptible of being reduced to *a priori* and necessary knowledge, are subjective also. In other words, according to Kant, the mind imposes its own forms of synthesis upon the unorganized and unrelated sensations which it receives from an unknown and unknowable source termed by him the " thing-in-itself." These forms and relations imposed by the mind upon its sensory material are divided by Kant into three groups, each group being ascribed to a distinct faculty of the ego. The first set of forms consist of space and time ; they are ascribed to the faculty of Sensibility. The second set are called by Kant " categories " ; they are twelve in number, and comprise such fundamental forms of relationship in the world of experience as unity and plurality, the degrees of quantity, substance and attribute, cause and effect, possibility, actuality, and necessity. The faculty to which these categories are assigned is called by Kant Understanding. The third set of synthetic forms are named " ideas." Their faculty is Reason. They are three in number, and represent the three senses in which the actual and possible objects of experience are regarded as woven together in such wise as to make up a completed totality or universe. In virtue of its possession of these three sets of synthetic forms, the human mind may be regarded as a " Legislator for Nature." For the laws of Nature are nothing other than laws of Mind writ large, as it were, and projected outward into a world which is apparently quite independent of the consciousness which informs it. Thus, when the scientist marvels over the unities and harmonies which geometry and mechanics reveal to him, he is but discovering in objective form the unities and harmonies of his own subjective nature. This is the view of the world known as Transcendental Idealism. Kant delighted to refer to it as the Copernican Revolution of Philosophy, for he believed that the change from the old view of the mind as a passive recipient of Nature's laws to the new view, according to which Nature derives its laws from the mind, was analogous in its revolutionary character to the change wrought by Copernicus in substituting the sun for the earth as centre of the planetary system.

Our purpose is not primarily historical ; hence we shall not attempt any detailed analysis of the extraordinary innovation in philosophical thinking proposed by Kant, nor can we enumerate the many arguments adduced by him in support of the various parts of his doctrine. We must, however, devote some attention to the more important arguments for transcendental idealism, and especially to those arguments which by their application of the principle that (selective) relativity implies subjectivity, constitute a logical continuation of the reasoning which had governed the development of subjectivism throughout its earlier and pre-Kantian stages. Even this meagre undertaking will be complicated by the fact that Kant's arguments for the subjectivity of the forms and laws of Nature vary somewhat, according to which of the three sets of laws he is considering. Inasmuch as his treatment of the subjectivity of space and time is both the clearest and, in our opinion, the most fundamental part of his transcendentalism, we shall follow it in preference to what appears to be the more involved and less essential discussion of the " categories " and the " ideas." Space and time are indeed the underlying bases of all physical relations, and if they can be proved to have no existence except as forms of our consciousness, the relegation to a subjective status of the other laws and relations of nature would follow more or less as a matter of course. There are four major arguments for the subjectivity of space and time, and we shall consider them in succession.

1. *The arguments from " adhesion " and " antecession."*— These arguments (the titles of which we borrow from *The Elements of Metaphysics* by the German philosopher and Orientalist, Paul Deussen) are so nearly identical in character that they may be treated together as constituting the first of the four principal proofs of Kantian idealism. It is possible, so the argument runs, to imagine the non-existence of all the bodies in space and of all the events in time, but it is impossible to imagine the non-existence of space and time themselves. We can no more escape in our thought from space and time than the bird can fly away from its own wings. The only explanation for this phenomenon is that space and time are as truly parts of our consciousness as the bird's wings are parts of his body and conditions of his movement. Were space and time independent of our consciousness, it would be possible for us to think of their absence or non-existence ; the fact that they " adhere " to the mind is proof of their subjectivity. The argument from " antecession " is quite similar to the above. We cannot conceive bodies to exist, except in a space antecedently provided for them. In other words, space is perceived to be logically and ontologically prior to the bodies that occupy it. And in the same way time must be conceived as real antecedently to the events that occur in it. Nothing could happen unless there was a time provided for it to happen in. In short, bodies and events cannot be conceived apart from or independently of the space and time which they respectively occupy ; but space and time can and must be conceived as independent of and prior to their occupants.

The foregoing arguments can be criticized briefly as follows : The difficulty of imagining the non-existence of space and time, and of imagining bodies and events apart from space and time, might, it is true, be due to the fact that space and time were forms of the mind, but it might equally be due to the fact that space and time are in themselves fundamental forms of being and pre-conditions of objects and events. The fact that we cannot think of redness without colour, and that we can think of colour without redness, does not prove that colour is more subjective than redness, but only that, like any other genus, it is logically prior to and implied by its species. If space and time were, as Newton and Spinoza believed, the most fundamental conditions of existence, it would be impossible for us to " think them away " or to imagine their destruction (adhesion), and equally impossible for us to avoid thinking of them as pre-conditions of bodies and events (antecession). There is at least one other thing which we are still less able to escape from in our thinking than from space and time, but which would not be regarded as therefore subjective, at least by Kant. This inescapable, yet not subjective, entity is *Being* itself which is presupposed by everything else. In short, the inescapability of an aspect of experience would seem to be no proper guarantee of its exclusively subjective status ; and the mere fact that space and time were in truth more fundamental than the objects in them, would in itself constitute a more natural explanation of their being experienced as fundamental than would the Kantian assumption that they are forms of the mind.

2. *The argument from a priority and necessity.*—This is the argument which seems to be favoured most by Kant himself. Our reasonings about the properties of space and time, and also about the causal law and kindred postulates of mechanics, possess a certainty and a necessity that in Kant's opinion can be explained only by the assumption that space and time and the underlying categories of mechanics are forms of the mind. How could we be so certain that every event must have a cause, that material substance can be neither created nor annihilated, that the sum of the angles of the triangle are equal to two right angles, that time can never run backwards, and that it is impossible to go from Tuesday to Thursday except by way of Wednesday, unless causality, substantiality, space and time were parts of the mind's own nature ? To know a thing with certainty we must create it, or be it. If, and only if, space, time, and the categories were forms of our own thought, could we possess that *a priori*

certainty independent of all experience which characterizes our reasonings on these subjects. I have an absolute assurance that if I could travel beyond the frontiers of the visible universe the triangles and circles that I should encounter in those unexperienced regions would have exactly the same properties as are possessed by the triangles and circles here at home. Kant feels it to be almost self-evident that the conclusion to be drawn from our arrogant but justifiable confidence in such matters is that triangles and circles are special modes of those rules of synthesis which must be applied to any sensory material before it can appear as a perceptual object of experience.

Two kinds of answer may be given to the above argument. With John Stuart Mill, we might challenge the assertion that mathematical conclusions were known to be true beyond all peradventure. Is it, after all, not open to doubt that the triangles beyond the Milky Way are different in their properties from those with which we are familiar ? As this line of opposition to Kant's transcendentalism appears to me more specious than convincing, I will not pursue it, but will turn at once to the second possible answer to the " argument from necessity." We may admit Kant's assumption of the *a priori* validity of mathematical reasoning, but deny that this implies the subjectivity of mathematical material. We may hold that the reason for the certainty of geometry and kindred sciences lies in the fact that the material dealt with is so simple and abstract, that it is easily possible to distinguish, in the case of a triangle, for example, the generic from the specific and individual characters, so that we may see at a glance that such a property as the equality of the sum of the angles to two right angles is not due to the peculiarities of the individual triangle used by the geometer in his demonstration, but only to the generic characters which any figure must possess if it is entitled to be called a triangle. Thus the necessary and *a priori* aspect of pure and applied mathematics is given a suitable explanation by appealing to the nature of the subject-matter, and not by what appears to Kant's opponents as a purely irrelevant appeal to the nature of the thinking process. Even supposing space and time to be forms of the mind, it would not follow that they were objects capable of being known *a priori*. No one, not even the Objectivist, would deny that thinking, feeling, and willing are processes inseparable from consciousness, and yet the science of psychology which deals with those processes is very far from possessing the clearness and necessity of mathematics. In short, our answer to the Kantian argument that would make necessity and *a priority* in a given field of investigation imply the subjectivity of that field is essentially the same as our answer to the first argument, in which the antecedence or primacy of space and time was made the basis for inferring their subjectivity; namely, that all such characteristics of the subject-matter of a science are to be explained by the nature of the subject-matter itself, and not by the quite irrelevant consideration of the relation in which that subject-matter stands to the mind that investigates it. In short, no light is cast upon the objects of thought by a study of the processes of thought.

3. *The indirect argument from the antinomies of space and time.*—This argument differs from the two preceding in that it does not content itself with merely proving that space and time are subjective, but undertakes to show further that they cannot be objective. The first and second arguments, even if their validity were granted, would not be incompatible with the assumption that space and time were objective as well as subjective, forms of things as well as forms of thought. But in the present argument Kant undertakes to demonstrate that if space and time were supposed to be independent of consciousness, they would have to be either finite or infinite ; and inasmuch as their *finitude* is made impossible by the necessity which we are under of passing in thought and imagination beyond any assignable limit of space or time, and inasmuch as their *infinitude* is made impossible by our realization that a completed or actually existent infinite would be self-contradictory, as it would imply the completion of what by definition is incompletable, it therefore follows that the initial assumption of the objective reality of space and time is untenable. It will be noted that this argument is the type known as the *reductio ad absurdum* ; it disproves a proposition by showing that the conclusions that would follow from it are false.

We have not space to give an adequate answer to the ingenious reasoning of Kant concerning the alleged antinomies

relating to space and time. We can only state very briefly
the grounds on which we feel justified in rejecting that part
of the proof which attempts to show that an objectively
existent infinite is self-contradictory. We agree with Kant
in his contention that space and time cannot be finite, but we
refuse to accept as valid his disproof of their infinity. It is
alleged that the infinite cannot exist, because existence means
completedness, and an infinite series is a series that cannot be
completed. Our answer is that the impossibility of completing
an infinite is contingent upon our having only a finite time in
which to accomplish that task. I could never count or enumerate an infinite number because I have only a finite number
of moments at my disposal. Suppose, however, that I could
command an infinite number of moments. It would then be
possible for me to complete the enumeration of an infinite
series; if all finite series of events or objects could be
enumerated in finite numbers of moments, then an infinite
series of moments would have to afford the possibility of
enumerating an infinite multitude of events or objects. In
fact, we would urge here against Kant the same point which
in Chapter VI, on Scepticism, we urged against Zeno. Zeno,
it will be remembered, had argued that Achilles could never
catch the tortoise because in order to do so he would have to
traverse an infinite number of space intervals, and we contended
that there would be no difficulty in his doing this if he were
provided with an infinite number of time intervals in which
to do it. In other words, the apparent difficulty depends on
a failure to realize that time is as infinitely divisible as space.
There are as many successions in a second as there are extensions
in an inch, and the one infinity perfectly suffices as an antidote
and offset to the other. When the Kantian bids us imagine
an actual infinity of space stretching before us, we have, it is
true, a feeling of the impossibility of accepting his challenge,
but the feeling of impossibility is not due at all to the character
of infinite space, but rather to the fact that we can only build
up by finite stages the magnitude which we are trying to
imagine. Whether we take as our unit a mile or a trillion
miles, our attempt to envisage the infinite will consist of a
number of acts in which we add our chosen units to one
another ; and as the number of acts is finite (being limited,

indeed, by our resistance to the fatigue and monotony attendant upon such a process), and as the units added are also finite, we find ourselves defeated. We cannot reach the infinite, and therefore we say the infinite cannot exist. It is as though we were challenged to conceive of the number 2 as being equal to the sum of the series $1 + \frac{1}{2} + \frac{1}{4} + \frac{1}{8} \ldots$, and we should strive desperately to reach the end of this series, and failing in our attempt should turn petulant and deny that 2 was the sum of the series, or even that it existed at all. Our failure would quite obviously be due to the defect in our method of counting by finite steps and would indicate nothing as to the non-existence of the goal of our journey. The difficulty which Kant felt in conceiving the infinite time which must have elapsed up to the present moment can be explained in the same way. Suppose that we are in agreement with Kant as to the impossibility of a finite origin of time and accept his challenge to imagine an infinite past. We start counting backwards in imagination, selecting any unit, such as a day, or a trillion years ; we heap these units upon one another until we are weary, and then find ourselves no nearer to our infinitely remote goal than when we started. As in the case of space, we overlook the fatal finitude in our method of travelling into the past, and attribute the failure of our journey to the non-existence of its goal—in short, we seem driven to deny the existence of an infinite past time. So far as I can see, all the contradictions and difficulties which have been alleged by Kant and others to permeate and vitiate the objectively existent infinite, are traceable to the defect of finitude in our mental processes and to nothing else whatsoever. If, instead of vainly and foolishly trying to reach the infinite by taking a finite number of finite steps, we scrutinize the concept itself, resolutely overlooking the abyss by which it is separated from us, our reason will disclose nothing that is logically repugnant or in any way incompatible with the existence of infinite space and time. In view of these considerations we must reject as invalid the third Kantian proof for transcendental idealism.

4. *The argument from* (*selective*) *relativity.*—We come now to that argument which, though, so far as I know, it is nowhere explicitly stated by Kant, is yet more or less implicit in all

his reasonings, and which is but a further and consistent application of the principle underlying all forms and degrees of subjectivism.   Let us state it once more : *Which objects a conscious self will experience will be determined primarily and directly by the nature and condition of that conscious self, and only secondarily and indirectly by whatever may exist outside of the self.* This principle of (selective) relativity was used, as we have seen, first by reflective common sense to prove the subjectivity of those unreal objects and situations which figure as the content of illusory or erroneous experience ; and, secondly, by the conservative epistemological dualist to prove the subjectivity of sense-data and of all things that enter into direct perception ;   thirdly, by the radical epistemological dualist to prove the subjectivity of the secondary qualities ; fourthly, by the Berkeleyan idealist to prove the subjectivity of the primary qualities ; and now, fifthly, it is used by the Kantian or transcendental idealist to prove the subjectivity of the categories, relations, and laws of nature. If we are to accept the validity of the principle in its applications to the first four stages of subjectivism, I can see no reason for denying its valid application to the fifth stage, which is the one under discussion.

When we look out upon nature and observe the web of relations uniting the objects of our experience into a system, it is difficult for us to realize that our experience has for its necessary condition not only the reception by the self of a multitude of separate sensory shocks conveyed to us by means of the various sense-organs and nerve-fibres, but also the interconnection of the sensory elements into an orderly and unified system ; and yet this latter condition, according to which the conscious self or its organism transforms the manifold of sensations into a world of law and order, is in reality more important than the first condition of mere sensibility. To do justice to Kant, and to get any sympathetic understanding of his theory, we must realize that before the world of objects can be perceived or conceived it must in some sense have passed through the mill of human faculty, and to that extent must be regarded as a function of sensations built up and unified by the experiencing self. No element or relation in the most abstract conceptual system but what has been derived from the synthesis of sensations, and unless we are willing to question the principle of (selective) relativity itself we must follow Kant to the extent of admitting that the relations or laws that hold between the objects of actual and possible perception are functional relata of the forms and relations imposed by mind upon our sensations. In other words, the human mind is, as Kant claimed, the law-giver to nature; and should there exist in a supposedly independent world a fact or law which was incompatible with the structure of the mind, and therefore incapable of being assimilated by the mind, it could never figure in any way as an object in the world of our experience. Or to put the matter in another way : If we are loath to admit that man creates that world of which he himself appears to constitute so small a part, we must at least admit that before he can either perceive it or conceive it he must *re-create* it out of the sensations which he receives. And yet, when all justice has been done to Kant's " Copernican Revolution," we cannot avoid feeling that something is gravely wrong, and that the position into which we have been led by apparently unanswerable reasoning is paradoxical. For the world which we are alleged to have created out of our sensations is the world of which we ourselves are the products ; and the laws which we are alleged to impose upon nature are laws to which our own actions are subject. Man is born at a certain place, his life is lived in a certain determinate portion of space and time, his death occurs at a definite place and at a definite moment. His powers of thought, like the rest of his faculties, develop according to spatial and temporal conditions, and are themselves capable of being explained by the law of causality and by the other less fundamental laws which pervade the objects of his experience. It is considerations such as these that make it difficult to accept the Kantian claim that man is a law-giver to that world in which he lives and moves and has his being.

The Kantian subjectivist is, however, fully aware of the paradoxical appearance of his doctrine, and he attempts to remove it by inventing the conception of the " transcendental self." It is not, he tells us, the finite and ordinarily recognized mind of an individual which is the legislator for nature, but rather that unrecognized deeper self in each of us which does not figure as an object in the world at all. This deeper, or transcendental, self is spaceless and timeless, as it would have to be if space and time are themselves only its forms of synthesis; and for the same reason that it is free from the limitations of space and time it is free also from the dominion of the categories by which it organizes its system of objects. Among the phenomenal objects which the transcendental ego produces out of the raw material of its sensations is the phenomenal duplicate of itself. The empirical self is frankly recognized by Kant to be subject to the same limitations of space and time and the same natural laws as any other object. It is, as it were, the incarnation in the world of experience of that transcendent entity which is the ground and condition of all experience. Of the intrinsic nature of this deeper self we can know no more than we know of the source of the sensations which it receives. Its nature is revealed to us only in so far as it is related to the world of experience. We know it, that is to say, as the possessor of the forms of synthesis by means of which our experience is formed and organized.

We cannot discuss at any length the merits of Kant's theory of the transcendental self, but there are two points to which we would call attention. First, we should note that there runs through the development of subjectivism a law of compensation or conservation in accordance with which the *losses sustained by the objective world in the process of its subjectivization are offset by corresponding gains in the nature of the mind or self.* When, for example, the objective world was deprived of the contents of hallucination and error, there was no place in which the plunder could be put except in the percipient self. In the same way, when sense-data, the secondary qualities, and the primary qualities were successively removed from the objective world, they were of necessity bestowed upon the mind. And, finally, when, under the Kantian Criticism, space and time and the formal laws of nature are deemed unworthy of objective existence, they, too, must perforce go to the enrichment of the self. Thus the epistemological situation, which at its commencement contained a self conceived as virtually without content (all content being ascribed to the objective factor), has been transformed into a situation in which the self is regarded as possessing almost all [1] the contents of experience, and the independent object as possessing almost nothing. Kant's invention of the transcendental self was nothing more than the logically necessary consequence of applying the subjectivistic principle to the realm of nature's laws.

The second point which we wish to make with regard to Kant's transcendental self has to do with the complete lack of experiential grounds for its postulation. The supposition that each of us possesses as the core of his nature a wonderful timeless and spaceless ego is necessitated by the dialectic of subjectivism, but by nothing else whatsoever. We may look into our own natures as carefully and as sympathetically as we choose without discovering anything other than the more or less helpless and commonplace self with which we are familiar. We may speculate as to whether this self is a product and outcome of the perishable body which it appears to inhabit, or whether it is the expression of an immaterial agent or soul, capable of existing apart from the body. But scrutinize it as we may, we cannot, I repeat, discover anything about it which could lead to the assumption that we are outside and above the space and time in which we live. It is only after we have first convinced ourselves, because of the (selective) relativity of objects to our consciousness, that therefore our consciousness must in some sense be the container and author of those objects, that we are tempted, and indeed compelled, to the flattering inference that we possess that deeper and transcendental ego which imposes laws upon nature.

VI

The Sixth Stage of Subjectivism: the Subjectivity of the Ground of Our Sensations, and the Reduction of the Many Transcendental Selves to One Absolute Self.

The transcendental idealism of Kant made no attempt to reduce the cause or ground of our sensations to a subjective

---

[1] That is to say, all but the external ground for the manifold of sense. It is the contingency of the latter which convinces Kant that it does not originate from the self.

status of dependence upon the self, nor did it ever deny that the transcendental selves were independent of one another. It remained for Kant's successors to apply the argument from (selective) relativity to prove : (1) that the deeper or transcendental selves in each of us are identical and constitute one universal and absolute self ; (2) that this single cosmic self is the ground of the existence and material of our sensations as well as of the forms and relations by means of which our experience is organized. We shall not concern ourselves with the intricate history of the transition from Kantian transcendental idealism to post-Kantian absolute idealism, nor with the differences between the intellectualistic interpretation of the absolute self, favoured by Fichte and Hegel, and the voluntaristic interpretation set forth by Schelling and Schopenhauer. It will suffice for our present purpose to show how the fifth stage of subjectivism must inevitably develop into the sixth or present stage if the principle that " (selective) relativity implies subjectivity " is consistently carried out.

The Post-Kantian subjectivist can call attention to the fact that my notion of another mind will be determined both in its general form and in all its details by the kind of mental processes which I have at the time when I entertain the notion. These modifications of myself may in their turn be caused by something external to me, but they themselves are the direct and primary determiners of what my thinking is to be about. As they change, the objects of my thought will change ; and this is true quite irrespective of whether those objects are bodies or other minds. Hence, if I am going to take seriously the great principle of subjectivism—that relativity to the thinker implies the subjectivity of the objects of his thought —I must hold that what I call the minds of other people are merely states of my own mind, and that the entire universe, in so far as it is thinkable for me, is an inseparable state of myself.

This startling conclusion can be temporarily robbed of its absurdity if we distinguish between two meanings of the term " myself." The *I* upon which the universe depends for its meaning and existence is the infinite and absolute self ; the *I* which writes these words is a finite and fragmentary self. " Myself " in the second sense of the term is but an insignificant part or aspect of myself in the first sense.

It will be remembered that this device of distinguishing two meanings of the self was used by Kant in developing his doctrine of transcendentalism. The self that is a " legislator for nature " imposes the forms of its thinking upon the raw material presented in sensation, and by so doing builds up the world of organized experience in which my finite or empirical self (both mind and body) exists as an object along with the minds and bodies of my neighbours.

Yet in spite of its similarity to Kantianism as respects the doctrine of the two selves, the stage of subjectivism which we are considering differs in two respects from the Kantian theory : (1) the many transcendental selves are replaced by one Absolute Self ; and (2) because of this unification it becomes possible to dispense with Kant's hypothesis of an unknowable X as the material source of sensations. The Absolute Ego which is my own deepest self suffices as the ground, not only of the form, but of the matter of experience, and the process of subjectivizing the universe appears complete.

VII

THE SEVENTH STAGE OF SUBJECTIVISM : THE SUBJECTIVITY OF THE ABSOLUTE SUBJECT.

There is, however, a final and disconcerting stage in the development of this line of thought of which we must now take account. We have already seen that according to subjectivism all objects of experience or knowledge are to be regarded as states of the experient or knower. Now, to a consistent subjectivist the alleged " absolute " must share the universal fate and be likewise denied independent existence. Thus the entire world of objects, including the minds of other persons, which for the sixth or penultimate stage of subjectivism was regarded as constituting the experience of an absolute self, is, by the relentless dialectic of subjectivism, itself reduced to the status of dependence on the finite self. This seventh and last stage of the subjectivistic epistemology is known as " solipsism." The doctrine in its pure form has probably never been held by any school of philosophers. Indeed, one can easily imagine the difficulty of a situation in which two solipsists should happen to meet and the sheepish manner in which, by averting their eyes, they would endeavour to escape the mutual refutation which their co-presence in the world would involve. Solipsism, however, in spite of its non-acceptance, is worthy of our serious consideration for two reasons : (1) It is by taking account of this final and complete form of subjectivism that we can best understand the nature and significance of the entire tendency ; (2) only after boldly facing this acute or solipsistic stage of subjectivism can we effectually guard against the lesser but more insidious forms of the doctrine.

Let us begin by noting that solipsism, carried out consistently, reduces our past self to the status of any other object. At any given moment it is the self of that moment that does the knowing and to which all things are (selectively) relative. The *I* on which the universe depends is the *I* of the present moment ; not the self for whose welfare I strive, but a mere mathematical point which for some reason the universe must accept as its centre of reference. There is no object conceivable that is not (selectively) relative to (and therefore—according to the principle of subjectivism—dependent upon) the one who conceives it at the time he conceives it. This is solipsism proper, or, as we might call it, *super-solipsism*. Just as the kind of (selective) relativity which the experience of objects displays, and on which the subjectivist must base his case, is not a relatedness to consciousness in general, but to some *particular* consciousness, and just as it is to *my* particular consciousness rather than to some other which I must primarily relate the universe, so also is it my conscious self at some particular moment—*viz.* the *present* moment—rather than at some future or past moment in relation to which my universe must be known. It is not only my self *here*, but it is also myself *now* that must figure as the primary subjective pole of my perceptual and conceptual experience. Any device that would release the universe from its bond of dependence upon the *now when* it is known would also release it from the *here where* it is known. Either the knower here and now can know what is other than and independent of himself, both locally and temporally, or he cannot know what is other than or independent of himself, either temporally *or* locally. The doctrine of super-solipsism is an absurdity, but it is an absurdity that is forced upon us if we admit the cardinal principle that (selective) relativity implies subjectivity.

Our exposition of subjectivism is now completed ; we have followed the theory through its seven principal stages, beginning with the seemingly reasonable doctrine of the dependence of the unreal objects of thought upon the thinking subject, and ending with the seemingly paradoxical doctrine of the dependence of all objects, real and unreal, minds and bodies, upon the self of the moment. We have sometimes paused in our exposition to consider the strong and weak points of a particular form of subjectivism, but we are postponing to the next chapter the question as to the validity of the assumption underlying all forms of subjectivist doctrine—the assumption, namely, that (*Selective*) *Relativity implies Subjectivity*. It has been by extending this principle with increasing consistency to class after class of the objects of perceptual and conceptual experience that the subjectivist has progressed from the first to the seventh stage of his theory.

CHAPTER XI

A REINTERPRETATION AND RECONCILIA-
TION OF THE THREE METHODS OF
EPISTEMOLOGY

It will be remembered that we began our treatment of the epistemological problem by distinguishing three types of theory—Objectivism, Dualism, and Subjectivism. These theories have been successively examined in the three preceding chapters ; our exposition has, however, been somewhat complicated by the fact that when we came to the third theory we found that from the standpoint of its dialectical and historical development the first two theories could be exhibited as stages or degrees of Subjectivism itself. Thus the standpoint of Extreme Objectivism (according to which all objects of experience are viewed as existing independently of our consciousness of them) reappeared as the starting-point or " Zero Stage of Subjectivism " ; while the less primitive Common-sense form of Objectivism (which accorded independent existence to all objects except those of illusion and error) reappeared in what we labelled the " First Stage of Subjectivism." In the same way the two forms of Epistemological Dualism (the first of which accorded independence to all the qualities of immediate experience, and the second to the primary or quantitative qualities only, when considered as the inferred causes of the immediately experienced objects) reappeared under the heads of the Second and Third Stages of Subjectivism. The four remaining degrees of Subjectivism exhibited the progress of the subjectivistic principle from the stage at which the world of merely material objects had been reduced to dependence upon conscious selves to the final or climactic stage of solipsism, according to which the entire universe is only the experience of a single self. From the

standpoint of the attempt which we are about to undertake—
the reconciliation of the epistemological methods—we shall do
well to neglect these finer shades of doctrine and return to
the basic three-fold division of epistemological theory
into :

I. Pure Objectivism, according to which all objects of
experience have a physical existence independent of consciousness.

II. Pure Dualism, according to which all immediately
experienced objects are dependent upon the self, and exist
solely in its consciousness, while at the same time all the truly
inferred causes of these sense-data are independent of them,
and exist solely in a world outside and beyond them.

III. Pure Subjectivism, according to which all objects—
both immediate and inferred—depend upon the self, and exist
solely within its experience.

I shall try to show that each of the three theories in its
original or "naïve" form can be condensed into two propositions ; that in each case one member of the pair of
propositions can be proved false and the other proved true ;
that the true propositions constitute adequate definitions of
what may be called " Critical Objectivism," " Critical Dualism,"
and " Critical Subjectivism " ; and that these theories, unlike
the "naïve" doctrines from which they were derived, can
be combined to form a complete and self-consistent solution
of the epistemological problem.

I

THE RE-INTERPRETATION OF OBJECTIVISM.

The objectivist holds that *all the objects which are experienced
exist physically or externally and are independent of mind.* I
contend that this doctrine is properly analysable into the
following pair of propositions :

1. All experienced objects have an independent meaning
or essence that gives them a status of *possible* physical existence.

2. All perceptually experienced objects (sense-data) enjoy
a status of *actual* physical existence.

Let us examine these propositions in turn.

1. *The truth of the first proposition of Objectivism.*—When a sphere appears at a given distance in front of our eyes, under normal conditions, no stereoscopic apparatus being present, it can usually be demonstrated by experiment that there is a real sphere in the same place as the apparent sphere. Or to put the same thought in other words : Under ordinary conditions the space that appears to be filled with a sphere also behaves as if it were filled with a sphere ; it connects up with all the objects experienced by our other senses, by our neighbours, and by ourselves at other times and from other positions ; and in each of these varying contexts it functions as a sphere ; and so finally the assumption that it is in reality what it appears to be in experience becomes overwhelmingly probable, because that assumption is the only presupposition that we can use to explain and reconcile the various groups of perceptions. In these cases of true perception the perceived object and the object whose existence we finally verify turn out to be one and the same, for they occupy the same position in the single spatio-temporal system which all our experiences imply, and to which, as its functions, they are all referred. The objectivist is therefore abundantly justified in that part of his first proposition in which he declares that an object of immediate experience may also be externally existent to the percipient.

Before concluding our examination of the first of the two propositions which define objectivism, there is a final point that we must consider, which bears equally upon all experienced objects, whether existent or non-existent. In the case of the stereoscope, in which an unreal sphere appears in experience, and in the case of normal vision, in which the sphere that appeared was real, we must recognize that, quite apart from the question of its status as an independent *existent*, the object experienced possessed in each case the status of an independent *logical entity*. So far as its qualities, nature, or meaning were concerned, it was something more than a mere *state* of the perceiver ; its character or " essence " was independent alike of the fact that it was experienced and of the fact that it was existent or non-existent. There is always a sense in which the logical meaning of an object is independent of its actual presence in a context. For example, we do not know whether "inhabitant of Mars" is a real or an unreal object, nor do we know whether anyone will ever have that object as the content either of an illusory or of a veridical perception; we do know, however, that what we now mean by the words "inhabitant of Mars" will in any eventuality remain the same. It is important to keep in mind this sense in which all objects, even those which are found to be illusory or unreal, enjoy an independent logical meaning or "subsistence," which makes them something more than mere inner states of consciousness; otherwise we shall be constantly confusing questions of psychology, which deal with the processes by which we experience things, with questions as to the nature of the things themselves. A psychologist, for example, might furnish a magnificently adequate explanation of why I happened to refer to the question as to whether Mars was inhabited, or of why a drunken sailor sees a sea-serpent, or of why a child understands that 5 and 7 make 12. But if we were interested in learning whether any of these propositions were true, we should wait to consult the astronomers or aviators of the future as to Mars, inquire of the marine zoologists as to the sea-serpent, and harken to arithmeticians in the matter of true and false numerical relations; we should not trouble the psychologist with any of these questions.

2. *The falsity of the second proposition of Objectivism.*— The statement that all experienced objects enjoy a status of actual physical existence cannot be defended without giving to the term "existence" a strained and unprofitable meaning. What it is to "exist" has been variously defined, but the definitions differ more in form than in substance. Perhaps the most natural of them is the following : To be real, or to exist, is to have a position in space or time, or to be implied as a condition of such positionality. Thus, to say that a body existed *nowhere*, or that an event had at *no time* occurred, would be exactly equivalent to saying that the body or the event referred to was non-existent or unreal. The reason that space and time themselves, together with the relations and laws which connect the concretely existing things, are also held to be real or existent is because (though

lacking position) they are logically implied or presupposed by the things that do occupy positions.[1]

Another definition of existence which has much to commend it is suggested by Professor Marvin in his book *A First Course in Metaphysics* (p. 40). According to this author, the existent is constituted of all the entities (terms or relations) which are implied or presupposed by whatever is experienced. Inasmuch as in every case the necessary presuppositions of a field of experience are found to be a system of entities, perceptual or conceptual, occupying positions in the unitary space and time in which we live, this second definition turns out to be identical in substance and meaning with the definition first given.

And now that we have a clear meaning for the term existence we may proceed at once to our question as to whether or not naïve objectivism is correct in claiming an actual existential status for every experienced object.

A. Let us begin by considering the objects experienced in dreams. While asleep in my bed at home in New York I have a clear experience of myself with a company of friends, some of whom are dead, taking a midday luncheon in San Francisco. I see and hear my friends; I see, smell, and taste the food. What must I say, on my awakening, as to the reality of the events of my dream? Of course I can say that the episode was "real for me," but that means only that I actually had the experience. As a matter of fact, I have never lunched anywhere with the friends who figured in my dream. The dreamed-of luncheon has no position in that spatio-temporal series of events. It is therefore non-existent, unreal, or, in Mr. Marvin's terminology, the luncheon is not one of the events that are presuppositions of the experience of myself and my friends; it is in fact actually incompatible with those presuppositions, and is therefore barred from the world of existence. But because it is unreal, it by no means follows that it is unexplained. I can explain my dream in terms of my waking experience, though I cannot

---

[1] In view of the universal and persistent usage of common sense, according to which " reality " and " existence " are treated as synonyms, it seems to me inadvisable to differentiate between them, as some authors have done, by restricting the term " existence " to the concrete things which alone can be said to occupy positions.

explain my waking experience in terms of my dream, otherwise I should have no means of knowing which was which. My San Francisco party becomes perfectly intelligible—that is, compatible with my total field of experience—when and only when I deprive it of the existence which it laid claim to, and relegate it to the status of an object experienced by me as the effect of various memories and desires, but in itself lacking membership in the world of spatio-temporal occurrences which are implied as the causes and presuppositions of our experience. All that is necessary for a person in bed in New York to get the experience of lunching in San Francisco is to have produced in his brain by causes within his organism the same sort of effects that would ordinarily be produced by the external causality of a luncheon in San Francisco.

B. Let us turn now from dreamed-of objects to the illusions of waking life n rder to test further the naïve objectivist's claim that all experienced objects exist externally to the observer. Consider, for example, the following typical case of an illusory experience : I perceive a sphere in front of me ; it turns out, however, that the space where the sphere appears is empty. This illusory appearance of a sphere where in reality there is no sphere is explained by the existence of two flat discs which, by means of a stereoscope, are made to stimulate my eyes separately, the left disc casting its image on my left eye, the right disc casting its image on my right eye. The physiological effect of the separate sets of light waves from the two flat discs, acting upon my brain, is the same as that normally produced by the light waves from a single sphere, and consequently the object which figures in my consciousness is the single sphere. In this case, as in the case of the dream, the object perceived cannot be said to exist in any sense in which it is profitable to use that term. The sphere is not real, but an appearance ; the discs are real, though they do not appear.

Our re-examination of epistemological objectivism is now complete. We have found that the second of the two propositions into which the theory resolved itself is false, and that the first proposition is true. The doctrine is wrong in claiming an *actual* external existence for every experienced object, but it is right in holding to a *possible* external existence for such objects, and in maintaining that, as the presupposition of this possibility of independent existence, all the objects of experience have a nature or meaning that is independent of their presence in anybody's experience. To this status of logical independence, which is a status above existence, and which does not pre-judge it either positively or negatively, we gave the name " subsistence."

II

THE RE-INTERPRETATION OF SUBJECTIVISM.

" Pure Subjectivism " is the theory that all objects, whether directly perceived or indirectly inferred, are relative to the self and contained within its experience, and that consequently they are incapable of existing independently of it or externally to it. Now, it is our contention that here, as in the case of the opposite theory of Objectivism, the defining statement is really composed of two propositions, one of which is true and the other false. In this case, as in the preceding one, we shall find it convenient to take up the true proposition first. Taking them in this order, our two propositions are as follows :

1. All entities are (selectively) relative to a self and *possible* objects of its experience.

2. All entities are (constitutively) relative to, or dependent upon, a self, and cannot exist except as *actual* objects of its experience.

1. *The truth of the first proposition of Subjectivism.*—In order to test the truth of the first statement, let us consider several kinds of objects which might seem to be in no wise relative to a conscious self or capable of being objects of its possible experience.

Take first the case of *imperceptible objects*, such as chemical atoms. An atom, asserted to be less than one billionth of the smallest visible particle, is postulated because the assumption of it appears as the simplest and most intellectually useful explanation of the behaviour of bodies in chemical combination. But because an atom is imperceptible, it need not be supposed to possess qualities other than those of perceptual experience. Size, weight, mobility, elasticity are all qualities of experience, and they are all attributed to the atom, which is imperceptible only because of its minuteness. 'Moreover, even that minuteness is indirectly expressible in terms of perception by a sort of " rule of three " process. For example, we might be able to say that an atom is as much smaller than a flea, as a flea is smaller than the visible expanse of the heavens. Such considerations can make us understand that the imperceptibility of conceptual entities like molecules and atoms is accidental rather than intrinsic ; and that, in the event of our senses being sufficiently acute, they would reveal these supposedly purely conceptual elements of physics and chemistry to be integral and homogeneous members of the perceptual world.

Let us consider secondly *remote objects*—temporally remote, such as the events on the earth prior to the appearance of conscious life, or spatially remote, such as the structure of a distant star. It is easy to see that these objects of scientific inference, which serve to explain the objects of actual experience, are, like the atoms, describable in terms of perception. When we say that the earth was at one time—or that a distant star is at the present time—a molten or a gaseous mass, the object which we are considering is composed of the same perceptual qualities as those of the objects under our eyes ; and even the spatial or temporal distance itself is, like the size of the atoms, imaginable, or indirectly perceptible in terms of the relations or multiples of actually perceived spatial and temporal magnitudes. In short, *the space and time of conceptual inference is one and the same with the space and time of perceptual experience, and all the objects of the former are continuous and homogeneous with all the objects of the latter.*

Consider thirdly *abstract and artificial objects*, such as a perfect circle or a perfect human being. Such objects of conception are admittedly derived from the contents of perception either by mere selective analysis—*i.e.* abstraction—or by a combination of analysis and synthesis. The most abstract and schematic fictions of science, no less than the most fantastic dreams of creative art, are such stuff as things are made of, *viz.* the quantities and relations of ordinary experience combined into new *ensembles*.

Fourthly and finally, let us consider *inaccessible objects*, such as other minds and their feelings. Nothing would appear to be so cut off from the direct experience of one self as the experiences of another self. I can never be certain of the existence of your mind and its states ; I can only infer them from your behaviour and from what you tell me. You may have a toothache, a memory of yesterday's breakfast, a perplexity over Kant's idea of the Deity—none of which things can I see, feel, or hear in the sense in which I can see, feel, or hear your body and its movements. And yet, after all, your thoughts and inner experiences which I conceive and infer to exist are all of them, in so far as they have any definite meaning for me, conceptual constructs from my own perceptual experiences. Your memories and your puzzlings, your feelings of pain and pleasure, are homogeneous with mine ; not always as mere duplicates, but at least as functional derivatives, in the sense in which the size of the atom is a functional derivative of sizes that have actually been perceived. Unless I knew their essence I could not doubt their existence.[1]

But now that we have pointed out the affinity of the various types of conceptual objects to the perceptual objects from which they are derived, it may still be said that there is nothing in all this to justify the contention of the subjectivist that all the things of the world are relative to the self and possible contents of its experience. To show that the inferred world of our conception is but an extension of the

[1] The homogeneity of these four classes of conceptual objects with the percepts from which they are derived is sometimes obscured by two points of difference between them, which result from the different ways in which they originate. A direct or perceptual experience is the effect of an external stimulus, and its content is (1) predominantly sensory in quality, and (2) definitely located in time and in its spatial relation to the body of the percipient. These two characteristics give a peculiar vividness and realness to perceptual objects which is lacking in the objects of imagination and conception, for these latter experiences arise from causes within the cerebrum ; and probably, by reason of their less definite relation to the motor reflexes, their contents do not possess definiteness of time or place in relation to the organism. Perhaps for the same reason they are relational rather than sensory in quality. It would, for example, be impossible to have a clear perception apart from a sensory quality such as colour or tone ; but when I *conceive* of an object like an atom, the sensory quality is faint and irrelevant ; its clearness of meaning is due to the relations in which it is felt to stand to other objects.

world that is perceived, and that it is determined by it and relative to it, is not the same as to prove that both worlds are relative to the self. It is, however, a definite step toward that conclusion, for it disposes of the false element in the theory of epistemological dualism, according to which there exists an inferred world of objects which cause the world of our experience, but never themselves enter into that world or share its vicissitudes. The inferred world of conceptual thought is part and parcel of the immediate world of perceptual experience, and if the latter is relative to the self, so also is the former.

Is the world that I perceive in some sense relative to me, the percipient ? It most assuredly is. Elementary psychology proves beyond a doubt that to every specific object in a field of perception there corresponds an equally specific state or process in the percipient's organism. Thus, if we are to perceive a chair, a mountain, a star, there must be for each a specific process in the organism. For every definite colour, shape, or tone to figure as a perceived object there must be an equally definite organic process. These neural processes are the only necessary and sufficient conditions of experience, and as they vary, the objects of our experience vary. The processes themselves are, of course, caused in various ways— by external stimuli and by influences from within the body, and particularly by the traces in the brain left by past stimuli— but, whatever the manner in which the cerebral process is produced, when once it *is* produced, the object determined by it appears in a perception. Thus, it will be remembered, in the case of the stereoscope the process produced in the brain was such as to yield the perception of a sphere. The fact that there did not exist a sphere in the place where the sphere was perceived made no difference to the perception. *The indirect determiners of our perceptual objects are many and varied, but the direct and final determiners are always and exclusively the processes or states of the organism.* As to the nature of these processes, there is room for disagreement. The majority of psychologists take the naturalistic or materialistic view that they are purely physical, but there are some who hold that the processes determining our experiences involve not merely the brain, but an immaterial entity or soul that co-operates with the brain during life. However this may be, there is no disagreement at all as to the fact that the specific content of every perceived object is determined by an equally specific process of some sort within the organism of the percipient. And so we are justified in holding that the world of perceived objects is in some sense " *relative to* " the percipient self, or that any perceived object is a " function of " some state or process of the percipient. Which means that for every member of the one class there is a corresponding member of the other class, and that for every change in the one class there is a corresponding change in the other class.[1]

Now we have already demonstrated that the supposedly imperceptible and transcendent causes of our immediate experience which are arrived at through conception and inference (such as atoms, remote events, artificial abstractions, and other minds) are not really transcendent at all, but are, on the contrary, located in the same space and time as that of the immediately experienced objects, and that they are homogeneous with and functions or derivatives of the latter. If Z is a function of Y, and Y is a function of X, then Z is a function of X. So if the system of conceptually inferred objects is relative to the system of perceived objects, and if the latter is relative to the system of processes of a certain sort within the percipient, it follows that the conceptually inferred objects, like all others, are relative to and determined by the self and its processes. Everything in the entire universe is in some sense relative to the self, and in that sense " subjective." If a thing can be talked about at all, it can and must be regarded as capable of entering in the fullest measure into the experience of the one who talks about it. The world in which we live is, as Kant said, " the world of possible experience."[2]

---

[1] This does not mean that all organic processes have percepts corresponding to them, but only that there is a certain species of organic processes for each member of which there is a corresponding percept.

[2] The basic premise in Kant's theory of knowledge is the thesis that the self creates the laws of nature by applying the mind's pure forms of synthesis to the manifold of its sensory material. From this it results, as we observed in the preceding chapter, that nothing can ever be perceived as a natural object except what has been through the mill of human faculties. In other words, anything that figures as a perceptual fact of science will have made

In our defence of the subjectivist's doctrine of relativity we have so far spoken of " the " self or " a " self, as though we meant only that the objects of the world could be regarded as relative to or included in some self or other, or in the totality of finite selves, or in an Absolute or world-self. But all that we have said applies with equal cogency to the support of solipsism, which is that most radical and final form of subjectivism according to which the entire universe is relative to *my* self and included within *my* possible experience. For the only thing that I can mean by the world or by any object in the world is something that *I* can conceive, and everything that *I* can conceive is an extension or reconstruction of what *I* perceive, and everything that I perceive is in some sense relative to and determined by my own inner states and processes. Hence with the solipsist I can and must exclaim,

its peace with and received the stamp of the conceptual structure of reason. The natural will have been proved rational in form, thus disposing of Hume's classic doubt as to how a subjectively grounded knowledge can agree with the objectively grounded course of natural phenomena. There are two great difficulties in this Kantian doctrine. First, the only self that we have any knowledge of as a recipient and combiner of sensations is a finite self, but the only self that could be capable of legislating for nature would be a transcendental self outside time and outside space. This latter self, not being given, must be postulated to meet the needs of the theory. Second, the ghost of Hume's objective " course of nature " comes back to plague Kant's system under the guise of the things-in-themselves on which the manifold of sensations is grounded. Why should these alien immigrants that constitute the " matter " of experience show such amazing docility and conformity to the net of schemata and categories which the mind throws over them ?

Now if we substitute for Kant's lordly assumption of knowing as a *creation* of nature's laws the modest assumption of knowing as a *re-creation* of nature's laws, we avoid the two difficulties above noted. For, in the first place, the self that re-creates the world of nature does not have to be outside nature ; it can be the finite self that we know as a part of nature. And in the second place, there is no longer any mystery in the fact that the mind's subjective forms harmonize with the " course of nature," for the reason that those forms themselves are now seen to be the results of nature's own prior operation. The mind, as a child of nature, renders back in her *knowing* the same structure that went into her *making*. It will indeed be true, as Kant said, that all objects that I can experience will have passed through my consciousness and conformed to its forms. But this will not longer entail the paradox that the objects that we know depend upon our knowing of them. *The created is (constitutively) relative to and therefore depends upon its creator, but the re-created is (selectively) relative to and therefore does not depend on its re-creator.* The words of a history book re-create the events of the past. Those events are functional relata or implicates of the symbols which reveal them, but they are not for that reason dependent upon them. To substitute re-creation for creation as an interpretation of the cognitive act enables us to preserve the truth of Kantian idealism while escaping its paradox.

" *The* world is *my* world." But, as we shall point out more at length in the next section, this relativity of all objects to a subject is selective rather than constitutive, and does not make the objects dependent on the self that knows them.

The first half of our re-examination of the epistemological theory of subjectivism is now complete. Of the two propositions which we took as defining the theory, the first has been proved true—" All objects are in some sense relative to the self and objects of its possible experience."

2. *The falsity of the second proposition of Subjectivism.*—We shall now consider the second of the two defining propositions, the proposition, namely, that " All objects are actual contents of the experience of a self and cannot exist independently of that experience." This latter assertion of the subjectivist we shall try to prove false.

To begin with, I would call attention to two statements which are, indeed, closely related in meaning, and the truth of which is obvious. (1) In general, one and the same object can be a member of different systems or relational contexts, simultaneously or in succession, without prejudice to its identity, and without having its meaning exhausted by any one of its contexts. (2) In general, a thing can be a possible member of a context without being an actual member of it. We contend that each of these statements is directly applicable to the perceptual and conceptual objects of consciousness. Consider, for example, the toothache from which our friend is suffering : it is present in our consciousnesses as an object of conception, and how we shall conceive it and when we shall conceive it depends upon how and when our brains are specifically excited. But the indubitable presence of our friend's toothache as a member of the system of objects conceptually apprehended by you and me has not the slightest direct effect upon its presence in the system of things felt by the sufferer. If either you or I cease to think of the painful event, it continues with undiminished intensity. Its presence in a knowledge-context is compatible with, but in no sense necessary to, its presence in the spatio-temporal context of existence. Nor does its membership in any one of these contexts exhaust its meaning. The fact that it is a possible object of your consciousness and of mine does not mean that it is an actual object in either. If you object that we are begging the question by using the word " it " to denote the toothache that our friend experiences, the toothache that you are thinking of, and the toothache that I am thinking of, and that in reality there are three numerically different toothaches instead of one toothache in three different contexts, I must reply that the objection can be shown to be self-contradictory. For it is self-contradictory to tell me that the thing that I am thinking of is not the thing that I am thinking of. If I am thinking of the toothache from which my friend is suffering, it is just that and nothing else which is the object of my thought ; and if you are thinking of our friend's toothache, then we are most assuredly thinking of the same thing, and the fields of our conscious thought overlap ; and if our friend is actually suffering from the toothache, as we think him to be, then there is one and the same thing which figures as the object of one man's perception and of two other men's conception. And as conceptual fields can overlap or contain identical members with one another and with perceptual fields, so also can two or more perceptual fields overlap one another ; and finally, any conscious field, conceptual or perceptual, can overlap a field of existence ; and these various fields, or contexts, despite their ability to contain the same objects, in no way interfere with or directly condition one another. If any doubt is felt as to these latter assertions, we must refer to the arguments given in the preceding section of this chapter, where in dealing with the element of truth in the theory of Objectivism we showed that an object which is perceived by one or more individuals may also exist externally and independently of the fact that it is so perceived. If you and I each perceive a content such as a sphere, which we describe in the same terms, and which is located by each of us in a given space outside of our organisms, there is at least a chance that we are perceiving one and the same thing, and there is at least a chance that the very thing that we are perceiving exists. For if two things are to be different, they must differ either in quality or in spatio-temporal position ; and if the sphere which I perceive agrees in its shape or quality and in its position in space and time with the sphere which I conceive as objective and independently existent, the " two " spheres must be one and the same ; the only difference is one of context.[1]

When we speak of the perceived sphere, we mean a sphere that stands in a certain unique relation to the cerebral processes of you and me ; when we speak of the existing sphere, we mean a sphere which stands in a certain relation to the totality of experienceable objects, the relation, namely, of being presupposed by them. The two expressions may denote the same object, just as the two expressions, " the book lying on my table " and " the book written by Colonel Roosevelt," may denote the same object.

What is the reason that this possible identity of perceived objects and existent objects is not generally recognized? [2] The reason is that the identity is only a possible identity, and by no means always actually realized. I can never be *certain* that the sphere that I perceive and the sphere that you perceive are identical with one another, or that either is identical with an actually existing sphere. The knowledge situation itself neither precludes nor ensures that identity of perceived object and existent object which constitutes perceptual truth. There is always the chance of error—the chance that the things which we perceive or conceive may not coincide in quality and position with the things which, because they are presupposed by the totality of experienceable objects, are called existent or real. There is no short cut to certainty in this matter. No single experience, perceptual or conceptual, contains intrinsic marks by which its truth or falsity are made evident. In each case it is necessary to proceed by the various methods of logical inquiry to compare the given experience with other experiences in order to test its claim to objective truth. But this necessity must not be taken by the subjectivist as justifying his claim that because all objects are experienceable they are all experienced ; or because an object can exist within an experience it is thereby rendered incapable

[1] The principle of the *Identity of Indiscernibles* is true when and only when there is an indiscernibility of spatio-temporal position as well as of quality or essence.
[2] It is in their denial of the possibility of an identity in spatio-temporal position of the perceptual content with the existent object that the " Critical Realists " or epistemological dualists differ from the position I am here defending.

of existing outside that experience ; or because the meaning and nature of objects can be discovered only through their presence as terms in an actual experience-relation (*ratio cognoscendi*) that therefore their meanings and natures are constituted by that relation (*ratio essendi*).

Our re-examination of Subjectivism is now completed. In its pure or naïve form the theory asserted that all objects— both immediate and inferred—depend upon the self and exist solely within its experience. This theory was analysed into two propositions : (1) " All entities are (selectively) relative to a self and objects of its *possible* experience " ; and (2) " All entities are (constitutively) relative to or dependent upon a self, and cannot exist except as objects of its *actual* experience." The first of these propositions we have found true, the second false. And now that we have shown that the two opposed methods of epistemology—Objectivism and Subjectivism—are each capable of being amended in such a way as to make them compatible with each other and with the facts of the knowledge-situation, it remains for us to show that the theory of Epistemological Dualism is susceptible of a similar analysis which will enable us to bring all three types of epistemological doctrine into a complete and final harmony.

III

THE RE-INTERPRETATION OF DUALISM.

The Epistemological Dualist holds that all immediately experienced objects of sense are dependent upon the self and incapable of existing apart from its experience, but that at the same time the conceptual objects which are inferred as the true causes of experience exist independently of the self and are never identical with the objects of consciousness. This pure or naïve dualism can be resolved into two propositions : (1) " *The system of objects experienced by a self and the system of objects existing externally to that self and causing its experience can vary independently of each other.*" (2) " *The experienced objects and the existent objects, because they vary independently of one another, are never coincident or identical, but constitute two mutually exclusive systems of metaphysical entities."* Of these two defining propositions we shall try to prove that the first is true and that the second is false.

1. *The truth of the first proposition of Dualism.*—Let us begin by considering two typical cases in which the experienced objects change while their externally existing prototypes remain constant, thus justifying the dualist in his claim that the experienced and the existent can vary independently. I see a table in front of me ; I close one eye and press the ball of the other eye ; the table that I see moves about as I press ; the table that exists remains stationary, as can be proved in many ways. In this case the perceived object changes while the real object stays constant. An instance of the same situation in the field of conceptual knowledge occurs in Shakespeare's *Othello*. The Desdemona of whom Othello is conscious is changed by the slanders of Iago from a loyal wife into the sweetheart of Cassius. The Desdemona who " exists " remains constant throughout the tragic change in her subjective double. Again, I look at the stars. To my consciousness they remain fixed, changeless. The astronomer tells me, however, that all the while the real stars are moving through space with incredible velocity, and that some of them may even have been destroyed years ago ; for the news of such destruction could reach us only after the light waves (which left the stars at the time their destruction occurred) had traversed the immense distance by which we are separated from them. In this case existing objects change, perceived objects remaining unaltered. An instance of the same sort, but in the conceptual field, can again be taken from *Othello*. Othello as he figures in Desdemona's consciousness appears unchanged in his love and trust through most of the period when he is being metamorphosed into a jealous murderer.

The four cases which we have chosen are fair and typical instances of the facts on which Dualism is founded ; they show the possibility of change taking place in experienced objects, whether perceptual or conceptual, while the real objects remain unchanged, or of experienced objects remaining unchanged while the real objects change. They show, in short, that, as the Dualist claims, the objects that are experienced may vary independently of the objects that exist. We have now to demonstrate that the second claim of the Dualist, to the effect that experienced and real objects are never coincident or identical, is as false as his first contention is true.

2. *The falsity of the second proposition of Dualism.*—As a rule, when two things vary independently of one another, they are thereby shown to be numerically or existentially non-identical; yet there are instances in which this is not the case. Consider, for example, two intersecting lines; each line can be viewed as a class of points or as generated by the movement of a point. The point of their intersection is one identical point, and yet it is a member of each of two separate series, and, as such, is in each case determined by a separate law or equation. If we conceive each line as produced by a point moving through a series of positions, then we must conceive of the two points coinciding at the intersection, though each of them continues to belong to separate systems, each of which varies independently of the other. That the systems vary independently does not prevent their possessing common or identical members. Now it is our contention that the relation between the two line-systems just mentioned is the same as the relation between the experience-system and the existence-system of objects. What I perceive in the visual field may be identical in every respect with what exists in the physical world outside my body; but what I perceive in the visual field depends primarily upon processes within my nervous system, and will vary only as those processes vary, while what exists in the physical world outside my body is primarily independent of processes within my nervous system, and will vary according to external conditions. In short, the existence-system of objects is controlled in its behaviour by extra-organic factors, while the experience-system is controlled by intra-organic factors. Although the two systems of objects *may* coincide to any extent, there is no necessity for such coincidence, and no guarantee that it will continue. The epistemological monists —both subjectivists and objectivists—have rightly emphasized the coincidence or identity of the two systems, which is realized whenever truth is attained; but they have neglected

the duality of causes owing to which the coincidence of the two systems is possible and occasional rather than uniform and necessary. The epistemological dualists, on the other hand, have rightly emphasized in their first proposition the duality of causes, but in their second proposition they have erred in assuming that such duality of causal contexts precludes a coincidence or identity of the objects that are experienced with the objects that exist. The theories which in their naïve or pure form were found to be false in themselves and hopelessly incompatible with one another, when re-examined and modified in the light of the facts turn out to be not only true in themselves, but harmonious and mutually supplementary.

Before leaving the subject of dualism there is one point which needs further explanation in order to guard against a possible misunderstanding. When we say that the causes determining the existence-system and the experience-system of objects respectively are separate and distinct, and to that extent independent, we do not mean to imply that they exert no influence upon one another. The extra-organic factors are continuously affecting the intra-organic processes upon which our experience depends, and conversely the revelations of experience enable us to influence through conscious action the world external to our organism. The fact that the experience-system and the existence-system are constantly overlapping and intersecting is far from being a matter of chance. What appears in our consciousness as a physical world is the indirect effect of the objects and forces of the environment which combine with the media through which they act and with the brain itself to produce the direct determiners of whatever we experience. Because of the indirectness and complexity of the process, the cerebral states that condition our experience give only a misplaced and distorted presentation of their extra-bodily causes—hence the existence of error. But the distortion involved in the immediate sensory picture is in large measure corrected by the happy capacity of the brain to retain the traces of previous effects which may combine with the impressions of the moment to produce an experience in which things appear as they are—which is truth. The way in which objects are distorted by the media through which they must operate, and the way in which the true perspective is restored by the corrective inference involved in both perception and conception was explained at some length in our chapter on Scepticism, and we need only repeat here two or three of the examples which were used there as illustrations.

Let us take first the cases in which the correction is made on the perceptual level. There is, we will suppose, a real circle in front of me. Because it lies in a plane not perpendicular to the line of sight, it casts upon my retina an elliptical rather than a circular image ; I see it nevertheless as a circle ; the retinal and sensory distortion have been corrected by the brain, which has been modified or trained by previous experiences, so that it automatically interprets that kind of elliptical presentation as circular. In the same way, when a man walks away from me, the image cast upon my retina and the resulting content of visual sensation decrease in size, yet I perceive the man as changing his distance rather than his size, because through past experience (or possibly through innate endowment) my brain has learned to associate this kind of sensory decrease in size with increase in distance.

On the conceptual level, the power of the brain to correct the distortions of peripheral perspective is shown by our ability not to be fooled by the apparent change in shape which a stick undergoes when partly immersed in water. The difference in the refractive powers of the two media of water and air produce the distortion, and it is only through a somewhat deliberate use of our past experience that we can attain the true belief that the stick itself has not changed its shape. An illustration of an even more refined conceptual correction of sensory distortion is afforded by our interpretation of the " setting sun " as due in reality to the rotation of the earth on its axis ; for here we draw not only upon our own past experience, but upon the scientific calculations of others.

The two great purposive activities that occupy our waking life are : (1) the activity of *knowing*, in which we strive to bring the experience-system of apprehended objects into harmonious coincidence with the existence-system, which coincidence, when attained, we call " the true " ; and (2) the activity of *willing*, in which we strive to bring the existence-system into harmonious coincidence with the experience-system of desired objects, which coincidence, when attained, we call " the good." [1]

It is the great merit of epistemological dualism that it recognizes, in the first of its two defining propositions, that the objects in experience and the objects in existence are determined by different sets of causes, and that consequently they can vary independently of one another, and will not of necessity coincide. Dualism errs in the second of its propositions, in which it asserts that, because the experience-system and the existence-system vary independently, therefore their objects can never coincide, and that we can be conscious never of reality itself, but only of more or less perfect copies of reality.

IV

CONCLUSION.

In order to illustrate the concordance of the three schools of epistemology, I wish now to show how the concept of truth can be stated adequately in terms of each theory and translated from one to the other without essential change of meaning.

1. For the Objectivist, the True is simply *the real considered as the object of a possible conscious belief or judgment*. And the real or existent comprises all those entities, and only those

---

[1] There is indeed a third type of equilibrium or adjustment between the individual and his environment which manifests itself in conscious experience, though not as a direct result of purposive activity. The stimuli of the environment, in so far as they affect the vital processes and tendencies of the organism and not merely its organs of sense, produce those forms of experience which we call feelings and emotions. When such stimuli are in accord with our needs and tendencies they give us the feeling of pleasure ; and when the pleasure is associated with the *form* of the object perceived, and is ascribed to its *intrinsic* character (rather than to our own individual mood), the pleasure is æsthetic, and the object causing it is termed " beautiful." Thus our experiences of the True, the Good, and the Beautiful are all of them cases in which the environment and the individual are in equilibrium ; but whereas the hedonic or æsthetic equilibrium is a matter of feeling and is brought about spontaneously, the true and the good are attained as the result of purposeful effort, and consist, as we have said, in an identity or coincidence of the objects of the experience-system with the objects of the existence-system.

entities, which are logically implied or presupposed by the totality of experienceable contents. To discover which of the contents of experience is real is usually possible only by a long process of induction ; but whenever we experience a content that turns out to be real, the experience in question turns out to have been true. That is to say, when our *object* of belief is *real*, our *attitude* of belief is *true*. Thus, for example, if the roundness of the earth is a fact or reality, then the judgment " The earth is round " is a true judgment.

2. For the Subjectivist, the True is *whatever would be confirmed by an all-comprehending or absolute experience*. A judgment such as " The earth is round " is true provided it would be made by an absolute mind. In short, truth to the Subjectivist means *confirmability by further experience*.

3. For the Dualist, the True is *whatever in the individual corresponds to what exists outside the individual*. Thus the judgment " The earth is round " is true if there is in the world external to my organism a relation of identity between the *earth* and *round*, corresponding to the relation of identity between my idea or experience " earth " and my idea or experience " round." In short, truth for the Dualist consists in *the correspondence of intra-individual with extra-individual identity-relations.*

Is it not easy to see that if any of these three theories is valid the other two must be equally valid ? For observe : If the Objectivist is correct in his theory that a judgment is true when what it asserts is real—that is, presupposed by the totality of experienceable objects—then it will follow that every judgment that conforms to this criterion of identity with reality will conform also to the Subjectivist's criterion of confirmability by a completer experience ; for the more complete or most complete experience will reveal the presuppositions that are necessary to make it self-consistent, and the objectively real and the subjectively apparent will coincide. In short, if our judgment that " The earth is round " is true in the sense of asserting a reality, it is equally true in the sense of being confirmable by, or maintaining itself unaltered in, a completer experience-system. The two criteria are based on two aspects of the same thing, and are no more incompatible than the concavity and convexity of a curved line. In the one case I define truth in terms of the relation of my judgment to the totality of possible objects ; in the other I define it in terms of the relation of my judgment to a possible totality of experience.   The same correlation and harmony is of course to be found in the application of the two criteria to falsity. The judgment " The earth is flat " is false to the Objectivist, because the object which the judgment asserts—*viz.* a " flat earth "—happens to have no position in the spatio-temporal system, and as such is not presupposed by the totality of possible objects or by that portion of the totality which we have experienced.   To the Subjectivist, the same judgment is termed false because it has been precluded rather than maintained and confirmed by those more complete experiences which were conceptually (and in part perceptually) attainable after the circumnavigation of the globe.

And the correspondence-criterion of the Dualist is as reciprocally implicatory of the criteria of the Objectivist and Subjectivist as those are of one another.   The Dualist, we remember, insists upon our noting that the objects that exist at any moment in the world outside the nervous system of an individual, and the objects which at that same moment the individual experiences as so existing, are determined by separate sets of causes (extra-neural and intra-neural respectively), and that therefore they vary independently of one another.   Truth then consists in the correspondence or agreement of the judgments contained in the narrow and transitory experience-system of the individual with the things and relations comprising the incomparably broader and more enduring existence-system of which the individual is himself a part.   But this dualistic kind of truth will be realized when and only when the content, object, or meaning of the judgment is identical with a part of reality, which, as we have seen, consists of that select class of entities which are presupposed by the totality of entities (objectivism), and which, as such, would be confirmed by a single all-inclusive and self-consistent experience (subjectivism).   What the epistemological Dualist, thinking in terms of psychology and physiology, interprets as a harmonious correspondence between two independently caused sets of events, the epistemological Monists, thinking in terms of ontology and logic, interpret as the simultaneous membership in two systems—that of experience and that of reality—of one identical object. Or to put it in other words, the "judgment-utterance," considered as a psychological process within the individual, will correspond to objects in the environment when and only when the "judgment-content," considered as a logical meaning, is also an existent fact. The Dualist's "correspondence of extra-organic with intra-organic occurrences" is a perfect translation of the Monists' identity of truth and reality. And here, again, we need hardly add that with respect to falsity there is a similarly complete conformity of the Dualist's criterion to those of the Monists. It is just because a "flat earth" is a member neither of the Objectivist's world of reality nor of the Subjectivist's completed experience that the Dualist who makes the judgment "The earth is flat" will find to his sorrow that there is a lack of harmonious correspondence between his inner mental states and his external environment.

It has been our aim in this chapter to show that all of the three epistemological theories can be re-interpreted in such a way as to bring them into accord with the facts with which they deal and with one another; and we hold that in each case this re-interpretation has preserved what is positive and essential in each of the warring theories, and has omitted from them only that which is unimportant and negative. Thus, the essential contention of Objectivism is that all objects of actual experience are also objects of possible existence, and that whether they are existent or not, they possess a logical meaning or "subsistence" that is independent of the fact that they are experienced. The essential contention of Subjectivism is that all objects of actual existence are also objects of possible experience, and that the entire universe is in some sense relative to each of the selves that it contains. The essential contention of Dualism is that the system of experienced objects and the system of existing objects are determined by separate sets of causes, and that consequently they vary independently of one another. The three propositions which severally express the traditionally irreconcilable types of epistemological theory are, when thus restated, in no way incompatible with one another. They are mutually supplementary and interchangeable. Each expresses a different aspect of the knowledge situation—or rather, each expresses the whole situation from a particular angle, making clear and explicit certain values which the other two leave vague and implicit.

If the foregoing analysis is valid, the epistemological problem is solved.

POSTSCRIPT

THE KNOWER AND THE KNOWN
A DIALOGUE

PARTICIPANTS

PARTRIDGE, an Objectivist.

BRYCE, a Subjectivist.

LOVELACE, a Dualist.

HYLANOUS, a Realist.

I

In which HYLANOUS, *after explaining the purpose of the meeting and defending the terms used in the discussion, proceeds to answer the objections that are brought forward by* PARTRIDGE.

HYLANOUS : I have asked you three gentlemen to meet me in order to see if by friendly and informal discussion we cannot arrive at a solution of the epistemological problem. Bryce will speak for subjectivism, Partridge for objectivism, Lovelace for epistemological dualism, while I as a realist will endeavour to show you how your warring theories can be re-formulated in such a way as to make them perfectly compatible with one another.

PARTRIDGE : It may be a small matter, but I should like to know first of all what right you have to describe yourself as a " Realist." You are not satisfied with giving our doctrines ugly and awkward names, but you must proceed to appropriate for your own doctrine a label which rightfully belongs to me.

LOVELACE : I feel somewhat as Partridge does. I don't mind so much your calling me a Dualist so long as you make it plain, as I think you do, that you are using the term in a purely epistemological sense, according to which mental states are different in position and not merely, or even necessarily, in nature, from the physical objects which we infer to exist. But I am not so well content with your monopolizing the term " Realism " for yourself, for I claim to be a realist no less than Partridge. And the mere fact that I hold that real external objects are *represented* in consciousness rather than directly *presented*, as he thinks, certainly does not make me any less realistic. It only means that I am an " old realist " or " critical realist " rather than one of the " new " or extreme type.

HYLANOUS : I am sorry that my terms have given offence, and without wishing to spend too much time in a purely verbal discussion, I may be permitted to explain that one reason for my refusing to apply the name " realist " to either of you was just because you both claimed it, and I wished to avoid the ambiguity that would have resulted. It is certainly true that Partridge, in dealing with the knowledge-relation, emphasizes the object as the important pole of that relation, and tends to think of consciousness as only a continuum, or cross-section or perspective of the totality of objects ; and it is equally true that Bryce in dealing with the same situation emphasizes the subject or the conscious self as the important term of the relation, the objects known being regarded as states or elements of conscious experience and inseparable from it ; while you, Lovelace, admit the reality both of external objects and of the conscious states by which they are known, but deny that they can ever be identical, and hence, as you have acknowledged, you may properly be called a Dualist. Now, my reason for calling myself a Realist is that my theory accepts all the positive or affirmative elements of the three theories which you severally maintain, and excludes only the negations and denials. Thus I believe that Partridge is right in his claim that the objects of which we are directly conscious can exist externally and in their own right, and that all objects have a meaning or subsistence independently of whether or not they are known ; but I also agree with Bryce that all objects are actual or possible elements of conscious experience, and in that sense always related to a conscious subject ; and finally with Lovelace I admit that the objective and subjective orders of events can vary independently of each other, thus constituting a true duality between them. On the other hand, however, I deny Partridge's imputation of unreality to the knowing subject and its ideas ; I deny Bryce's imputation of unreality to a world of independent and externally existent objects ; and finally I deny my friend Lovelace's imputation of unreality to that experience of identity of the perceived and the existent which is the very essence of true knowledge. In short, I refuse to relegate to a status of unreality any of the important elements in the knowledge-situation ; for this reason I think I have the best right to the term Realism as a name for my eclectic solution.   Does that satisfy you ?

LOVELACE : It satisfies me.

PARTRIDGE : I must confess that I think your reasons are a little thin ; but I suppose you want to retain the name Realist because you once were really such, and if you like the word so much I shan't object any more to your using it for your new compromise.

HYLANOUS : How about you, Bryce ?   Are you angry at my calling you a Subjectivist ?

BRYCE : Oh no ; that silly epithet makes me too tired to be angry.   I am an idealist, and as such I am used to being misrepresented, and I suppose that it is quite hopeless for you realists ever to see anything in my philosophy except what you call " subjectivism."   Though I confess that it always surprises me to be stigmatized in this way when I furnish the only intelligible interpretation of objective reality.

HYLANOUS : I mean no offence by the term " subjectivist," and I understand perfectly well that your idealistic philosophy, whether in its British or in its German form, is not exclusively a theory of knowledge.   But I am interested just now in trying to isolate the epistemological problem ; and although you are quite convinced that you provide adequately for our common-sense conviction of the world's reality, it is true, is it not, that you hold that everything that is real, or even capable of being discussed intelligibly, is of necessity an element of conscious experience ?

BRYCE : That is my belief, of course ; but there is nothing in such a view to indicate a failure to distinguish adequately between the two classes of phenomena which common sense describes as " physical " and " psychical."   I am, in short, an *Objective* Idealist.

HYLANOUS : I know it, my dear fellow, nor am I for one instant unmindful of it.   Nevertheless, you must admit that your theory that no object can possess either meaning or existence apart from its relation to a subject (empirical or transcendental) that experiences it may properly enough be termed " Subjectivism "—especially when it is discussed in relation to a theory such as that of Partridge, according to which objects are asserted to have not only a meaning but an actual existence quite independently of whether or not they are experienced by a conscious subject.

BRYCE : Well, if that is all you mean to indicate by calling me a " Subjectivist," I don't suppose I need object any longer to the name. But I want it clearly understood throughout the discussion that this so-called " subjectivism " applies only to the idealistic theory of knowledge, which is but a small part of the great philosophy of idealism; and secondly, that even as such it does not confuse what we mean by " physically real objects " with what we mean by " mere ideas."

HYLANOUS : I am sure we all understand that, Bryce, and you may count on us not to caricature your doctrine in any way. And now that we are agreed on the matter of terminology, I should like to discuss the possibility of our arriving at some sort of epistemological eirenicon or compromise in which full justice will be done to each of your three theories. And as Partridge is perhaps most familiar with my general attitude toward the problems of knowledge, I will ask him to begin the discussion.

PARTRIDGE : Well, Hylanous, I suppose my distrust of any such compromise as you propose centres on your idea of " subsistence." That term has been used in the philosophical discussions of recent years to denote objects of thought other than particular existents, but as I understand it, you employ the term to denote any possible object of thought, whether universal or particular, and whether existent or non-existent. In short, the subsistent is for you a true *summum genus*, the one class for which there is no negative. Is that correct ?

HYLANOUS : That is it exactly ; universals and particulars, real objects and unreal objects, are all species of the subsistent.

PARTRIDGE : Precisely. Now, I object to the introduction of such a category on the ground that it is artificial and misleading, and I particularly object to your well-meaning attempt to amend my theory by classing as an " unreal subsistent " the content of a so-called sensory illusion, such as the appearance of a solid object produced by means of viewing two flat objects through a stereoscope, or such as the appearance of a bent stick produced in accordance with the laws of physics by means of the partial immersion of a straight stick in water. It is bad enough for epistemological dualists like Lovelace to call such phenomena " ideas," and to declare that they exist only " in the mind." That notion is a foolish one, but it is at least intelligible. Whereas your attempt to introduce under the term of " unreal subsistents " a class of sensory objects which are independent of our experience of them, and which at the same time are to have no place in the world of material existence, is a sheer absurdity.

HYLANOUS : You understand why it seems to me to be necessary to give to the objects of sensory illusion this new status, do you not ?

PARTRIDGE : Why, yes, I understand your intention or motive. You want to avoid what you and I both feel to be the fallacy of dualism. You and I agree that, if we once start putting the objects of so-called illusory sensory experience in the mind, that is, reducing them to mere dependent states of the perceiver, we must end by regarding all the objects of perception as in the same predicament, and that we shall then have no means of cognizing, even by means of conceptual inference, any world beyond our own mental states. You are right enough in wanting to avoid the complete subjectivism to which epistemological dualism always leads. But your method of avoiding subjectivism is fantastic and unnecessary. Instead of dividing sensory objects into existent and non-existent (the existent being regarded as the exclusive occupants of positions in an absolute space and time, while the non-existent are left to " subsist," suspended as it were in mysterious independence outside of the space and time in which they appear), you should recognize that position is relative, not absolute, and that all sensory objects exist, but that each of them exists *in relation to* other objects of which the percipient organism may be one. You would then under-- stand that the solid object seen through the stereoscope, and the stick that is seen as bent when partly immersed in water, are actual physical existents, although their existence is of course relative to the peculiar visual contexts in which they respectively figure.

HYLANOUS : Would you extend this conception of the physical existentiality of all sensory objects to such things as those stars which, though they still appear in the sky, may well have become extinct in the interval of time separating the moment when the light-waves left the star and the moment they reach our eyes ?

PARTRIDGE : Of course. The stars which, from the astronomer's conceptual point of view, no longer exist, may perfectly well exist from the point of view of a visual observer on the surface of the earth. What else would you expect, knowing as we do the length of time which it takes light from such stars to reach the earth ?

HYLANOUS : How about the objects that appear in dreams and hallucinations? Do they also enjoy this relative existence ?

PARTRIDGE : Certainly ; only in their case the distortion of perspective is far greater than in the case of the bent stick or the extinct star. For the projection-system which is always involved in perception is complicated by the mediation of that elaborate network of association-paths in the brain on which memory depends, so that, although the events of a dream or hallucination like all other objects of sense-experience do exist, yet they exist in a peculiar way, which is, I admit, quite different from the way in which the objects of our so-called true perceptions exist.

LOVELACE: I like that! Partridge generously admits that objects which are definitely known to be unreal exist only in a peculiar sense. Non-existence is indeed a peculiar kind of existence ; infernally peculiar, I should call it.

HYLANOUS : Be patient, Lovelace, please. I think I understand what Partridge means, and strange as it may seem, I believe we are much nearer to an agreement than ever before. And now tell me, Partridge, if I will agree for the moment to use the term " existence," as you do, to characterize all of the actual and possible objects of sense-experience, will you in return agree to recognize that " existents " as thus defined can be divided into two classes, (1) " ordinary existents," that is, such objects and events as would be regarded as real by ordinary people, whether they were experienced or not ; and (2) " peculiar existents," that is, such things as the solid body which appears when two flat disks are viewed through a stereoscope, or the bent stick which appears when a straight stick partly immersed in water is viewed obliquely, or the star which appears as the result of the light-waves from a star which is extinct, or finally the objects that figure in dreams and hallucinations ?

PARTRIDGE : Why, yes, I don't mind admitting that ; though the word " ordinary " which you use to characterize the first class of existents savours a little of question-begging.

HYLANOUS : Well, really, Partridge, inasmuch as you yourself chose the word " peculiar " for the one class of existents, you hardly have the right to object to my designating the non-peculiar kind as " ordinary."

PARTRIDGE : Oh well, let it pass. And now tell me what use you want to make of this division of existences which you have persuaded me to admit.

HYLANOUS : Why simply this : I should like to know your opinion as to the reason why people in general restrict the term existence to what we have agreed to call " ordinary existents " and prefer to describe your " peculiar existents," that is, the objects of illusory experience, as non-existent ?

PARTRIDGE : Why, I suppose the reason for that is purely pragmatic. We select certain of the objects of experience on account of their practical importance and call them existent or real, while other objects such as the solid objects seen through the stereoscope are more or less peculiar, and for the purposes of ordinary life quite unimportant, and hence we term them non-existent. The one class is as real as the other and the distinction is purely relative.

HYLANOUS : Granted, my friend ; but while you and I both recognize the extent to which practical interests determine our classifications, and in that sense are in sympathy with the pragmatists, we are also realists, and as such we know that, although the recognition and selection of differences may be motivated by practical interests, the differences themselves are grounded in the nature of the objects. I ask you then to tell us what it is about certain objects of experience which makes it practically important to class them as existent, in distinction from other experienced objects which we term illusory or unreal ?

PARTRIDGE : Well, I suppose that the objects that are ordinarily called real are those which we are finally compelled to assign to a definite position in the single conceptual space and time recognized by science. This public or conceptual space-time must of course be distinguished from the private space-time or perspective of the individual.

HYLANOUS : You would say, then, that the solid object which appears when two flat disks are viewed through a stereoscope has no position in space ?

PARTRIDGE : It exists in the private space or perspective of the individual, but when we try to reconcile its existence in the space where it appears with the rest of our experiences, we cannot do it, hence for purposes of practical convenience we may deny it a place in public space, and in that sense call it non-existent.

HYLANOUS : And you would agree, would you not, that the reconstructed system of things which for practical purposes we select as having positions in the space and time of science is composed of those objects, some of them perceptual and some conceptual, which are presupposed or implied by the totality of experienced objects, and which are therefore to be called *real* ?

PARTRIDGE : Yes, I admit that the objects and relations which are presupposed by the totality of experience may be called real in a more fundamental sense than other objects.

HYLANOUS : Very good ; will you not admit further that the objects which appear in experience, but which are not presupposed by it, can have no place in the real world as you have just defined it ?

PARTRIDGE : You mean such objects as the solid that appears in the stereoscope ?

HYLANOUS : I mean all the objects that are generally classed as illusory or non-existent, and which you have termed " peculiar existents."

PARTRIDGE : Yes, it is true that these existents have no positions in the system of existents which we have called real. They fall outside the space and time of physical science.

HYLANOUS : But why then do you wish to call them existent ? " Unreal existence " seems self-contradictory. You have accepted my theory, why not accept my terminology and use the word subsistence to denominate the actual or possible appearance of an object in experience, and reserve the word existence for that much smaller class of objects which, whether they themselves appear or not, must be presupposed to explain and harmonize the host of conflicting experiences ?

PARTRIDGE : You mean that my so-called peculiar existents are in fact identical with what you have termed " unreal subsistents " ?

HYLANOUS : That is exactly what I mean. The solid sphere seen through the stereoscope " exists " only in the sense that it *appears*. It has no position of its own in the space occupied by the two flat disks. We can explain its appearance only by presupposing the two flat disks and the stereoscopic apparatus. It should be termed unreal or non-existent for the same reason that we term the events of a dream non-existent—*viz.* the dream presupposes the world of waking life and can be explained in terms of it, while the world of waking life does not presuppose the world of the dream and cannot be explained in terms of that world.

PARTRIDGE : I suppose that my real reason for objecting to your terminology is that it suggests an unnecessary and illegitimate dualism. It makes a chasm between the two classes of existences.

HYLANOUS : But you have yourself just admitted that there is an urgent practical necessity for making the distinction, and that this practical necessity was not arbitrary or relative to the observer, but was based on the objective difference between actual and possible appearances as such ; and you have also admitted that there is one select group of appearances which must be finally presupposed to explain the rest and which therefore have a special claim to be called real or existent.

PARTRIDGE : Yes, I know I have admitted all that, but nevertheless I feel strongly that a so-called non-existent object, such as the stereoscopic solid, is part and parcel of the physical world. Its appearance to the eye is determined entirely by the laws of physics and physiology. There is nothing psychical or spiritual about it. It is as much a function of the physical order as the images on a photographic plate. And the same is true of all illusory objects ; even the space-times of dreams and hallucinations are nothing more than purely visible perspectives which are the natural products of the complicated projection system composed of sense-organs and brain interacting with other parts of the physical world. If we call these irregular or distorted perspectives " non-existent subsistences," we make a separation as artificial as that between a photographic image and its cause. The one is as physical as the other.

LOVELACE : If I may interrupt for a moment I should like to remind Partridge that the objection which he thinks fatal to my dualism—*viz.* the supposed difficulty of passing from intra-mental data to their extra-mental causes—is just as great a difficulty in his own system. How is he to get from any of his private space-times or individual perspectives of sense-data to the conceptual space-time of science ? He uses the blessed word *physical* for his private space-times as well as for the public space-time. But the gulf between the two domains is just as great as if he had called one psychical and the other physical.

HYLANOUS : I think your *ad hominem* criticism is sound in part, Lovelace, but unless you object, I would like to postpone for a little while the problem of how under any system we are to deal with the power of the individual to transcend in thought his own internal states, be they physical or psychical.

And now, Partridge, to return to our discussion. I fully grant you that the appearance of a non-existent object is itself a physical phenomenon, explicable in terms of physical laws, and that the illusory objects are determinate functions of the real or existent objects. The straight stick half immersed in water would produce an image of a bent stick in the camera as well as to the eye ; in each case the image of the bent stick would be a function of the straight stick, and would be explained in purely physical terms. But the fact that an illusion has a physical cause does not make it any less of an illusion. The very condition of the stick appearing bent is that it is in reality straight. It is only by assuming that it is a straight stick that projects its light rays through the differently refracting media of air and water that we can understand how an image of a bent stick appears. And in the same way it is only by assuming the existence of the two flat disks projecting their light-waves through the lenses of a stereoscope that we can understand how and why there is produced the appearance of a solid sphere in a space which in reality is empty. In short, *if you promote the object of an illusory experience to membership in the order of existent objects you have deprived yourself of that very physical explanation of its appearance on which you are so eagerly insisting.*

PARTRIDGE : You mean, that the appearance of illusory objects can be explained only by postulating a system of objects from whose membership they are excluded?

HYLANOUS : Exactly so ; and it is for that reason that I wish you to overcome your final scruple and admit that illusory experience presents a situation which forces us to divide objects into two classes: (1) a class of objects that have positions in the space and time of science and that exist in the sense that they are presupposed by the totality of experience ; and (2) a class of objects that do not exist, that have no true position in the space and time of science, but whose appearance in space and time is determined according to physical laws as a product or function of the objects composing the first class.

PARTRIDGE : Well, I think that that way of putting it removes my objections to your theory. Let me make sure that I understand you. You hold, first, that all thinkable objects, the total contents of actual and possible experience, are to be called *subsistent*, and that each of these *subsistents* has a meaning, character, or essence that is objective in the sense of being independent of whether or not it is actually experienced and of whether or not it actually exists. In short, your realm of subsistence is an all-inclusive *summum genus*, outside of which there is nothing. It embraces both terms and relations, both particulars and universals ; it is the totality of things, within which the actually existent and the actually non-existent figure as constituent parts.

HYLANOUS : You have stated my meaning exactly.

PARTRIDGE : Then, secondly, you hold that this totality of logically subsistent entities presupposes or implies a certain small part of itself—which you term " existence " or "reality," those terms being used interchangeably. **These existent** elements and relations constitute the spatio-temporal manifold in which each element has a definite and exclusive position in time and space. Among the objects of this existent world are living organisms which act upon and which are acted upon by the things outside them. As a result of this interaction within the existent world there arises in connection with each organism a unified system of objects; and each such unified system of objects is called a field of experience or consciousness. The objects figuring in an experience are in part the same objects as those that compose the fields of existence; and an experience, in so far as it contains such real or existent objects, is said to be a true or valid experience. But because of the complicated process of interaction between an organism and its environment, the experience produced by the interaction contains elements and relations that are other than those of the system of existent objects. An experience is termed false, illusory, or erroneous just in so far as its constituent objects (perceptual or conceptual) are unreal or non-existent. Thus the one existence-system and the many experience-systems are only partly identical; objects may exist without being experienced, and they may be experienced without existing. An experienced object may or may not exist, and the only way in which conscious individuals can discover which of their experienced objects are real is by comparing the various fields of experience and deriving from that comparison a system of elements and relations in terms of which the totality of their experiences can be harmonized and explained. Because of the limited number of experiences available for this purpose, our knowledge of reality is never either complete or certain, but both the extent and the degree of probability of our knowledge increases with the number of our experiences and the multiplicity of their interrelations and mutual corroborations.

HYLANOUS: You have stated my theory exactly. Are you satisfied with it?

PARTRIDGE: Yes, I think so. My main objection was based on what seemed to me to be the false dualism which you erected between the existent and the merely subsistent, but now that you have made it clear not only that the experienced and the existent may be actually identical, but that even the objects of an illusory or erroneous experience, though not themselves existent, are nevertheless physically determinate functions of existence, and explicable as natural products of natural law, my objection is removed, and I accept your theory as doing adequate justice to the claims of an objectivistic epistemology. You will permit me to add, however, that this very fact makes me doubtful as to whether you can make the theory satisfactory to Bryce and Lovelace.

II

In which HYLANOUS *discusses with* BRYCE *the arguments for idealism based on the ego-centric predicament and the relativity of perception.*

HYLANOUS : And now that Partridge and I have reached an agreement, I should like to see whether it may not be possible to reach a similar agreement with Bryce. And to begin with, I might say that in my opinion such an agreement can be attained quite simply by substituting " possible experience " for " actual experience." The idealists maintain that every object *must* be present in experience, while I would say that it is sufficient to admit that every object *may* be present in experience.

BRYCE : There are two objections to any such compromise. In the first place there is the ego-centric structure of reality —of any reality that we can know or even discuss. You realists try to belittle this great fact by talking about an *ego-centric predicament*, but to us idealists it is no " predicament " at all, but rather the axiomatic foundation of our whole system. In the second place we should object to your compromise because it implies a denial of our belief in the organic unity of reality. You call this belief " the theory of internal relations," and you reject it, at least so far as the cognitive relation is concerned, when you claim that the act of knowing or experiencing makes no difference to the content

We regard your doctrine of the separability of the content and the process of experience as an artificial and illegitimate abstraction.

HYLANOUS : Let us take up these two objections in turn, beginning with the ego-centric predicament. I would ask you first if you believe that in every case in which one thing A is found with another thing B, it follows logically that A cannot exist apart from B.

BRYCE : I would not say that the separability of two things was absolutely precluded by the fact that we always found them together, but only that we had no right to believe in it, and that there was a presumption against it.

HYLANOUS : Take the sea and the sky, for example : we never find the sea with the sky absent ; but does that create a presumption that the sea could not exist apart from the sky ?

BRYCE : Perhaps not ; but that is because the situation itself determines the concurrence of the two, so there is nothing to indicate a causal connection between them. If, however, every time the ace of spades was drawn from a pack of cards we heard a thunder-clap, we should unhesitatingly conclude to some sort of causal connection, even though we were unable to conceive of any possible mechanism by which they could be related.

HYLANOUS : Exactly so. When the situation under which an observation is made does itself determine the concurrence of two phenomena, then and then only is there no presumption of a causal relation created by their concurrence. Now, it is obviously impossible to be conscious of an object without both consciousness and the object being present together. The situation under which the observation is made determines the concurrence, and hence nothing is indicated as to the dependence of objects upon the observer's consciousness.

BRYCE : The fact remains, nevertheless, that we have no direct evidence and no possibility of getting it as to what happens to objects when there is no consciousness of them.

HYLANOUS : Yes, but that absence of direct evidence does not mean the absence of all evidence. The Method of Difference is not the only inductive method. The causal independence of sea and sky cannot be tested by direct evidence, but, as we saw, that does not prevent our concluding that the one is independent of the other. We observe that the changes in the sea (other than those of colour) are in no way governed by corresponding changes in the sky. In the same way we can observe that the behaviour of objects is determined by physical rather than by psychical conditions. Thus we look for a time at the second hand of a watch as it pursues its circular motion, and then we look away, and on looking back we find the hand to be in the same position that it would have been had we been watching it for the same period. We could even arrange by means of sand or smoked paper to have the hand leave a trace of its movement when unobserved that would resemble exactly the trace left by it during a period when it was under observation. In such ways as these we can demonstrate with overwhelming probability that the course of events is not affected by being present in consciousness.

BRYCE : Surely, Hylanous, you do not regard the idealist as guilty of the absurdity of claiming that the mere act of looking at the hands of a watch determines the law of their motion. In your use of such an illustration you are attacking a man of straw, a conveniently fantastic opponent of your own making ; and you are not refuting idealism at all.

HYLANOUS : I am quite aware that your common sense makes you disavow the implication of the idealistic theory of knowledge when the issue is pressed in a particular case such as this. When asked whether the existence or behaviour of a given clock, chair, tree, or river depends in any way upon whether or not it figures as an object of experience, you answer No. Yet through it all you remain convinced of the general or abstract truth of the theory that nothing can be real outside of conscious experience. It is as though you were to say, " Of course Socrates is dead, Cæsar is dead, this, that, and the other man is dead, but Man as such is immortal."

BRYCE : That is not fair ; you forget the Absolute. When I hold that nothing can be real apart from experience, or except as experienced, I do not mean your finite experience or mine—I mean the Absolute experience which is assuredly presupposed by each and all of our fragmentary consciousnesses. Hence there is no inconsistency in my rejecting with indignation the belief which you would impute to me, that any individual by looking at a watch can change it, and yet at the same time insisting that to be at all means to be an element of experience. In short, I must remind you once more that I am an objective idealist, and not that absurd and probably non-existent creature known as a subjective idealist.

HYLANOUS : You hold, then, that the objects and processes of the material world exist independently of our finite experiences, that they come in and go out of these fields of consciousness without undergoing alteration, but that all the while they are elements in the experience of the one Absolute Being, which is the self of ourselves ?

BRYCE : I suppose that my view could be expressed in some such manner by a realist. Of course, no idealist would ever talk of objects " going in and out of consciousness."

HYLANOUS : Tell me, then, what evidence have you for believing in the reality of this Absolute. If you admit that particular material things like the hands of a watch exist independently of our perception or thought, why not stop there and accept the realist's doctrine of a system of physical objects capable indeed of being experienced by any and all individuals, but capable also of existing in and by itself without the aid of any spectator ? In other words, why drag in a hypothetical Absolute ? Why not trust the world to take care of itself in the intervals in whicn it is not being experienced by finite beings ?

BRYCE : There are two reasons for " dragging in " the Absolute as you call it. In the first place, ever since Berkeley it has been clear to all but the crudest minds that the nature and existence of what are called " material objects " can be defined only in terms of experience, that *esse est percipi*, and that the realist's world of objects existing independently of any consciousness is as senseless as it is useless. Now, if you accept this proposition of Berkeley, that nothing can exist outside of experience, and if you accept also the proposition (which Berkeley himself failed to attain, or at least to make clear) that no material object depends for its existence or behaviour upon the experience of you or me, there will follow from these two propositions as premises the conclusion that an Absolute exists. In short, if objects depend upon experience, but not upon finite experience, they must depend upon a superfinite or absolute experience. The partial truth of Berkeley's subjective idealism and the partial truth of common-sense realism combine to produce the complete truth of Absolute or Objective Idealism.

HYLANOUS: I understand now why you feel that the Absolute is not dragged in irrelevantly; but your argument seems to me none the less to be seriously fallacious. The Berkeleyan arguments which go to establish the first of your premises all turn on the relativity of individual perception, and if they prove anything they prove that a material object depends not upon experience in general, but upon your experience or mine. If the arguments are good, they make the Absolute unnecessary. If they are bad, as we realists believe, there is no support for the proposition that material objects depend upon any experience, finite or absolute.

BRYCE: You would claim that I ought either to admit that material objects were proved by their relativity to human experience to depend upon human experience, or else that because their behaviour was independent of our perceiving them therefore they were real independently of any experience, even that of the Absolute?

HYLANOUS: Certainly; I don't see how you can use the Berkeleyan argument from relativity to prove the identity of existence with experience, and then repudiate it in order to prove the need of the Absolute.

BRYCE: Well, I suppose it is because I feel a certain amount of sympathy with Berkeley's subjectivism, and also with your realism, that the doctrine of Absolute Idealism seems to me to do justice to both.

HYLANOUS: Undoubtedly that is the way you feel, but I am pointing out that the two parts of your argument turn out, when analysed, to be inconsistent with each other. It is undoubtedly true that the way in which objects appear to any individual depends at least in part upon the condition of the mind and senses of the perceiver. Now, either this dependence on the individual of the appearance of objects implies also the dependence of their existence, or it does not. If it does, the Absolute is unnecessary, because the world of physical objects depends on the perception of finite individuals ; if on the other hand this relativity of appearance does not imply dependence of existence, then also the Absolute is unnecessary, for the world of material objects, in the absence of any evidence to the contrary, can exist independently of any experience.

BRYCE : Well, Hylanous, you may have exposed a certain difficulty in combining the belief in the relativity of objects to human perception with the belief in an Absolute Experience ; but nevertheless it still seems to me that each of these beliefs can be proved true in turn, and must therefore be somehow combined. Take first the matter of relativity : how can you possibly explain the admitted facts about the mechanism of perception without concluding, as Berkeley did, that the nature and existence of physical objects are inseparable from the sensory experiences in which they figure ? What answer can your realism give to this question ?

HYLANOUS : I suppose you are referring to the changes in the appearance of things, their colours, shapes, and positions, that depend upon the condition of the percipient organism ?

BRYCE : Yes.

HYLANOUS : Well, in the first place we realists hold that all cognition, whether of the direct perceptual kind or of the indirect sort which we get in conception and judgment, is selective rather than creative. In our view nature is not a poor indeterminate canvas upon which we project the patterns of our minds ; it is rather a being of infinite variety, and which of the many aspects we select for apprehension will depend not only on the nature of the object and its mode of stimulating us, but on our condition and our interests, theoretical or practical. And we believe that the so-called relativity of knowledge is just as compatible with our view that knowledge is selective as with the idealist's view that it is creative. Thus, to borrow from one of the illustrations of William James : If we have been expecting twenty-five dollars, and twenty-seven dollars is suddenly handed to us, we apprehend the twenty-seven as twenty-five plus two. If, on the other hand, we had been expecting thirty dollars, we should apprehend the twenty-seven as thirty minus three. This does not mean that the twenty-seven dollars was in itself an indeterminate something, lacking either of the relations to the other numbers—each of the latter being added to the objective reality by the cognizing subject.   It means rather that the twenty-seven is *both* 25 + 2 and 30 − 3, and we *select* for attention whichever of these really existent aspects is the most congruous with our interest or expectation at the time.   Or again, if to our right hand water feels cool and to our left hand it feels warm, we do not follow Berkeley in concluding from this relativity that the water in itself has no temperature at all.   We hold that the situation shows on the contrary that the temperature of the water is objective and definite, not subjective and indefinite ; and that just as one and the same 27 can be 25 + 2 and 30 − 3, so one and the same temperature can be higher than that of our left hand and lower than that of our right hand, without prejudice to its identity as an independent reality.

BRYCE : I might accept your realistic conception of the cognitive act as being selective rather than creative, if it were not for the cases of illusion and error.   It may be that the number 27 can in itself be both 30 − 3 and 25 + 2, and that to apprehend it as either is a mere selection *from* reality rather than a creative addition *to* reality ; but how about the times when 27 is apprehended as 25, or when two flat objects are apprehended (through the stereoscope) as one solid object ?   Can you deny that at least all unreal objects and all false propositions are created by the mind and exist only within its experience ?

HYLANOUS : Of course I deny it.   The belief in a proposition (*i.e.* its open or tacit expression as the content of a judgment) has no relevancy to the truth or falsity of the proposition itself.   The proposition " The earth is flat " was at one time believed by everybody, while at the present time it is believed by nobody.   The proposition itself, however, has always been false.   And its falsity has been quite un-affected by the change in men's attitudes of belief.   It is no more false now than it was in the heyday of its popularity. The falsity of a false proposition, like the truth of a true proposition, is independent of whether or not it is believed.

BRYCE : Do you mean that false propositions are as objective in their status as true propositions ?

HYLANOUS : Certainly ; and if you will reflect for a moment, you will see that it could not be otherwise. We can consider a proposition as to its specific content, and as to its status of truth or falsity. Now, will you not admit that the content of a proposition is inseparably bound up with and determined by the content of its contradictory ?

BRYCE : Yes, if I understand you correctly. Do you mean that if you have given a proposition such as *All A is B*, or *Some C is not D*, or *No apes can talk*, the contradictory propositions are also given, namely, *Some A is not B*, *All C is D*, and *Some apes can talk* ?

HYLANOUS : Yes, that is what I mean. The content of any proposition is determined absolutely and completely by the content of its contradictory. And it is the same with the status as with the content. For if the original three propositions chosen by you in your illustration have the status of truth, then the second three propositions which contradicted them have the status of falsity. To say that a true proposition is objective and independent of an apprehension or belief, but that its false contradictory is subjective and dependent on consciousness, would be as absurd as to say that the convex aspect of a curve was objective, but that the concavity, correlated with it and determined by it, was subjective.

BRYCE : But if false propositions are as objective as true propositions, what is error ? and how comes it that we use the terms true and false to apply to such undeniably mental acts as beliefs and judgments ?

HYLANOUS : Error is that relation of a conscious individual to his objective environment in which a false proposition is made an object of belief or the content of a judgment. " True " and " false " are terms applied to judgments and beliefs only in a borrowed sense, not for what they are in themselves, but in virtue of the objects to which they are directed. Thus, when we say that my assertion " Man is mortal " is a true judgment, we mean that the proposition or identity-relation which the judgment takes as its content is a fact or reality.

BRYCE : Well, Hylanous, even if we admit this ultra-realism of yours in virtue of which you extend so curiously the categories of objectivity and independence to include even the realm of the false, it still remains to show how this realism in the field of logic could be applied to matters of perceptual error or illusion.

HYLANOUS: I can only answer by repeating briefly the doctrine of unreal subsistence which came up in the discussion with Partridge: Every real object is identical with the content of a true proposition, and every unreal object is identical with the content of a false proposition. Real and unreal have respectively the same denotations as true and false. The proposition "American soldiers are fighting in France" means that the complex conceptual object American-soldiers-fighting-in-France is also a real object. In order that a complex of qualities or essences should constitute a unitary object, the qualities or essences must have one position; this oneness of position constitutes the identity-relation signified by the copula *is*. The propositional manner of designating an object stresses this identity-relation. Thus the judgment "This table is brown" has for its content a unitary object constituted by the quality "brown" together with the other qualities denoted by "this table"—the whole complex occupying one position in the spatio-temporal system.

BRYCE: I can understand your conception of the numerical identity expressed by the copula as being an identity of position when the judgment is particular; for then the position is spatio-temporal, as in the illustration just cited. But how can you interpret the copula of a proposition as expressing oneness of position in the case of a universal proposition such as "7 + 5 = 12," or "Black is the opposite of white"? The identity between the subject- and predicate-essences does not seem to be one of position in space and time, but that deeper kind of union which differentiates the necessary and universal from the contingent and particular.

HYLANOUS: There is indeed the distinction you speak of. But position is constituted by any complete system of relations, and not merely by the spatio-temporal system. Thus "12" and "7 + 5" are distinguishable essences which have the same position in the number series in that their relations to all the other numbers are the same. The "*position*" of an entity is constituted by its relations to all other entities of the same system. In the same way, " black " and " the opposite of white," though distinguishable as such, are not distinguishable or in any way different in the set of relations in which each stands to the other colours. This " logical position " is as real as spatio-temporal position ; but whereas this oneness of spatio-temporal identity of position is contingent and not dependent on the essences which participate in it, but caused rather by external circumstances, the identity of " logical position " is necessary or inseparable from the essences which participate in it. Thus the genuinely true and necessary universal proposition expresses an object whose several qualities have an indissoluble identity of position in a system of logical relations, and its opposite is impossible ; while the particular proposition, empirical and contingent, expresses only a spatio-temporal identity of position, and it is both conceivable and possible for the qualities which participate here and now in the same position to have on another occasion a diversity of position. Thus 7 + 5 must always be 12, but *this table* need not always be *brown*.

BRYCE : Well, Hylanous, I suppose I must grant all this ; but, after all, what bearing does it have on the strength of the idealist's argument from the relativity of perceptions ? I admitted that the realist's argument that cognition was selective and not additive or creative, could be reconciled with the relativity of perception, except where the perception was definitely erroneous, as in the case of the stereoscope ; and you were to show me how even in such cases where false objects and relations were perceived it would still be possible to hold that the unrealities thus experienced were the result of selection rather than creation by the percipient.

HYLANOUS : You ask me what bearing this discussion of the contents of propositions as identical with objects has on the question of perceptual error as an argument for idealism. When it is once made clear that the contents of true and false propositions are respectively the same as real and unreal objects, it will also be clear that as every true proposition has a false proposition corresponding to it as its contradictory, so every real object has corresponding to it an unreal object. The percipient organisms are acted upon by the other real objects which surround them, and the effects produced upon a man's brain determine the content of his perceptual experience. Since the process by which an object affects the brain is complex and indirect, it often happens that the simple action of the object is modified and changed by the media of air or ether, of nerves or brain, through which the action takes place. The result is that the final effect produced in the brain will be subject to the same sort of distortion of perspective and general aberration that befalls the light reflected in a mirror or registered on a photographic plate. And despite the capacity of the brain to correct such aberrations by its memories or traces of past stimulation, it will often happen that a real object will produce upon the brain an effect that is uncharacteristic or misrepresentative of its cause, the consequence of which will be the perception of an unreal or non-existent object—in short, an illusion.

BRYCE : As conceptual error is belief in a false proposition, so perceptual error is the apprehension of a non-existent object ?

HYLANOUS : Exactly so. All perception carries with it a *prima facie* attitude of belief in the reality of what is perceived. And so when the perceived object is non-existent we have the so-called error of the senses, or illusion. The aberration may be of quality simply, or of locus simply, or, as in the case of the stereoscope, it may be both. And it may be a simply correctible distortion due to the physical media through which the senses are acted upon, or it may be the more radical distortion produced by disturbances within the brain itself. In the latter case the error is of that pronounced type found in hallucinations and dreams. But in either case perceptual error is due to the distortion of the action of an object upon the brain, resulting in the perception of a non-existent object.

BRYCE : And these non-existent objects that figure as the content of erroneous perception are selected and not created ?

HYLANOUS : Certainly. Each of them is a perfectly definite causal product or function of an existent object whose action is distorted by other existent objects. It was the fact that every illusion, no matter how extreme, was the product of perfectly definite physical causes that was the basis of Partridge's contention that every perceived object enjoyed physical existence. We found that though a perceived object need not itself exist, it was at least a physically determinate function or perspective of existence.

BRYCE : You claim then that these non-existent objects which figure in perceptual error are the distorted perspectives of existent objects which act upon the brain of the percipient, and that they are selected from the multitude of possible objects, real and unreal, by the complex mechanism, physical and physiological, which conditions all cerebral stimulation ?

HYLANOUS : That is it exactly.

BRYCE : I think I can agree to that. But here is a point that I do not understand : If every real object corresponds to a true proposition and every unreal object to a false proposition, then inasmuch as the number of false propositions is equal to the number of true propositions—each being the contradictory of the other—it would follow that the number of unreal objects is exactly equal to the number of real objects—that to each existent object available as the content of a true perception there would correspond one and only one non-existent object available as the content of a false or erroneous perception.

HYLANOUS : Yes, that is correct. Where is your difficulty ?

BRYCE : Why just this—the number of non-existent objects that we can conceive of is infinitely greater than the number of existent objects. Truth is one and error is many. To one way of hitting a mark there are a thousand ways of missing. For example, here in front of me is a brown table of definite size, shape, and weight. To this existent object there corresponds an infinite multitude of non-existent objects, even of non-existent tables, that is, tables of any other size, shape, or colour than the true one. Hence, while I accept your account of error as the false perspective of existence that is made possible by the complexity of the process leading to perception, I cannot reconcile it with your notion of an objective realm of unrealities which in the case of error are selected and not created by consciousness.

HYLANOUS : Your puzzle is natural enough, but it can be easily cleared up. The true propositions which express the world of existence or reality are most of them negative, and only a tiny minority are affirmative; while of the false propositions which contradict the true judgments and which express the shadow world of unreality, the great majority are affirmative and a correspondingly small minority are negative. Thus in your illustration of the table—there is, to be sure, only the one affirmative proposition that is true, *viz.*, " This table is brown," but there is an infinite number of negative judgments about the table which are true, each of them asserting the absence of some object other than that which confronts you.

BRYCE : And do you include the absences of all the non-existent objects from a situation as real characteristics of that situation ?

HYLANOUS : Certainly; it is only by doing so that we can characterize the world adequately. Ordinarily, we are more interested in the fact that a thing is present than that some other thing is absent ; but there are times when the absent unreality is more important. If, for example, you wanted a chair rather than a table, or a white table rather than a brown one, you would select from the true propositions characterizing the situation, not merely the affirmative one which you used as your illustration, but the negative pro-positions : " This table is not a chair," or " This table is not white," etc. In short, as each proposition has one and only one contradictory, the number of false propositions, with the unreal objects that they express, is exactly equal to the number of true propositions with the real objects, negative as well as positive, which they express.

BRYCE : I must confess, Hylanous, that it seems a little queer to include in an objective and independent realm not only the whole mass of unrealities, but also the totality of negations, the greater part of the latter being not only sub-sistent but actually existent. Still, I suppose I ought not to regard this wealth of objectivity as in itself an objection, because the Absolute would of necessity have for the con-tent of its experience the same rich manifold of all conceiv-able propositions, true and false, affirmative and negative, universal and particular. But since you yourself believe that this totality of the conceivable is capable of enjoying a status of objectivity independently of any mind, finite or absolute,

I wish you would tell me why you think it is that not only idealists but many who have held the realistic theory have regarded unreal objects as purely subjective, and have believed that the act of judging was creative, or at least alterative, of the reality about which the judgment was made.

HYLANOUS: Well, I suppose that the reasons have been in large measure the same as those which you advanced in support of the idealist's position. The relativity of perception naturally suggests the subjectivity of its content, unless the objectivity of the false or unreal objects as distorted perspectives of the real is recognized ; and inasmuch as the unreal objects do not produce any effects except as they figure as the contents of a real experience, it is natural to think of them as owing their entire nature to the cognitive situation in which alone they are efficacious. Then, too, the fact that there are certain very general and universal laws which are not restricted to any particular subject matter, but which hold good of all implicative relations between propositions, such as the *dictum de omni et nullo* ; and that these laws of being have for want of any specific subject matter been foolishly characterized as "laws of thought," although they are no more psychological or subjective than the laws of geometry or geology, has undoubtedly operated to produce a confused feeling that propositional relations pertain to, or depend upon, the mind. And lastly, we must remember that by reason of our limited powers of apprehension, we usually cognize the aspects of an object not simultaneously but sequentially in the order of their prominence ; thus we see a thing having the general character of a material body before we see that it is a table, and we see it as a table before we see that it is brown ; so that this sequentiality of apprehension expresses itself as " This is a . . . ? table," and " This table is . . . ? brown." The necessary sequentiality of speech re-inforces the successiveness of perception, and we get the feeling that the object itself is undergoing the process of change and evolution which is really taking place solely in ourselves ; and that by our act of judging we have somehow modified, or made, the compound of qualities in the identity relation which constitutes the propositional object expressed in our judgment.

III

In which HYLANOUS *proves to* BRYCE *that the theory of Internal Relations when modified in two respects does not necessitate Idealism.*

BRYCE : You may be right, Hylanous, in your account of the reasons for my holding the idealistic view that judgment is creative rather than selective, and you may also have succeeded in meeting the arguments for idealism which I based on the relativity of perception ; but there is another argument for the theory of absolute idealism which I have not mentioned, and which would not be affected by anything which you have so far brought out in defence of realism.

HYLANOUS : If you will state it, I will promise to give it full consideration.

BRYCE : It is the argument from " internal relations." We Absolutists claim that inasmuch as any relation must be " internal " in the sense that its terms are incapable of existence or meaning apart from the relations in which they stand, so also the cognitive relation must conform to this general internality ; and that would make it impossible and meaningless for the object of any experience, conceptual or perceptual, to exist apart from consciousness. And we hold, further, that as a consequence of the internality of all relations, the totality of conceivable Being forms an organic unity of conscious experience constituting an Eternal Absolute Self. Each seemingly separate element is in truth an inseparable aspect of this Absolute Whole. And it is only by a process of vicious abstraction that an object can be conceived to have that independence of the cognitive relation or of any other relation which you realists believe in.

HYLANOUS : I think I understand you. According to this new proof of idealism you do not start with the cognitive relation and argue that the objects which are found in that relation do not behave in such a way as to indicate their independent existence during the intervals when they are not perceived ; instead of this empirical method of inquiry, you propose to argue deductively from the nature of relations in general to the nature of the cognitive relation in particular ; and to show that because the terms of any relation depend upon and are constituted by the relations in which they stand, it must follow that the terms of the cognitive relation are constituted by and dependent upon the cognitive relation.

BRYCE : Just so.

HYLANOUS : You must admit, Bryce, that your new procedure savours somewhat of question-begging ; but nevertheless I expect to find myself in a closer agreement with you in this whole matter of the nature of relations than you may suppose ; and in any event I shall be glad to hear your argument. What is there about a relation as such that proves the dependence of its terms ?

BRYCE : Well, for example, consider two simple qualities such as white and black : the relation between them is that of oppositeness, and it is utterly impossible to think of either apart from its relation to the other.   The quality of whiteness could not be other than it is without bringing about a change in its relation to blackness ; the intrinsic natures of the terms determine absolutely and completely the nature of the relation between them.

HYLANOUS : Let me be clear on this point : You claim that the terms depend upon the relation in which they stand because that relation is determined and implied by them ?

BRYCE : Exactly so.   If A implies B, then A depends upon B, and cannot be conceived apart from it.   Hence it follows that if you grant that the nature of the terms implies or presupposes the nature of the relation between them, they will be unable to be conceived apart from that relation.   In other words, a thing is inseparable from its implication ; the ground is inseparable from its consequence.

HYLANOUS : I accept your general statement that relations are " internal " in so far as they are determined by the nature of their terms, and that in such cases the terms cannot be conceived apart from them ; but is it true that all entities do determine the nature of the relations obtaining between them ?   Can you show that the relation between white and black is typical of any relation between any two conceivable things ?

BRYCE : Certainly I can show it ; or rather you can see

it for yourself, if you will try. The relation between any two colours is like the relation between black and white—determined by the nature of the colours themselves. Take for example the relation between yellow and purple : it is a perfectly definite blend of similarities and dissimilarities, which could not be other than it is, the terms being what they are. It is the same with any two different types of sensation, such as the relations between red and the sound of a trumpet, or between red and the smell of musk ; the relation in each case has the character of irrelevancy and incongruity, but in each case it is an irrelevancy and incongruity of a quite specific and definite kind, not analysable perhaps, but none the less fixed and determined by the intrinsic natures of the terms in question, which could not be what they are without standing in just the relations that they do stand in. And it is the same with any two conceivable entities. You have but to consider them to see that their relations to one another and to all other conceivable entities are irrevocably fixed and determinate. Moreover, each entity is related to every other not only directly, as already illustrated, but indirectly ; that is to say, yellow and purple are not only directly related to one another, but each is related to the other through their common relation to red, green, and the rest of the colours. Thus any entity is related to any other through their mutual relations to all the rest of the entities ; and the totality of conceivable objects forms an organic system such as is found in a field of consciousness.

HYLANOUS : I don't think I object to this doctrine so far, Bryce, but just how does it apply to the cognitive relation ? Can you show in the same manner that the natures of the object known and of the mind that knows it determine the relation between them ?.

BRYCE : Certainly. Consider any object of knowledge that you wish ; when it is present in your experience does it not enter into the most intimate relations with the other objects that are present, and in co-operation with them generate feelings of meaning and of pleasantness and un-pleasantness ? And are not those relations obviously determined by the natures of their terms, the object known and the mind for which it is an object ? Must we not agree with

Berkeley that the so-called primary or spatial qualities of bodies cannot become objects of visual experience without taking on the so-called secondary or specific qualities, and that the qualities thus engendered react with the knower himself, and with his instincts and needs, to engender in their turn the so-called tertiary or affective qualities of feeling and sentiment ? Berkeley's own example of this last type of fusion is based on our experience of the indissoluble unity of the secondary quality of intense hotness, and the tertiary quality of the pain that accompanies it. In short, the general " internality " of relations is more strikingly exemplified in the cognitive relation than in any other. Will you not, as a realist, admit that any unexperienced and supposedly independent object, such as the interior of the earth or the other side of the moon, as soon as it becomes experienced engenders definite relations with the mind of the knower, and the other elements in the field of consciousness, so that the whole system of elements thus related forms an organic unity within which there could be distinction indeed, but no separate existence ?

HYLANOUS : Yes, Bryce, I will admit that there is no independently existing object whose nature in connection with the nature of the mind that perceived it would not determine relations of a definite kind, and definite tertiary qualities associated with such relations. And as I have already admitted that if the terms imply a certain relation they are by that token incapable of being conceived apart from it, it will follow that no object can be conceived as internally or intrinsically dissociated from the properties which it acquires by standing in relation to any mind, or for that matter to any other object. Every object of actual or possible experience has for its nature that infinitely rich complex of qualities, meanings, and values which are bound up with relations to each and all of the other objects, including of course each and all of the minds into the experience of which it might enter.

BRYCE : Now at last you seem to have grasped the meaning of the Absolute of idealistic philosophers. The totality of experienceable objects forms an eternal organic system, no element of which can be conceived independently of the great unity of which it is a part, or rather, a fragmentary aspect. And this Absolute Whole of truth and reality is implied by each finite experience, as its necessary correlate, and as its ideal completion and justification. In short, the Absolute as the single deeper Self of all our transitory selves supplements and corrects the relativities of finite experiences by affording an objectivity and self-consistency which you realists are always demanding. But it secures this objective transcendence of finite experience without going outside of experience in general, and without involving us in the absurdities of a realism which can purchase objectivity only at the price of postulating a world of independent entities existing outside of all experience, and therefore outside of the domain of intelligent discussion.

HYLANOUS: I must admit, Bryce, that this Absolute of yours grows more and more attractive. And your present method of procedure, based as it is on the logical implications of the internality of all relations between essences, does not seem open to the objections which, as you agreed, proved so disastrous to your earlier attempts to establish idealism on the psychological analysis of sense-perceptions and the relativities thereof. But it seems to me that you may go even farther than you have already in the praise of your Absolute ; for is it not true that the nature of the lower implies the nature of the higher, and that in order to measure or even to appreciate the imperfect in any domain it is necessary to refer to a norm or standard of perfection in that same domain ? And would it not follow from this that the Absolute supplements and completes our finite experience not only *logically*, but also *ethically*, and that we may regard it therefore, not only as a self-consistent totality of essences, but as an embodiment of all those perfections which the world so sadly lacks ?

BRYCE : Yes, Hylanous, what you say is indeed true. I had not spoken of this aspect of the Absolute before, because you were yielding so generously to my argument that I did not wish to touch upon what I feared might alarm you. But since you have yourself introduced the subject, I do not mind admitting to you that with many of us idealists the moral and religious motives for a belief in the Absolute are stronger than the purely logical. The knowledge that in the Absolute all perfection is eternally realized, enables us to endure the spectacle of the woes and tragedies of this world of mere appearance with a lofty equanimity that you realists can scarcely understand.

HYLANOUS : Perhaps our difficulty, Bryce, is not so much a difficulty in understanding the consolations of your philosophy as in approving them. But, apart from this, there is one point in connection with this conception of the Absolute which greatly puzzles me. Why is it that, having developed this wonderful notion of an organic and unified totality of essences, you take so little interest in inquiring as to whether any part of it is real ? I should think the demonstration of the existence of the Absolute would be a much more exciting enterprise than a dialectical elaboration of its essence such as we have just been engaged upon.

BRYCE : What on earth are you talking about ? You surely don't mean to go back on what you have said and deny the Absolute.

HYLANOUS : Certainly, I don't deny the Absolute ; I simply raised the question of its existence.

BRYCE : Would you mind explaining what you mean, and telling me how you could have followed all my arguments so sensibly, as I thought, and still raise a question as to the Absolute's reality ?

HYLANOUS : Why, Bryce, we have been talking about essences, not existences. We found that the relations between essences followed from their nature, and that therefore the essences could not be conceived apart from their relations, and that hence the totality of conceivable qualities formed an organic unity which we called the Absolute.

BRYCE : This distinction between essence and existence is a miserable relic of Scholasticism ; it is one of those vicious abstractions which you realists are always making, and which I thought I had persuaded you to abandon when you acquiesced in my doctrine of the Absolute.

HYLANOUS : But, Bryce, how unreasonable you are. I didn't make the difference between essence and existence. The universe made it, and if there is any blame in the matter it should be put on the universe. We realists believe that our minds only discover what is there, and that they don't make anything.

BRYCE : They certainly don't make sense. I agree with you to that extent. But give me some illustrations of the way in which your distinction between essence and existence bears upon the matter which we have been discussing, and with regard to which I had supposed we had reached complete agreement.

HYLANOUS : Why, we might begin with the illustration used before. We agreed that Black was the opposite of White, and that White could not be what it is without having Black for its opposite. Thus the nature of White implies the nature of Black ; but this does not mean that the *existence* of White implies the *existence* of Black. If you have a piece of white ribbon, it does not follow that you must also have a piece of black ribbon. And still more clearly, the nature of any number implies the nature of all the other numbers, but that does not mean that if you have three apples you must also have twelve apples. Three apples implies the essence of twelve, but certainly not its existence.

BRYCE : Would you use this wretched Scholastic distinction as an excuse for going back on your admission that all imperfection implies a perfection in terms of which it is measured and appreciated, and that therefore the Absolute as the sum-total of all perfections is implied as the necessary corollary of the imperfect world of Appearance ?

HYLANOUS : I will let you answer the question for yourself. You will admit, will you not; that the Bolshevik Russian State is an imperfect Socialism ?

BRYCE : Very imperfect indeed.

HYLANOUS : Good. And the basis on which you make this judgment is your conception of what a perfect Russian Socialism would be, and your apprehension of the extent to which the actual condition in Russia deviates from your more or less clearly formulated ideal ?

BRYCE : Of course ; all imperfection implies deviation from a norm or standard assumed to be perfect, and imperfect socialism in Russia is in this respect just like any other imperfection.

HYLANOUS : And do you then believe that a perfect Russian Socialism is anywhere realized ?

BRYCE : No, my friend, I do not. And not being so optimistic as you, I feel pretty sure that a perfect socialism, Russian or otherwise, cannot exist either now or at any future time.

HYLANOUS : Indeed! Yet you admit the ideal of a perfect socialism ?

BRYCE : Yes, Hylanous, I admit the ideal, if that is any comfort to you. It is only the reality of your Utopia that I am denying.

HYLANOUS : Exactly ; and as it is your logic rather than my politics which we are discussing, I feel at liberty to call your attention to the fact that in your admission that you can have an ideal of what Russian Socialism ought to be without believing in the realization of that ideal, you have contradicted your theory of the Absolute. For, as you will remember, you took exception to my compromise notion of an Absolute which contained all essences, including all those ideal perfections which we postulate as the standards by which we measure imperfections, but which might nonetheless lack any existence or reality. And you declared that it was a repulsive Scholastic subtlety to conceive of essence apart from existence. Yet in the case of the essence or nature of perfect socialism you have done that very thing. And speaking of Scholasticism for which you neo-Hegelian idealists have developed such a contempt, may I remind you that all of your attempts to pass from the necessity of postulating the nature of ideals of perfection to the equal necessity of postulating their realization in the Absolute, are but thinly disguised revivals of that triumph of Scholastic philosophy, the Ontological Proof. I need not repeat Kant's demonstration of the doctrine that existence is a relation in which an essence may or not stand to the totality of possible experience, and in no sense an essence or character itself ; as an idealist, you should be sufficiently familiar with that famous refutation.

BRYCE : You would have me accept an Absolute that consists only of possibilities or " essences " as you call them, and that lacks reality or actual existence ?

HYLANOUS : I do not deny the reality of the Absolute, I insist merely that the exigencies of logic and epistemology to which you have appealed in your argument do not themselves prove the Absolute to be more than a totality of essences or objective meanings. Other and more empirical evidence might conceivably provide grounds for a belief in the Absolute's existence.

BRYCE: If you think that there is a doubt as to the existence of the Absolute, why do you speak of it as " objective " ?

HYLANOUS: That point was discussed in my talk with Partridge. Any topic of discourse, whether a universal or a particular, and whether real or unreal, has a logical objectivity. That is to say, the nature or meaning of what we talk about is not dependent upon, or in any way altered by, the fact that we talk about it. That was one of the elements of truth in the type of epistemology that we termed " objectivism." Thus " perfect Russian Socialism," though we both hold it to be non-existent, has a nature and meaning that is independent of our discussing it, or of our being in any way conscious of it.

BRYCE: Was it this strange kind of objectivity which is independent, alike of existence and of consciousness, which you called " subsistence " ?

HYLANOUS: Yes, Bryce, it was. And though this doctrine of logical realism may seem strange to you, it is not only true, but it is the pre-requisite of all discourse. Unless we can suppose that the things we talk about retain their meanings throughout our talking, and in the intervals when we are not talking, there would be nothing about which we could talk.

BRYCE: But is it not obvious that the things which we discuss often change their meaning as a result of the clarifying influence of the discussion ? A person may begin a talk with a certain conception, say of the meaning of socialism, and end by attaching to the term a quite different meaning.

HYLANOUS: To be sure ; but the nature or essence of what he first called socialism remains what it was, after his conversion, otherwise he would be unable to confess that he had formerly meant one thing and now meant another by the term socialism. When we are converted from a false belief that the earth is flat to the true belief that it is round, the proposition " The earth is flat " has itself undergone no change of meaning ; the only change is in our attitude toward the proposition. If the proposition or topic itself had altered, there would be no way of registering our change from error to truth, or from an inadequate to an adequate understanding of a situation. We go from one phase of a topic to another just as we go from one place to another, and the condition of our movement, whether in thinking or in walking, is the objective permanence of the logical or physical *track* along which we move.

BRYCE : But does this realm of changeless essences to which you would relegate our Absolute differ from Plato's realm of Ideas ?

HYLANOUS : The world of subsistence was indeed discovered by Plato, as America was discovered by Columbus ; but like America, the new world of logically objective meanings was more extensive and diversified than its discoverer realized. It differs from the Platonic Ideas principally in two respects : in the first place, it is not separate from the world of existence, as were the Ideas, but contains that world within it, as terms contain their relations or as the ocean contains its waves ; and in the second place, the subsistent is not restricted in its contents, as were the Ideas, to the more lordly and generic essences, ethical and logical, but includes all that is conceivable, the logically specific as well as the logically generic, the ethically base as well as the ethically good. And among the specific contents of the world of subsistence are those perspectives which constitute fields of consciousness, the fragmentary and human, as well as the complete or absolute. In short, the totality of essences is an organic unity of internal relations and is ego-centric throughout.

BRYCE : That sounds more like my Absolute. But what do you mean by saying that this realm differs from the Platonic Ideas in not being separate from the world of existence ? I thought that you believed in its priority and in its superiority to the world of existence.

HYLANOUS : It is logically prior to the existent as the genus is prior to the species, or as the atoms of hydrogen and oxygen are prior to the molecule of water which expresses their union. These terms of the chemical relation are logically prior to their product, but not transcendent or separate from it when it is formed. In the same way, the genus *man* is logically prior to the species *good man*, but the latter is not therefore separate from the former. The species *good man* is the genus *man* combined with or determined by the other genus *good*.

BRYCE : You mean that the existent is the mere subsistent or essence with something added to or combined with it ?

HYLANOUS : Yes.

BRYCE : What is this something which must be combined with a mere possibility or nature in order to make it actual ? Is it simply another essence ?

HYLANOUS : No, Bryce ; for one possibility or essence to combine with another would only produce a third essence, more specific or complex than its components ; but that in itself is not sufficient to constitute existence. It is true, however, that no group of essences, *i.e.* no identity-complex of forms or qualities, can exist unless it is completely individuated.

BRYCE : What do you mean by " individuated " ?

HYLANOUS : Any existent object at any given moment involves by positive or negative determination all possible essences in the realm of subsistence, and is therefore a kind of monad or microcosm. Thus while table in general can be both red and not red, round and not round, etc., any existent table must be either red or not red, round or not round, and so on with respect to every conceivable predicate. Hence, if we represent the totality of possible positive essences (both simple and complex) by the letters $\overset{+}{A}, \overset{+}{B}, \overset{+}{C}, \overset{+}{D} \ldots \overset{+}{Z}$, and the totality of their negatives by $\overset{-}{A}, \overset{-}{B}, \overset{-}{C}, \overset{-}{D} \ldots \overset{-}{Z}$, then any existent object at a given moment will be of the form $\overset{\pm}{A}, \overset{\pm}{B}, \overset{\pm}{C}, \overset{\pm}{D} \ldots \overset{\pm}{Z}$, every letter appearing once in either its positive or negative phase. But while individuation, as thus defined, is *necessary* to existence, it is not in itself *sufficient*, for every existent in addition to complete logical individuation must possess for its final differentia a definite *position* in the continua of space and time. When any merely conceivable object adds to its essence or qualitative nature a spatio-temporal position, it ceases to be merely subsistent and becomes existent. Thus *existence* is *individuated essence united to position*, just as water is hydrogen united to oxygen.

BRYCE : What is this positionality, and how is it related to the mere essences which by its means attain the status of existence ?

HYLANOUS : The answer would be long and difficult. Space and time are such simple notions that the further analysis which their definition would require is hard to give. Their denotation is so clear that for ordinary purposes, or even for the purpose in hand, we can let their connotation remain unanalysed. Every term or object of thought has, in addition to the qualities which constitute its intrinsic nature, relations of a serial order to the other terms of the group. These latter relations (which are quite distinct from internal similarities and differences) constitute the extrinsic nature or position of the object. If two different qualities have the same position, they are numerically identical, and the word " is " expresses their relation. Thus when we say " Black *is* the opposite of white," or " 2 + 2 *is* 4," or " This round table *is* red," we mean by the copula " is " to symbolize the fact that the complex of qualities connoted by the predicate term occupies the same position in the system as the qualities connoted by the subject term. In other words, the two terms, though intrinsically diverse, have one and the same set of extrinsic relations to the other terms in the group.

BRYCE : Well, Hylanous, I think I understand what you mean by position, and the reasons why you regard identity of position as the kind of identity expressed by the copula of a judgment. But I do not understand how you differentiate the positionality of a spatio-temporal kind which you regard as requisite for existence from the more abstract kind of position expressed in such judgments as $2 + 2 = 4$.

HYLANOUS : To answer your question properly would require, as I said before, a full definition or analysis of space and time. And that I shall not attempt. There is, however, one negative though basic character which differentiates the forms of serial order which we call space and time from every other form of serial order. The position of an object in space or of an event in time is independent of its intrinsic character, whereas in all other forms of order the position or extrinsic relations of an essence is determined by its nature or intrinsic character. Thus 4 and 2 + 2 occupy the same position in the number series because of their intrinsic natures. But it is not because of their natures that *this round table* and *this red table* occupy the same position in space ; hence the proposition " This round table is red " is a contingent proposition, while 2 + 2 = 4 is a necessary proposition. In the latter case the identity in position or denotation of the terms follows from the nature of their essence or connotations ; in the former case it does not.

BRYCE : In order for a thing to exist it must in the first place be completely individuated with respect to the totality of essences, and in the second place it must possess the two determinate sets of purely external relations to other individuals which we call space and time. Is that your idea ?

HYLANOUS : Yes.

BRYCE : How does consciousness enter into this system of subsisting essences ? Granting that the world of existing objects can be differentiated from the totality of conceivable essences by the spatio-temporal relations which unite its members, what further differentia is necessary to define a field of conscious experience ?

HYLANOUS : The concept of consciousness like the concepts of space and time is by reason of its simplicity difficult to define. For to define it we should have to analyse it and express it as a complex of elements simpler and more generic than itself. For the purpose of your question, however, it may be sufficient to point out a characteristic of consciousness about which everyone will, I think, agree, and which will serve as a provisional definition. Whatever else it may be, consciousness or experience is at least a relation between an individual that exists or occupies a spatio-temporal position and other objects existent and non-existent, such that these other objects, in addition to their own proper efficacies, physical or merely logical, acquire a secondary or vicarious efficacy within the states of the individual to whom they are related, *i.e.* by whom they are experienced.

BRYCE : You say that any object of which a man is conscious is by virtue of that relation capable of acting in the place where the man is as well as in its own place ?

HYLANOUS : Yes, Bryce ; to be conscious of an object means that that object functions as part of yourself, as one of your own states. However distant it may be in space or in time, it is brought by the relation of consciousness into direct and immediate causal connection with the passions and actions of your organism.

BRYCE : You seem to make of consciousness a paradoxical form of relationship, which overrides spatial and temporal distances, and which enables a thing to be and to act in a place where it is not. Will you give us some concrete illustrations of this aspect of consciousness ?

HYLANOUS : Cæsar's crossing of the Rubicon is an event which happened at a date many years ago, and at a place many miles away, yet we, here and now, can think of that distant event ; and as an object in the field of our conceptual consciousness it acts upon our feelings and thoughts, and controls our speech-movements as we discuss it. In short, it has a real though secondary efficacy upon our brains, even though its primary and proper efficacy was upon the remote things spatially and temporally contiguous to it in its own place and time.

BRYCE : Of course I see what you are driving at, but would it not be less sensational and more accurate to say that it is not Cæsar crossing the Rubicon that is acting upon our brains, but only our description or image of that event ?

HYLANOUS : No, Bryce, I do not think so. The object of my thought is the event itself, and not an image or verbal description. I can have the latter also, now that you have mentioned it, as an object of thought, but I did not until you spoke of it. There is, indeed, a very simple way to prove that we are conscious of things rather than of our images of things. For, observe, you could not claim that the objects of your conceptual thought were images of things rather than the things themselves without distinguishing between them, and as you can only distinguish between objects which are contents of your experience, it would be a self-contradiction to say that you could not think of a distant object, but only of a present copy of it. You could not distinguish your thought or description of a thing from the thing itself unless both of them were objects in your consciousness.

BRYCE : Well, give some other illustration of your idea of consciousness. Cæsar's crossing the Rubicon was a case of conceptual consciousness—choose something from that more direct and intimate form of awareness which we term perception.

HYLANOUS : Very well, take the sun which we see up there in the heavens. Its proper place is ninety million miles away, and its direct efficacy as a physical object radiating energy is upon the ether or other physical objects immediately contiguous to it. Yet that same sun is also an element in our present field of consciousness, and as such it causes feelings of interest and pleasure, and serves as an illustration of our discussion. It has, for example, made me say things about it which are different from those which I would have said about the moon or a comet. In short, it functions as an effective determiner of our psycho-cerebral activities here in this room.

BRYCE : By no means all of our conscious experience is of existent things. There are cases of illusion and dreams, and also those cases in which, without false belief, we entertain in imagination the thoughts of non-existent objects such as fairies and mermaids, or of abstract universals such as justice or redness. How would your provisional definition of consciousness as a condition of the vicarious efficacy or presence of a thing in a place other than its proper place apply here ? These latter objects have no places of their own in time and space.

HYLANOUS : Non-existent objects, whether particulars like mermaids, or universals like justice, have indeed, as you say, no proper places of their own in the spatio-temporal world of existence. But, in so far as they figure as objects of experience, they gain an efficacy and a presence in the life of the individual who experiences them. Existent objects in addition to the effects they produce in their own places may act also in as many secondary places as there are individuals by whom they are experienced ; but non-existent particulars have their only efficacies in the lives of conscious individuals. Sirens and goddesses have been potent factors in the world's history, but their efficacy has been parasitic or vicarious. The only changes which non-existent things have wrought have taken place in and through the existent individuals who have imagined them.

BRYCE : According to your view, Hylanous, the universe of conceivable objects could be divided with respect to their relations to consciousness into four classes. (1) Things which have a primary or intrinsic presence and efficacy in the spatio-temporal world of existence, and also a secondary or vicarious presence and efficacy in the consciousness of individuals. These would be the things that exist, and that are also experienced—such as the sun and earth. (2) Those things which neither exist nor are experienced, and which therefore lack both intrinsic and vicarious efficacy—such as non-existent objects which nobody has ever thought of. (3) Things which are present in men's experience, but not present in existence—such as the sirens and mermaids of which we were speaking a moment ago. And (4) Things which exist and enjoy a primary efficacy in the spatio-temporal continuum, but which have never been experienced, and hence have never possessed a vicarious efficacy in the consciousness of individuals.

HYLANOUS : Yes, Bryce, there would be the four classes that you have given. And may I add that the reason that has led philosophers from the earliest times to conceive of non-existent objects as purely psychical or subjective rather than as objectively subsisting independently of consciousness, is the fact that while an existent object can operate both in its own place, and also in the individual who experiences it, a non-existent object is efficacious only in somebody's experience. It has only a single and secondary efficacy, and hence is supposed to have its entire nature determined by the mind.

BRYCE : How do you explain the origin of this capacity for vicarious presence which you call consciousness ? Is it an omnipresent relation by which any existent individual is united to the rest of the universe, or is it restricted to a certain limited class of individuals, for example those which possess a highly developed nervous system ?

HYLANOUS : The question of the causes and conditions of consciousness is a matter of cosmology rather than epistemology, and I should prefer to stick to the purely empirical and non-controversial definition which I have given. But since you have raised the point, I will confess that I believe that any entity is conscious in so far as its states are the effects produced upon it by past events, and are the causes of future events ; and that the objects in the field of such consciousness will consist of the simplest or most probable causes of those states.

BRYCE : You mean that a thing's consciousness is nothing but the capacity of its states to refer backward to their causes ?

HYLANOUS : Yes ; consciousness is nothing but the retrospective or retroactive correlate of causality or energy.

BRYCE : What do you mean by the retroactive correlate of energy ?

HYLANOUS : By the retroactive correlate of energy I mean the not externally observable characteristic of a thing at any instant which embodies its past, and is correlated with the potentiality of its future behaviour. A moving body, for example, at any one position is in all its externally observable characters exactly like a motionless body in the same position. The moving body, however, has that in it which ensures its occupancy of a new position in the following instant. Though this energy is invisible at any one instant, it is as real as the shape or size of the body possessing it.

BRYCE : But, Hylanous, nothing is more visible than motion.

HYLANOUS : Yes, through a finite interval of time. But the energy is real at each instant of that interval, and at such single instants it is not visible. The essential privacy or invisibility of energy may, however, seem more clear in the case of what is called potential energy. A coiled spring, for example, contains in its system of invisible accelerations the capacity for its future movements. And here, as in the case of any system of energy, the potentiality of its future is embodied in the invisible summation of the results of its past. In short, energy and its retroactive correlate constitute that inner property of a body which refers to what is outside and beyond it in space and time.

BRYCE : If you really take seriously this absurdly

materialistic correlation of consciousness with energy, how are you going to differentiate what we ordinarily call consciousness from this universal property of matter ?

HYLANOUS : The carbon compound known as protoplasm, and in particular that most highly developed form of protoplasm known as the human cortex, possesses the curious capacity for retaining as specific forms of potential energy minute portions of the specific kinetic energies of the neural currents which stream through it. These traces of potential energy are built up into vastly complex systems, which give to the brain possessing them the power of referring to the past and future in time and to the beyond in space. It is by reason of the extraordinary richness in form and vastness in range, of its system of potential energies, that the human brain possesses that capacity to remember the remote past and to plan for the distant future which distinguishes man as a self-determining and rational being from other living beings and from the inanimate bodies whose stores of energy are simple in form, and not sufficient in range to prevent their behaviour from being controlled by the bodies immediately contiguous to them. Do you like the theory, Bryce ?

BRYCE : No, Hylanous, I cannot say that I do. The only part of it that appeals to me is the doctrine that we are somehow made conscious of the things external to us by the effects that those things produce upon us. This is true enough ; but I am not at all convinced that the effects thus produced upon us by things are summed up and stored in our brains as forms of potential energy ; or that even if they were they would of themselves suffice to reveal to us the objects which were their causes. Still less am I convinced that every existent particular merely in virtue of its causal efficiency or energy possesses an awareness of its past causes.

HYLANOUS : Well, Bryce, it is not at all necessary that my special theory of the psycho-physical relation be accepted as a basis for the epistemological eirenicon which we are discussing. The ultimate nature and grounds of consciousness may be whatever you please. So long as you will admit my purely empirical or descriptive definition of consciousness as the condition or property of a thing in virtue of which other things distant from it in time and space can enjoy a vicarious presence and efficacy through the effects that they produce upon it, that is all that is needed. Consciousness conceived in this way constitutes a new form of relationship between things. It is conditioned by space and time for its actualization, but it transcends those relations in the sense that it affords any existent being the possibility of an immediate *rapport* with all other things actual and possible. Any individual so far as he is conscious occupies the central point or focus of a field of objects. And these objects, when considered as related to one another through their relation to the central point, make up what we may call, after Mr. Bertrand Russell, a " perspective." And in so far as an individual's consciousness can be conceived as possibly extended to all the things in the universe, we can say that the universe in addition to its other characters and relations constitutes a permanently possible perspective system or field of experience.

BRYCE : Do you mean that any and all the members of your realistic universe can be considered as not only existing and subsisting in their various physical and logical relations, but also that each and all of them can in addition be considered as members of the possible experience-system or, as you call it, the perspective of an individual ?

HYLANOUS : Yes. Everything in the universe is an object of possible experience, and can be described as such.

BRYCE : What individual are you considering as possessing the universe as a field of possible experience ? The Absolute, I suppose ?

HYLANOUS : Why, any individual at all could have the universe as a field of possible experience.

BRYCE : You mean that there are as many total systems of possible experience as there are individuals ?

HYLANOUS : Why certainly. Any system or array of objects from the universe down to the things in this room can be considered as constituting as many perspective-fields as there are possible individuals to serve as the *foci* or experiencers of such fields.

BRYCE : A plurality of Absolutes ! Horrible !

HYLANOUS : Only of *possible* Absolutes, Bryce. Remember here may not be even one that is actual ; and remember also that their fields of objects can coincide with one another, and with the field of existence to any extent.

BRYCE : But could one and the same set of objects figure in more than one of these perspectives ?

HYLANOUS : Certainly ; take the objects here in the room. You and I each see them from different positions, and hence for each of us they make up a different perspective. As members of a new perspective they acquire new relations which do not in any way interfere with their relations as independent existents or as members of other perspective systems. The fields of the various perspectives overlap and interpenetrate one another, and in so far as they are true they overlap and inter-penetrate the field of existence, but they cannot interfere with one another because the members of a perspective-system enjoy causal efficacy only through the agency of the states of the perceiving individuals, each of whom occupies a different spatial position. Thus you and I see the same objects in the room—an arm-chair, a bookcase, etc.—but as members of my experience the chair and the bookcase, despite their spatial and qualitative differences, have for me (as they have not for you) a particular association and interaction through my memory of having bought them at the same shop. And again, you may press your eyeball, and some of the objects in your perspective of the room will dance about together, while those same objects in my perspective and in the field of physical existence will remain unmoved. In short, the relation between any two objects in a field of conscious experience is primarily triadic and indirect, for it is only through the medium of the states of the perceiver that they can influence each other.

BRYCE : How many of these possible perspectives or fields of experience are there ?

HYLANOUS : Just as many as there are possible positions in the spatio-temporal continuum and possible kinds of individuals to occupy them and serve as foci or organizing points. Thus, if the infinitely infinite totality of conceivable objects is termed the " objective universe," the number of ways in which that universe can figure as a system of possible experience will be an infinite of an infinitely higher order than that of the universe itself. For each individual at each point in space at each instant will be the centre of a definite separate field of possible experience. Thus the universe would yield a system of possible experience to the Kaiser that would be different from that which it would present to Napoleon or to any other individual, even if put in the same place and time with the Kaiser. And each and all of these different individuals could get a different totality of experience for each and all of the points in space or instants in time. So, Bryce, you will realize that a realistic universe, instead of being a *thing-in-itself* beyond the bounds of possible experience, is, on the contrary, through and through experienceable. And any object in it can without prejudice to its status of realistic independence be described in terms of any one of an infinity of possible experiences.

BRYCE : I think I could admit most of what you have said, but I feel a little doubtful as to your extending the term " perspective," which properly applies solely to the field of visual perception, to characterize an entire system of consciousness, conceptual as well as perceptual.

HYLANOUS : Perspective in the strict sense denotes, as you say, the visual field as it appears from a single point in space. The essential characteristic of a perspective consists in the facts (1) that the objects in it are related and organized with respect to a central point or focus on which they are projected as effects. And (2) that the new orientation which the objects gain through their vicarious presence at the focus, can, since it is a derivative causal function of their independent existential system, supervene upon that system with a more or less perfect coincidence, and without directly interfering either with it or with other perspective views of it. Now, these essential characters of an ordinary visual perspective are the essential characters of any field of conscious experience. Any of the objects in the universe can directly or indirectly produce upon my brain a set of effects and somehow or other, by means of these effects and depending upon them, there arises *in* me a consciousness of objects *outside* of me in time as well as in space. Some of these objects are apprehended directly, and in definite spatial and temporal relation to the apprehending organism, as, for example, the sight of the window in front of us, or the sound of the clock that has just ceased striking. These we call perceptions. Other objects in the field of experience are apprehended indirectly, *i.e.* in terms of their connections with other things, and do not appear in any definite relation to the apprehending organism, as for example Cæsar's crossing the Rubicon, the coming of the millennium, the other side of the moon, mermaids, or the square root of minus one. These we call conceptions. But any perceived or conceived object is related to any other object in the field of consciousness through the agency of the brain of the apprehending organism at the moment of the apprehension. This is the first essential of a perspective. And the various relations which the objects sustain to one another supervene without any causal interference upon the physical or logical relations which the objects enjoy in their own right as independent of the apprehending organism. Thus the illustrations just used might lead me to wonder whether the moon was full when Cæsar crossed the Rubicon, and whether Cæsar himself believed in mermaids, and had ever had the conception of the square roots of negative numbers. By such idle fantasies, the various objects—Cæsar, moon, mermaids, square root of minus one—are all brought into a set of relations quite irrelevant to their proper natures, and wholly determined by my own psycho-physical states. The true relations between these objects are in no way affected by their secondary or vicarious relations to my thoughts and feelings. In short, the objects of the universe, in addition to their primary natures and positions, are all of them members of each of the actual and possible perspective systems, total or partial, of which any individual at any time or place can be the centre.

BRYCE : It is your opinion, then, that any and all objects can be characterized in their entirety as elements of possible experience ?

HYLANOUS : Yes ; and, as I have said, whether or not there is anywhere an actual absolute, there is certainly an infinity of possible absolutes, with respect to whose ideal perfection any finite experience may be measured and evaluated.

BRYCE : Well, tell me, Hylanous, do the objects of the universe, when considered as members of a possible experience or perspective, form an organic unity ? In other words : *are their relations internal ?*

HYLANOUS : Yes ; in the sense in which we have been using these conceptions, the elements in a perspective are internally related, and so form an organic unity in which each part is determined by its relations to the whole. That is to say, any object of thought has by reason of its potential relations to the other objects in a possible perspective certain characteristics which would pertain to it as a result of standing in such relations. Thus, for example, the nature of moonlight could be fully known only if one knew all the tertiary qualities, such as the tender values which all possible lovers under all possible circumstances might ascribe to it.

BRYCE :   How then does your conception of internal relations differ from that of the idealist ?

HYLANOUS : My conception of relational internality differs from that of the idealist in two respects.   First, the internal relation of two essences does not imply a corresponding internality of relation between their existences.   Thus the essence or nature of a " half-dozen apples " implies the essence or nature of a " dozen apples," but the existence of half a dozen apples does not imply the existence of a dozen apples. And the nature or essence of imperfection implies the essence or nature of an absolute perfection with reference to which the imperfection is judged and measured ; but the existence of an imperfect thing of any type by no means implies the existence of a perfect thing of the same type.

BRYCE :   This was the principle that you used before in denying that I could infer the existence of an absolute experience in which the fragmentary meanings and values of our finite experience were all completed.

HYLANOUS : Exactly. I admitted to you that we were obliged to accept, not one, indeed, but an infinite number of absolute selves, potential completions of our actual selves, in relation to which our finite experiences could be estimated ; but I denied that we could for that reason alone infer the existence of even one of these potential absolutes.

BRYCE : What is the second point in which your conception of internal relations or " organic unity " differs from that of the neo-Hegelian idealist ?

HYLANOUS : My second point of difference is this : in the realm of essences to which internal relations are applicable and which consequently form an organic unity, the characters which belong to a term in virtue of its relations to a second term are in no way negated or changed by the other characters which belong to the term in virtue of its relations to still other terms.   Thus a given term, say " whiteness," acquires a certain supplementary character in virtue of its being related to a second term, " blackness," as its opposite ; but this character is not negated or changed by the other supplementary characters that belong to whiteness in virtue of its relations to blueness and redness.   So, while I can say with the idealist that each entity in the ·realm of essences is a " logical microcosm " possessing as rich a manifold of internal attributes as there are relations in which it stands to other entities, yet I can also say, with the modern neo-realistic logicians, that nothing that is true about some of these aspects will be made false by what may be later found out about other aspects.

BRYCE : I never could see why the neo-realistic logicians objected so bitterly to our doctrine of internal relations.   It is obvious that the nature of a thing gets modified by its relations to each and ·every other thing, and that therefore each fragment of the universe is a function of the whole and presupposes it.   And a system, the parts of which imply the whole, is an organic unity.

HYLANOUS : The neo-realistic logicians object to the doctrine of internal relations because, in its ordinary form, it throws logic into confusion, and makes knowledge impossible. For according to that doctrine it would be impossible to know the truth about a part of the universe without knowing the truth about the whole.   If every object of thought owed its entire nature to its relations to everything else, then we should have to know everything before we could know any-thing, which is both empirically impossible and logically self-contradictory.

BRYCE : How does your own modified form of the theory of internal relations escape this difficulty, if difficulty it be ?

HYLANOUS : By maintaining that the secondary relations, and the secondary characters which they produce in the terms related, supervene upon and add to, without in anyway destroying or negating the primary relations and the primary characters produced by them.

BRYCE : Please illustrate your meaning.

HYLANOUS : Certainly. Take the term " north." Here is a notion that appears to be all shot through with relationality from the very start, for north presupposes south even in its primary intent. Now, when north is considered in relation to east and west and up and down it gains new attributes or shades of meaning which constitute something of its secondary intent. But the new modifications do not in any way interfere with the original nature of north. They only add to it. When considered in relation to contingent and existential entities like the American Civil War and the Pole discovered by Peary, the entity " north " gains further modifications which add to the previous connotation, but which do not in any way take away from it. And while we can and must admit that if north could be known as by an Absolute in all its infinity of relations to the rest of the conceivable universe, it would be found to have acquired thereby an infinite wealth of internal secondary intent, its original or primary intent would be preserved intact, and all the propositions which were true of the primary intent would maintain their status of truth quite unembarrassed by the introduction of the new truths concerning the secondary intent. Or, to take another illustration drawn from that system in which internal relations have their most complete exemplification—the number system. Consider the numbers 7 and 8 : a child can know a great deal that is true and worthwhile about these numbers before he learns that when multiplied together they make 56. And when he learns this latter relation the old truths are in no way discredited, although 7 considered as a joint factor with 8 in producing the relatively formidable 56 takes on new colours and a richer interest. And in the same way I doubt not that if we knew the various relations in which the number 7 stands to any and all of the members of the number series it would acquire in addition to its primary intent of $6 + 1$ an infinitely rich system of attributes which would, however, in no way interfere with one another.

BRYCE : Well, Hylanous, I admit that you have satisfied

my demand that the conceivable world be treated as an organic unity in which each member is, as it were, a logical microcosm in which the nature of the whole is somehow incarnate. And I admit too that the theory of internal relations is helped rather than hurt by the modification involved in your insistence that the various relations do not interfere with one another. But would you, as a realist, be willing to allow this conception of modified internality to apply to the cognitive relation ?

HYLANOUS: Certainly; every conceivable thing stands in the relation of " experienceable object " to every possible consciousness. And from each of these relations it gains a new quality. Thus the other side of the moon in addition to its commonplace physical properties possesses all those qualities of sentimental significance which could be attributed to it by the non-existent lovers who under other astronomic conditions would be able to enjoy the luminous contours which are to us unknown. But the new properties which objects possess in virtue of their relation to the conscious life-histories of actual or possible individuals in no way negate those other properties which they possess as their primary intent or as the result of their relations to objects other than conscious individuals. And while the full and complete nature of any conceivable entity includes the appearances and values which it would have for every possible consciousness, it does not imply or need the *existence* of any consciousness whatever.

BRYCE: You mean, in short, that everything in the universe, existent and subsistent, implies a possible experience to which it is internally related, but that at the same time nothing in the universe, existent or subsistent, implies actual consciousness; and that consequently the objects of any actual conscious individual are externally related to him as an existent being, and so capable themselves of existing or subsisting independently of his cognizing them ?

HYLANOUS: Yes, Bryce, that is it exactly. That is the compromise that I am offering you on the subject of idealism and its theory of the internality of all relations, and in particular of the cognitive relation.

BRYCE : Well, Hylanous, in this matter of internal relations, and in most of the other subjects that we have discussed, you have properly enough addressed your arguments to the view that I represent, namely, Absolute Idealism. But I am curious to know how your compromise theory would apply to another view that is sometimes called idealism, though its correct designation is Phenomenalism. Phenomenalism or " Empirical Idealism " is opposed to our absolute idealism in most points, and its scientific method and spirit are very different from the philosophic method and spirit of absolutism ; but there is one point in epistemology on which we are agreed, and which would, I suppose, seem to you as a realist to be an erroneous one. Phenomenalists like Ernst Mach and John Stuart Mill, and absolutists like the Cairds and Professor Royce all agree on the basic doctrine that objects exist, and have their meaning only within experience. But whereas the phenomenalists declare that the so-called objective world consists of past, present, and future experiences of finite beings like ourselves, and that truth is the confirmation of ideas by later sensations, we absolutists, as you know, hold that the objective world cannot be adequately expressed in terms of finite experience, and that the truth of an idea consists not merely or mainly in its confirmation in the perceptions which it anticipates or to which it may lead, but rather in its consistency and harmony with the eternally actualized system of absolute experience which is implied by our world of appearance. Now, how does your epistemological eirenicon apply to empirical idealism or phenomenalism as I have defined it ?

HYLANOUS : I think that my compromise applies to the empirical idealism that you have referred to in quite the same way that it applies to your own absolute idealism. We realists object to idealism because it makes the existence of things depend upon their presence in experience. And empirical idealists with their attempt to restrict the reality of the mighty cosmos, infinite in space and in time, to the narrow field of human and animal experience, are quite as obnoxious to us as are the objective idealists like yourself, who think it necessary to postulate a transcendental Absolute Being for whose existence there is no evidence, in order to justify the being of the world in which we live. Before the revival of realism the philosophical writings of modern philosophy were largely made up of discussions between the upholders of these two forms of the idealistic epistemology. Empirical idealism had the advantage in sticking to the facts and not postulating gratuitous entities of a transcendental kind. The only experience known to exist is finite experience, so if you have to make experience the container of reality it is better to take the finite experience that you know rather than to invoke a hypothetical absolute. On the other hand, you absolutists had the grace to recognize that the world of things and laws was too vast an affair to be made to depend upon the experience of animals who have inhabited one planet for a few million years. You were right in rejecting finite experience as inadequate to contain the universe, but wrong in supposing that you could help matters by invoking an Absolute. The transcendental assumptions of such idealists as Josiah Royce are not proper remedies for the poor flux of sensations and behaviour to the compass of which such phenomenalists as Professor Karl Pearson would reduce the earth and the starry heavens. The absolutist cure is indeed no better than the phenomenalist disease. So it was that while you two schools of subjectivists abused one another politely and subsisted prosperously on the validity of your mutual refutations, we realists were not prevented by your differences in logic and cosmology from recognizing the epistemological fallacy that you shared in common—the fallacy, namely, of supposing that it is necessary to make the universe depend upon *any* experience, finite *or* absolute.

BRYCE : Really, Hylanous, the purpose of my question as to the bearing of your theory upon empirical idealism was to elicit information and not an abusive sermon.

HYLANOUS : Please excuse me. I was just on the point of answering you quite definitely. The compromise theory that I propose is based on the substitution for the idealist's notion of *actual experience*, of the notion of *possible experience*. The world must be *experienceable*, but it need not be *experienced*. From this it follows that while in their old form Absolute Idealism and Empirical Idealism are each of them incompatible with the other and both of them false, in their amended form they are compatible with each other and both of them true. For observe : in the realistic universe which I offer you, any object can figure as an element of a possible finite and imperfect experience, and at the same time it can figure as an element in an absolute and perfect experience. And because it is possible, and not actual experience to which all things are related, the existence and subsistence of those things is in no way dependent upon or restricted to the existence of any experience whatsoever, finite or absolute, yours or another's. The nature and the reality of the universe and of all parts of the universe are what they are irrespective of whether any individual, human or divine, is so fortunate as to be conscious of them. But at the same time the universe and all parts of the universe, though externally related to any actual experience, are internally related to every possible experience. *Things are what they can be experienced as because things can be experienced for what they are.*

BRYCE : But, Hylanous, you seem to forget that this conception of real things as possible experiences has been put forward both by the objective or transcendental idealist, Kant, and by the phenomenalist or empirical idealist, J. S. Mill. For Kant, the objects of nature are elements in a system of possible experience, and the laws of nature are the relational forms of possible experience ; while for Mill, material objects are defined as permanent possibilities of experience.

HYLANOUS : My position differs from the positions of Kant and Mill in that I believe that the possibility of being subjectively experienced is a supplement to objective reality, and not a substitute for it. There is no such thing as a mere possibility, in the sense in which Kant, Mill, and other epistemological idealists use the notion. The permanent possibility of experiencing a chair implies the chair as existent in its own right. And it is because things are real, regardless of whether they are actually experienced, that they constitute possibilities of experience. If I were to ask you at breakfast whether you would like to eat the possibility of a chicken, you would probably express a preference for something more hearty—an egg, for example. Now an egg is a possible chicken only because it is an actual egg ; so the objects in a realistic universe are possible experiences only because they are actual existents and subsistents. Indeed, the very conditions and method of their possibility of being experienced can be explained only by assuming their antecedent objectivity.

BRYCE : I admit that your realistic theory uses the concept of possible experience in a different sense from that of idealism ; but does not that very difference deprive the realist of the undoubted advantage from a methodological standpoint of conceiving of all things in terms of possible experience ?

HYLANOUS : Not at all. What you think of as the methodological advantage of the " possible experience " doctrine is the feature of it which frees you from the bugaboo of a reality which is a thing-in-itself outside of all experience and therefore unknowable.

BRYCE : Yes, Hylanous, to be quite frank with you, one of the main reasons for our opposition to realism has consisted in our hatred of any theory which seemed to posit a " reality " that was not only inaccessible to knowledge, but incommensurate with all that appears real in our everyday life.

HYLANOUS : Exactly so. We realists recognize fully the need of avoiding the mock reality of a world beyond experience. We hold with you that the only reality that is worth discussing is a reality that can be experienced, and that can be expressed in terms of experience. But at the same time we insist that this experienceable reality constitutes a system of self-subsisting entities, which are in no way dependent for their nature or reality upon the extent to which they enter into actual experience. Instead of making the universe as small as the field of actual experience, the realist makes the scope of possible experience as broad as the universe; and while nothing is real by reason of being experienced, yet everything is experienceable by reason of its being existent or subsistent.

BRYCE : You have indicated the manner in which your realistic compromise on the basis of possible experience applies to empirical idealism as well as to absolute idealism. How does the theory apply to that bugaboo, solipsism, which you realists have always declared to be implicit in any idealism carried out to its logical conclusion ?

HYLANOUS : To the realist, solipsism is indeed nothing but idealism carried out to its logical conclusion. If you once start to make the content of any experience, perceptual or conceptual, dependent for its nature or reality upon the fact that it figures as a term of the experience-relation, you cannot consistently stop until you have reduced everything in the universe, including your own past existence, not to mention the Absolute, to the status of dependence upon your consciousness at the moment. It is perfectly true that most idealists have stopped far short of this abyss to which their dialectic would lead them. They have preferred inconsistency to absurdity. Thus we find Berkeley reducing the primary or spatial qualities of the experienceable world to the same status of dependence on the conscious subject to which Cartesianism had been so ill-advised as to reduce the secondary or non-spatial qualities of material bodies. But there Berkeley stopped short, and insisted that while knowledge by perceptions made the known dependent upon the knower, there was a knowledge by means of " notions " that was quite different, in that it enabled the knower to apprehend both the relational order in which ideas are given to us, and also the minds of our fellows, without thereby reducing these objects to the dependent mental states of the knower. Kant went much farther in that he extended the principle of subjectivism from the particular *facts* of the world to its *laws*, and so made the human mind into a legislator for nature. He accomplished this " Copernican revolution " by substituting for the independent world of known objects an unknowable " thing-in-itself," and for the empirical self in each of us a transcendental self outside of time and space. Kant's successors went still farther, for they abolished the " thing-in-itself," which was all that was left of the independent material world, and then proceeded to replace Kant's plurality of transcendental selves with a single absolute self for whom and in whom the universe has its being. But here again, as in the case of Berkeley, the same subjectivistic arguments that had sufficed for the relegation of nature and nature's laws to a status of dependence upon a transcendental or an absolute self, had to be arbitrarily brought to an end ; for if worked out consistently the absolute self and all other selves would have been reduced to the speaker's self, which is solipsism. Just as Berkeley had preserved the independent reality of the realm of relations and of other minds by abandoning, through the use of the term " notion," the conception of knowledge as an internal relation in accordance with which all known objects must be regarded as states of the knower, so with a quite similar inconsistency Fichte and Hegel refused to apply their subjectivistic principles to our knowledge of the absolute self. For them, the Absolute Ego, on which all else depends, can itself be known without being thereby reduced to dependence upon the knowing. To it is accorded the same realistic status that for ordinary folk is ascribed to the material universe.

BRYCE : Well, Hylanous, I feel somewhat doubtful as to the justness of your charge that Berkeley and the Post-Kantians were guilty of the same kind of inconsistency in stopping their arguments before reaching the stage of solipsism. But how does your realistic interpretation of " possible experience " make matters any better ?

HYLANOUS : Why, just in this way. If objects in addition to their independent existence and subsistence have the possibility of entering into any experience, then I can regard the entire universe, including not only all material bodies, but other minds as well, and even the absolute self, if there be such a thing, as objects of my possible experience. And I can perform this solipsistic reduction of the universe to terms of my experience without absurdity, and without in any way belittling the world of which I am so humble a member.

BRYCE : Do you mean that you can regard other minds as mere thoughts in our own mind ? Do you consider me, for example, as being only a figment of your imagination ?

HYLANOUS : I didn't say that you were a *mere* thought of mine, Bryce. Nothing is a *mere* thought. But it is certainly true that you are an object of my thought ; like everything else, you are such that you can enter into my conceptual or perceptual experience. You are not a Kantian thing-in-itself, and I can conceive of you only in terms of the experiences which I might have of you. There is nothing derogatory in this. Just as an egg does not lose anything of its independent reality when we recognize that it is the possibility of a chicken, so you lose none of your independent reality in virtue of being a possible object in the experience of someone else. It is because things stand in those primary relations which constitute their existence or subsistence that they are able to figure in the secondary relational systems which constitute the perspectives or experiences of beings other than themselves. If I believed that you were nothing but one of my thoughts, and if you believed the same of me, we could not pass one another in the street without each of us feeling embarrassed. But if our actual or possible knowledge of one another is the consequence rather than the cause of our existence, there is nothing in any way embarrassing or contradictory about my being one of your thoughts, and you being one of mine.

BRYCE : You would maintain that a realistic universe, whose every part is independent of whether or not it is actually experienced, is nevertheless of a nature such that each part can contain as possible experience the very whole of which it is a part ?

HYLANOUS : Yes, Bryce. It is because the whole contains the parts in its existence that each part contains the whole in essence, or as possible experience. In short, I offer you a doctrine which affords a universal justification of epistemological idealism, objective and absolutistic, or empirical and phenomenalistic. And you can carry either form of idealism to the point of solipsism without the slightest danger. In return I ask only that while retaining all your positive sympathies for idealism, you give up the unnecessary and purely negative notion that a world whose nature is definable in terms of experience must therefore depend for its existence upon experience. And now, if you have no objection, we might go over very briefly the various stages of our discussion. Like most modern idealists, you put forward three main lines of argument in support of your position : (1) The seemingly axiomatic argument based on an analysis of the " ego-centric predicament," *i.e.* the necessity of apprehending everything in terms of experience and in relation to the conscious self ; (2) the mainly psychological arguments from the relativity of perception and the occurrence of error ; (3) the arguments based mainly on certain purely logical considerations as to the necessary internality of all relations, and consequently of the cognitive relation.

BRYCE : Yes, those were the three principal considerations on which I founded my idealism. They do not operate in isolation but in relation to one another.

HYLANOUS : Now, with regard to the first argument we found that the mere fact that a thing such as a chair stands as object in the cognitive relation to an individual does not in itself justify the assumption that the cognitive relation uniting the individual and the chair is an internal relation such that the chair as it appears could not also exist during the intervals when it does not appear. In other words, you agreed that we had no right to prejudge the nature of the cognitive relation by assuming that an object *before* the mind was an inseparable state *of* the mind.

BRYCE : Yes, Hylanous, I did agree with you to the extent of admitting that it was abstractly conceivable that the objects which are related to us in experience might remain the same when not experienced, but you will remember that, even so, I maintained that the burden of proof was upon the realist. For since we can only apprehend objects when they stand in the experience-relation to us, it remains at best sheer guesswork as to what they would be when not experienced by us.

HYLANOUS : That is true, but this burden of proof that would seem to rest on the realist was greatly lightened, if not altogether removed, by the reflection that from the nature of the case the ego-centric predicament would be unavoidable, irrespective of whether cognition were an external relation which had no effect on the objects cognized, or an internal relation which constituted its terms. In either case we could apprehend objects only by having them related to us, and therefore no further assumption would be necessary to explain the fact that we can see objects only when we are looking at them.

BRYCE : Yes, I did admit that the realistic analysis of the ego-centric predicament had a certain degree of validity, and consented to your proposal to give up at least for the time the claim that the truth of idealism is self-evident.

HYLANOUS : And so by mutual agreement we decided that as it was impossible from the nature of the case to determine by direct observation what happened to an object when it passed from observation, we would try to determine that question indirectly by studying the behaviour of objects. And we thought that the way in which things behaved when in consciousness might give a clue to their probable fate when we ceased to be conscious of them.

BRYCE : Yes ; and it was in this connection that I advanced my second line of arguments for idealism which were based on the relativity of perception and the occurrence of error.

HYLANOUS : You insisted that the fact that how an object appeared depended on the condition of the perceiver, and that the manner in which he was related to the object proved that the object was essentially and inseparably bound up with conscious experience, and that consequently it could not be believed to exist apart from it. Then I dared you to apply this theory that relativity implied subjectivity to particular objects such as the hands of a watch, and asked if you really believed that because a watch appeared differently to different observers, and to one observer at different times, it followed that the watch and the movement of its hands depended upon their being experienced by you or me.

BRYCE : And in reply I pointed out that of course the watch existed independently of its relation to this or that observer, and that the relativity of perception only indicated the dependence of things upon consciousness in general, or rather upon an absolute consciousness which was immanent in and also transcendent of our finite minds.

HYLANOUS : Yes ; and I objected that the relativity which we find in experience is always relativity to some particular observer, and not to a general or absolute consciousness. So that although your Absolute might suffice to restore to objects the status of reality independent of individual consciousness, it was a purely gratuitous invention, at least in the sense that it in no way followed from the relativity of perception, and in no way helped to cure or to explain the errors resulting from it. In short, if relativity proves anything in the way of subjective dependence, it proves a dependence upon the finite individuals, which was a conclusion that you rejected as being a mere caricature of genuine objective idealism.

BRYCE : That is correct according to my memory, Hylanous. And then you went on to show how the phenomena of relativity, and even of illusion, were compatible with the realistic view that cognition was selective rather than creative. And that the fact that an object appears as having various sizes, shapes, and colours to various individuals does not prove that it is in itself without size, shape, or colour, but that on the contrary it is just by conceiving it to have such specific qualities, independently and in its own right, that we can understand how the different aberrations of perspective in different individuals are produced. You closed by pointing out the way in which both common sense and science take account of the personal equation or distortion of perspective and succeed, by a process of comparison, in eliminating it without eliminating or in any way damaging the independent reality of the object.

HYLANOUS: Exactly so; and as I recall it you admitted that on the whole you were convinced of the validity of my answers, and confessed that after all the Berkeleyan appeal to the relativity of sensory experience was an ineffective method for the modern idealist to use.

BRYCE: That brought us to the third line of argument for idealism according to which the internality of the cognitive relation, and the consequent restriction of the world of reality to the world of experience, is proved by the internality of all relations, and the necessarily organic unity pervading the universe. And when we dealt with this argument you led me on to believe that you accepted it fully, admitting that the totality of conceivable objects forms a network of internal relations, and that the full nature of anything implies the nature of everything.

HYLANOUS: Yes, Bryce, and I admitted further that consciousness or the cognitive relation is no exception to the general internality of relations as such; and that consequently the full nature, meaning, and value of every object would have to include its relations to every possible consciousness. And, finally, inasmuch as any sort of individual at any point in space at any instant in time could be conceived as the focus of a possible perspective or experience-system in which the universe would be included, I maintained that each object could be defined as a possible experience in an infinite number of finite selves, and also in an infinite number of absolute selves.

BRYCE : I know you admitted all that, and offered me a universe more manifoldly subjectivistic and experiential than I had ever dreamed of. And then, as it seemed to me at the time, you spoiled it all by insisting that while every object implied the possibility of being experienced, yet no object implied an actual experience. And that not only its nature, but also its status of reality or unreality were quite independent of any existent consciousness, finite or absolute.

HYLANOUS : In other words, I tried to convince you that while relations between essences or subsistents were internal, yet relations between existents were external. I illustrated this doctrine by reminding you that while the nature and meaning of five implies the nature and meaning of ten, yet the existence of five apples by no means implies the existence of ten apples ; and that while the nature and meaning of imperfection implies the nature and meaning of perfection, yet the existence of the former by no means implies the existence of the latter. In short, a relation to your special kind of idealistic Absolute, or to any other consciousness, is implied as a possibility, but not as an actuality.

And then, you will recall, I proposed a second modification of the theory of internal relations to the effect that while all essences imply and so depend upon the relations between them, yet the resulting modifications in the terms are supplementary rather than destructive, so that the truths discovered about things in certain relations are not altered, but only added to by the discovery of further truths about them due to other relations in which they stand. It was this second modification of the theory of internal relations that enabled it to meet successfully the neo-realist charge of the absurdity of any doctrine which would not permit a proposition to be wholly true unless it expressed the whole truth.

And, finally, I pointed out that in distinction to the doctrine of Kant and Mill, the possibility possessed by objects of entering into any and all fields of experience was in no sense a substitute for their independent existence or subsistence, but that on the contrary the universal experience-ability of things is a result of their reality, and would be impossible without it.

BRYCE : That was the ·tenor of your argument, and I

confess that I was pretty much convinced by it. For after all, Hylanous, as I said at the time, what we idealists have wanted most is to get a view of things that would do away with that repulsive and self-contradictory conception which was held by some of the older realists—the conception, namely, of a reality that lies outside the scope of experience, and that consequently cannot be described in any intelligible terms. Since your eirenicon does away with the thing-in-itself, and at the same time does full justice to the organic and ego-centric character of our universe, and to the thoroughgoing experienceableness of all things, I suppose we can forgive you for your realistic insistence that things are independently real irrespective of their presence in any existent consciousness, and that it is possible, rather than actual, experience which is coextensive with the universe.

IV

In which HYLANOUS *persuades* LOVELACE *that the duality of objective and subjective results from a difference of causal context rather than from a difference of nature or existence.*

HYLANOUS : Now that both Bryce, as representing sub-jectivism, and Partridge, as representing objectivism, have assented to my compromise, I am hopeful of winning over the dualistic member of our group. For it seems to me that a solution of the epistemological problem which satisfies representatives of the two extremist attitudes ought to appeal to Lovelace even more. For his dualism, like my realism, is an attempt to mediate between the opposite positions of objectivism and subjectivism in epistemology.

LOVELACE : Well, Hylanous, your realism, as you call it, and my dualism might superficially appear to resemble one another as compromise doctrines. But in reality they are quite different. For while your compromise would include the points essential to both objectivism and subjectivism, my compromise has a less ambitious, and—if you will pardon my saying so—a more sensible aim. You try to combine the merits of the two opposed theories, and, in my opinion, succeed only in combining their errors. My dualism, on the other hand, is frankly incompatible with each of the extremes in epistemology. Without any pretence at a higher synthesis, I aim to steer a straight common-sense course midway between the Scylla of objectivism and the Charybdis of subjectivism.

HYLANOUS : Why, Lovelace, I thought you agreed with Partridge in holding that there is a real world independent of our experience, and that at the same time you thought that Bryce was right in his theory that any object of which we can be *directly* conscious is an inseparable state of the knower, that is, a mere idea or sensation.

LOVELACE : Of course, in that sense and to that extent, my view, like yours, recognizes an element of truth in each of the epistemological extremes. But there the resemblance between us ends. For I believe that the situation in which an individual cognizes the world outside him is clearly and irremediably dualistic, involving on the one side a set of internal states or ideas which constitute the individual's consciousness, and on the other hand, a set of absolutely external things which make up the world of reality. The second set is the cause of the first set, but is in no sense identical with it. Extra-organic things are not ideas, and ideas are not extra-organic things. And in view of this duality, I reject as futile the epistemological monism of the objectivist for whom the content of experience is an aspect of the material world ; and I reject as equally futile the epistemological monism of the idealist for whom physical objects are aspects of experience. While as for your attempt to combine both of these monisms, it seems to me, as I said, to involve a double set of errors. You took the objectivism of Partridge, and after admitting to him that every content of experience had an objective nature and status that was independent of consciousness, you proceeded to modify his doctrine by denying his claim that the objects of illusion and dreams were existent objects. Yet even on this, your only point of criticism, you conceded that the non-existent objects of experience, such as the straight stick that appears bent in the water, and the parallel rails that appear to converge, were existential in the sense that they were physically explicable effects of the actually existent, and might to that extent be regarded as distorted aspects of extra-organic bodies. In short, you conceded to Partridge the essentials of his objectivistic monism, merely substituting potential existence (or, if definitely illusory, a distorted and relative existence) for the actual existence which he wished to attribute to every particular object in a perceptual field. Again, in dealing with the idealism of Bryce you gave in to his epistemological monism of the subjectivistic variety, merely substituting possible experience for the actual experience to which he wished to reduce all reality.

HYLANOUS : Yes, Lovelace, that was it exactly. I thought to eliminate the paradoxes of epistemological monism by substituting the concept of *possible* for the concept of *actual*. To the Partridge-monists I said : " *The immediately experienced is numerically identical with what might be (but need not be) an independent existence.*" To the Bryce-monists I said : " *The independently existent is numerically identical with what might be (but need not be) immediately experienced.*" Why do you object to this way of dealing with the situation ?

LOVELACE : Well, for one thing, the whole business is too far-fetched and complicated to suit me. There is a chair on the floor in front of me. I press my eyeball in and out and the chair that I directly experience jumps up and down ; but in the meantime the real external chair that you and I believe in, and that we can sit upon, remains quite unmoved by the gyrations of my perceptual image. The one chair varies independently of the other, so why not recognize their obvious duality ? The chair in my experience is one thing, the chair in the physical world is another. Why should you go to work and by an elaborate *tour de force* attempt to show with the Objectivist that the chair in my consciousness is an aspect or even a potentiality of the physical chair, and then with the Subjectivist attempt with equal elaboration to prove that the physical chair is a potentiality of the chair inside my mind ? I tell you the thing is artificial and fantastic.

HYLANOUS : Do you use this epistemological dualism in teaching your classes ? I admit that it sounds very simple and clear.

LOVELACE : Yes, Hylanous, I do use it in my classes,

and it works very well. And what is more, just by way of experiment, I have tried several times to interpret the knowledge situation and to define truth and error in terms of each of the opposed forms of epistemological monism. Those efforts of mine were not successful. After learning the elements of the physiology of sense-perception, as generally taught in a beginners' course in psychology, the students found it difficult to see any sense in which states of consciousness could be identical with material objects. For that reason I returned to my dualism, and I have never since had any trouble. In teaching, I usually represent the bodies and events in the external world by the large letters of the alphabet A, B, C, . . ., and the corresponding mental states which are their effects and from which their existence is inferred by the small letters *a, b, c,* . . .

HYLANOUS : I understand ; and when our ideas are good copies of the things outside we have truth, and when they are bad copies we have error ; is that it ?

LOVELACE : Well, yes. Only, you must remember that the essential point about this so-called copying is not that the specific ideas and sensations shall resemble the bodies and properties, but only that the *relations* between the terms in the one system shall resemble the *relations* between the terms in the other system. Or, to put it in another way, there must be a correspondence rather than a similarity between the two sets of entities. For example, it is not necessary that the ether waves which cause a colour sensation should themselves have any quality resembling the colour quality of the sensation which they cause ; it is sufficient if there is a one-to-one correspondence between specific colour qualities and specific ether vibrations.

HYLANOUS : Then, if I understand you, your epistemological dualism is concerned to defend only a numerical duality or non-identity of the contents of a person's experience on the one side and the external causes of those contents on the other ; while as to the *ontological nature* of the internal experiences and the external things that cause them, your epistemology is neutral. Is that the case ?

LOVELACE : Yes, Hylanous, that is the case. The internal states or contents of which alone we have direct awareness may be the states of a psychic agent, a soul or a transcendental ego ; or, on the other hand, the self may be only the brain, and the states of consciousness may be modifications of neural substance or forms of neural energy ; or, finally, the self and its experience may be partly material and partly immaterial. With respect to these rival theories as to the nature of the self and its states, our dualistic epistemology is, as you have said, wholly neutral. While as for the external realities themselves, they may be (1) exact duplicates of the effects which they produce in consciousness (naïve realism) ; or (2) similar to our experience only as regards the primary or spatial properties (scientific or critical realism) ; or (3) of a nature quite unknown to us (agnostic realism) ; or (4) psychic in their own right, either (*a*) as aspects of a cosmic self, or (*b*) as complete souls like the Leibnizian monads, or finally (*c*) as aggregates of " mind-stuff " or " mind-dust," which is panpsychism, the view which most of the present group of epistemological dualists are inclined to accept, though our epistemological dualism as such is compatible with any of the ontological theories which I have mentioned.

HYLANOUS : Yes, I understand. It is only the so-called numerical duality or difference in position which you insist upon, from the standpoint of epistemology. What we can be aware of directly are the states inside our brains, and from these internal data we can infer with more or less probability the nature of the causes outside.

LOVELACE : Precisely.

HYLANOUS : You have said that you always found it easy to convince students of the soundness of your epistemology and to make clear to them the nature and the causes of true knowledge and of error by using the large letters A, B, C, . . . to symbolize the external realities of the physical world, and the small letters *a, b, c,* . . . to symbolize the internal effects or ideas, of which alone we can have direct apprehension. But tell me honestly, did you never have any objections or criticisms of this copy theory of knowledge ?

LOVELACE : Well, I must admit that once or twice objections were made to this procedure.

HYLANOUS : What were the objections, Lovelace ?

LOVELACE : Well, one of them was the old objection that

is usually advanced against Locke's form of our theory. It runs as follows: If we can never apprehend anything but our ideas, which are copies of objects, how can we ever tell whether these copies resemble their originals, that is to say, how do we know anything about things as they really are? This apparent difficulty I have always disposed of by appealing frankly to probability. If, for example, the assumption of a system of atoms and electro-magnetic vibrations enables me to predict successfully the sequences of sensations that will ensue when wood is set on fire or when any two chemicals as they appear in experience are mixed together, there is a probability (which becomes stronger with the multiplication of instances) that the reason why the assumption tallies with our experience is because it is true. In other words, if instead of atoms and ether the world were made of something quite different, it would be extremely unlikely that the effects of that something could be explained and predicted by the atom and ether assumptions. It is here very much as with our inference of other minds. If from my auditory and visual sensations of you, I infer the existence of you as a human being like myself, with an interest in the epistemological problem, I am able to rationalize and predict those future experiences of mine which I describe as seeing your behaviour and hearing your remarks. And so, although it is possible that you have no objective existence at all, and that the cause of my visual and auditory experience is wholly different from what I assume, yet this latter possibility is extremely improbable, as you yourself will be the first to admit!

HYLANOUS: Yes, I feel the force of that, Lovelace. And I suppose that we must admit that the experience of any complex of qualities is conditioned not only by external causes but also by our own natures; and that consequently it must always be a matter of inference and probability as to just which of the experienced qualities are the existent properties of things in their own right, apart from their relation to the organism. And we should probably agree that there is sufficient ground for regarding the primary or spatio-temporal qualities as existentially objective irrespective of any relation to the knowing self, but that the status of the secondary or non-spatial qualities, such as colour, tone, odour, and savour, is

more doubtful.   That is to say, it is possible that the secondary
qualities are only effects produced upon the brain or self by
energies which are themselves lacking in those qualities.   In
short, we should both agree that the extent to which things
out of relation to the organism resemble their appearance
when related to the organism is a matter for empirical investigation, and that whatever difference there might be between
things   and   their   appearances   would   depend   upon   the
distortion of the forms and periodicities of the energies in
the passage from their extra-bodily origin to their terminals
in the brain.

LOVELACE :   Indeed, Hylanous, all that you say is correct ;
but you are speaking quite in the manner of an epistemological
dualist.

HYLANOUS :   I have much more sympathy for your dualism
than you give me credit for.   But now I wish to go back to
something you said a little while ago in connection with your
success in teaching epistemological dualism as compared with
your experience with both forms of epistemological monism.
Did not your students ever point out any further difficulties
in the dualistic conception ?   Did they always find it satisfactory ?

LOVELACE :   Well, I must confess that some of the more
acute students raised one or two other objections which led
to a good deal of confusion.

HYLANOUS :   What were those objections ?

LOVELACE :   Two or three of the students asked how it
was possible to differentiate between the conceptual space
and time in which the external causes of perceived objects
are inferred to exist and the space and time which are actually
experienced.   These students claimed that any conceptual
or inferred space and time could be thought of only as a continuation of the space and time we immediately apprehend
as containing and relating our perceptual objects.   And they
went on to illustrate their objection by pointing out that if
the space in which the stars are perceived to be located is
assumed by the dualist to be merely an intra-cranial copy of
a genuinely real extra-cranial space, the latter can be conceived
only as spatially beyond or outside the space that we perceive.   But inasmuch as the extent of perceived space has no

limits except the accidental limits put upon it by clouds, stars, and other opaque objects, it seems impossible to conceive of or believe in any space outside of that of the alleged copy-space of perceptive experience. Hence they concluded that if *perceived* space is inside us, *conceived* or inferred space must be equally so. And as to perceptual and conceptual time, this same claim for identity was made. Thereupon the class divided into two groups : one group insisted that this identification of perceptual space and time with the space and time that we infer meant that the so-called external objects of inference were as subjectively internal and dependent on consciousness as were the objects of perception ; while the other group took the opposite position of extreme objectivism, and argued that the realm of so-called internal percepts was as externally objective as anything could be. My class of contented dualists was thus transformed into two warring factions : subjectivists and objectivists ! And my own position seemed as foolish as that of a pacifist in the middle of a battlefield, neglected by all and respected by none.

HYLANOUS : I see. The claim was that inferred space and perceptual space must be identical ; and therefore that if you are to get to a world beyond your own states in inference, you must in perception. In short, if you don't get outside your head in perception you can't get outside at all.

LOVELACE : Yes ; and those who accepted the subjectivist horn of the dilemma urged that the objects that a man infers to exist are as relative to his condition and prejudices and as dependent upon his mental states as are the objects of perceptual experience. It was argued that men differ at least as much in what they believe as in what they see.

HYLANOUS : How did you deal with this disintegration of the dualistic epistemology ?

LOVELACE : Well, I admitted that there was a puzzle about the independence and externality of perceptual space and time as such, but I reverted to the rock-fact on which dualism is founded, namely, the demonstrable independence of the sensory experience of objects, and the system of causes outside the organism which we must infer in order to explain the order of our perceptions. In the case of the stereoscope, for example, it cannot be denied that I see a spherical object in front of me ; but neither can it be denied that the cause of that apparent sphere is two flat disks acting separately upon my two eyes.

HYLANOUS : But in what place do you locate the stereo-scopically apparent sphere ?

LOVELACE : In the space in front of me.

HYLANOUS : And in what place are the two flat disks located ?

LOVELACE : In the space in front of me.

HYLANOUS : Is it not plain, then, according to your own admission that the space of the illusory sphere and of the existent disks is the same ? And, in general, that the space of real objects in which you believe is no more and no less external than the space of immediate perception ?

LOVELACE : It would seem so ; and yet to admit it would be absurd. For it would do away with the duality of the merely apparent and the real.

HYLANOUS : No, Lovelace. We can do full justice to the duality on which you rightly insist by making it a duality of *context* and of *causal conditions* rather than of *position*.

LOVELACE : I do not understand you.

HYLANOUS : Take once more the illustration of the stereo-scopic illusion which was discussed at length with Partridge. In this case the real objects and the apparent object are differentiated by their internal natures—flat disks on the one hand and solid sphere on the other. But why do you call the sphere merely apparent, and the disks real ?

LOVELACE : Because the disks stand in relations of causal efficiency to photographic plates, to scales, and in general to the totality of other objects in addition to and independently of their effect upon my consciousness ; while the sphere has no effects except upon my conscious states at the moment of perception.

HYLANOUS : Just so ; the actual and practical reason for condemning certain contents of experience to a status of illusion is not that they are located in an intra-cranial space, (for, as we have seen, real and unreal are located in the same space), but that their *effective relations* are restricted to an individual's private field of experience ; while what we call the real objects are not thus restricted, but exert their effects upon the totality of other objects, regardless of their membership in anyone's private experience. This difference of behaviour is the practical criterion for distinguishing between the real and the illusory ; why is it not also adequate to serve as the theoretical or final criterion of the difference ?

LOVELACE : Do you mean that illusory objects such as the stereoscopic sphere, the convergent appearance of the rails of a train track, and the chair that dances up and down as the result of my pressing my eyeball, are actually located in the same external space as that of the real objects which are the bases for these distorted images ?

HYLANOUS : For a thing to be apparent it must operate through the brain of an individual. For a thing to be only apparent, it must operate only through the brain of an individual. Real objects operate causally on the totality of things. The duality between the immediately perceived and the independently existent is a duality of behaviouristic context and not of spatial location.

LOVELACE : What is the advantage of substituting your duality of relational context for my duality of spatial location ?

HYLANOUS : There are two points of advantage. In the first place, my view makes the theoretical criterion for distinguishing the objectively real from the merely subjective or illusory, identical with the practical criterion that we actually use. In the second place, my view of the situation makes it possible to explain how in the case of true perception the object perceived can be identical with the real object.

LOVELACE : I do not understand this second point of advantage.

HYLANOUS : Why, according to your view all immediately apprehended objects are internal states of the knower, and as such can never be identical with the objects external to his organism whose existence he infers. You can never know external reality ; the nearest you can come to it is to apprehend mental states which stand in one-to-one correspondence with external objects. Moreover, as we have already seen, even conception and inference cannot properly avail to give you a consciousness of anything outside yourself. For the conceptual order of extra-organic objects in which you believe is no more than a rearrangement of perceptual qualities ; and

the space and time of the inferred objects, if it means anything at all, must mean the same space and time as that of
your perceptual objects. In short, if you are correct in your
assumption that the realm of perception is intra-cranial, you
are forced to admit that the realm of conception and inference
is equally intra-cranial, and your dualism degenerates into a
monistic subjectivism. Now the view which I am proposing
substitutes for the impossible duality of locus a duality of
relational context. It defines a content as subjective in so
far as it stands in immediate causal relations to your other
perceptions and to your cerebral processes. It defines a
content as objective and externally real in so far as it stands
in immediate causal relations to the totality of other objects.
This definite duality of subjective and objective contexts does
not preclude any content from having membership in both
orders simultaneously. The private field of an individual
experience and the public field of extra-organic objects can
intersect and overlap. Whenever a thing is known truly it
is known *as it is*. The known object and the real object are
identical. Consider two curves which are continually intersecting. Each curve is a system of points determined by a
law or formula of its own. The points of intersection enjoy
membership in both systems without prejudice to their
identity. Their duality of context is no bar to their oneness
of essence and existence. So it is with the subjective order
of events in consciousness and the objective order of events
in the physical world. The one order of events is determined
by intra-organic processes of the individual knower, the other
by the extra-organic processes of the physical world. Yet
despite this duality of causal conditions there is constant
intersection and overlapping of the two orders, so that one
and the same event can be a member of both orders, which is
the situation involved in true apprehension.

LOVELACE : Will you give a concrete illustration of the
way in which this duality of context would permit of intersection or identity of the perceived and the real ?

HYLANOUS : Certainly. Take the case of the chair which
you perceive in front of you. Apart from the question of its
secondary qualities, you infer and believe, for all sorts of
reasons, that there is really, out there, independent of your

consciousness, an object that in shape, size, mass, and position is indistinguishable from the object that you perceive. The chair in the room and the chair in your consciousness are one and the same thing. Now, press your eyeball and the chair which you experience dances about, while the chair on which you can sit and which you can photograph remains at rest. In short, you are no longer apprehending a reality. The dancing chair is purely subjective. Now this shows that the chair that you perceive depends for its behaviour primarily and directly upon causes within your organism, while the behaviour of the real chair depends upon causes quite different. So that the one can vary independently of the other. Your view interprets this situation to mean that the perceived chair is inside your brain. My view would hold, on the contrary, that it is only the determiners of the perceived chair that are inside your brain, and that the perceived chair may be in exactly the same extra-bodily space as the chair which we infer to exist.

LOVELACE : You say that the chair in consciousness is controlled by intra-organic conditions, and that so long as these conditions are such as to make the chair *appear* in the space where the real chair actually is, the two chairs are identical and our perception is true ?

HYLANOUS : Yes.

LOVELACE : And that as soon as the intra-cerebral processes (which are themselves in part, though only in part, the effect of the external chair's activity upon the sense-organs) become such as to produce the appearance of a chair different in nature or position from the external chair, that then our perception becomes false ?

HYLANOUS : Yes.

LOVELACE : Well, to make your view clearer, tell me just how many combinations of the subjective and objective orders there are and to what situations they correspond.

HYLANOUS : There are obviously four logically possible combinations of the two orders with respect to any element or object.

(1) An object can have membership in both the subjective or intra-organic and in the objective or extra-organic orders. It is then both apprehended and

externally existent. For example, the stationary chair perceived as such. This is the situation of *actualized truth*.

(2) An object can have membership in the subjective or intra-organic order and no membership, or no corresponding membership, in the objective or extra-organic order. It is then apprehended, but not externally existent. For example, the chair in a dream or the chair that dances when the eyeball is pressed. That is the situation of *actualized error*.

(3) An object can have membership in the objective or extra-organic order, but not in the subjective or intra-organic order. It exists externally, but is not apprehended. For example, the things on the other side of the moon. This is the situation of *potential truth*.

(4) An object can have membership neither in the objective or extra-organic order nor in the subjective or intra-organic order. It neither exists nor is apprehended. For example, any of the unreal objects which have not been believed in or thought of, such as a moon made of purple cheese. This is the situation of *potential error*.

LOVELACE : Well, Hylanous, I think that I might accept this compromise of yours, according to which the duality of the apprehended and the real is interpreted in terms of separate causal conditions rather than separate places, were it not for the fact that consideration of the mechanism by which perceptions are produced shows quite clearly that the qualitative natures of the things which we perceive and also the spatial and temporal relations between them are just what we should expect to appear if the world were mirrored in our brains, or represented in the system of brain-states, which are the effects of extra-organic causes. You admit that the happenings in the brain determine the objects of perception. But you hold that the latter are genuinely extra-organic in their location. How could intra-organic processes determine extra-organic objects ? What could be the means by which perceived objects were re-projected into that outer space and past time from which their causes initiated their action ? How much simpler it would be to make the perceived objects identical with the intra-organic effects of the real objects.

HYLANOUS : I will admit that the cerebral states of an individual constitute a kind of simulacrum or reflection of the world outside his organism.

LOVELACE : Will you admit that that simulacrum might be perceived by an external observer, if the brains of the observer and the subject could be grafted together ?

HYLANOUS : Yes ; but in such a situation the observer would perceive only the brain-states of the subject and not the extra-organic world which the subject himself perceived by means of those brain-states. It would be like seeing the words without seeing the meanings.

LOVELACE : If the subject's brain-states in a case of true perception have a one-to-one correspondence with the contents of his perception, why do you fear to identify them ?

HYLANOUS : I fear to identify the brain-states of the subject with the objects which are perceived by them for the same reason that I fear to identify the words in a book with the things outside the book which they mean and reveal. The words are in one-to-one correspondence with their meanings, they might even be pictures resembling their meanings, but they are not identical with the things which they mean. The things meant may be existent or merely subsistent, real or unreal, but the words designating them are always existent and particular. Even the idealists admit a difference between the mental state or image and the meaning attached to it. You have now, let us say, the thought of Socrates. Perhaps there is in your brain or in your mind a more or less accurate image of the man. But that image, visual, kinesthetic or what not, is located in some sense within your organism and occurs at the present moment. It gives you the thought of Socrates, but it is not Socrates. Nothing that exists in your head to-day can be identical with what existed outside your head and in the distant past.

LOVELACE : I understand ; you do not deny the possibility that the world outside an individual can produce an image of itself inside that individual, but you hold that these cerebral or mental states, like words, have a meaning or implication of what is outside them, in the sense of occurring in other times and spaces than their own, and that it is this implication of the brain-states rather than the brain-states themselves which the individual apprehends.

HYLANOUS: Exactly so. What a man will perceive or conceive depends entirely upon the processes or states of his nervous system, just as what a book describes depends entirely upon .what words are printed on its pages; but to argue from this that a man could apprehend only his own states would be as absurd as to argue that a book could describe only its own words and pictures.

LOVELACE: Your analogy between words and brain-states makes clear your meaning, but it leaves totally unexplained the manner in which the effects produced in the brain can imply or reveal their extra-cerebral causes. Words reveal the things for which they stand in virtue of a mind which comprehends their meanings. But in your theory the brain-states are like words which interpret themselves. They are at once the book and the reader.

HYLANOUS: I admit that my analogy as such offers no explanation of the manner in which the cortical states transcend themselves and afford an experience of objects other than themselves. The question of how this is possible is a matter for psychology rather than epistemology. I have on various occasions expressed my belief that the self-transcending implications of the brain-states could be understood as a corollary of the truth that they are forms of potential energy into which the kinetic energies of the sensory nerve currents had been converted, and that as such they could contain, intensively, reference to other times and places than those which they occupy. But I am not concerned here to defend this particular psycho-physical theory as to the nature of brain-states and the manner in which they refer to a world beyond themselves. It is necessary only to accept the fact that in some manner the internal states of an organism are the indispensable conditions for an apprehension or consciousness by that organism of a space and time other than that of the states themselves. And that in so far as the internal states agree with or correspond to the objects existing in the outer world, there is consciousness of reality or truth; while in so far as the brain-states, by reason of the distorting influence of the media, physical and physiological, through which the stimuli must pass before they can affect the brain, are not in correspondence or agreement with their extra-organic causes, then there will be consciousness of what does not exist—in other words, error.   In either case, inner states of the brain reveal an outer world, but in the one case that outer world will be real, in the other case it will be unreal.

LOVELACE :   I think I understand.   Outer things, in so far as they are implied by a system of self-transcending brain-states, are members of a subjective order, and are controlled by intra-organic causes ; while in so far as they are in inter-action with the totality of other objects in space, and not merely with any one brain, they are members of the objective or existential order, and are controlled by extra-organic causes.   An object such as a chair can have membership in both orders together, in either singly, or in neither.   And the duality of what is apprehended and what is real expresses a duality of intra-organic and extra-organic causal conditions, and not a duality of intra-organic and extra-organic location.

HYLANOUS: Yes. Your own epistemological dualism noted correctly the capacity of real objects and perceived objects to vary independently of one another, and it also noted correctly the existence in every percipient organism of a set of internal states by which consciousness was determined. But in interpreting this situation by identifying the objects *of* which we are conscious with the brain-states *through* which we are conscious, it made a chasm between an inner world that we can know but which is not real and an outer world which is real but which we cannot know.   The compromise which I offer does full justice to the power of the real and the perceived to vary independently, and it does equally full justice to the duality involved in the intra-cerebral images of an extra-cerebral world ; but by refusing to make the brain-states their own objects we permit the real objects and the known objects to be members of intersecting contexts rather than of separate realms.   They are independent without being mutually exclusive.

LOVELACE :   Well, I am more nearly satisfied than I expected to be by your compromise.   But I cannot quite see how you can grant so much of my epistemological dualism and still keep your theory satisfactory to the monistic objectivism of Partridge and the equally monistic subjectivism of Bryce.

HYLANOUS : I have contended throughout our whole discussion that it was possible to reconcile the three classic types of epistemological theory which you three friends respectively represent. And the eirenicon which I have proposed is constructed by cutting out from each of your three theories that element which, unessential in itself, has nevertheless sufficed to keep you in disagreement with one another, and if I may say it without offence, in equal disagreement with the facts of the knowledge situation.

V

In which HYLANOUS *shows how in the light of his eirenicon such concepts as truth and error can be translated without loss of meaning from any epistemology into any other ; whereupon the dialogue concludes with a discussion of the importance and the unimportance of epistemology.*

BRYCE : Well, Hylanous, now that you have wrung from each of us individually a more or less reluctant consent to accept the restatement of each of our views of the knowledge situation considered in its bearings upon the independence of objects from the cognitive relation, I would propose that you give your own definition of truth and error and compare it with the definition given by objectivists, subjectivists, and dualists, so that we may see how our revised theories appear when put side by side with one another and studied in the light of your compromise.

HYLANOUS : I shall be glad to comply with your request, and I shall hope to show that your three theories in their revised forms are not only compatible but equivalent and interchangeable. But as a preliminary to undertaking a real definition of truth and error in terms of the three standpoints which you severally accept, I must ask you all to admit a certain nominal definition of truth—namely, that regardless of any epistemological theory, the word " true " in its primary sense means the same as the word " real."

LOVELACE : I should like to oblige you, Hylanous, by making this admission, but I am afraid I cannot ; for every judgment that a man makes is *real*, but not every judgment is *true*. Hence real and true are obviously different in their meanings.

HYLANOUS : I only wished to identify truth in its primary or objective sense with reality. When the thing asserted by a judgment is true, then the act of asserting is called true in a secondary or subjective sense. *Charles I dying on the scaffold* is a reality, a fact, a truth in the objective sense. For that reason and for that alone any judgment that asserts it is called a true judgment. *Charles I dying in his bed* is an unreality, it is not a fact, it is not so, it is not a truth ; for that reason, and for that alone, the judgment " Charles I died in his bed " is a false judgment, an error. In short, judgments and assertions are not true or false primarily or in their own right, but only in virtue of the truth or falsity of the object which they assert. A judgment is true when what it asserts is true or real. " Buck-shot " means shot intended to kill a buck, and " bird-shot " is shot intended to kill a bird. We do not by those terms mean that shot is buck like or bird like in appearance. The words " buck " and " bird " when used as adjectives for shot are used in a secondary sense, derived from the kind of object which the shot is to hit. So " true " and " false " when applied to judgments are used only in the secondary sense derived from the kinds of objects which the judgment asserts.

LOVELACE : I don't feel sure whether this distinction between the primary and secondary sense of the terms true and false is itself true, and if it is true, I doubt if it is important.

HYLANOUS : Well, Lovelace, you can satisfy yourself that it is true very easily—see if you can find any case in which a judgment that you would call true fails to assert something that is real, or *so*. Can you find any such case ?

LOVELACE : I must confess I can't think of any.

HYLANOUS : Very well. Now make the converse attempt

and see if you find any case in which a judgment which, though it asserts something that is a reality or fact, would yet not be called true.

LOVELACE : I confess again that I cannot think of any such case.

HYLANOUS : Very well; can you succeed any better in the matter of false judgments ?   Can you think of a case in which a judgment that you consider false owes its falsity to anything except that what it asserts is not real or not a fact ?

LOVELACE : I admit I cannot.

HYLANOUS : So much for the truth of my distinction between the true in its primary sense as identical with the real, and the true in its secondary sense as applying to judgments which assert what is real.   Now for the importance of this distinction—it is best shown by considering the confusions that result from failing to make it.   Those relativists and pragmatists who have thrilled the world with the announcement that truth changes and progresses as much as anything else, and that consequently evolution is as true for the supposedly eternal realm of logic as it is for biology, have in my opinion played fast and loose with the two senses of the word truth.   People's assertions and beliefs do change and progress. ⌣Men call true in one century what in the next they regard as false.   But although existence is itself full of change, yet that something existed at a given time is a fact or truth which does not change.   Once true always true.   To say then that truth in its objective or primary sense evolves is a paradox.   To say that men's knowledge and beliefs evolve is a truism.   Mix the truism and the paradox by mixing the objective and subjective meanings of the word true, and you get what appears to be an exciting extension of the theory of evolution, but what in reality is an arrant confusion.   Hence I hold it to be important to distinguish between truth in its primary sense as reality and truth in its secondary sense as an assertion of reality.

LOVELACE : All right then, for my part I am willing to grant that a judgment is true when what it asserts is a reality.   But I wonder whether Partridge and Bryce would be equally willing.

PARTRIDGE : For me, as an epistemological monist, it is perfectly natural to admit that the true is the real and that any judgment may be called true just to the extent that what it asserts is real.

BRYCE : I, too, as an epistemological monist, will agree with what Hylanous calls his nominal definition of truth and his distinction between the objective and subjective uses of the term. Only we must remember that the definition is, as he says, merely nominal. Granted that the true is the real, the point at issue turns on what we are to mean by reality.

HYLANOUS : Just so. Now, unless I am mistaken, Reality can be defined in three ways : (1) For an objectivist, the *real* is that which is logically presupposed or implied by the totality of what is experienced. (2) For a subjectivist the *real* is that which would appear to an absolute mind who experienced each object in the light of the totality of objects. (3) For a dualist the *real* is that which possesses its temporal and spatial position and relations independently of any individual per-spective. Now, on the basis of these three conceptions of the *real*, let me suggest the three epistemological conceptions of the *true* to which they respectively correspond. For you, Partridge, a proposition (by which I shall mean any object of conceptual or perceptual experience involving an identity relation between two or more contents) is *true* if and when it would also turn out to be a logical presupposition of all possibly experienceable objects. Would you, as an objectivist, accept that as an adequate definition of truth ?

PARTRIDGE : Yes.

HYLANOUS : And for you, Bryce, a proposition is true if and when it would also remain acceptable when viewed in the light of its relations to the totality of possible experience by an Absolute consciousness. Would you, as an idealist, regard this as a proper definition of truth ?

BRYCE : Yes.

HYLANOUS : And would you, Lovelace, regard a proposi-tion as true if and when the judgment expressing it corre-sponded to a spatial and temporal reality that was external to and independent of the private experience of the individual by whom the judgment was made ?

LOVELACE : Yes, Hylanous ; and I should hold that the status of independence and externality which characterizes the reality with which our judgments must agree, if they are

to be called true, can be ascertained with increasing
probability by the extent to which any given judgment is
confirmed by future experience, by the experience of others,
and by the indirect evidence of its causal relations to the other
objects of belief.

HYLANOUS : You not only accept the definition of truth
which I offered you in terms of the dualistic epistemology,
but you state a criterion by which the dualist could discover
truth.   Let me be sure that I understand you.   You say
that we can tell to what extent our ideas and judgments
correspond to a reality outside us by the extent to which
they are confirmed by future experience, by the experience
of others, and indirectly by their relations to other objects.
What do you mean by this *indirect* confirmation ?

LOVELACE : I mean that, for example, if your judgment
that a sea-serpent was swimming across the bow of your boat
were true, the truth would be manifest not only by getting
future perceptions of him at positions farther along, and by
other people corroborating your experience with theirs, but
also by seeing a row-boat upset and waves put in commotion,
and other similar phenomena such as would result from the
presence of a real as distinguished from an unreal sea-serpent.
A thing which exists in its own right in the world of space
and time will naturally be the cause not only of direct perceptions of itself in the minds of various individuals in the
neighbourhood, but will also be the indirect cause of experiences
arising from the changes which it produces in other objects.

HYLANOUS : I understand ; and I assume that Partridge
and Bryce would also hold that there were certain criteria for
ascertaining the truth in the sense in which they use the term.
How about it, Partridge ? Have you any criterion for ascertaining the truth in an objectivistic sense of any judgment
which you might make ?

PARTRIDGE : Of course I have.   If an object which we
experience really exists in the sense that it is presupposed by
the totality of other experienced objects, why, the more I can
get of confirmatory experience, direct or indirect, my own or
other people's, the more it will tend to be the only hypothesis
justified by the situation.   In other words, its truth or reality
will be proven.

HYLANOUS : Would you also accept these criteria, Bryce ?

BRYCE : Why, yes ; at least in a general way. Of course, we finite minds have no perfect means of knowing how a given proposition or object in our finite experience would appear to an Absolute consciousness, for whom it would figure as an inseparable aspect of the organic totality of things ; nor can we guess the additional meanings and values which it would thus acquire.   There is thus an element of scepticism which any epistemology must recognize in view of the ever present possibility of such knowledge being revised in the light of more complete vision.   But I think that an idealist can admit that as we increase the extent of finite experience confirmatory of a given judgment, the probability of that judgment being rendered false in the Absolute will be correspondingly decreased.   In other words, the more evidence there is in favour of a proposition the less the probability of its being falsified by a completed or Absolute experience.   A judgment which was confirmed by all finite experience would be supplemented but not refuted by Absolute experience. And as to your illustration of the sea-serpent, I should willingly grant that a sea-serpent which was seen by many observers, and which could overturn row-boats and affect photographic plates, would enjoy a greater degree of truth and reality in the absolute mind than that accorded to an hallucinatory serpent which was present in only a single individual consciousness and which left no effect upon objects in the physical world.

HYLANOUS : Very well, then, it seems to me that the agreement as to the general criteria for testing the truth of a proposition to which you three epistemologists have confessed is a clear indication of the harmony and compatibility of your theories of the meaning of truth. For Partridge, the true is that which would be logically implied by the totality of experienced objects. For Bryce, it is that which would appear unaltered in the light of an Absolute experience.   For Lovelace, the true or real is that which is independent of any individual perspective or private system of ideas and beliefs. It is, in short, the single external spatio-temporal order with which the internal events in an individual's nervous system must be in one-to-one correspondence if the individual in question is to apprehend reality. Now, my contention is that these three epistemological theories of truth are but three aspects of the same thing, and that if any one of them is correct the other two will be equally correct.

LOVELACE : Well, Hylanous, if what you say is true, you ought to be able to show how, for example, my dualism would lead to the subjectivistic and objectivistic monisms which are defended respectively by Bryce and by Partridge.

HYLANOUS : Certainly I can show how your dualism, in the revised form which I prevailed upon you to accept, implies the truth of the equally revised forms of objectivism and subjectivism. If reality is, as you describe it, the single external system of nature which produces, in the various individuals contained in it, more or less distorted copies or perspectives of itself, it will follow that these cerebrally determined effects will, when taken together in their totality, imply their extra-cerebral causes. But the real, conceived as the implicate or presupposition of the totality of the apparent, is identical with the real as Partridge conceives it. This same reality which is at once the extra-cerebral cause of the intra-cerebral effects, and also and therefore the implicate of those effects, will, thirdly, be identical with the order of an Absolute experience, or with reality as Bryce conceives it. For a thing would appear, if viewed in the light of its relations to the totality, exactly as what it was implied by that totality to be. In the completed vision of the Absolute, appearance would coincide with reality and the psychological would be one with the logical. Will not you, Bryce, admit that this is so ?

BRYCE : Why, yes, I will admit that in the organic unity of an absolute experience the elements which make up our world of appearance would be re-arranged and combined in accordance with the principle of self-consistency. And for a system as a whole to be self-consistent it would be necessary for the order of that system to be identical with the order presupposed by the totality of its appearances. If that is what you meant by saying that in the Absolute the psychologically apparent would coincide with the logically real or true, I am in agreement.

HYLANOUS : And you, Partridge ? Are you too satisfied

that my epistemological eirenicon succeeds in harmonizing the three theories of knowledge ?

PARTRIDGE : Please remember that your epistemological eirenicon, as you call it, achieved its result only by mutilating each one of our theories. You took from my objectivism its wholesome emphasis on the external existence of all objects of perception. You took from Bryce the reality of that Absolute self upon which his subjectivism was founded. And finally, you deprived Lovelace of the dual world of things and ideas of which he was always so proud. It is the tatters and remnants of our theories that you have shown to be identical, not the theories themselves.

HYLANOUS : That is not fair. You each admitted the revisions I suggested at the time; we discussed them very thoroughly, and it is too late to go back on them now. And why should you wish to ? You yourself started by insisting that every content of experience had a logical meaning or essence that was independent of the fact that it figured as an object of anybody's apprehension, and I fully granted the justice of that contention. Objectivism is a belief that sub-sistence or essence is not dependent upon being actually experienced. In this respect it is identical with what is sometimes called " logical realism," and it is certainly valid. But when you wished to supplement this subsistential objectivism with an existential objectivism, and asserted that every experienced object possessed physical existence, and that the bent stick, which appeared as the result of a straight stick being partially immersed in water, was a genuine occupant of external space, I objected, and persuaded you to admit that what you called "relative existence," or "existence merely in a visual context," was really a non-existence, and that all these appearances of non existent objects—such as the bent stick, the convergent rails of the train track, and the stereoscopic solids—presupposed a perfectly definite set of objects in space and time, of which the apparent objects were the more or less distorted perspectives. Thus the assumption that the rails of the train track are actually and physically parallel is the only explanation of the fact that the laws of light being what they are, the camera no less than the human eye will get variously distorted prespectives of the single physical fact. You consented to admit all this, and consoled yourself by insisting that the non-existent objects which figure in our perceptual experience could all be regarded as distorted but genuinely objective perspectives or derivatives of the physical world. And to this I assented. My revision of your theory robbed it only of an embarrassment and a weakness. For instead of having to maintain that any experienced object must as such be physically existent, you need only maintain that experienced objects may be (though they need not be) also physically existent ; and that physically existent objects may be (though they need not be) also elements in a person's experience.

My revision of Bryce's theory was similar in that it preserved its essential meaning and deprived it only of that element of weakness which had made it incompatible with the other theories and with the facts. I suggested that any conceivable object could be described completely in terms of possible experience, finite or absolute. But this possibility of being experienced, as Bryce finally admitted, was compatible with the realist's claim that knowledge is selective rather than creative, and implies a dependence on possible rather than on actual experience. Just as the necessity of defining imperfection in terms of perfection in no way implies the reality of that perfection, so a thing can have its meaning determined by reference to an Absolute consciousness without implying the reality of that Absolute.

And finally, with regard to Lovelace's dualism, I admitted his central contention that for an individual to know the world, he must have some sort of copy of it inside his head. But I succeeded in convincing Lovelace that this intra-cerebral copy of extra-cerebral causes did not necessitate the disastrous assumption that an individual could apprehend nothing but his own mental states. *The objects of apprehension are the external meanings or implicates of the cerebral copies, and not the copies themselves.* The world that we experience is inside our heads no more and no less than the events described in a book are inside the book. In view of all this, I repeat that it is unfair to accuse my epistemological eirenicon of a failure to provide a true reconciliation of the objectivistic, subjectivistic and dualistic theories of the knowledge situation.

I might conclude this defence against Partridge's charge, and perhaps clarify my suggested synthesis of your theories, by an analogy. The general situation involved in any awareness of objects, perceptual or conceptual, whether that awareness involves " acquaintance " or inferential " knowledge about "—to use the terms employed by William James—is fairly comparable to the situation involved in the motion of the planets in relation to the earth.   1. It is possible to measure that planetary motion in the Copernican manner by taking the fixed stars as the frame or system of reference. From this point of view the movements of the planets as they appear to an observer on the earth will be explained and corrected by treating them as a derivative and partly distorted aspect of the movements as they actually are. This heliocentric astronomical method has for its analogue the epistemological method which we have called Objectivism. The individual's private sensations and ideas are explained and corrected by being treated as a genuinely objective but derivative and distorted perspective of physical reality.   2. It is possible to measure planetary motion in the Ptolemaic manner by taking the earth as the fixed point of reference. From this point of view the movements of the planets as they appear to an observer on the earth will be explained in terms of the hypothetical assumption of a system of possibly observable movements of a cycloidal and epicycloidal character. This geocentric astronomical method is the analogue of the epistemological method called Subjectivism or Idealism. The individual's private experience will be explained and corrected by being treated as a partial or fragmentary appearance of a hypothetical Absolute—the Absolute being conceived as the deeper self of the individual, the completion and supplementation which his private experience would undergo if extended so as to include in an organic unity the totality of things. 3. It would be possible to measure planetary motion in both the Copernican and the Ptolemaic manner simultaneously. We could conceive of two sets of planetary motions, set over against each other, the planetary motions in relation to the fixed stars and the planetary motions in relation to a fixed earth. We could then compare the latter system with the former and work out a scheme of correspondence between them whereby the geocentric appearance supplemented by its hypothetical cycloids and epicycloids could be checked up and corrected by the measure of its agreement with the heliocentric reality. This combined method of astronomical procedure would be the analogue of the dualistic method of epistemology. The many systems of individual and private experience, actual and potential, are explained and corrected if we determine the extent to which they are in one-to-one correspondence with the single public system which is their common cause and of which they are the more or less similar effects.

The three methods of epistemology, like the three methods of astronomic procedure, can all be stated in such a way as to be not only mutually compatible but mutually implicatory. It is as though we had an identical situation described by a Frenchman, an Italian, and a Spaniard, where each spoke in his own language and each complicated his just contention that he was right with an unsound and irrelevant contention that the other two descriptions must therefore be false. If we could purge the three descriptions of their negative and conflicting claims to an exclusive validity by restating the situation in a neutral language comprehensible to the three, we should have established victory for each, defeat for none, and peace for all.

BRYCE : I think that your answer to Partridge's accusation that you have had to mutilate our theories in order to reconcile them is satisfactory on the whole, though the analogies with which you have concluded the answer are not so convincing as you appear to think. The astronomic analogy is somewhat vague, especially in that part of it in which you liken Lovelace's dualism to a fantastic and purely hypothetical combination of the Copernican and Ptolemaic standpoints. As for the fable of the three linguists, it is of course frankly question-begging. But quite aside from all this, I have an objection to your whole enterprise which I should like you to consider. It is an objection of a different kind from any that has been brought up, and I feel a little embarrassed in presenting it ; but after all, it involves what might be a pretty serious economic problem for all of us.

HYLANOUS : An *economic* problem ? What on earth do you mean ?

BRYCE : Why just this. If the whole business of epistemology should ever be disposed of in any such manner as you propose, we professors of philosophy might find ourselves out of a job. You know that in many of our courses in " Introduction to Philosophy " the first term is taken up with the endeavour to make the student believe that the world exists only as the sum-total of sensations and ideas. And that leaves us free during the second term to show how it is and why it is that this seemingly startling discovery is after all a truth which makes no real difference to common sense or to the various theories of science and of religion. The more advanced courses of the curriculum in philosophy will naturally be concerned with showing the tremendously important conflicts between such thinkers as Berkeley, Hume, and Kant, in interpreting the theory that the only real objects of our knowledge are our own ideas. Now don't you realize that if the various epistemologies were shown to be nothing more than different languages, in which the same situation was described, the student might get the idea that the whole subject of epistemology was unimportant ? And as most modern philosophy is centred in epistemology, a loss of interest in the latter might result in a neglect of all branches of philosophy.

HYLANOUS : But, Bryce, I don't think epistemology *is* very important.

BRYCE : I see ; I suppose that is why you have devoted such an interminable time to discussing it ?

HYLANOUS : Oh, come now! Is a speck of dust important ?

BRYCE : No, Hylanous, it is not ; or at least not to me. It may be to you.

HYLANOUS : But the speck of dust may become very important to you if it gets into your eye, may it not ?

BRYCE : Well, naturally. But in that case the thing to do is to wash it out and then forget it.

HYLANOUS : So it is with epistemology. As long as people think that the key to unlock the secrets of the universe consists in the discovery that there is a certain sense in which the material world can be interpreted in terms of human experience, and as long as idealists believe that God, Freedom and Immortality, and in general the primacy of spirit over nature, can be established by an analysis of the knowledge situation—just so long will epistemology be important. In short, the epistemological problem is important in the sense that while it remains unsolved or wrongly solved it functions like the speck of dust in one's eye as a source of distraction and confusion. But when the problem of knowledge is solved, it ceases to be of importance, and philosophy is set free for the study of objective questions. To the realist and to him alone the fact that a thing is known has no direct bearing whatever upon its nature. The Greeks realized this for the most part, and their philosophy was vital and fruitful.

BRYCE : That is all very fine. But the Greeks lived when science was in its infancy, and, in the absence of exact knowledge and the technique for acquiring it, it was permissible for them to speculate about the phenomena and the laws of nature. Modern science has taken that task to itself, and it would be vain and presumptuous for the philosopher to invade its domain. We idealists have not forgotten the disastrous attempt to invade the domain of physical science which was expressed in the *Natur-Philosophie* of Schelling and Hegel a century ago. The ambition to anticipate the results of the laboratory by intuition and *a priori* speculation was a failure ; and that failure resulted in a great loss of prestige to philosophy and particularly to idealism. We English-speaking idealists have profited by the experience of our German ancestors, and so when in the last third of the nineteenth century we resurrected Hegelianism and brought it over to the universities of England and America as an offset to the increasing popularity of materialistic ideas as set forth in the writings of Spencer and Huxley, which seemed to menace the stability of religion, we were careful to purge our Teutonic transcendentalism of most of its romantic cosmology. In the main we have confined ourselves to logic and epistemology, with the result that nothing in our philosophy has given offence to our scientific brethren. We have not even taken sides on such issues as that of mechanism and vitalism, and as the price of our consistent neutrality on almost all of the problems in which ordinary men are interested, there is hardly anybody except Dr. Schiller who has accused us of saying anything that is actually false.

HYLANOUS : Yes, Bryce, but there are a great many people, including Dr. Schiller, who would claim that your scrupulous restriction of philosophy to the field of epistemology and your insistence upon keeping yourselves and your Absolute neutral on all concrete issues has resulted in a considerable degree of intellectual aridity. To avoid the risk of saying anything false is to incur the risk of saying nothing important. However, I am not pleading that philosophy should abandon the problem of epistemology in order to invade the territory of the sciences. There are three great inquiries in which men have been interested but with which the scientists themselves are not primarily concerned.

BRYCE : What are they ?

HYLANOUS : I might call them Analytic Metaphysics or Ontology ; Synthetic Metaphysics or Cosmology ; and Evaluative Metaphysics or Religion. By Analytic Metaphysics, I mean the definition, analysis, and comparison of the basic concepts or categories which the various sciences assume. The technique of experiment and calculation is used by the special scientist to discover the relations of sequence and co-existence, to disentangle from the variable conjunctions of experienced phenomena the invariant laws which make possible the explanation and prediction of nature's doings. The scientist's ability to use and apply his technique of discovery no more implies the ability to criticize the categories with which he works than the ability to speak a language implies an interest in its etymology. And as science becomes more and more specialized there is less and less time for the scientific worker to analyse his assumptions and to study their relations to the assumptions of his fellow-specialists in other lines of research. Not science itself, but the logic, or, if you choose, the grammar of science, should engage the atten tion of philosophy. You, Bryce, should be interested in this on account of the importance ascribed to it by Kant and his followers ; though in recent years I think the best work in this branch of philosophy has been done by Partridge and his friends under the leadership of Mr. Bertrand Russell.

As for Synthetic Metaphysics, the second department of philosophic inquiry, it resembles Analytic Metaphysics in being related to the sciences without being a part of them.

The varied armies of scientists need "*liaison* officers" not only at their base but also on the line of their farthest advance. If each specialist is increasingly preoccupied with attaining his own particular objective, it is increasingly necessary for somebody to put together and organize the various principal discoveries, so that people can get a bird's-eye view of the universe, as science reveals it, and realize where they stand. The philosophers should essay this task of sizing up the world in Cosmology or Synthetic Metaphysics.

LOVELACE : I like this idea ; but for the philosopher to make any sort of respectable show either in synthetic or in analytic metaphysics, as you have defined them, he would have to be much better equipped in the elements of science than most of us are.   And even then I think that the scientists might often prefer to furnish their own "*liaison* officers*" rather than accept them from the non-scientific laity.

HYLANOUS : We certainly should be better equipped ; and if we can once get rid of the need of wasting so much energy in epistemology we can employ the time thus saved in attaining that equipment.   As to the chance that the scientists themselves will want to delegate some of their own people to undertake the work of constructing cosmologies, we should welcome it.   Men like Huxley and Driesch, Pearson and Arrhenius, who have deigned to devote their time to a general survey of the results of science, ought to be regarded with much more respect and interest by professional philosophers than has been customary.   Such attempts on the part of scientists are all too few, and we need have no fear that they will be sufficiently numerous to satisfy the great and growing demand for synthetic surveys of nature.

The third line of objective inquiry to which philosophy can devote itself in lieu of epistemology is what I just spoke of as evaluative metaphysics.   Quite apart from ethics or the study of values as such and in their relation to man's conduct, there is the great question as to the place of human values in the cosmic economy.   To what extent does our present knowledge of nature permit us to ascribe to the universe a concern for those ideals which play so essential a rôle in the life and history of man ?   This is the problem of theology in the broadest sense of that term.   Interest in this branch of philosophy is an original and continuing interest.   Unless one is indifferent to the fate of men, one cannot be indifferent to the fate of men's ideals, as determined by the degree to which they are embodied and conserved in the objective universe.

LOVELACE : In this line of philosophic inquiry as in the two others the scientists might wish to coöperate ?

BRYCE : And why not also the professional theologians and the men of letters ?

HYLANOUS : We should hope so.   Religious men, artists, and poets will naturally share with the scientists that universal human concern as to whether man is an alien in the world, his spirit the product of blind forces and its continuance at their mercy, or whether, on the contrary, there is warrant for the ancient hope that man and his world are kin, and that what is highest in the one is deepest in the other.

It seems to me that there is more need for the study of these problems in objective metaphysics and more hope of advancing their solution than ever before.   Knowledge is good food for those who love wisdom, and science in its present advanced stage should afford ample nourishment for philosophy.   But to avail ourselves of the opportunities for the study of objective problems, we must see to it that either the epistemological problem is solved, or if that is too much to expect, we must at least segregate it along with other purely methodological questions.   Philosophy's primary interest is in the ways of things rather than in the ways of knowing them.

INDEX

INDEX

417

Constants of gravitation and light, 116
Constituents of time and space, 180
Constitutive—
relativity, 297, 303
and see Selective
Context—
true in a, 244
difference of, 305
Contingent propositions, 88, 89
Continuum—
logical interdependence in, 116
infinitieth as constituent of, 180
Contradictory propositions, one true, 175
Convenience as criterion, 220
Copernican—
theory, 144, 145
revolution, 276, 284
Copy theory, 33, 242, 250, 257, 311, 385, 386
Correspondence—
of ideas and things, 218
truth as agreement or, 250, 257, 312
not similarity, 385
Corroboration—
by many witnesses, 207
by several senses, 208
of elements as test of truth, 210
of other methods by empiricism, 230
Cosmo-centric and bio-centric, 230
Cosmology—
as synthetic metaphysics, 31, 411
phenomenalism as theory of, 174
Cosmos, possible mind of, 58
Creation—
as selection, 124
and see Re-creation
Creative imagination, 56, 57
Credulity, natural, 39
Creighton, J. E., *see* Bryce, 317 ff.
Criterion—
for discovering truth, 34
of scientific hypothesis, 140
of good hypothesis, 144
satisfaction as, 157, 160
of truth, 162
Critical—
form of epistemological theories, 292
realists, 305 note, 319
Curiosity—
instinctive nature of, 155 note
growth of theoretical, 158
Customs and institutions revered, 44

Deductive reasoning, 219, 229
Democritus, 174
Denotation—
nominalistic conception of, 73
expressed by judgments, 79
as relative, 80
compared with connotation, 80
relativity of, 81
as position in series, 82
of same object by different names, 305
Descartes, 214, 254
Description—
compared with explanation, 229
of physical facts, 255
quantitative, 256

Determiner—
of perception, 252, 270
direct and indirect, 300
Deussen, P., 277
Development, scientific, stages of, 128
Dewey, J., 133, 134, 135 note, 136, 137, 149, 154 note, 156, 157
Dialectical—
rationalism, 118
process, 119
argument for scepticism, 175
Dictum de omni et nullo, 344
Difference, kinds of, 304
Dilemma of denial of reason or sense, 177
Direct determiner of percepts, 300
Distance infinitesimal, 179
Distortion of objects, 309, 310
Diversity implied by identity judgment, 82 ff.
Domains, the five, 225
Drake, D., *see* Lovelace, 317 ff.
Driesch, H., 167
Dualism—
cosmological, 174
psycho-physical, 248
epistemological, 33, 237, 248 ff., 305 note
as second stage of subjectivism, 267
and subjectivism in agreement, 274
reinterpretation of, 306 ff.
definition of truth for, 312
fallacy of, 323
Duality—
numerical, 248 ff.
qualitative, 260 f.
of inferred and perceived, numerical, 261
of context or of position, 390 f.
of conditions, 397
Duration, infinitesimal, 179
Dyadic relations, relativist denial of, 244

Ecstasy, religious, 56
Eddy, Mrs., 58, 60
Education, evils of elective system in 142
Ego-centric predicament, 331, 377
Einstein, A., 116
Emotion, relation to intellect, 136
Empirical—
pragmatism, 148
self, 285
Empiricism—
and Rationalism, general treatment of, Chapters III and IV
as logical theory, 34
defined, 69
and innate ideas, 76
extreme, 110
and rationalism complementary, 126
dangers and nature of, 127
and pragmatism, 182, 222
and authoritarianism, 212
and mysticism, 215
and rationalism, 219
and scepticism, 223
and fourth domain, 230
End as justification of means, 48
Ends, plurality of, 48

INDEX

Golden Age, 44, 45, 168
Good—
 and the true, 152, 230
 for utilitarianism, 160
 attainment of, 311.
Gorgias, 176
Gravity, sense of, 190 note.

Haeckel, 174
Haldane, R. B., see Bryce, 317 ff.
Hallucination—
 and intuition, 215
 and theory of knowledge, 243
Hamilton, W., 124 note, 176, 222
Hedonism criticized, 161
Hegel, 118, 119, 121, 221, 287, 376, 410
Hicks, G. Dawes, see Partridge, 317 ff.
History—
 interpretation of, 45
 its dependence on testimony, 225
Hobbes, T., 170
Hobhouse, L. T., 89 note, 99, 210
Hocking, W. E., see Bryce, 317 ff.
Holt, E. B., 249 note
 and see Partridge, 317 ff.
Homogeneous series of qualities, 253
Humanism, 135, 136
Humanistic practicalism, 149 ff., 153
Hume, D., 199, 275
Huxley, T., 170
Hylanous, a realist, 317 ff.
Hyper-syllogism, Aristotelian syllogisms
 reduced to, 95, 98
Hypnotism and credulity, 39
Hypotheses—
 scientific, criteria of, 140
 good, 144
 rival, 221
 working, 233
 test of, 258, 259
Hypothetical character of universal
 propositions, 122

Idealism—
 as subjectivism, 33
 absolute, 135
 revolutionary, needed, 172
 conflict with materialism, 174
 objective, 321, 335
 empirical, 371
 absolute and empirical, 372
Ideas—
 innate, 76
 of Plato, 109, 354
 more, 241
 routine of, not an idea, 274
 physical objects as, 275
 as forms, 275
Identity—
 logic of, 84
 the basic relation, 78
 and implication, 83, 93
 relation, judgment as, 85
 numerical, 252, 269, 356, 384
 of real and perceived, 293
 of membership in different systems,
  303, 304
 of indiscernibles, 305 note
 possible and actual, 305

Identity—(continued)
 denial of, 306
 of membership in lines, 308
 relations in truth, 312
 dualist's denial of, 320
 of position, 339
Idols, Bacon's, 151
Illusion, explanation of, 249
Illusionism as tendency of mysticism, 60
Illusory—
 objects, 240
 experience, 246
Imagination—
 as inheritance, 56
 as basis of creation, 64
 touched with conviction, intuition as,
  66
 power of, 72, 76
Imperceptible objects, 297
Implication—
 as partial identity, 82
 and identity, 83, 93
Impossibility of finitude or infinitude of
 space, 280
Improbable always happens, 203
Independent—
 variables, 121, 185, 252
 percepts and causes, 249
 psychical states as, 269
 world, 274
 meaning or essence, 292 f.
 variation of objects and experience,
  306
 variation and non-identity, 308
 and see Objective
India, 59, 60
Indirect—
 method of measurement, 256 note
 inference instead of observation, 259,
  260
 determiners of perception, 300
Indiscernibles, identity of, 305 note
Individual, concept of, 72
Individuation, nature of, 355
Induction—
 for deriving universal propositions, 86
 nature of, 99 ff.
Inductive—
 proof, 88 note, 89 note
 method, 103
 deductive cycle, 128
Inference—
 correct, 33
 involved in perception, 187
 of independent objects, 237
 false, 251
 indirect, 259, 260
 cannot transcend sense-data, 273
 of other minds, 299
Infinite—
 divisibility of space and time, 178, 281
 probability of causality, 206
 completed, 280, 281
Infinitesimal distances and durations, 179
Infinitieth as constituent of continua,
 180
Innate ideas, 76
Inspiration, supernatural, 55
Instants not sole constituents of time, 180

GEORGE ALLEN & UNWIN LTD

London: 40 Museum Street, W.C.1
Auckland: 24 Wyndham Street
Bombay: 15 Graham Road, Ballard Estate, Bombay 1
Buenos Aires: Escritorio 454-459, Florida 165
Calcutta: 17 Chittaranjan Avenue, Calcutta 13
Cape Town: 109 Long Street
Hong Kong: F1/12 Mirador Mansions, Kowloon
Ibadan: P.O. Box 62
Karachi: Karachi Chambers, McLeod Road
Madras: Mohan Mansion, 38c Mount Road, Madras 6
Mexico: Villalongin 32-10, Piso, Mexico 5, D.F.
Nairobi: P.O. Box 12446
New Delhi: 13-14 Ajmeri Gate Extension, New Delhi 1
São Paulo: Avenida 9 de Julho 1138-Ap. 51
Singapore: 36c Prinsep Street, Singapore 7
Sydney, N.S.W.: Bradbury House, 55 York Street
Toronto: 91 Wellington Street West